Moral Psychology

Developmental Psychology Series
Series Editor, Wendell E. Jeffrey

Moral Psychology

Daniel K. Lapsley

Westview Press

A Member of the Perseus Books Group

Developmental Psychology

Copyright © 1996 by Westview Press, A Member of the Perseus Books Group

Published in 1996 in the United States of America by Westview Press, 5500 Central Avenue, Boulder,
Colorado 80301-2877, and in the United Kingdom by Westview Press, 12 Hid's Copse Road, Cumnor
Hill, Oxford OX2 9JJ

Library of Congress Cataloging-in-Publication Data
Lapsley, Daniel K.
Moral Psychology /Daniel K. Lapsley.
      p. cm.—(Developmental psychology series)
     Includes bibliographical references and index.
     ISBN 0-8133-3032-7 ISBN 0-8133-3033-5 (pbk.)
       1. Moral Development. 2. Judgment (Ethics). 3. Psychology—Philosophy. I. Title. II.
     Series: Developmental psychology series (Boulder, Colo.)
     BF723.M54L38   1996
     155.2′5—dc20   96–6852
                                                                       CIP
The paper used in this publication meets the requirements of the American National Standard for
Permanence of Paper for Printed Library Materials Z39.48-1984.

10   9   8   7   6   5   4   3   2

PERSEUS
POD
ON DEMAND

Contents

Tables

Preface

The study of moral functioning has been one of the most enduring and central of all the various research enterprises to be found within the scholarly psychological literature. It is conceptualized by diverse theoretical perspectives that span many domains of psychology. In addition, it is informed in important ways by ethics and other developments in philosophy. Perhaps the study of moral conduct, ethical thinking, and values is so preeminent in the social sciences just because moral qualities appear to be what are so distinctive about the human species.

A literature that sprawls over so many domains and disciplines, however, and attracts so much research interest and controversy is hard to distill for purposes of teaching. As someone who has taught numerous seminars on moral development, I can well attest to the sheer frustration of trying to represent the field in a fair way with isolated readings drawn from very diverse sources. What clearly seemed required was a textbook that brought together the various literatures in a coherent way and in a way that encouraged further reflection, criticism, and, one hopes, new lines of research. I do hope that this text will be found useful in this respect.

I attempted to present each theoretical approach in a complete and balanced way and with a large measure of sympathy and fairness. But I also tried to appraise strengths and weaknesses, to confront each theory with the empirical literature, and to capture some of the back-and-forth of scholarly dialogue. It is a mistake, I believe, for textbook authors to simply catalog the various theories and findings as if every point of view is equally well-considered and equally valid. This "textbook neutrality" does not capture the sense of excitement and dynamism that working scholars encounter in their academic labors, and it conveys a bad impression to students, too, namely that one idea is just as good as any other. I do hope, of course, that any critical comments that I do make are found suitably gentle and useful, but I am comforted by the fact that if some should misfire, even these should serve the useful purpose of generating a good critical class discussion.

The reader will note that although the text is decidedly focused on the psychological literatures, there are, nonetheless, numerous references to allied philosophical issues and literatures. I make no apology for this. As Habermas (1990) has pointed out, the division of labor between philosophy and the social sciences is untenable, and besides, I think some of the best work in moral psychology can be found in some recent philosophical works.

This text was written for students taking upper-division undergraduate courses and for use in graduate seminars on moral psychology. These courses are typically taught in departments of psychology, education, and philosophy. I do assume that students have at least a glancing acquaintance with some of the broad intellectual movements in psychology. A prior course in developmental psychology would be helpful for many students. That said, I do hope that the text will be fully accessible to and appreciated by a general readership.

There are many individuals whose assistance was critical for bringing this book to fruition. My thanks, first, to Michael Lange for encouraging me to write a book on this topic and to Dr. Wendell Jeffrey, series editor, for his consideration of the project. I am also grateful to Michelle Baxter and the staff at Westview Press and Jennifer Maughan at Interactive Composition Corporation for moving the project along and to Diane Hess, whose editorial services have prevented me from inflicting any number of stylistic and grammatical offenses on the reader.

This text profited a great deal from the criticism of Larry Nucci, Dan Hart, and Donald R.C. Reed. I am grateful for their generous comments, their suggestions, and the hard work that was evident in their respective commentaries. I also want to express my appreciation to a number of colleagues and friends who have over the years provided me with support, inspiration, feedback, and example: Bob Enright, Clark Power, John Borkowski, Gus Blasi, Rev. Michael Himes, Mark McDaniel, Sister Joris Binder, and Ron Serlin. I am grateful, as well, for the continuing support and friendship of my former students at the University of Notre Dame. This textbook was written during my tenure in Brandon, and there are so many here who generously offered their friendship and whose support has meant so much to me. I particularly want to mention Ken and Dianne Fox, Dr. Ron Richert and Gail Richert, David and Bernice Lewis (and their children, Danny, Anthony, and Juliana), Nicole Varshney, Rev. Louis McClosky, Jason Edgerton, Sanjam Grewal, Dan Roy, Dr. Chris Breneman, Jeff Malfait, Chris Bidinosti, among others.

Finally, I dedicate this text to Sarah, Vanessa, Billy, Joey, Cara, Katie, and Amber Cate, my nephews and nieces, who don't get to see their Uncle Dan quite often enough.

Daniel K. Lapsley

1

Piaget's Theory: Stage and Structure

Our understanding of human development is influenced in large measure by the vision and genius of the great Swiss intellectual Jean Piaget (1896–1980). It is not an extravagance to say that Piaget was the greatest child psychologist that ever lived. The modern study of moral development, and many other topics besides, would look very impoverished were it not for his pioneering achievements. Yet Piaget did not consider himself to be a child psychologist; nor did he believe that his contribution was primarily psychological in nature (Piaget, 1977). Although his views on cognitive development are widely characterized as a "stage theory," stage may not be the most central category for understanding Piaget's project (Broughton, 1981a).

But if Piaget did not envision his work as a simple contribution to developmental (genetic) psychology, how did he conceive it? What was the problem that motivated his research on children's cognitive development, and how do the various Piagetian findings contribute to the solution of this problem? If stage is not, in fact, the central category for understanding the Piagetian project, what categories would be better candidates? We must make some attempt to answer these questions, for two reasons. First, examining the key features of Piaget's theory of intellectual development will allow us to place his own pioneering work on moral judgment in the context of his larger project. Second, understanding the Piagetian paradigm provides us with the necessary tools to understand and evaluate subsequent moral psychological theories. As we will see in later chapters, the Piagetian notions of stage and structure are featured in most theories of moral reasoning. For example, Lawrence Kohlberg's theory of moral development, which I take up in Chapter 3, is a sophisticated extension of the Piagetian cognitive developmental approach to the moral domain. Many issues that swirl around Kohlberg's theory will be better considered when the Piagetian foundations of the theory are well understood. Indeed, the Piagetian paradigm has been an important source of insights, and criticism, for many decades, and no foray into developmental matters can get very far without a working grasp of some key Piagetian concepts. In this first chapter, then, I examine in broad stroke the Piagetian approach to intellectual development with a particular focus on the twin notions of stage and structure. In the next chapter, I examine Piaget's (1932/1965) landmark study of moral judgment. Let us begin with some of the principle themes that framed Piaget's account of intellectual development.

Genetic Epistemology

Piaget was primarily interested in accounting for the development of scientific knowledge. How is it that scientific practice is able to discover anomalies and novelties? What are the mechanisms that allow knowledge to be constructed? How is scientific knowledge organized or formalized, and how can it be said to progress from less-developed to better-developed organizations? By what criteria can we judge later-occurring formalizations of knowledge as better or more adequate than earlier formalizations of knowledge, and how can we characterize the various transitions from less adequate to more adequate? Piaget's lifework can be seen as an attempt to provide answers to these sorts of questions. His pursuit gave rise to a new discipline of inquiry that he called *genetic epistemology*. So Piaget considered himself a genetic epistemologist, and he saw his empirical investigations of children's reasoning as the groundbreaking articulation of this new discipline.

What is genetic epistemology? Genetic epistemology is concerned with the developmental origins of knowledge, especially scientific knowledge. It attempts "to explain knowledge on the basis of its history, its sociogenesis, and especially the psychological origins of the notions and operations on which it is based" (Piaget, 1970, p. 1). In other words, in Piaget's view, there is a complementary relationship between the psychological formation of knowledge as it might occur within the development of individual human subjects and the formation of knowledge as it might occur within the various scientific disciplines, mathematics, and logic. This being so, it becomes possible to delineate the growth of knowledge in the disciplines of logic, mathematics, and science by examining how concepts specific to these disciplines are constructed in ontogenesis, that is, in the cognitive developmental history of individuals. As Chapman (1988, p. 332) puts it, "The study of children's cognitive development was a way of answering certain questions regarding the evolution of knowledge that in turn would provide criteria for deciding among different forms of judgment involving questions of truth and value."

Hence, in the study of children's cognitive development, Piaget would be interested in describing how children's understanding of various logicomathematical concepts (e.g., space, time, number, and causality) is organized, how these organized understandings can be said to develop from less adequate to more adequate forms, and how we can know the difference. Consequently, the same questions that Piaget addressed concerning the progress and formalization of knowledge *in science* are addressed as well when Piaget turned his attention to the progress and formalization of scientific knowledge *in individuals*. Epistemological questions, that is, questions concerning the nature of knowing and of knowledge, require both historical investigations of the scientific enterprise and developmental investigations of the "epistemic subject" (Kitchener, 1980). The formation or constitution of knowledge is to be studied in all of its aspects, in history, in sociogenesis, and in ontogenesis, and this is the task of genetic epistemology.

Piaget's epistemological focus, then, is revealed by his concern with the characterization of knowledge, and in the range of topics that he investigated (for example, the categories of knowledge—space, time, number, causality, morality, etc.). The way he defined intelligence and the way he characterized developmental transition and progress, however, strongly reflected his formal biological training (Piaget's doctoral dissertation was on mollusks, and his earliest professional writings dealt with issues concerning species classification and adaptation). Indeed, in an autobiography, Piaget (1952a) remarked that in his earliest youth he became committed to providing a biological explanation of knowledge and that he did so by creating a new "science of types" he thought could bring biological themes to bear on epistemological issues. This youthful fascination with the possibility of deriving a biologically based epistemology resonated throughout Piaget's long, productive career. In fact, Michael Chapman (1988) has argued that the central categories of Piaget's mature theory can be fully grasped only when seen in the light of his early, formative ideas. A consideration of these early ideas, then, will pay some dividends.

Biology, Genera, Holism, Equilibria

It occurred to the adolescent Piaget that if one could penetrate the structure of living things and discern the principles of organization and operation, one might be in a position to address questions of ultimate value, including questions of religious, moral, and aesthetic values. Indeed, it might even be possible to reconcile science and religion. Piaget's optimism on this score was motivated by his conviction that God was coterminous with life itself and that the more one learned of the biological processes of all life—the organizational structure and operational functioning of living entities—the more one learned of divinity. As Piaget (1952a, p. 240) remarks, "The identification of God with life itself was an idea that stirred me almost to ecstasy because it now enabled me to see in biology the explanation of all things and of the mind itself." In a thinly disguised autobiographical novel entitled *Recherche* (published 1918), the youthful Piaget, who had just been awarded his doctorate from the University of Neuchâtel, worked out a scheme whereby science and religion could be reconciled. Some of the preliminary ideas that would govern his life's work would also surface in this novel (Gruber & Voneche, 1977; Chapman, 1988).

The reconciliation of science and religion seemed to hinge on the notions of totality and equilibrium. All living entities, all biological processes, are coherently organized in certain ways so as to permit adaptive functioning. Indeed, structural organization is a general feature of living processes, and this can be detected on multiple levels of reality. Hence, at various levels of nature and in human psychological and social life, one readily detects patterns of organization and modes of relating that exist in a state of partial (or "real") equilibrium. In every "relational totality," that is, in every organized structure, in living entities of all kinds, there exists a relationship between the structural whole (*structure d'ensemble*) of the entity and its constitutive parts.

For Piaget, it is the relationship between the totality of the structure (the whole) and its parts that is primary. This is worth pointing out because Piaget's theory emphasizes intellectual form, pattern, organization, and structure, and so is often taken to represent the view called *holism,* which is often contraposed to *elementarism.*

Holism is the view that the whole is not merely the sum of its elements (contra elementarism, which holds that the whole is the additive sum of its parts). Rather, the whole is more than the sum of its parts; that is, the whole takes on an emergent quality that is quite unlike its constitutive parts. For example, when two hydrogen atoms are combined with an oxygen atom, the resulting structure is not a gas—that is, the resulting entity is not merely the sum of the two gaseous elements that compose it but is rather another entity (water) that has very different qualities (fluidity, wetness) that emerge in the union of elements.

Hence, a whole or totality has properties that are not possessed by its individual parts, elements, or members. A mathematical structure, for example, has certain holistic properties (transitivity, communicativity, associativity) that are not possessed by individual integers (Kitchener, 1986). In this sense the whole is greater than the sum of its parts. Yet Piaget extends the basic notion of holism by stressing the dynamic relationship that exists between parts and whole, a view that has been called "relational holism" (Kitchener, 1985). What is primary in Piaget's relational structuralism is the part-whole *relationship*, or rather, the relationship among the elements. In Piaget's words, "Logical *procedures* or natural *processes* by which the whole are formed are primary, not the whole, which is consequent on the systems laws of composition, or the elements" (Piaget, 1968/1971, pp. 8–9, my emphasis). This suggests that what is whole and what is part are never absolute, or even stable, because the primary relationship between them is transformative. What is structure at one stage becomes transformed so that it is integrated as an element or part in the succeeding stage. The boundary between structure and element, between whole and part, is itself a developmental construction and will change (Kitchener, 1986). Or to put it differently, structures are not to be understood apart from the constructive, transformative activities (for example, reflective abstraction, equilibration) that generate them (Turner, 1973; Broughton, 1981b).

The interaction of parts and wholes can be observed at all levels of reality. In biology, it is reflected in the interaction between cells (parts) and the organism (whole). In social affairs, it is reflected in the interaction between individuals (parts) and society (whole). In psychology, between cognitive operations (parts) and the *structure d'ensemble* of intelligence. In logic, between general concepts and particular instances of the concept.

Perhaps the best example is to be found in the philosophy of science (of which genetic epistemology is one approach). Here Piaget's relational holism is reflected in the view that neither empirical data (the facts) nor holistic theory are fundamental. Rather, what is fundamental are the procedural operations, the methodologies, or the transformational relations that mediate facts and theory. In this case, the theory and the discrete data are mutually derived from such transformational operations (Kitchener, 1986). Similarly, and more generally, part-whole structural relations are mutually derived from and are secondary to the transformative operations that relate them. This is the meaning of Piaget's claim, noted previously, that "logical procedures are primary" and that the whole is a consequence of "laws of composition."

In a number of his earliest investigations Piaget (1926, 1928) focused on some of the consequences of failing to grasp the relationship between parts and whole in children's representational thought. *Syncretism* describes a mode of reasoning and perceiving that tends toward globality and lacks differentiation. That is, it proceeds from global, comprehensive schemes, from the whole to the part(s). It is a tendency to think in terms of wholes, to assimilate perceptions and ideas to totalizing points of view and subjective schemas without corrective adaptations to objective standpoints. In a metaphoric sense, syncretism is a failure to see the trees because of the forest. *Egocentrism*, the well-known Piagetian concept, is an example of syncretistic thinking. Egocentrism describes a lack of differentiation between some aspect of self and other. It describes an inability to infer the visual, affective, or cognitive perspective of another insofar as these perspectives are undifferentiated from one's own. *Realism* is another example of syncretistic thinking. Piaget (1951) calls realism an "anthropocentric illusion." It, too, is a kind of egocentrism in the sense that the child fails to distinguish the subjectivity of the self (what is internal and psychical) from the objectivity of the external world (what is external and physical). Believing in the external reality of dreams—that names are inherent attributes of the objects they signify—and that thought is bound up with objects are examples of realistic thinking. Syncretism, egocentrism, realism, then, all reflect the tendency to view external reality in an undifferentiated way, that is, in a way that reflects the predominance of the whole over the parts.

Juxtaposition is a complementary mode of reasoning and perceiving that proceeds from the part to the whole. That is, it focuses on discrete details in isolation from any attempt to integrate them into a coherent whole; metaphorically, juxtaposition is a failure to see the forest because of the trees. Syncretism (and its variants) and juxtaposition are the result of a particular kind of part-whole relationship. They reflect an unstable resolution of the part-whole structural relationship because they yield a way of thinking and perceiving that is not adaptive. And it is not adaptive because each mode represents, in its own way, a failure to adequately grasp the relationship between parts and whole. In one case, the parts predominate over the whole (juxtaposition); in the other, the whole predominates over the parts (syncretism). What is missing, and what would constitute greater adaptation, is the ability to flexibly move from parts to whole and back (reversibility). Structures that are characterized by reversible part-whole operations yield greater developmental stability and adaptation. The part-whole notions of syncretism (moral constraint), juxtaposition (moral egocentrism), and reversibility (morality of cooperation) surface again in Chapter 2 when I consider Piaget's theory of moral judgment.

The part-whole relationship can be described, then, as a particular kind of organization or structure. It is a particular organization of elements. The organization is always an imperfect one, that is, the part-whole relationship exists as an unstable (real) equilibrium. By "unstable equilibrium" Piaget means that the relationship between parts and whole are such that either the whole predominates over the parts (syncretism) or the parts predominate over the whole (juxtaposition). As noted previously, unstable equilibria are imperfectly adaptive because syncretism can lead to rigidity and juxtaposition can lead to disintegration (Chapman, 1988). Yet unstable part-whole relationships always tend toward a more ideal organization. In this ideal equilibrium toward which structural organizations tend, parts and wholes are mutually and dynamically conserved in a system of perfect compensations, thereby preserving the integrity of the structure by precluding either rigidity or disintegration. In other words, structural organizations, at whatever level, tend to progress toward an ideal equilibrium, which is an adaptive perfection of the operation of the system.

Once again examples can be drawn from many areas. In biology, one can describe the relationship between organisms (parts) and the species (the whole) as an evolutionary equilibrium that is stable, adaptive, and ideal. In psychology, cognitive operations are increasingly organized into an articulated *structure d'ensemble* that takes on greater power and stability in later stages of cognitive development. In society, the ideal equilibrium between individuals and society is governed by notions of justice and morality.

For the youthful Piaget the notion of ideal equilibrium provided a ready criterion by which to appraise moral (the good) and aesthetic (the beautiful) judgments (Chapman, 1988). Structural organizations that approach the ideal form are judged to be better than structural organizations that are partial and far from ideal. The tendency of structural forms to develop in the direction of increasing adaptation and more perfected modes of operation provided Piaget with an epistemological criterion by which to judge different forms of knowing. And the criterion is quite simple: Forms of knowing that appear later are better and more adequate because they are the result of a process of development. Development has its own internal standard of adequacy. The developmental process transforms the relationship between parts and wholes in the direction of increased articulation and differentiation (Werner, 1957), so that a more adaptive mode of functioning is gradually attained, that is, until an ideal equilibrium is reached. Hence "development" implies a standard of adequacy that sets apart more developed from less developed forms of knowing or else distinguishes modes of operation that are temporary, unstable, partial, and less adaptive from operations that are enduring, stable, ideal, and more perfectly adaptive.

There is an important consequence to this view. When one says that the goal or aim of development is to attain a particular end point, in this case an ideal state of structural equilibrium, one is not simply making an empirical claim about the natural course of development. One is also making an evaluative and normative claim. When you say that something is developing, you are implicitly making reference to some standard of reference that allows you to distinguish progressive development from mere temporal change, and it is the ideal end point, or final stage, that serves as this standard of reference. Developmental change is evaluated or explained in terms of how well or how closely it approximates the attainment of the normative end point, typically conceived as the final stage of development (Kitchener, 1983). "Thus the developmental end-state is a normative standard of reference by means of which we can evaluate the direction of development and its degree of progress towards this goal" (Kitchener, 1986, p. 29).

And there is a second consequence to this view. In the study of development, one cannot help but mix empirical claims about the "natural" course of development with normative (value-laden) claims about what constitutes "good" development. The final stage will have some intrinsic worth such that to approximate it during the course of development is "good." It is "good" and "better" for cognitive structures to be adaptive rather than nonadaptive, to be ideal rather than partial, to be enduring rather than temporary, to be stable rather than unstable. To make a claim about development, then, is to say that the system has progressed to a more desirable and better mode of operation, and one cannot help but make this sort of value judgment when describing a natural course of developmental change. Factual (what is natural) and normative (what is good) issues will always be mutually implicated in developmental studies (Kitchener, 1986; Piaget, 1971a). Later we will see (1) how Kohlberg (1971) uses these Piagetian notions to good advantage to press his claim that his higher moral stages are better than lower stages in both a psychological and normative (moral) sense and (2) that the study of moral development necessarily entails some mixing of factual ("is") and normative ("ought") moral claims, a mix that has traditionally been denounced as the *naturalistic fallacy* in moral philosophy (Hudson, 1969).

Before turning to Piaget's theory of moral judgment, we need to consider one additional Piagetian theme, that being the question of stages.

Stages as Morphological Taxonomies

To this point I have not been too concerned with the notion of stages of development. This might seem surprising given the fact that stage is widely thought to be the central concept in the Piagetian tradition. The stage concept is, of course, an important way of characterizing developmental change, although its range of meaning has been subjected to many important conceptual analyses (e.g., Bickhard, 1978; Brainerd, 1978; Flavell, 1971; Flavell & Wohlwill, 1969; Kohlberg, 1969; Pinard & Laurendeau, 1969). Yet Piaget's own use of the stage concept has been far from uniform, and there is now reason to believe that Piaget's understanding of stage and the understanding of stage by many Piagetians, especially Kohlberg, may not at all coincide.

Let's step back for a moment. We have seen that Piaget's understanding of intelligence is thoroughly infused with biological themes. Indeed, Piaget's genetic epistemology was an attempt both to account for the construction of intellectual novelty and to appraise growth in knowledge. He did this by appealing to the development of increasingly more adequate forms of structural equilibria in children's thinking (and in the history of science)—adequate in the sense that adaptation is more perfectly served as thinking approximates the ideal equilibrium.

Piaget's attempt to derive a biologically based epistemology spilled over into his definition of intelligence. Hence, in one definition, Piaget (1952b, pp. 3–4) suggests that intelligence is a kind of biological achievement. It is a "particular instance of biological adaptation" at the psychological level. Along the same lines he also notes that intelligence is a "form of equilibrium towards which all [cognitive] structures tend" (Piaget, 1950, p. 6). By calling intelligence a form, Piaget draws attention to its organizational features. By calling it a form of *equilibrium*, Piaget is suggesting that the function of intelligence is to permit ideal adaptation to all sorts of intellectual environments. By calling it a form of equilibrium toward which all structures tend, Piaget is drawing attention to the fact that this adaptive equilibrium is not attained immediately but only gradually and over the course of development. And progress toward this ideal, this "tending" or gradual approximation of intellectual equilibrium, can be charted as a series of stages. The various stages of cognitive development describe the succession of increasingly more powerful forms of structural equilibria, with formal operations (the final stage) being the final equilibrium attained by thought (Ginsberg & Opper, 1969). The gradual evolution of increasingly more powerful intellectual structures, then, can be demarcated into a series of stages, which is exactly the strategy that Piaget adopts. How, then, are we to think about stages?

The received view is that the Piagetian tradition has established some "hard" criteria for applying a stage typology to a developmental process. Indeed, one source of the received view is undoubtedly Piaget himself. In one paper, for example, Piaget (1960) outlined the following developmental criteria for governing the use of "stage": (1) Stages describe qualitative differences in children's modes of reasoning. (2) These qualitatively different modes of reasoning form an *invariant sequence*, or a constant order of succession that cannot be altered by cultural factors. (3) Each mode of reasoning forms a structured whole (*structure d'ensemble*), which is an underlying thought organization or pattern of reasoning, or a deep structure that unifies superficially dissimilar "surface" responses. This seems to imply that underlying a range of different content areas may be a single structural organization. (4) Stages are *hierarchical integrations*. That is, each succeeding stage is not simply a replacement of the preceding stage. Rather, lower-order structures are reorganized and reintegrated into structures that define higher-order stages. What is whole at one stage becomes a part at the succeeding stage.

This characterization of developmental stages was taken to be the Piagetian standard. It was given added currency by the fact that Kohlberg's influential theory of moral development, and his "cognitive developmental approach" to socialization more generally, embraced this "hard," demanding notion of stage (Kohlberg, 1969, 1971). With this notion of stage the empirical assessment of Piagetian (and, later, Kohlbergian) claims seemed straightforward enough: Simply focus on whether observed developmental change for some domain in question meets the exacting standard of the "hard" stage criteria. If the subjects' responses show too much stage mixture, if change seems too quantitative and continuous, if there is evidence that children give a range of responses on stage-relevant tasks (which seems to violate the "structured whole" understanding of stage), then considerable doubt can be cast on the validity of Piagetian (and Kohlbergian) claims (e.g., Case, 1985).

But is the received view the most appropriate way of characterizing the Piagetian conception of stage development? Perhaps not. Chapman (1988) has argued, for example, that Piaget's biological and zoological intentions regarding the notion of stage were never fully grasped by North American researchers. North American researchers have tended to make (at least) three errors in their evaluation of Piaget's use of stage. The first error was to think of a stage as a functional explanatory construct that somehow summarized an antecedent-consequent relationship between environmental conditions and behavioral outcomes. In other words, the Piagetian project was thought to explain developmental outcomes in terms of causal, functional antecedents (Chapman, 1988).

One variant of this view is the B = f(stage) type of explanation. Performance on some task, or some exhibition of behavior (B), was explained as a function of the stage (f[stage]) the child was thought to be in. For example, a child can solve class-inclusion and conservation problems because the child is in the stage of concrete operations. This suggested that stages were classifications of children (as opposed to classifications of forms of reasoning at an epistemic level).

The second error concerned the interpretation of the structured-whole assumption. The notion that stages are a structured whole was thought to imply that there should be uniform performance across a wide range of contents (tasks, problems) thought to be appropriate for a given stage. It was thought that at a given stage children would perform with uniform consistency across a wide range of problems and tasks. Hence, to observe asynchrony in development, to observe, for example, that the conservation tasks are in fact solved at widely different ages (*horizontal decalage*) even though their solution ostensibly requires the same underlying logical structure was thought to be an empirical embarrassment for the stage concept (Case, 1985). Similarly, evidence that individuals give a range of responses to the same or similar task was also thought to have unfortunate consequences for Piagetian stage theories, as this, too, appeared to violate expectations bound up with the notion of *structure d'ensemble*. Remember, an underlying form of reasoning, or an underlying thought organization (*structure d'ensemble*), was thought to unify superficially different content domains and to preclude, therefore, within-stage variation in reasoning or behavior.

Finally, the third error was the demand to see sharp, abrupt discontinuities in the behavioral data as the warrant for validly using stages even as descriptive devices. Hence, empirical evidence that a course of change was gradual and smooth was thought to be inconsistent with the view that a stage sequence should describe a progression of qualitative discontinuities in performance, that is, should describe differences in kind, not in amount.

The difficulty with these three expectations is that they are at variance with Piaget's own use of the stage concept. One looks in vain for stage sequences in Piaget's many books that actually adhere to hard-stage criteria (Rest, n.d.). Asynchrony in development and *decalage* appear to be the rule. In some instances individual children give answers that range across a variety of stages. Otherwise there is considerable stage overlap and mixture, development seems gradual and incremental, and there are frequent acknowledgments that research conclusions are very much tied to particular methods or to particular kinds of children and the

like. All of this could mean that Piaget's account of the development of various scientific, mathematical, and logical concepts fails even his own standard of adequacy
insofar as these sequences do not comport with the received view regarding what
a proper stage sequence should look like. Yet there is reason to believe that the
received view does not adequately capture the Piagetian understanding of stage.

How should Piaget's notion of stage be properly characterized? One clue is
to keep in mind Piaget's early fascination with embryological matters, his biological training, and his attempt to derive a biologically based theory of knowledge. Chapman (1988) argues, for example, that the classification of children's
thinking into various stages according to certain formal and structural criteria
was not unlike the classification of various biological species into zoological categories based on formal morphological characteristics. The young Piaget who
had, as a naturalist, collected and classified specimens of mollusks is continuous
with the older Piaget who had, as a genetic psychologist, collected and classified
specimens of children's thinking. Hence, stages were not considered by Piaget to
be explanatory devices. From the very beginning they served as descriptive tax-
onomic categories that classified not children but rather formal properties of
children's reasoning (Langer, 1969). Just as biologists use formal morphological
criteria to distinguish plant and animal species, so too does the genetic epistemologist use formal structural criteria to distinguish different "species" of
knowledge. And "if the developmental classifications of forms of thinking and
reasoning can be compared to the classification of biological species, then the
attempt to explain the mechanisms of transition from one stage to another can
be likened to the attempt to explain the origins and evolution of species"
(Chapman, 1988, p. 337).

Yet what is to be made of the structured-whole assumption? Does this
assumption entail the view that an underlying stage structure must necessarily
unify a range of contents into a uniform and consistent mode of responding? Does
this assumption entail the view that variation in stage responding—the observance,
for example, of content *decalages*—is to be regarded as an empirical embarrassment
for the structural notion of stage? This was certainly Kohlberg's (1969) understanding of what the *structure d'ensemble* assumption entailed. Indeed, Kohlberg and
his colleagues went to great efforts to ensure that the Kolhbergian moral-stage
sequence was in accordance with the received view on the structured-whole
assumption. For example, over the years the technology of moral-stage scoring was
progressively revised in order to more sharply distinguish underlying moral structure (form) from mere surface content, and this (1) to limit variation in responding
and decalage, (2) to ensure greater uniformity in stage responding, and (3) to
improve the developmental trajectory of the sequence (Colby, 1978; Levine, 1979).

Kohlberg's commitment to the received view on the structured-whole
assumption may be justly motivated by other considerations, but it is not driven by
Piaget's theory (Kohlberg's own view of the matter notwithstanding). Chapman
(1988, p. 347) argues, for example, that "contrary to widely accepted interpretations of his theory, Piaget did not believe in general stages of development charac-

terized by developmental synchrony across domains of content, and such an interpretation of stage development cannot be derived from the concept of *structures d'ensemble*." According to Chapman (1988) there is no implication in Piaget's theory that behaviors of a given stage are bound into a functional unity, regardless of content, and must therefore develop in synchrony.

Indeed, Piaget (1960, p. 14) is quite explicit about the matter. "There are no general stages," he writes. Although developmental processes are obviously related to one another, their relationship cannot be characterized in any uniform way; nor do these processes obey a common developmental (temporal) rhythm, "there being no reason why these processes should constitute a unique structural whole at each level" (Piaget, 1960, p. 15). Piaget denied that *structures d'ensemble* entail the notion of structural unity across domains of content or entail temporal uniformity in the appearance of formally similar abilities or cognitive understandings (Broughton, 1981a). He did not believe that individuals are structural unities in the sense that the totality of their stage-related behavior can be the result of a single general structure: "Nowhere have I seen structural unity, at no stage in the development of the child. . . . And if there is no structural unity, there are no general stages that permit fixed correspondences, verifiable in all domains, and between all functions" (Piaget, cited in Chapman, 1988, pp. 346–347).

But what is the proper understanding of *structures d'ensemble*? If they do not, in fact, have anything to do with either (1) uniformity of responding across stage-related domains or (2) temporal synchrony in the appearance or transformation of stage-related abilities—if they have nothing to do with these things, to what do they refer?

Structured Totalities and Relational Holism

Once again we can appeal to the part-whole model of structure and Piaget's understanding of relational holism to help us understand this difficult concept. For Piaget a structure is an inferred organizational property of intellectual functioning. A structure is a particular composition of elements. It is a kind of totality, that is, a whole that is formed by the relationship (laws of composition) among the parts. Hence, a structure is a relational totality—a structural totality formed by the relationship among constitutive elements or parts. Piaget (1950) identified these relational totalities as *structures d'ensemble*.

Different stages are characterized by different kinds of structural organizations, or structures. That is, different stages are defined by different part-whole configurations. For example, during infancy, discrete reflexive behaviors (parts, or elements) are organized into coherent behavioral patterns called *schemes* (wholes). The infant possesses, then, an organized way of looking, of seeing, of grasping, of hearing, of sucking. These primitive sensorimotor schemes are wholes in the sense that they are the result of a relationship among parts, in this case, discrete reflexive behaviors. However, these sensory schemes are uncoordinated with each other in the early phases of the sensorimotor period. They will themselves be organized as elements (parts) into higher-order habits. For example, *visual schemes* (organized ways of looking) and *prehensive schemes* (organized ways of grasping) will themselves be coordinated, as elements, into a higher-order whole through the process (law of composition) of *reciprocal assimilation*. With reciprocal assimilation, behavioral and sensory schemes mutually assimilate one another. Thus, a higher-order organization emerges when through reciprocal assimilation, the visual scheme assimilates the grasping scheme (permitting an infant to grasp what she sees); the grasping scheme assimilates the visual scheme (permitting an infant to see what she grasps). In this way two lower-level organized wholes (looking scheme, grasping scheme) are now organized as parts or elements into a new, higher-order, organized whole (coordinated looking-grasping scheme through reciprocal assimilation).

Yet the coordination of sensorimotor schemes is a slow, gradual process that unfolds in a continuous and uneven way throughout infancy. Some coordinations (sucking-grasping, looking-sucking) are achieved before others (looking-grasping). But whenever a particular coordination does emerge, it has the same formal properties as all the other coordinations. It represents a formally similar part-whole organization. It comes about because of a formally similar process that bears a strong analogical relationship to other, related sensorimotor coordinations. So if one refers to the *structures d'ensemble* of the sensorimotor period, one is making reference to these formal, analogical similarities among the various sensorimotor coordinations. One is *not* making the claim that a general sensorimotor structure organizes the totality of infantile behavior into a functional unity across a range of contents. If that were so, one would have to claim that once there is coordination of, say, the looking-sucking scheme, the infant must also be capable of other sensorimotor coordinations, which is not the case at all.

Let's continue our analysis of the notion of *structures d'ensemble* by bearing down on the content *decalages* of concrete operations. Let's begin by considering some examples from Piaget's famous studies of conservation.

The conservation-of-physical-quantity task works something like this: The child is shown an amount of some physical quantity, say, a lump of clay. The lump is divided into two balls of equal amount. After the child acknowledges that the two balls are indeed equal in amount, one of the balls is transformed, say, it is flattened so that it appears to have more than the untransformed ball (even though nothing is added or taken away from the balls). The child is now asked if the two balls are still equal in amount. If the child answers yes, which is the correct response, and assuming that the child is not guessing and can give a suitable rationale for her answer, we may conclude that the child has conserved physical quantity in spite of the distorting perceptual bias (that one ball was transformed and now looks like it has more).

Now consider a related task: the conservation of weight. This task works in a way very similar to the physical-quantity task. Present the child with two amounts (clay balls) that weigh the same. Transform one of the balls. Ask the child if, given the transformation, the two balls still weigh the same. Again, if the child says yes, and assuming that the child is not guessing and can give a suitable rationale for her answer, we can assume that the child has conserved weight in spite of a perturbing transformation of the objects.

The received view assumes that the two conservation tasks should be solved at about the same time (age). Why? Because the solution of either task rests on the child having cognitive structures that are operational. When a child is in the stage of concrete operations, she has operational cognitive structures that permit her to annul, correct, or reverse a series of transformations by taking their inverse and thereby restoring the cognitive equilibrium. The underlying logical structure of conservation tasks is identical across all of the tasks. If the child has the cognitive ability to solve one conservation task, she can solve them all, since the underlying structure of the various conservation tasks is identical.

In other words, the various kinds of conservation problems (e.g., physical quantity, weight, liquid volume, area) are simply content domains that are organized by the same underlying deep structure. So if the child can cognitively reverse the transformation, that is, annul or undue it, then the child can balance the perturbing transformation with compensatory cognitive acts, thereby conserving the original amount or weight. In this way cognitive equilibrium is maintained. And reversible cognitive operations are a hallmark of the stage of concrete operations. Again, to continue the received-view assumption, if the child has the cognitive ability to solve one task (physical quantity), she should solve the other (weight) as well. And why not, since the underlying logical structure of the tasks is the same; if her structures are operational (reversible) enough to solve one, they should be reversible enough to solve the other.

Unfortunately, the two tasks are solved at widely different ages. Typically, children who solve the conservation-of-quantity task will have to wait an additional two years before they will be able to solve the conservation-of-weight task. This gap, or delay, in the ability of children to solve formally similar tasks characteristic of a given stage (in this case, concrete operations) is an example of *horizontal decalage*, and many researchers (e.g., Case, 1985) consider this phenomenon to be a failure of the structured-whole requirement of the stage concept. Presumably, because a stage is a structured whole, there should be a certain uniformity in responding across a range of contents. If a child is in a stage, the child should be able to solve all the tasks appropriate to that stage—and horizontal decalage would seem to frustrate this expectation.

Yet horizontal decalage should not be viewed as an empirical refutation of the structured-whole requirement after all (Gelman & Baillargeon, 1983; Pinard & Laurendeau, 1969; Broughton, 1981a). To see this one must consider how it is that cognitive structures are said to emerge. Let's consider the case of concrete operations and the two conservation tasks described previously. The various structures of concrete operations are called groupings. How do the cognitive groupings that are characteristic of concrete operations emerge? Groupings are based on overt actions that have become interiorized, that is, made part of mental cognitive activity. This is a basic Piagetian claim, that the origin of thought is interiorized action, or action that is internally (mentally) represented in cognitive form. When overt actions become interiorized, they are grouped in certain ways, and there are eight such groupings peculiar to concrete operations. These groupings are ways of organizing specific content, since they are based on different kinds of overt actions. Hence, one grouping of concrete operations could be functionally different from another grouping of concrete operations because the two groups of operations are derived from different kinds of actions. In other words, the two groupings could be functionally different, since they are based on operations that have their source in actions that have different content, but they are formally the same, since they are nonetheless groupings of concrete operations.

An example should make this clear. In order to solve the conservation-of-physical-quantity task, one has to be able to perform certain reversible mental operations. What is the source of these reversible mental operations relating to physical quantity? The source is overt behavior. That is, these mental operations are themselves interiorized versions of overt behavior that involved manipulation of objects—putting objects together, taking them apart, transforming their shape, and the like. So the mental operations involved in the conservation of physical quantity derive from interiorized actions of manipulating objects. The mental operations involved in the conservation of weight are very different. These mental operations are interiorized versions of actions that pertain to overt acts of a different sort, in this case, of weighing. Hence, in the mind of the child, mental operations that pertain to physical quantity are organized into one group, and operations that pertain to weight are organized into another. Each grouping of operations is adaptive for its particular content. That is, the structural grouping based on manipulation of objects is adaptive for dealing with questions of physical objects, including the conservation of physical quantity. The structural grouping based on actions of weighing is adaptive to questions regarding weight, including the conservation of weight. Again, the two groupings of operations have formal similarities, but functionally they are very different, since the two groupings are adaptive for different content problems (conservation of amount, weight) and they are derived from different sources of interiorized actions (manipulating objects, weighing them).

But some actions are easier to group than others (Piaget, 1971b). Different tasks or content materials present certain resistances to grouping structures, and herein lies the cause of horizontal decalage (Flavell & Wohlwill, 1969). The extension of formally similar grouping operations to different kinds of content may result in lags or delays because of the resistance of some contents to grouping operations. Consequently, formally similar cognitive structures, or formally similar understandings, need not appear in different areas of content at the same time or develop in temporal synchrony (Broughton, 1981a; Chapman, 1988). As Piaget (1952/1965, p. 204) points out, a formal structure "will not be acquired all at once, irrespective of its content, but will need to be reacquired as many times as there are different contents to which it is applied." A formal structure, he continues, is simply a "coordination at a given level," a coordination that is possible, however, only if the elements, terms, or relations to be coordinated are well understood. Consequently, the formal structure "must be reconstructed as a new coordination each time a new class of notions is involved." This is a very clear indication that horizontal decalage does not at all violate Piaget's understanding of cognitive structure and is therefore not the empirical embarrassment that the received view has led us to believe (Gelman & Baillargeon, 1983).

It was noted previously that according to Piaget's relational holism, the relationship between parts and whole is primary. Indeed, part-whole totalities were said to be derivative of transformative operations such that structures could not be understood apart from the constructive activities that generated them. Intelligence is *constructive*. It now appears that structures cannot exist apart from specific content as well. The *structure d'ensemble*, as a relational totality, is a particular organization or composition of parts or elements. Hence form (structure) and content are inseparable (Piaget & Inhelder, 1974), and, consequently, structures will always reflect a certain content specificity (Chapman, 1988). There is content *decalage* (in the conservation tasks) because the grouping structures of concrete operations are constructed for and adapted to specific content, which explains why these operations appear at different points within the concrete period for different conservation problems.

Summary

Piaget's influence on child development is so pervasive that any consideration of the moral domain must necessarily begin with his theory. My examination of Piaget's genetic epistemology revealed the fact that Piaget had a long-standing interest in developing criteria for judging growth and progress in the construction and formalization of knowledge and values, including moral values. Formalizations that approximate an ideal equilibrium over the course of development are better than formalizations that are developmentally prior to, or further from, the ideal. I also examined Piaget's understanding of structure and took up the issue of stages, particularly the issue of what the *structure d'ensemble* assumption reasonably allows one to expect of stage development. I concluded that content *decalages* do not violate this assumption and that structures are content-specific. These latter conclusions will help us better understand the Kohlbergian project and the numerous theories that take Kohlberg's project as a point of departure. For example, over the years there have been a number of important adjustments made in the way the Kohlberg group scores moral-judgment interviews (Colby, 1978). As we will see in Chapter 3, these revisions were motivated by a desire to address a number of important criticisms of the moral-stage sequence. In order to address these criticisms, it was thought necessary to come up with a scoring procedure that sharply distinguishes between structure and content. However, whether it is sensible to conceive of contentless structures is very controversial (Döbert, 1990) and is otherwise not driven by Piaget's notion of cognitive structure, as we have seen. Kohlberg's theory embraces a number of other Piagetian themes, including some themes from Piaget's writings on morality. So I now need to continue my introduction to the cognitive developmental approach by considering Piaget's seminal work on moral development.

2

Piaget's *Moral Judgment of the Child*

The Two Moralities: Constraint and Cooperation

All of morality, in Piaget's view, consists of a system of rules, and the task of genetic psychology is to determine how it is that children come to know these rules and, critically, come to respect them. One obvious way children come to know moral rules is that they adopt the injunctions and prescriptions of adult authorities. Indeed, it is broadly assumed that children are socialized into moral realities by the coaxing and posturing of adult socialization agents, especially parents. Moral socialization is complete when the child comes to submit to the tutoring of these agents and when the child abides by the discipline of the group (Durkheim, 1925/1973).

This view seems natural enough. Parents have greater physical, intellectual, and social power than do children, and they can therefore exert their will and enforce their perspective with relative ease. They also have greater knowledge of the work-ings of the world and can better appreciate (than can children) the place of rules in managing social affairs. The young child, who has no knowledge of such things, must be made to adopt the judgments of the "wiser" more powerful adults and to con-form her behavior accordingly. This is a rather standard view of moral socialization.

Yet Piaget's book is a sustained polemic against the standard view. He did not question the fact that moral socialization begins by inculcating in children a sense of respect for the rule-making authority of great adults, but he believed that breed-ing heteronomous respect for adult authority was a very mediocre moral stance, and one that is not well suited for further development. Indeed, he argued that in the area of moral socialization, the usual parental practices are likely to retard moral development, not promote it.

Parents are typically pleased to coerce obedience to their rules by asserting their power. Typically this assertion meets no resistance on the part of children because they have *unilateral respect* for the magnificence and moral perfection of parents, and there is hence a natural desire on their part to take on the wishes of adults as their own. But because of cognitive limitations, children do not under-stand the rationale behind adult injunctions, do not see the necessary role of moral rules in coordinating activities, and do not understand the genesis of moral rules or their flexibility. For young children moral rules have force not because the rules summarize what is right or just but rather because these children are commanded by adult authority. Rules are respected not because they allow us to coordinate interpersonal interactions or to achieve mutually desired ends in a fair way but rather because adult perfection is to be admired and adult power is feared.

Consequently, parents require children to respect rules that they cannot possibly understand. Children, for their part, feel constrained by their sense of duty and obligation to conform to parental injunctions, yet this conformity is undermined by a lack of understanding of the purpose and function of these rules. Hence, the more children are under the power of adult constraint and the more their moral sensitivities are framed by unilateral respect for adult authority, the less likely it is that real moral understanding is possible. Adult constraint and unilateral respect, then, work against the development of sophisticated moral understandings.

Piaget calls this first phase of moral development the *morality of constraint*. The young child is awed by the superiority of adults and is constrained by it. Hence, the wishes of adults are viewed as requests for blind obedience. Moral obligation and duty are judged in terms of whatever upholds the commands of adults. The child has an absolutistic sense of morality: There is an absolute sense of right and wrong, and parents will tell us. There is an absolute source of morality and it is to be found in adults. There is an absolute moral perspective, and it is the point of view of those with power and authority. There is an absolute sense of moral duty, and it is to obey. There is an absolute sense of justice, and it is revealed whenever parents punish or praise—whatever is punished is morally bad and whatever is praised is morally good.

This heteronomous orientation to moral rules, motivated by unilateral respect, is an example of a kind of syncretism in social life—a dominance of the whole (adult influence) on the parts (children). As such it is an imperfect and unstable equilibrium. It will be supplanted later in development by a second moral orientation that is marked not by unilateral respect but by reversible social relationships, that is, by mutual respect, by reciprocity, equality, and cooperation. Given the fact that parent-child relationships are inherently asymmetrical, this more equilibrated moral orientation must necessarily be nourished elsewhere, within the context of relationships that are inherently equalitarian. These relationships are found within the society of peers.

In Piaget's view, the fundamental understanding of morality is transformed as the child gains greater experience with peers. It is through cooperative exchanges with agemates that children come to learn that rules are not blind requests for obedience but are instead socially constructed flexible arrangements that serve pragmatic ends and are binding as long as consensus prevails, mutual interests are served, and the bonds of solidarity are protected. Because social power is more evenly distributed within a peer group, peers must be won over with reasons. Rules must be established that draw wide support. When rules fail the test of consensus, they can be flexibly renegotiated so as to maintain cohesion and solidarity. This second orientation Piaget aptly calls the *morality of cooperation*. Whereas the morality of constraint is grounded by the unilateral respect that children have for adult authority, the morality of cooperation is grounded by the mutual respect that characterizes a society of equals.

In *The Moral Judgment of the Child* (1932/1965) Piaget reports a wide range of empirical evidence that documents the developmental characteristics of these two broad moral orientations. What seems startling about this account is Piaget's claim that the more adequate, more "equilibrated" moral orientation is one found not in the context of the family but rather in the peer group. The give-and-take of peer negotiations, learning how to cooperate, the way plans are made and disputes settled—these common features of children's friendships provide ample opportunity for moral education. What children learn through these exchanges is a keener appreciation of the purposes and functions of social rules. What they learn is how the benefits and burdens of cooperation can be fairly shared in ways that are responsive to the demands of peer solidarity (Rest, 1983).

The notion that adult-child relations favor only an unstable and mediocre kind of moral orientation must come as a shock to those who assume that the moral formation of the child is a family affair and that only the worst is to be expected of peer influence. Yet Piaget is quite harsh in his estimation of what passes for moral education in the home. "The majority of parents," he writes, "are poor psychologists, and give their children the most questionable of moral teachings" (Piaget, 1932/1965, p. 191). Oftentimes adults are overbearing, opaque, and harsh in their dealings with a child, to such an extent that moral and intellectual egocentrism is strengthened rather than overcome. Simply observe the "average parent" deal with a child "in trains, especially on Sunday evenings after a days outing" (p. 192). Piaget continues:

> How can one fail to be struck on such occasions by the psychological inanity of what goes on: the efforts which parents make to catch their children in wrongdoing instead of anticipating catastrophes and preventing the child by some little artifice or other. . . ; the pleasure taken in inflicting punishments; the pleasure taken in using authority, and the sort of sadism which one sees so often in perfectly respectable folk, whose motto is that 'the child's will must be broken,' or that he must be 'made to feel a stronger will than his.'

The constraint exercised by one generation upon another explains the source and persistence of childish moral notions, in Piaget's view notions that are subverted only by the more equalitarian interactions to be found in the peer arena.

Hence, Piaget identifies two broad stages in the moral judgment of the child, one characterized by constraint, heteronomy, and unilateral respect, the other by cooperation, reciprocity, and mutual respect. I will now flesh out these two stages by examining some specific empirical findings reported.

The Practice and Consciousness of Rules

Piaget begins his study of child morality by investigating what it is children know about rules and, given this understanding, how they put rules into practice. On the playgrounds of Neuchâtel and surrounding communities Piaget engaged children in respectful conversation about the game of marbles. In his view the game of marbles is imbued with its own sense of implicit morality. It contains a complex set of rules, a "code of laws" and a "jurisprudence all its own" (Piaget, 1932/1965, p. 13). These rules are handed down from one generation to the next, just like moral rules, and are preserved and practiced just to the extent that they command respect. If respect for rules is the beginning of morality, then it would seem that investigating children's consciousness and practice of rules in the game of marbles was a good place to start a general investigation of children's moral judgment insofar as marbles is a social game that already has features of an implicit moral system.

How, then, does Piaget describe the *practice of rules*. The practice of rules has its developmental origins in *ritualized motor schemes*. That is, the child simply handles marbles in accordance with certain motor habits. In the second stage (age two to five) the practice of rules is egocentric. This stage emerges when the child is initially exposed to codified rules. Although the child attempts to follow the rules and, indeed, is convinced that she is doing so in fidelity to the examples provided her by her elders, she nonetheless practices the rules in a highly individualistic manner. That is, although the child believes that she is in possession of the whole truth about the rules of the game, that she is playing correctly and just like everyone else, that she is indeed sharing the larger group perspective, in reality she is shut up in her own egocentric perspective. In Piaget's words, the child "plays in an individualistic manner with material that is social. Such is egocentrism" (Piaget, 1932/1965, p. 37). Hence, egocentric play is an intermediate position between the strictly individualistic-motor use of marbles in the first stage and true social play, which will emerge in the next stage.

What happens when two egocentric children sit down to play a game of marbles? They both play for themselves, in a highly individualistic way, according to different sets of rules. Both children attempt to put into practice rules they believe to have come from some mystical adult source (the "elders"). But they do so each according to their own perspective. Because the game is not, therefore, being governed by common rules, there is no real sense of competition, no sense of trying to win by besting the opponent. There is no real concern with what the companion is doing, since each child is playing for himself according to idiosyncratically applied rules that are imperfectly understood.

A third stage, incipient cooperation, emerges between the ages of 7 and 10. Here children genuinely try to win, which means that there must be some concern for seeking agreement about common rules. However, many of these cooperative agreements are unstable, rarely lasting longer than the duration of a single game. Children are still vague about the rules, many contradictory opinions abound, and attempts to legislate unusual or controversial aspects of a game typically fail. This *codification of rules* is the hallmark of the fourth stage (11–12). Here every detail is fixed and the rules are widely known and shared. Indeed, there appears to be an interest in rules for their own sake at this stage.

What is the child's consciousness of rules? During the first stage (which corresponds to the first stage in the practice of rules) the child has some notion that rules must apply to marbles. This is because his entire life up to this point has been permeated with natural (e.g., alternation of day and night) and imposed (meals, bedtime) regularities that have all the appearance of laws. Hence, although the child assimilates the "practice" of marbles to repetitive, individualized action schemes, the child is probably aware that some lawlike regularity must apply here too. When the child is made aware of rules from some outside source and desires to imitate them, the second stage emerges.

The second stage corresponds to the egocentric stage in the practice of rules. Here rules are thought to be sacred and unchangeable, since they emanate from powerful adults and partake of adult authority. Hence there is an almost mystical respect for rules: They have always existed, they have never changed, they cannot be altered, and they were handed down by Noah, or by God or by the elders. This applies even to rules just learned or recently revised! In this case innovation is not real innovation because the child cannot yet distinguish between before and after, old and new. That is, the child does not clearly distinguish between what is learned and what is remembered. She cannot distinguish innovation from reminiscence. Because of this "the child is led to think that he has always known something which in fact he has just learned" (Piaget, 1932/1965, p. 57). In the third stage the rule is no longer an external imposition from above but is rather the result of collaboration and mutual consent among peers. The rule is respected because of loyalty and peer solidarity, but it can be altered if there is sufficient consensus. The rule is now internal in the sense that the child makes it her own as an act of autonomous free choice and mutual agreement.

Perhaps the astute reader has noticed a contradiction. In the practice of rules the egocentric child plays the game of marbles in a highly individualistic way, in seeming disregard for the rules of the game. Yet this child is also one who, in the consciousness of rules, nonetheless regards the rules of the game as immutable, unchangeable, and sacred. That is, the child appears to have mystical respect for rules that she nonetheless routinely and casually violates. Yet the explanation of this curious phenomenon is straightforward. Because of the child's egocentrism, she fails to distinguish between her own impulses and wishes and rules imposed from above. The child is unable to make genuine, mutual contact with adults and hence remains bound up within her own perspective. And the child is not easily liberated from egocentrism because the adult-child relationship is one of constraint, which implies unilateral respect for authority, prestige, and power. Constraint, Piaget argued, is always the ally of egocentrism and serves to nourish it. Consequently, regarding moral rules, the child submits to them, or at least thinks she does, out of deference to the authority and prestige of the adult. But because the rules are external to her, because they come down from adults and she is not the equal of adults and does not understand them, rules do not really transform her conduct. The child intends to conform but cannot, since she does not really understand the rule-making perspective of adults. "The child is, on the one hand, too apt to have the illusion of agreement when actually he is only following his own fantasy; the adult, on the other, takes advantage of the situation instead of seeking "equality" (Piaget, 1932/1965, pp. 61–62). When constraint gives way to cooperation, when unilateral respect gives way to mutual respect, then moral egocentrism will be eliminated from the child's thought.

By way of summary we can ask the genetic psychology question—What does a child know about rules, and how can we characterize growth in knowledge? In his study of social games Piaget identified three types of rules that children come to know: the *motor rule*, traced to habitual action schemes; the *coercive rule*, traced to relations of unilateral respect; and the *rational rule*, traced to relations of mutual respect. The motor rule results from a feeling of repetition that arises out of the ritualization of motor schemes. Motor habits, however, are not yet marked with a sense of obligation. When a child first encounters marbles, then, they are simply assimilated to various action schemes. Rules proper begin when the experience of regularity is imbued with a sense of obligation. That is, when motor rituals are subjected to the social constraint of adults, then the coercive rule, marked by unilateral respect and egocentrism, emerges. This will be supplanted by the rational rule under the social conditions of mutual respect and reciprocity. If intelligence is a "form of equilibrium towards which all structures tend," then mutual respect is the more ideal equilibrium toward which unilateral respect is tending (Piaget, 1932/1965, p. 96), making mutual respect more developed and hence more intelligent. It is a more stable social equilibrium, is more reversible, and hence is more rational. As Piaget puts it, "What is this rational rule but the primitive motor rule freed from individual caprice [egocentrism] and submitted to the control of reciprocity" (p. 88). In political terms, rational development is a movement away from theocracy or gerontocracy to democracy. That is, rational development, in both ontogenesis and in political development, is a movement *away* from the external imposition of sacred laws by elders, away from heteronomy, unilateral respect, and constraint, *to* autonomy, mutual repect, and democratic cooperation.

Moral Realism and the Idea of Justice

It was noted in Chapter 1 that realism is a general feature of the thought of the young child (Piaget, 1951). Realism reflects egocentrism, that is, the inability to distinguish between the objective and subjective, between what is psychical and internal and what is physical and external. Realism is an external projection of mental subjectivity into the material processes of the real world. Hence, dreams have an objective locus, names are aspects of the objects named, and so on. *Moral realism* is the tendency to see moral duty as something that is external to the self and that imposes obligations regardless of circumstances. It is forbidden to lie, to steal, and these laws have an independent existence and are applicable regardless of motive, intention, or special circumstance. Indeed, there is a systematic confusion of moral and physical. The world is permeated with moral rules. Rules, like names, are part of the physical stuff of the universe. For example, sometimes we trip and fall even when we are trying to be careful. In this case falling always follows tripping, according to the physical law of gravity. Similarly, if we are unwittingly careless with the truth, it is a lie, and punishment must follow with just as much inevitability as does falling when one unwittingly and carelessly trips. It is as if nature obeys moral as well as physical laws. This belief Piaget called *immanent justice*, and it is an outgrowth of moral realism.

Immanent justice is the belief that moral laws are immanent in the forces of nature and that the physical universe will automatically exact retribution even when adults fail to detect a transgression. In this case what does motive or intention matter? "A great many children think that a fall or cut constitutes a punishment because their parents have said to them 'It serves you right,' or 'That will be a punishment for you,' or 'God made it happen'" (Piaget, 1932/1965, p. 260). Hence immanent justice, and moral realism more generally, are nurtured by adult constraint and the habit of punishment; hence the child attributes to nature the same power of applying punishments that is possessed by adults.

Moral realism is marked by at least three features. (1) Duty is heteronomous. Obedience to a rule, or to anything at all commanded by an adult, is good. (2) What is to be obeyed is the letter of the law, not the spirit. (3) Acts are judged not according to motives or intentions but in terms of objective consequences, or in terms of exact conformity to the rules. For example, consider two boys, Ron and Ray. Ron wishes to help his mother set the table for dinner, but in his zeal to be of service, he breaks 10 cups. Ray, in an act of mischief, breaks 2 cups. Who is more naughty? More culpable? The young moral realist would hold Ron more culpable, because is not 10 cups an objectively more serious amount of damage than 2 cups—Ron's more praiseworthy intentions notwithstanding? Hence the moral realist believes in the primacy of *objective responsibility*. Objective consequences, not subjective intentions, are the measure of moral responsibility. I will have more to say about this dimension of moral judgment a bit later.

As another example, consider the case of lying. For the moral realist, to lie is to commit a moral fault by the use of language. Hence, swearing, lying, and even unwittingly telling a falsehood are abuses of language and are equated. Lying is thus defined in a purely objective manner without reference to intentionality or to subjective motives.

Moral realism is a reflection of egocentrism, but it is made to flourish by adult constraint and unilateral respect. The commands of adults are invariably external to the child. Their rules are as inscrutable to the child as are the regularities of the physical universe and are on the same plane: "One must eat after going for a walk, go to bed at night, have a bath before going to bed, etc., exactly as the sun shines by day and the moon by night, or as pebbles sink while boats remain afloat" (Piaget, 1932/1965, p. 191). Realistic thought will attenuate, however, with movement to relationships of mutual respect and reciprocity. Relations that are marked by equality and interactions that are marked by reciprocity will force the child to occupy and compare the points of view of others. The child will then come to value the primacy of intentions and motives. Hence, when appraising conduct, the child will favor subjective responsibility. Immanent justice will be rejected in favor of social justice. Lying will be judged as intentional deception. Once again the morality of constraint will yield to the morality of cooperation.

Piaget also investigated the child's understanding of what is just and what is fair. The notion of justice, in Piaget's view, develops independently of adult influence and is more a result of the mutual respect and sense of solidarity that develops among children themselves. Indeed, Piaget argues that adult authority cannot be the source of the sense of justice, since the development of justice presupposes autonomy (Piaget, 1932/1965, p. 319). Hence, immature conceptions of justice are characteristic of the morality of adult constraint and relations of unilateral respect. Mature conceptions of justice are characteristic of the morality of cooperation and relations of mutual respect.

In summary, the morality of constraint is driven by notions of heteronomy and unilateral respect and is associated with a variety of immature moral notions: It encourages moral realism, objective responsibility, and the perception of immanent justice. It reduces moral duty to obedience. It identifies justice with the prerogatives of authority. Indeed, whatever conforms to authority is just; whatever is unpunished is good. Punishment itself is arbitrary expiative, severe, and necessary. In contrast, the morality of cooperation is driven by notions of equality and mutual respect. It is attuned to subjective responsibility and the social nature of justice. It is responsive to peer solidarity, to cooperation, to equalitarianism in all aspects of social life. Indeed, reciprocal peer relations are a more perfect social equilibrium, and moral notions forged in the context of reciprocity are hence more rational. By the onset of adolescence the thoroughgoing equalitarianism of the morality of cooperation will be refined so that notions of equity will be more common. That is, strict equality will be augmented by considerations of situational complexities and extenuating circumstances.

What Is the Empirical Status of the Theory?

What is the empirical status of Piaget's moral-stage theory? It must first be noted that in no way is the theory to be evaluated in terms of how well it fits the so-called hard-stage criteria. The received view would suggest that the moral stages must show sharp discontinuity in development and that performance on the various dimensions of moral judgment must cluster together into unitary stages. Research shows, however, that the various dimensions of moral judgment are not strongly intercorrelated and do not appear to cluster into tightly knit stages (Boehm & Nass, 1962; MacRae, 1954; Johnson, 1962b). This is a lethal finding only if the stage theory is to be evaluated in light of the received-view understanding of *structure d'ensemble*.

Piaget addressed the issue of discontinuity more directly. He emphatically argued in numerous places throughout the book that too much emphasis is laid upon discontinuity. "Let it be understood once and for all," he writes, "that any over-sharp discontinuities are analytical devices, and not objective results." Piaget also acknowledged, again in numerous places throughout the book, that his results may well vary as a function of social class, national origin, religious upbringing, and the like, a claim that subsequent research has documented (Boehm, 1962, 1966; Boehm & Nass, 1962; Harrower, 1934).

With this said, it appears that much of the empirical research does tend to support Piaget's work on moral judgment, at least in broad outline (Lickona, 1976; Rest, 1983). Indeed, Lickona (1976) suggested that perhaps the verdict of a generation of research is that more research is not needed and that Piaget's "intuition is probably sound" (p. 239). Let's examine a few of these dimensions.

In broad outline there is evidence that children become increasingly adept at taking more and different points of view as they get older (Shantz 1983; Flavell,

Botkin, Fry, Wright, & Jarvis, 1968) and that this generally improves the quality of moral judging (Ambron, 1973; DeRemer & Gruen, 1979). Young children do seem to believe in immanent justice, and this belief tends to attenuate as they get older (MacRae, 1954; Medinnus, 1959; Percival & Haviland, 1975; Grinder, 1964; Jahoda, 1958; Najarian-Svajian, 1966). Indeed, a recent study suggested that the accumulated evidence supports Piagetian claims about immanent justice reasoning and that the phenomenon is "real and robust" (Jose, 1991).

There are interesting variations to this general trend. In some cultural groups (e.g., Native Americans) immanent-justice responses may not decline at all, or they may dramatically increase with age (Havighurst & Neugarten, 1955). Immanent justice responses also appear to be associated with fundamentalist religious upbringing, where fortune or misfortune is often associated with whether one is sinful (Curdin, 1966, cited in Lickona, 1976). Why did Arun fall off his bicycle?—because he is a sinner, and sin is always punished! Along similar lines one study showed that preschool children tended to understand the causes of illness in terms of immanent justice (Kister & Patterson, 1980). Why did Arun catch a cold?—because he was bad! Older children, in this study, tended to invoke more rational causes of illness and had a better understanding of contagion.

The idea that children gradually come to consider intentions in their moral judgments and to forsake objective responsibility in their moral evaluations is, according to Lickona (1976, p. 224), "the best documented of all Piaget's moral judgment dimensions." Piaget's claim that peer group participation should have a good effect on moral development is largely supported (Brody & Shaffer, 1982; Keasey, 1971; Hendy & Butter, 1981). Research has shown, for example, that children who are altruistic and children who are advanced in moral reasoning tend to be more popular and belong to more social organizations than children who are not so popular or socially active (Enright & Sutterfield, 1980; Mannerino, 1976; Harris, Mussen, & Rutherford, 1976). In addition, children who actively participate in the forming of rules (of a game) are less rigid and more flexible about changing rules than are children who play with rules devised by others (Merchant & Rebelsky, 1972).

In the area of retributive justice, there is evidence that young children do favor expiative punishments, whereas older children endorse restitutive punishments (Harrower, 1934; Johnson, 1962b). In a study of first-, third-, and fifth-graders, Haviland (1971) found an age-related shift from an early preference for punitive, authoritarian responses toward a later preference for restitutive, equalitarian responses. Furthermore, mature restitutive responses were more likely at each age when the conflict involved two children as opposed to an adult-child conflict and when children had a classroom teacher who favored restitutive discipline. Amplifying on this research in a second study, Haviland (1979) found that schools, particularly those that permit corporal punishment, actually promote punitive beliefs in their children (and teachers). Teachers who were punitive in their discipline tended to have children who gave punitive retributive justice responses. Another study showed that a child's understanding of punishment may even affect how fairy tales are appreciated. In this study young children (age four) who were in the expiative stage showed greater appreciation of fairy tales where the main character (the "good prince") exacted harsh, severe retaliation on the "bad prince." Older children, in contrast, who were presumed to be in the equitable stage, appreciated tales that featured more equitable retaliation (Zillman & Bryant, 1975).

Although much of this early research is apparently more favorable to Piaget's theory than not, there are significant challenges to note as well. These challenges can be grouped under three main headings. First, there have been attempts to develop *information-processing* explanations of moral judgment. Second, the Piagetian account of moral development has been challenged by *social learning* theorists, who invoke such categories as imitation, modeling, and reinforcement (and not structures or stages) to explain moral behavior. Third, there is a line of research that challenges the idea that children are uniformly heteronomous or show unilateral respect toward adult authority, proposing that children have a more sophisticated understanding of social rules than can be shown with the standard Piagetian paradigm. Elliot Turiel (1983a) and his colleagues have pressed this attack. I will examine Turiel's research program in more detail in Chapter 6, but for now, let's call this challenge the *domains approach* to social knowledge. A few words, now, about each area of research.

Rival Theoretical Explanations

Information-Processing Explanations

The information-processing paradigm attempts to model human cognition using the metaphor of the computer. The human brain, like the computer, encodes information, formats the information in certain ways, places it in memory storage (which is variously conceptualized), then retrieves it. How children encode, manipulate, store, process, and retrieve information, then, are the problems set before the information-processing paradigm. This approach requires one to describe or model the cognitive processes used at each step in the information-processing sequence. It also requires one to examine the nature of the information to be processed, since various stimulus requirements (e.g., task complexity, story format, kinds of information, mode of presentation) interact with cognitive processing capabilities. Over the years a number of Piagetian moral-judgment dimensions have been subjected to this sort of analysis.

One line of research attempted to provide alternative explanations for the sort of performances that were often seen on Piagetian moral-judgment tasks. Rotenberg (1980) argued, for example, that young children are more impulsive than older children, and hence their search for relevant information in a story is limited and inefficient compared to the more reflective cognitive style of older children. When young children in this study received "reflectivity" instructions, they made greater use of intentional information when judging the moral blameworthiness of story characters. That is, children who were told to "think about all the reasons why the protagonist might be bad or might not be bad" prior to hearing the story and prior to making their evaluation of the character appealed to the intentions of the character more frequently than did children who did not receive the reflectivity instructions. Rotenberg (1980) suggested that young children tend to focus on consequences (vs. intentions) in the traditional Piagetian assessment not so much because they are victims of egocentrism or moral constraint but rather because they use a limited search strategy that is linked to their impulsive cognitive style. Anything that short-circuits their impulsivity, such as the reflectivity instructions that encourage more thorough information-gathering, should improve moral judgment.

Whereas Rotenberg attempted to reconceptualize the objective-responsibility domain, Rachel Karniol (1980) has focused on the domain of immanent justice. In her view, children tend to have an immanent view of causality not because they are burdened with moral realism, or with egocentrism, but because they fail to use causal chains to explain the relationship between misdeed and adversity. Let's take a simple example: Jonathan Brown stole some money. When he got home, he fell down the stairs. If we ask young children why Jonathan fell down the stairs, some might say that he fell down because he stole the money. A causal relationship is established between two events, a theft and falling down. If Jonathan didn't want to fall down, he shouldn't have stolen the money, because misdeeds are always punished—by God, bad luck, or some other nonnatural mechanism. A child who says this is expressing a belief in immanent justice. This child has an immanent view of causality. In Piaget's view, the belief in immanent justice is an important characteristic of the morality of constraint. It is also possible, of course, to see no relationship at all between the theft of money and falling down the stairs. It is possible to see the adversity as just a chance event unrelated to the prior theft or as due to some natural cause. It is possible to see that the prior theft is neither necessary nor sufficient for explaining Jonathan's tumble down the stairs. But this understanding, in Piaget's view, is a later developmental achievement, characteristic of the morality of cooperation.

In Karniol's (1980) view things are more complex than this. She developed an analysis of the immanent justice domain that was based on theories that attempt to explain how episodic information in prose passages is integrated, comprehended, and remembered (see, e.g., Rumelhart, 1975; Schank, 1975). The analysis goes something like this: Any given narrative passage consists of a set of propositions (e.g., "Jonathan stole some money. Jonathan fell down some stairs"). Readers tend to automatically impute cause-and-effect relationships among these propositions. That is, we try to integrate the assertions we read into some coherent unity. We construct causal chains. If we didn't, comprehension would be very difficult to achieve. These causal chains help us understand the stories we encounter. We make sense of events just because we see how they are causally linked. Furthermore, what helps us construct these causal chains is our understanding of the world. Our real-world knowledge, the way we represent what we know to be the case, helps us infer causal relationships among events. This suggests that young children, who are relatively deficient in such representational knowledge, may be prone to construct unsophisticated causal chains or to make illegitimate causal inferences. Young children may tend to make a causal linkage between, say, Jonathan's theft of money and his later falling down the stairs.

Karniol (1980) suggests that the tendency to impute this sort of immanent causality may be the simple result of the fact that the misdeed and the adversity are related to the child in a story format. When a child is told to listen to a story about Jonathan, a comprehension schema may get activated that alerts the child to causal relationships among the propositions of the narrative. So when the child hears that Jonathan stole some money and then later fell down the stairs, the two events tend to get yoked into a causal chain: He fell down the stairs *because* he stole the money. This is unsophisticated, of course, but the kinds of causal chains that are constructed may well vary with age and depend upon the extent of real-world knowledge and chaining ability.

What other kinds of causal chains might there be? Karniol (1980) notes three additional categories of causal explanation. There are, first, *asyndetic* explanations. An asyndetic explanation is one that jumbles together two independent causal events to account for the same adversity with no attempt to say how it all works. Here is an example:

Q. Why did Jonathan fall down the stairs?
A. Because he stole some money.
Q. Would Jonathan have fallen down if he didn't steal?
A. No.
Q. Why?
A. Because then he would be watching where he was going.

Jonathan fell down, then, for two reasons: (1) because he stole the money and (2) because he wasn't watching. Note that one part of this answer is still based on an immanent justice understanding of causality (because he stole), but now something more is required (watching) in order to account for the adversity. It may be necessary to include the fact that Jonathan stole in order to account for his falling, but this fact must be coupled with his not watching. The two causal events (stealing, watching), however, are not reconciled. No attempt is made to establish a mediating linkage between them.

In addition to immanent and asyndetic causality, there is a class of mediated causal explanations. Mediated explanations posit a causal chain between the misdeed and the adversity. As with asyndetic explanations, the misdeed (stealing) is not viewed as sufficient for causing the adversity (falling). But now some attempt is made to link the two by reference to some physical or psychological process. Here is an example:

Q. Why did Jonathan fall down the stairs?
A. Because he stole some money.
Q. Would he have fallen down if he hadn't stolen the money?
A. No. Because if he hadn't stolen the money, his pockets would not have been crammed with coins, and he would not have slipped on them when they poured out of his pocket (*physical mediation*).

A. No. Because if he hadn't stolen the money, he would not have been distracted by thoughts about lying, and he wouldn't have been so careless as to fall down the stairs (*psychological mediation*).

The fourth class of causal explanation is simply to note that the two events (misdeed and adversity) are unrelated. They are chance events linked only by contiguity.

Piaget's account of immanent justice does not make room for the class of mediated causal explanations, only for *immanent* causality (morality of constraint) and for *chance contiguity* (morality of cooperation). In theory, immanent causal explanations should decrease with age, and chance contiguity explanations should increase. Karniol (1980) showed, however, across three studies, that this expectation was not supported. No developmental trends were evident for either immanent causality (which was not prevalent, at any rate) or for chance contiguity. Significant developmental trends were observed, however, for asyndetic and mediated causal explanations. With age children tended to abandon asyndetic explanations and to increasingly favor mediated (physical and psychological) causal explanations.

Karniol also showed that children tended to use mediated causal explanations in order to make sense of the stories. That is, children use mediated causality in order to coherently integrate the elements of a story. In her Study 3, for example, Karniol (1980) tested children who had already indicated a preference for the mediated causality category. One-half of these children heard a story where the adversity was caused by some external event (e.g., Jonathan is struck by lightning). The other half heard stories where the adversity was self-produced (e.g., Jonathan falls off a bike). Karniol predicted that children who heard about the externally produced adversity would shift away from mediated causality (which they had previously favored and endorsed) and endorse chance contiguity explanations. Why? Simply because it is more difficult to find a natural mediation between a misdeed and adversity when the adversity is something externally produced, such as lightning. Because mediation is more difficult to imagine, in this case, children more often invoked chance contiguity. Hence, the kind of causal chains that are invoked depend upon the kind of adversity that is encountered in the story. Causal mediation is easier to provide for some kinds of adversity (self-produced: falling off a bike) but not for others (externally produced: being hit by lightning). And when mediation cannot easily be provided, chance contiguity is invoked. It can be argued that children are not so much making moral judgments when they struggle with these kinds of causal chains but are rather trying to comprehend what they are being told.

Karniol (1980) concluded, then, that Piaget's immanent justice data simply reflect a young child's inability to use causal chains to explain the contiguity between misdeed and adversity and that "at least one area of 'moral judgment' is interpretable in nonmoral terms" (Piaget, 1932/1965, p. 129) insofar as the information-processing approach provides a parsimonious account of the data.

We have seen how two Piagetian moral dimensions have been reconceptualized in terms of information-processing theories. Research has also suggested that performance on at least some of the Piagetian moral dimensions is the result of methodological artifacts. Research also suggests that Piaget's assessment may unduly tax the memory abilities of young children and that perhaps this is why their moral judgments seem so unsophisticated. Clearly, then, if the information-processing demands of the Piagetian stories can be simplified or if measures can be taken to ensure retention, perhaps even young children would be able to show more competence at moral judgment than has been possible with the traditional Piagetian methodology.

This question has attracted a great deal of research, much of it focusing on the dimension of objective responsibility. Let's review the standard assessment. In the traditional format, children are told stories about two characters, John and Henry. In the first story John is called to dinner. He enters the dining room through a door. As he opens the door, it hits a chair. On the chair is a tray with 15 cups. "John couldn't have known that there was all this behind the door. He goes in, the door knocks against the tray, bang go the fifteen cups and they all get broken" (Piaget, 1932/1965, p. 122). In the second story Henry tries to reach for some jam while his mother is out of the house. He climbs on a chair, but the jam is still out of reach. But in the process of reaching he knocks over a cup, which breaks. Who is more naughty, John or Henry?

The first character, John, opens a door, and this results in significant accidental damage (breaks 15 cups). The second character, Henry, performs a purposive action (reaching for jam), and the accidental consequence is slight (breaks 1 cup). Who is more naughty? Recall that Piaget claimed that younger children, in the morality of constraint, tended to judge John more severely—did not John break 15 cups, and does not breaking 15 cups involve an objectively more serious consequence than breaking only 1 cup? For young children, then, objective consequences are what guides moral evaluation. Older children, in the morality of cooperation, would attend not to objective consequences but to subjective intentions for the purposes of evaluating moral culpability (and would hold Henry more culpable).

But this standard format has been severely faulted. In the traditional presentation of information (the story-pair method), motives are presented first, followed by consequences. But this ordering of motive-consequence information may be a problem. A number of studies have shown that the evaluative judgments reached on this sort of task are strongly influenced by *recency effects* (Nummendal & Bass, 1976; Feldman, Klosson, Parsons, Rholes, & Ruble, 1976; Parsons, Ruble, Klosson, Feldman, & Rholes, 1976; Austin, Ruble, & Trabasso, 1977). In other words, how young children (under age 9–10) evaluate characters like John and Henry seems to depend on the order in which intentions and consequences were presented, with stronger recency effects being evident among younger children. When intentions were mentioned first, evaluative judgments were based largely on consequences. When consequences were mentioned first, intentions were more important to the evaluative judgment. Hence, whatever was *most recent* in the order of presentation played a larger role in determining how children evaluated the protagonists.

The problem of order effects was vividly shown by Royal Grueneich (1982a). He reported that 75 percent of third-grade children in his study made consequence-based moral judgments when the order of presentation was intention-consequence; about 75 percent of the children made intention-based moral judgments when the order of presentation was consequence-intention; and there were developmental trends evident when the order was intention-consequence (which is the traditional order of presentation) but not when the order was consequence-intention. Grueneich (1982a, p. 893) concluded that the standard Piagetian format "is seriously limited in its ability to make valid conclusions about children's criteria for making moral judgments."

When children's performance on a task is influenced by recency effects, it is often assumed that they cannot remember the prior information. Hence, what we may be seeing on this task is memory failure and not some developmental difference in how children weigh intentions and consequences (Feldman et al., 1976). What is more, when measures are taken to ensure that young children remember the details of the story, say, by asking them to repeat the story before making their judgments, age differences between younger and older children are often eliminated (Austin et al., 1977), although this process does not always eliminate the recency effect (Surber, 1982; Austin et al., 1977). This suggests that the stage differences reported by Piaget may reflect differences due to memory and information-processing and not moral decision-making.

Grueneich (1982b) highlights a number of additional problems with this paradigm. He notes, first, that intention and consequences are not simple notions; nor do they constitute a simple dichotomy. Yet the complex structure of these concepts are not adequately represented in the typical research in this area. Just to give you a feel for the complexity of these concepts, let's look at his analysis of these concepts.

When evaluating an actor we must first determine if the actor caused a given outcome. In other words, did the actor physically produce the outcome? If the actor did not, we must still decide if the actor is to be held responsible nonetheless (since one is sometimes held responsible for outcomes that one did not physically cause). If the actor did cause the outcome, we must next determine if the behavior was accidental or intended. If accidental, a number of additional judgments must be made. Was the actor's behavior voluntary or involuntary? Did the actor exercise proper care and caution, or was he or she acting carelessly? Were the actor's motives positive, negative, or neutral? In Piaget's Henry story, for example, Henry's behavior was causal (his action broke the cup), accidental (he did not intend to break the cup, just to reach the jam), voluntary (the cup was broken by voluntary reaching for jam), and careless (proper care was not taken while reaching for jam). If this were all there was to the story, our evaluation of Henry might not be too harsh. But Piaget's story insinuates that Henry was sneaking into the jam against his mother's wishes (since the story emphasizes the fact that the mother was out of the house). Hence we have grounds for thinking that Henry's motives were negative. This attribution would certainly alter our appraisal of what Henry was up to.

The previous analysis applies if the outcome was causally but accidentally produced. What if the outcome was produced intentionally? Once again, additional judgments are necessary. Was the motivation behind the intentional behavior positive, negative, or neutral? Was the action spontaneous, or was it the result of duress or provocation? Additional complexity accompanies the analysis of consequences. Is the outcome of the actor's action positive or negative? Are the consequences physical or social? If physical, do they involve objects or persons (see Elkind & Dabeck, 1977)? If social, how did the actor or victim-beneficiary react? Did the actor apologize? Did the victim forgive? Did some authority figure intervene?

It should be clear that our moral evaluation of an actor will vary depending on how we answer these sorts of questions. What is more, as this analysis reveals, the concepts of intention and consequence are a good deal more complex than the Piagetian paradigm has recognized. In Grueneich's (1982b, p. 340) view, "it seems likely that the most important developmental trend concerns not so much the relative extent to which intent as opposed to consequence information is used to make judgments as it does children's ability to make use of increasingly differentiated information about both." Perhaps children, as they get older, come to understand many more features of intention and consequence. Perhaps the difference between children and adults is that adults simply know more about the various complexities that go into our assessment of intentions and consequences. In contrast, it is also possible that children are, in fact, well aware of these complexities but weigh them differently than do adults or else fail to sufficiently integrate them during the course of making a moral judgment (Grueneich, 1982b).

How children weigh and integrate intention and consequence information has also attracted a good deal of research, much of it inspired by Norman Anderson's (1971, 1974; Lane and Anderson, 1976; Anderson & Butzin, 1978) information-integration theory. According to this theory, moral judgments are not different in kind from other sorts of judgments that we are called upon to make. In order to make a judgment or reach a decision, we must attend to the stimulus cues that are embedded in the information that confronts us; then we must integrate them into a coherent, unified judgment. The integration of information can be modeled mathematically. Indeed, the theory suggests that all human judgment follows simple algebraic rules. In other words, each piece of information has some weighted psychological value, and these values are combined to form a unitary judgment. The combination of psychological values is represented mathematically in terms of various algebraic rules, a cognitive algebra, the use of which is said to be pervasive in human information-processing (Anderson, 1971, 1974).

Let's take the sample case of gratitude (Lane & Anderson, 1976; Tessor, Gatewood, & Driver, 1968). Consider this simple example: Rick receives a gift from Terry. What is our judgment of Rick's gratitude? One factor that we must consider is Terry's intention in giving the gift. It is easy to see that Terry's intentions could vary considerably. On one extreme Terry could benefit Rick quite unknowingly, by mistake, or as the result of some accidental behavior, in which case there is no intention at all (and Rick need not feel grateful). On the other extreme Terry could go to great lengths on Rick's behalf, exerting much effort with good cheer. Between these two extremes one can imagine various other levels of commitment (grudging, slight, perfunctory, moderate, high). It seems reasonable to think that judgments of gratitude would increase for every increase in intention. That is, for every increase of intention, we feel a corresponding increase in gratitude. For example, we ordinarily would not feel very grateful for an action that was done for us in a very perfunctory, grudging manner. Yet we are very grateful indeed if the agent exerts much effort on our behalf. A similar analysis can be done for the stimulus cue value. If Terry gave Rick a gift of one dollar, his sense of gratitude would probably be very slight. But if the gift was considerably more or if the gift was something Rick really desired or needed, he would feel considerably more grateful. Once again, it is reasonable to suppose that gratitude tends to increase for every increase in value.

If I reach my judgment of gratitude using one or the other of these cues but not both, then my judgment is said to be based on a unidimensional rule. For example, if my judgment of gratitude hinges only on the intention of my benefactor, regardless of how I actually value the gift, then I am using a unidimensional rule. To put it in statistical terms, intention is a *main effect* in my judgment process (and value and the intention × value interaction are both nonsignificant). Similarly, if my judgment hinges only on the recipient's evaluation of the value of the gift and not on the giver's intention, then a unidimensional rule is being used, since only one dimension is being used to construct the judgment of gratitude. In statistical terms, we would have a main effect due to value (but no significant effect for intention and no intention × value interaction).

Most of us, however, use both dimensions in our judgments of gratitude. In other words, our judgments tend to be multidimensional. Both the value of the gift and the intention of the giver are relevant for our judgment of gratitude. But how do we integrate these two sources of information? According to Anderson (1974), the process of integrating information follows simple rules of ordinary algebra (and analysis-of-variance procedures). One major purpose of research on integration theory is to work out the cognitive algebraic models that apply to different areas of human judgment. The three models that have received the most attention are additive, averaging, and multiplicative models. I will focus on the additive and averaging models, since they more relevant for understanding moral judgment.

As our gratitude example illustrates, the psychological judgment of gratitude can be thought of as the additive effects of both intention and value. But note that intention and value are independent effects that are summed. If we keep intention constant (say, low) we should still see an increase in gratitude for each incremental increase (low, medium, high) in value. For example, I would have a hard time working up much gratitude if someone grudgingly gave me $1 (low intention, low value). But if I were grudgingly given $100 (low intention, higher value), I would be considerably more grateful. Similarly, if we keep value constant but vary intention, we should see incremental improvements in gratitude for every increase in intention.

In short, the additive rule says that intention and value are independent main effects that can be summed to yield corresponding judgments of gratitude. What is the averaging rule, and how can it be distinguished from the additive rule? This is best illustrated with an example. Consider the following scenario. Let's say that Terry gives Rick a gift with only low intentions. In this case, Rick's gratitude is correspondingly low. But let's say that the gift, given with low intentions, is nonetheless of medium value to Rick. Under the additive rule, the low intention should combine with the medium value to produce an additive increase in gratitude.

Or alternatively, let's say that Terry gives Rick a gift with very high intentions. Rick's gratitude should be correspondingly high, of course. But let's say that the gift, given with high intentions, is only of medium value. Once again, under the additive rule, we would expect the high intention to combine with the medium value to yield an additive increase in gratitude. But this is not what we would expect under the averaging rule. Under this rule, the medium value, when combined with high intention, should lower Rick's gratitude, not increase it. To put it differently, 10 units of intention plus 5 units of value should equal 15 units of gratitude under the additive rule, but only 7.5 units under the averaging rule. The additional test that must be performed, then, is to elicit judgments of gratitude with just the single cue (in this case, medium value). In statistical (ANOVA) terms, we should observe a significant intention $\times$ value interaction. Research has shown that intention and value are, in fact, integrated according to an averaging rule when adults construct judgments of gratitude (Lane and Anderson, 1976).

Developmental studies have applied Anderson's integration theory to Piaget's dimension of moral responsibility. Here the question concerns how intention and consequence combine to form a judgment of moral culpability (who is more naughty?). Colleen Surber (1977, 1982) pioneered the use of integration theory in the study of Piagetian moral judgment. She showed that children integrate intention and consequence information according to an averaging rule. The judgment of moral responsibility is influenced by both kinds of cues, at all ages. What changes, developmentally, are the weights assigned to intention and consequence cues. The weights assigned to consequence information decrease with age; the weights assigned to intentional information increase with age.

Along similar lines Leon (1982) found that most young children (age six to seven) use additive rules for combining information regarding intent, damage, and rationale. This suggests that young children do not simply make consequence-only moral judgments, then shift toward intention-only judgments when they get older. Rather, there is a developmental trend toward increasing integration of intention and consequence information with age (Grueneich, 1982a). Although younger children do seem to show a preference for unidimensional rules, there is nonetheless an integration or coordination of information with age, and this trend toward increasing integration is evident on many kinds of cognitive tasks (e.g., Anderson

& Cuneo, 1978; Siegler, 1978). Indeed, Grueneich (1982a, p. 893) remarked that the "use of the information integration approach calls attention to important similarities between children's moral judgments and their judgments in other areas," a theme that we have previously encountered.

Grueneich (1982b) also faults this literature for using stories that are poorly constructed and for paying insufficient attention to children's memory and comprehension of story information. Rachel Karniol (1978) was one of the first scholars to point out some of these difficulties. She noted that the material damage that is described in both stories is not the result of good or bad intentions but of clumsiness. Indeed, the intentions of John and Henry are by no means clearly stated. Surely John did not mean to break 15 cups; he just wanted to get his dinner. Presumably his intentions were benign and the cups were broken accidentally. What about Henry? Are we to assume that Henry's intentions were malevolent? Are we to assume that the Henry story is presenting us with a case of a boy who does something with bad intentions but slight consequences and is therefore more naughty? Are we to assume that children easily see that John's is a case of good intentions—much damage and Henry's is a case of bad intentions—small damage? Young children may not see things so clearly and may interpret the depicted actions quite differently from the interpretation intended by the researcher.

One study suggested, for example, that young children are much less severe with someone like Henry, who is simply judged to be clumsy but not bad (Farnill, 1974). In other words, Henry is inept, Henry is clumsy, but his motives are not questioned. But the point of the Henry story was to show him as a boy with malevolent intentions. This suggests, as Karniol (1978) points out, that the observed difference between younger children who endorse objective responsibility and older children to endorse subjective responsibility may simply be due to the fact that they have widely divergent interpretations of depicted events when intentional cues are ambiguous or unspecified, rather than reflecting cognitive differences in the ability to utilize intentional information. Indeed, Henry's intentions are quite ambiguous and are open to different interpretations. Under these conditions his breaking of just a single cup really does seem less naughty.

It is thus difficult to assess the use of intention cues by using the standard format, particularly when the damage, in either story, is not intended but is the result of accident. The two stories, then, do not adequately contrast intentional actions with unintentional actions. If young children focus on consequences when intentional cues are ambiguous (as in the standard Henry story), perhaps they will shift their focus toward subjective responsibility if intentional cues are made more explicit and clear. This has, in fact, been shown in a number of studies (Armsby, 1971; Buchanan & Thompson, 1973; Farnill, 1974). Even young children seem to know that an actor with malicious intent is to be judged more naughty, regardless of objective consequences, than is an actor who causes accidental outcomes (Suls, Gutkin, & Kalle, 1979). When objective consequences (material damage) are held constant, even three-year-old children can use information about intentions (Gutkin, 1972; Irwin & Moore, 1971). Five- and six-year-old children are just as likely as adults to recommend a reduction in punishment for transgressors if the transgression was motivated by legitimate reasons (Darley, Klosson, & Zanna, 1978).

Children of this age also use intentional information in subtle ways. An agent who harms for hostile reasons or for personal gain, for example, is held more culpable than one who harms for prosocial reasons (Rule, Nesdale, & McAra, 1974). One study found that young children were sensitive to different levels of intentions and were even willing to recommend punishment for a child who did harm at the behest of a powerful adult authority—which suggests that the respect that young children have for the authority of adults is not as absolute or as unilateral as Piaget envisioned (Berg-Cross, 1975). Similarly, Suls and Kalle (1978) showed that when adults and children commit the same act, adults are evaluated just as severely as are the children, a finding that again casts doubt on any strict notion of unilateral respect. In addition, behavior that is motivated by bad intentions is judged to be wrong by young children regardless of whether the social consequences are positive or negative, but the moral evaluation of good-intentioned behavior appears to depend on consequences (Suls, Gutkin, & Kalle, 1979).

A number of studies have shown that intention cues become more significant with age (Keasey, 1977; Suls & Gutkin, 1976). Clearly, in light of the evidence we have been considering, this does not mean that younger children are incapable of inferring or utilizing intentional information. Although young children may not spontaneously infer the intentions of another, they can certainly infer and utilize intentional information for constructing moral judgments when prompted to do so (Bearison & Isaacs, 1975). This suggests that young children have a *production deficiency*, that is, they do not know how or when to use intention information in their moral judgments. When they are instructed how and when to produce or utilize the information, their judgments show greater sophistication. It may also be the case that young children can access the subjective states of others, that is, can infer intentions and motives yet not use them in making responsibility judgments (Walden, 1982). In this case, the preference of young children for objective consequences in their judgments may reflect a mediation deficiency as well. In the area of memory development, the debate has been settled in favor of the production deficiency explanation—young children do not know how or when to rehearse, but when they are given suitable instruction, their memory abilities show marked improvement. Perhaps future research will settle the debate within moral psychology.

Finally, Vikan (1976a, 1976b) argued that objective and subjective responsibility were two "formally equal forms of cognitive organization" and that these two forms have "equal structural status." In one experiment Vikan (1976b) had children reason about desert and punishment in a legal court paradigm. When children took the role of the offender, they insisted that the court take into account their intentions (i.e., ignore the consequences of their action to the victim—offended party). When they took the role of the offended party, however, they insisted that the court consider what happened to them, that is, the consequences of the offender's action. In other words, as offenders children endorsed objective responsibility. As offended, they endorsed subjective responsibility. In another study Vikan (1976a) showed that moral judgment once again varied as a function of role-playing instructions in a legal court paradigm. Here children used more subjective psychological terms when they were acquitting, but not when they were sentencing.

All of this calls into question the Piagetian claim that young children are unable to access the subjective intentions of others when making moral judgments of responsibility. Age differences observed on the various Piagetian tasks are perhaps better explained by information-processing variables—by how information is encoded, weighed, integrated, comprehended, stored, retrieved from memory, and not by appeal to such global cognitive developmental variables such as egocentrism and moral realism. The real abilities of young children are obscured, this line of argument goes, because the complex nature of the tasks overtaxes the information-processing capabilities of young children. Berg-Cross (1975, pp. 973–974) spoke for many in the information-processing camp when she remarked, "It seems that Piaget's methodology may be over stressing the memory abilities and parallel processing abilities of young children, and they are forced to adopt a simplifying strategy. *The whole phenomenon of moral realism may thus turn out to be nothing more than a strategy for dealing with highly ambiguous, complex material*" (my emphasis). One theme that runs through the information-processing approach to moral judgment is that the process of making moral judgments is not very different from the process of making other kinds of judgments. Decision-making in moral matters is to be explained by the same sorts of information-processing variables that are invoked to explain decision-making in nonmoral domains. The cognitive architecture (hardware) that is required for decision-making in general is required for moral decision-making in particular. The cognitive processes (software) that are involved with making judgments in nonmoral domains are involved as well when it comes to making moral judgments.

The upshot of this analysis is that Piagetian moral phenomena are better explained by reference to information-processing theories and not by such Piagetian constructs as structure, stage, egocentrism, and realism. A similar theme is evident in the early social learning critique of Piaget's theory.

The Social Learning Approach

If one is interested in showing that Piagetian age trends in moral judgment were better explained with reference to social learning theory (and not in terms of stage, structure, realism, and the like), one would want to show that children's moral judgments could be manipulated by the mechanisms of social learning, that is, by imitation, modeling, and reinforcement. At issue is the notion of stage. Presumably, if one is at a given stage, this stage of reasoning should be stable and enduring. It should provide a unified set of operations that would influence how one solves problems and makes decisions. For example, if Desmond makes objective moral decisions, then this should be a rather stable way for him to make judgments about moral responsibility. In contrast, if Desmond focuses on subjective intentions, then this, too, should be a stable and enduring way for him to approach moral questions of this sort. First Desmond is in the stage of objective responsibility; then he moves into the stage of subjective responsibility. The stage theory suggests that he cannot be in both stages at once. He is first in one stage (objective consequences); then, later on in development, he enters the second stage (subjective intentions). When he moves to the later stage (subjective responsibility) he should not yield to the temptation to reason from the perspective of the earlier stage (objective responsibility), since, presumably, this stage has been deemed inadequate.

But what if you can manipulate the responses Desmond makes on this sort of moral task so that sometimes he gives objective responses and other times he gives subjective responses? What would you conclude if you took an objective child (i.e., a child who always gives objective responses) and trained her to always give subjective responses? In this case a younger child is giving responses that are characteristic of older children. Similarly, and more dramatically, what if you took a subjective child and trained her to always give objective responses? In this case, an older child is giving responses that are characteristic of younger children. In this case, you have taken a child whose moral reasoning was advanced and mature and conditioned her to reason from a stage perspective that is not advanced and not mature, indeed, from a stage perspective that she has already rejected as inadequate. If all of this was possible, it would certainly seem to turn Piaget's stage theory on its head.

But this is just what a number of experiments purported to show. In a classic experiment, Bandura and McDonald (1963) exposed objective and subjective children to adult models who gave responses counter to the child's predominant moral orientation. In other words, children who made judgments of responsibility (who is more naughty?) based on objective damage were exposed to models who gave judgments based on subjective intentions. Children who typically gave responses based on subjective intentions were exposed to models who gave responses based on objective consequences. The authors found that children changed their responses in the direction modeled by the adults. Subjective children were "conditioned down" to moral objectivity. Objective children were "conditioned up" to moral subjectivity. Bandura and McDonald (1963, p. 280) concluded that these results "fail to substantiate Piaget's theory of demarcated sequential stages of moral development [and that] the utility of Piaget's stage theory of morality is further limited by the finding that children's judgmental responses *are readily modifiable, particularly through the utilization of adult modeling cues*" (my emphasis). Although this conclusion has been challenged (e.g., Turiel, 1966; Crowley, 1968), it has also been replicated by a number of other experiments (Cowan, Langer, Heavenrich, & Nathanson, 1969; Bandura, 1969; Walker & Richards, 1976). Indeed, Walker and Richards (1976) showed that children's moral orientation could be influenced not just by exposure to live models but by exposure to narrated models as well. In this experiment children were exposed to narratives whose literary characters modeled moral judgments contrary to the child's predominant moral orientation (objective consequences vs. subjective intentions). The results showed that children were influenced by these models. Children tended to increase their responding in the direction of the moral orientation of the models to which they were exposed, and they maintained this mode of responding on a delayed posttest.

How much this kind of research counts against Piaget's theory is a matter of dispute (e.g., Bandura, 1969; Turiel, 1966). Some argue that modeling affects only discrete, isolated verbal responses, and not the structure of thought in its entirety, and that trained responses, especially those that run in a contradevelopmental direction, tend not to generalize to related tasks or endure over time (e.g., Sternlieb & Youniss, 1975; Crowley, 1968). The social learning approach, in contrast, suggests that moral judgments are learned the way other behaviors are learned, through imitation, modeling, and reinforcement. This early confrontation over how to characterize moral judgment was just part of the more general paradigm argument between learning theory and Piaget's structural developmentalism. It would be played out in numerous other Piagetian domains. The terms of the debate have been dramatically altered in recent years given the decline of interest in Piaget's moral-stage theory (which Piaget always regarded as preliminary, in any event) and given the important revisions in Bandura's social learning theory that have occurred over the years. I will have more to say about Bandura's social-cognitive approach to moral socialization in Chapter 10. Let's now turn to a third area of research that is problematic for Piaget's moral-stage theory.

The Domains Approach

Elliot Turiel (1983a) has faulted Piaget's moral-stage theory on a number of grounds. As we have seen, Piaget (1932/1965) argued that young children are heteronomous because they are cognitively egocentric and because they are subjected to interpersonal relationships that are marked by unilateral respect and adult constraint. Egocentrism and constraint breed moral realism. Recall that moral realism is characterized by three features. First, duty is defined as obedience to authority. This implies that rule-following is good and that adult authority is supreme. Second, children have a sacred view of rules that disposes them to obey the letter of the law and not its spirit. Rules are immutable and unchangeable and are invested with the prestige of powerful adults. Third, just because rules are taken literally and just because the good is defined as obedience, the child evaluates behavior only with respect to that which adheres exactly to the letter of the law. This means that objective consequences and not subjective motives are the sole evaluative criteria of moral judgments. A child abandons this heteronomous orientation when egocentrism gives way to perpectivism, when constraint gives way to cooperation, and when unilateral respect between child and adult gives way to mutual respect among equals.

This is the very foundation of Piaget's theory. Yet Turiel (1983a) argues that each of these features of moral realism is found wanting on empirical grounds. Turiel and his colleagues are responsible for an important line of research that draws a clear distinction between two domains of social knowledge. There is moral knowledge, on the one hand, and *social-conventional* knowledge, on the other. I will examine this research in greater detail in Chapter 5. But for now, let us say that moral rules and social-conventional rules each have defining characteristics. Moral rules are universal, prescriptive, unalterable by consensus, obligatory, and point toward intrinsic features of acts (e.g., harm, injury). Conventional rules help us organize social life, but they are arbitrary and can be altered by consensus. We must come to agreement about the rules we want to live by. Hence we establish a set of conventions to organize our common life. But moral rules are not like this. We don't establish the force of moral rules by agreement; nor can we change them by consensus. We don't say: "On Tuesdays, it will be permissible to steal from your neighbor." For even if we all agree that thievery is a good thing to do on Tuesdays, this would not, by virtue of agreement, make theft a morally permissible option. It is a moral rule not to hit or cause injury; it is a conventional rule not to address teachers by their first names. It is a conventional rule that peas should not be eaten with a knife or that boys should not use the girls' bathroom, but it is a moral rule that one should not lie or steal.

Research in this tradition clearly shows that even very young children are aware of the difference between moral and social-conventional rules. When the practices of adults violate moral (but not social-conventional) standards, they are judged to be wrong (Weston & Turiel, 1980). This shows that children's understanding of morality is not simply whatever it is that adults command. Something is not moral just because an adult commands it. Children are not heteronomous across the board. As Marie Tisak (1986) demonstrated, children draw boundaries around parental authority. When they evaluate the legitimacy of parental injunctions, children take note of the domain in question. Parents are seen to have greater legitimacy when they make rules around moral issues (e.g., stealing) than when they make rules around conventional and personal issues such as family chores and choice of friends. What is more, children see that they have a greater obligation to obey the moral injunctions of parents than the conventional injunctions. Hence, childrens' judgments regarding legitimacy and obligation hinge on their evaluation of the social events in question (Tisak, 1986).

Consequently, the rules of adults are not considered sacred, absolute, and immutable. All rules are not treated alike (Turiel, 1983a). This shows up in children's understanding of punishment. Research shows, for example, that young children make fine discriminations about punishment based on their understanding of domains of social knowledge. Piaget would have us believe that young children call for all transgressions to be severely punished. But young children believe that only moral transgressions should be punished, or punished severely (Smetana, 1981). And practices are not invariably judged wrong just because they are punished by authority. Just because a moral rule violation goes unpunished does not make it right, and even young children know it.

It is clear, then, that some practices are evaluated by children with moral criteria in mind, others are evaluated with conventional criteria, and children are sensitive to this domain distinction from an early age. For this reason, even the game of marbles is held to be an illegitimate way of assessing moral judgment, since games are conventional practices and therefore do not fall within the moral domain. To use the game of marbles as a means of indexing children's moral judgment is to assume that children do not distinguish between moral and nonmoral rules—that they are all the same to the young child, since they have a heteronomous respect for rules in general. But this is just what Turiel's (1983a) research denies.

The critique of the domains approach goes to the very heart of Piaget's theory of moral judgment. It appears that when combined with the criticisms of the information-processing and social learning traditions, Piaget's theory is now in tatters. Perhaps this explains why interest in Piaget's moral theory has waned in recent years. This does not mean that Piaget's influence is still not keenly felt in moral psychology, Indeed, the Piagetian cognitive developmental approach has yielded what is arguably one of the most important theories in the history of psychology: Lawrence Kohlberg's theory of moral development. Kohlberg's moral theory has supplanted Piaget's, to be sure, but as we will see in the next chapter, it is Piagetian to its very core.

3

Kohlberg's Theory: An Overview

Biographical Introduction

In Chapter 2, we saw how Piaget's adolescent fascination with the problem of how to reconcile science and values led him to pursue a life's work devoted to the articulation of a biologically based epistemology (Chapman, 1988). Similarly, one can point to important formative experiences in Kohlberg's youth that directed him to the study of moral development and the practice of moral education. Indeed, as Augusto Blasi remarked in a memorial tribute, Kohlberg was "a mind concentrated on an idea" to such an extent that his very life became the "obsessive personification" of this idea. What was this idea? What were these early formative experiences that gave rise to it? Simply put, the idea was bound up with the possibility of articulating a conception of moral development that was adequate to the task of defending moral universality and defeating moral relativism. The formative experience that gave rise to this project was Kohlberg's firsthand experience of brutality and injustice (Reed, 1991; Power, 1991a; Noam & Wolf, 1991)

Kohlberg (1927–1987) was profoundly moved by the horrors of the Holocaust. Indeed, he viewed his own theory as a response to the Nazi ethos that could sanction the murder of millions of Jews and as a response to the prevailing social science systems (behaviorism, psychoanalysis) that could provide no resources by which to combat genocidal ideologies. Indeed, positivist social science and Freudian psychoanalysis, each in its own way, assumed the relativity of moral values and were hence inadequate for responding to the sort of Nazi justifications that made genocide possible.

As a young man just out of high school, Kohlberg put his idealism in practice by joining the American merchant marine for a two-year tour of duty in the European theater. Upon his discharge, at age 20, he again took direct action against injustice, this time signing on as a second engineer on an old navy icebreaker called the *Paducah*. The *Paducah* was bought by the Jewish defense force (the Haganah) for the purposes of smuggling Jewish refugees from war-ravaged Europe to Palestine. This activity was forbidden by Allied, especially British, policy, and consequently, the *Paducah* was required to run a British blockade of Palestine—which it failed to do. The ship was intercepted by the British navy, and the crew and passengers, including Kohlberg, were subsequently interred in a British concentration camp in Cyprus. With the help of the Haganah, however, Kohlberg and others escaped from the camp and took refuge on a kibbutz in Israel. From there Kohlberg eventually made his way back to the United States. Kohlberg's (1948) first published article, entitled "Beds for Bananas," was a wry account of this episode. The title of the article was taken from a headline that appeared in a French

41

port-city newspaper. Reporters from the paper quizzed the *Paducah* crew about the shelving that lined the cargo holds of the ship. The reporters suspected that the ship was hauling not commercial freight but refugees, a suspicion fueled by the unusually high number of Jewish crew members assigned to the ship. The crew claimed, however, that they were simply hauling bananas.

As a very young man, then, just three years after high school and before he entered college, Kohlberg encountered firsthand the genocidal "morality" of Naziism, the injustice of postwar Allied policy regarding Jewish refugees, the violence of the Haganah, and the experience of kibbutzim community life in Israel. These experiences had convulsed Kohlberg with profound ethical questions. The central question concerned the very possibility of moral universals, that is, are moral notions universally applicable or are they uniquely applicable only to particular societies? Do moral notions transcend the particularities of culture, social class, nationality, and historical period or is morality relative to these things? Do different societies spawn their own unique moralities given the particularities of their experience, and if so, are they not then incommensurable with the moralities spawned by other societies that have their own unique sociohistorical experiences? And if morality is relative to culture, to society, to some particular perspective or point of view, then on what grounds can one rationally criticize alien moralities?

Some anthropologists (Herskovitz, 1955) and psychologists (L. Berkowitz, 1964) argue, for example, that a valid moral judgment is one that accords with the norms of one's social group, or that proper moral conduct is anything that a society deems worthy of positive reinforcement (Skinner, 1971). Yet if this is true, on what grounds do we reject Nazi morality, for example? Or Haganah violence? On what grounds do we embrace liberal democratic values or endorse the practices of kibbutzim socialization? Are we entitled to criticize the reinforcement structure of apartheid or Jim Crow morality? On what objective basis do we engage in any kind of moral discussion at all without moral argument simply being reduced to emotive preferences? It was hard for Kohlberg to see how any rational response to the Holocaust was at all possible if one assumed the validity of moral relativism. Indeed, it was difficult to see how any moral conflicts whatsoever could be resolved, even in democratic politics, if the truth of moral relativism was assumed. Later Kohlberg would view any psychological approach to moralization as philosophically suspect if it was seen to give intellectual support for relativism or to assume it.

Upon his return to the United States Kohlberg took up undergraduate studies at the University of Chicago, where he became familiar with the great moral traditions in the West that stretched back to antiquity (Socrates, Plato, Aristotle) and the Enlightenment (Kant, J. S. Mill, Locke) but that included John Dewey and Émile Durkheim (Gewirtz, 1991). Reading Kant was a particularly important formative experience, for in Kantian formalism Kohlberg would find the rudiments of what would later become Stage 6 in his stage sequence (Power, 1991a) and also the moral principle (the categorical imperative) that would undergird his claims for the universality of human rights (Reed, 1991). Kohlberg would come to argue, for example, following Kant, that a distinctly moral judgment must be grounded by reasons that have universal intent and that it is a profound moral duty to respect persons as ends in themselves. As Noam and Wolf (1991, p. 23) put it, "By his focus on the development of rationality and moral respect, [Kohlberg] gave concrete reality to the often empty slogan 'Never Again.'"

Kohlberg also did his graduate work at the University of Chicago, specializing in clinical psychology. He chose clinical psychology (over philosophy and the law) because he saw it as an opportunity to pursue his philosophical interests while being of personal service to others. During his graduate school years he became acquainted with the work of James Mark Baldwin and Jean Piaget, whose theories were either forgotten (Baldwin) or inaccessible (Piaget) to the American psychological community. Indeed, Kohlberg was one of the first to recognize the enormous importance of Piaget's work, and he would see in it a powerful alternative to the then-prevailing schools of thought in academic psychology (DeVries, 1991). Such an alternative seemed desirable because it became apparent to Kohlberg that mainstream academic psychology tended to neglect moral issues (Power, 1991a) or else dealt with them in ways that Kohlberg thought naive (DeVries, 1991). After a dispute with his training supervisor (Kohlberg had complained, unsuccessfully, about unfair treatment of a patient) Kohlberg abandoned clinical psychology and focused on his doctoral dissertation, which he completed in 1958. In this work Kohlberg took up the question of moral-stage typology using a developmental approach strongly influenced by Piagetian theory. This dissertation has to rank as one of the most important of unpublished documents in the history of academic psychology. And for the next 30 years Kohlberg would become "a mind concentrated on an idea," articulating a paradigm of research that would revolutionize our understanding of moral psychology, development, and education—so much so that his work is indeed a whole climate of opinion that defines so much of the discipline of moral psychology.

Piagetian Roots

It is perhaps easy to see why Kohlberg would find Piaget's theory so appealing. Kohlberg was keen to show that there were lawful ontogenetic variations in how children formulated moral knowledge and that it was possible to appraise these various forms of moral knowledge along a continuum of adequacy. In a sense the child was a naive moral philosopher who approached moral notions in a coherent way, yet one whose philosophy also changed with development. So during the course of moral development, it might be possible for an individual to embrace six philosophies about what is justice and what is moral with each succeeding philosophy being more adequate than the prior version. Hence, if one was in possession of a criterion by which to assess the adequacy of moral knowledge, that is, a criterion that would allow one to distinguish less adaptive forms from more adaptive forms of moral knowledge, then one would be in a position to resist the lure of moral relativism—a position that claims that no such criterion is possible, that different moral positions are, in fact, incommensurable (Gellner, 1985; Krause & Meiland, 1982).

This was, of course, Piaget's project, as we saw in Chapter 2. Piaget's genetic epistemology was an attempt to explain the growth of (scientific) knowledge from its less adequate forms to its more advanced forms such that one could detect genuine progress or development. In many ways this goal makes genetic epistemology a kind of philosophy of science. The great debates in the philosophy of science in this century have centered on the possibility of giving a rational account of scientific activity (Popper, 1959; Kuhn, 1970; Newton-Smith, 1981) and on whether this activity is such that it yields scientific change that is developmental, that is, change that is cumulative and progressive and not just different (Lakatos & Musgrave, 1970; Radnitzsky & Anderson, 1978; Niiniluota, 1984; Laudan, 1977). According to the philosopher Imre Lakatos (1978), one cannot appraise the rationality of scientific theories without some notion of what scientific growth amounts to. In his view growth is the defining feature of science. It is what gives science its scientific character. Hence a theory is appraised not so much in terms of how well it stands up to the evidence but rather how well it stands up historically (does it lead to progress, growth, development) when compared to rival, touchstone theories. In his view it is "a deeply entrenched dogma. . . that evidential support depends on the theory and the evidence and not on the growth that they represent in relation to former knowledge" (Lakatos, 1978, p. 183).

Lakatos's view that scientific rationality is conveyed by progressive growth in knowledge is very similar to Piaget's genetic epistemology (Kitchener, 1986). Piaget's criterion of adequacy was whether there was suitable development toward an ideal equilibrium, which he characterized as the final stage of development. Hence, structural organizations of knowledge that approached the ideal form (the final stage) are better than organizations that are some distance from the ideal. These latter organizations are partial, unstable, temporary, but they will become ideal, stable, and enduring later in development.

Consequently, to say that structural organizations develop is to make a dual claim: (1) an empirical claim about what is the case (X is developing); and (2) a normative, value-laden claim about what ought to be the case (X ought to develop in this way, since development yields greater adaptation, and more perfected adaptation is good and is better than partial adaptation). It is to say that more developed forms are good and are better than less developed forms—better in the sense that development conveys an ideally adequate, stable, and enduring adaptability and a more perfected mode of operation.

Development, then, has its own internal standard of adequacy. It also puts a premium on what is considered the final stage of development. As I noted in Chapter 2, the last stage has intrinsic worth in the sense that to approach it in development is good. It is the normative standard of reference, the touchstone, by which growth in scientific (Piaget) and moral (Kohlberg) knowledge is to be appraised. Consequently, any developmental explanation must make reference to this stage. As the philosopher Richard Kitchener (1983, p. 800) puts it, "Developmental explanations are diachronic pattern explanations in which a part (a stage) is explained when one understands how it fits into the whole (sequence)—that is, how it fits into a temporal process directed towards a goal [final stage]—and what contributing role (function) it played in the realization of this goal."

Piaget conceptualized the final stage of intellectual development (formal operations) as an ideal equilibrium that was sufficiently agile in its operations to permit adaptability in all sorts of intellectual environments. Kohlberg conceptualized the final stage of moral development (Stage 6) as a moral ideal, ideal in the sense that it entails a point of view that seeks universal applicability of principled moral judgments and is committed to seeking consensus and agreement in cases of moral conflict and disagreement. In addition, Kohlberg endorsed the Piagetian claim that development has its own internal standard of adequacy, namely that each succeeding stage in the sequence is psychologically better than the preceding stage—better in the sense that each new stage yields an advance in structural articulation, differentiation, and integration and is hence more psychologically adaptive than the preceding stage. Or to put it differently, each new stage is a closer approximation of the moral ideal described by the last stage.

But what seemed unproblematic when applied to stages of intellectual development takes on a certain urgency when applied to moral stages. That is, the notion that Piagetian stage development necessarily entails the mixing of factual ("is") and normative ("ought") claims does not seem terribly controversial as long as one is talking about the development of mathematical, logical, or scientific knowledge. But when the discussion shifts to the matter of moral development, things become much more contentious.

Kohlberg claimed that his sequence described the developmental elaboration of moral structures. He argued that how one reasons about moral dilemmas undergoes structural transformation with development, transformations that can be demarcated along a sequence of six stages. However, if development has its own internal standard of adequacy, indeed if the final stage is the normative standard that makes developmental explanation possible, then Kohlberg is forced to make the following two claims: (1) Each succeeding stage is better than the preceding stage on psychological grounds, that is, each new stage is more differentiated and articulated than its predecessor, since the new stage employs cognitive operations that are more stable, more reversible, more equilibrated, and the like. This claim holds because, after all, Kohlberg is describing the development of moral structures, and the Piagetian approach has shown that structural development takes just this form. (2) Each succeeding stage is better than the preceding stage on moral grounds as well—since, after all, the sequence describes the development of moral structures. Hence, because Kohlberg describes the development of moral *structures*, each new stage is better than the preceding stage on strictly psychological grounds. But because he describes the development of *moral* structures, each new stage is better on moral grounds as well.

Further, the final stage (Stage 6) is not only an ideal equilibrium but also a moral ideal. Hence it follows that Stage 6 is the normative reference point that yields judgments of psychological and ethical adequacy. It is a normative reference point that serves as the standard of evaluation. It allows one to appraise growth in moral knowledge. It provides criteria for assessing the adequacy of moral positions and, important for Kohlberg, the grounds for rejecting ethical relativism. Relativism is combated by the natural developmental tendency to seek the highest stage of development, at which point one is best able to distinguish the prescriptive and universalizable elements of a moral judgment from mere conventional considerations. One sees, at the highest stage, that moral reasoning has a universalizable intent and that agreement and consensus are necessary and desirable features of moral discourse (Lapsley, 1992a). A commitment to ethical relativism is just not an option at the highest stages of moral development.

Hence, relativism is combated by the fact that development takes us to a stage where the moral point of view forbids relativism as an option. Relativism is also rejected by the fact that moral judgments develop, and development has its own internal standard of adequacy. In contrast to ethical relativism, there is a criterion after all that allows us to appraise various moral philosophies, and this criterion is development. Moral-stage development is rational because it represents growth in knowledge, with the last stage serving as the model of perfected operation and as the evaluative standard. Indeed, in Kohlberg's view, the aim of moral education is precisely to promote development, ideally to the highest stages, where the moral point of view is most clearly accessible to reasoning (Kohlberg & Mayer, 1972; Kohlberg, 1987).

Two Sources of Resistance: Aretaic Judgments and the Naturalistic Fallacy

Why is Kohlberg's view controversial? There are at least two sources of resistance. First, some object to it as a way of grading individuals on their character or morality. That is, if development is a criterion of adequacy, then those who fall at lower stages of moral reasoning are falling short of the moral mark. Because their reasoning is less developed, those individuals who exemplify lower stages must also be less adequate in matters of morality, or less moral perhaps. Certainly grading or appraising the moral worthiness of individuals would be an unseemly use of the moral-judgment stage sequence. A second objection is more philosophical: Empirical ("is") and evaluative ("ought") claims cannot be so casually conflated on logical grounds. If moral development entails both an empirical claim about what is the case and a normative, value-laden claim about what is desirable and ought to be the case, then Kohlberg is committing the *naturalistic fallacy*. Let's examine these two objections in more detail.

Does Kohlberg's stage sequence present us with a way of grading the moral worthiness of individuals or societies? One can imagine an argument to the effect that individuals who reason at higher stages are more moral and better than individuals who plod along at lower stages. After all, isn't it a basic Piagetian claim that the notion of development invariably makes reference to an internal standard of adequacy? The very notion that there are higher and lower stages would seem to entail the view that there are higher and lower kinds of people who are characterized by more adequate and less adequate forms of moral reasoning, respectively.

Yet Kohlberg rejects this reading of his moral stages. He makes a distinction, following Frankena (1973), between two kinds of moral judgments. *Deontic* judgments are judgments about rights, duties, and obligations. *Aretaic* judgments concern the moral worthiness of individuals or of actions. Kohlberg's theory is about deontic judgments. This position, too, follows the Piagetian line. As we saw in Chapter 2, Piaget's stages are best thought of as morphological taxonomies that classify not children but rather formal properties of children's reasoning (Chapman, 1988). Stages describe species of knowledge, not kinds of children. Similarly, moral "stages are not boxes for classifying and evaluating persons" (Colby, Kohlberg, Levine, and Hewer, 1983 p.11). Indeed, just as Piaget abstracted from the performances of his concrete subjects to the perspective of what is the competence of the epistemic subject, so too do Kohlberg's stages reflect the abstract perspective of the rational moral subject. Piaget's epistemic subject and Kohlberg's rational moral subject are idealized, abstract subjects who are defined by "those consistent rational forms of thought organizations [structures] logically abstracted from the use of sets of logical operations identified in diverse content" (Kohlberg, et al., 1983, p. 36). In other words, stages describe sets of logical (Piaget) or sociomoral (Kohlberg) operations and are not "reflections upon the self" (p. 36). Kohlberg does leave room, however, for evaluating actions as moral actions. Moral actions are those actions that are motivated by moral principles. Hence, the intentions of the actor are critical for assessing the distinctly moral character of some line of behavior. The stage theory does not appear to leave room for anything more than this very restricted sort of assessment. As Kohlberg (1971, p. 217) puts it, "We . . . do not think a stage 6 normative ethic can justifiably generate a theory of the good or of virtue, or rules for praise, blame and punishment," and hence principles of justice "do not *directly* obligate us to blame and punish."

Let's consider the second source of resistance. What is the naturalistic fallacy, and in what sense (if at all) does Kohlberg's theory fall prey to it? It is often claimed, following Hume, that no valid argument can move from factual premises to a moral or evaluative conclusion. The chasm between fact and value, between what is descriptive and what is normative, between is and ought, is said to be wide and logical. Similarly, within morality (the ought), there is the additional distinction to be made between moral form and moral content (Nozick, 1981). Fundamental moral principles are thought to be noncontingent on any set of descriptive facts. And so it is illegitimate to derive ethical conclusions from factual premises. To do so is to commit the naturalistic fallacy.

This term derives from a famous argument of G. E. Moore in his *Principia Ethica*. Moore argued that ethical terms such as "good" and "right" point to indefinable, nonnatural properties. Hence, what is good cannot be defined by reference to any set of natural properties. What is nonnatural cannot be defined by what is natural, and to attempt such an equation is to commit the naturalistic fallacy. Similarly, any attempt to define ethical terms by reference to nonethical terms is to commit a species of this fallacy (Frankena, 1973). One is not entitled, on pain of incoherence, to derive a prescriptive judgment about what ought to be the case from a set of factual observations about what is, in fact, the case. Hence, we have the is–ought gap.

Moore's argument suggests that moral judgments are basic, irreducible imperatives that are discerned by intuition or reason but are not to be justified by empirical premises (Buchanan, 1977). Moral rules are objective in the sense that they cannot be derived from and are independent of psychological foundations. Kohlberg (1971) endorses this view: "Morality is a unique, *sui generis*, realm" (p. 215), and "Moral autonomy is king, and values are different from facts for moral discourse" (p. 223). This accords well with Kohlberg's campaign against ethical relativism. Indeed, Kohlberg's project is bound up with the general problem of the Enlightenment—how to provide rational foundations for an objective morality (MacIntyre, 1984). If morality is objective and autonomous, then on pain of committing the naturalistic fallacy, it cannot be grounded or given a foundation by reference to the particular practices of any given culture, society, or concrete historical circumstance. But Kohlberg's dilemma is perhaps now apparent. He desires not to commit the naturalistic fallacy, at least not too crudely (Kohlberg, 1971; Boyd, 1986) but is committed nonetheless to a Piagetian view of development that necessarily entails, as we have seen, the conflating of factual and normative elements.

It is interesting that for all of Kohlberg's antipathy toward logical positivism generally and toward behaviorism specifically, the desire to provide rational foundations for morality independently of content is itself a hold-over from a discredited positivist epistemology. According to Kornblith (1980), for example, the desire to divorce epistemological questions from psychological questions is a positivist legacy. "Epistemology is a normative discipline; it is concerned, among other things, with questions about how reasoning ought to proceed. Such questions can be answered, we are told, independently of investigations into the processes that in fact occur when reasoning takes place" (Kornblith, 1980, p. 597). That is, epistemology is concerned with "proper knowing," with how reasoning ought to proceed in some ideal sense, and this concern is logically independent (so it goes) from any set of descriptions about how reasoning actually does proceed.

Perhaps an analogy to the positivist view of science will make this clear. Positivists are wont to maintain a dualistic distinction not only between fact and value, is and ought, descriptive and normative, and the like but also between fact and theory. Facts are theory-free basic statements by which theories are assessed. Facts are an infallible set of observations against which fallible conjectures are tested. In this way irrationalism and skepticism are kept at bay because there exists an autonomous factual realm of observations against which theories should have to conform. There is nothing relative about scientific belief, since scientific assertions can always be checked by reference to hard facts. Indeed, it is the autonomy of facts that gives scientific activity its rational foundation. Rational belief in science is justified by the existence of hard, objective facts. In ethics *foundationalism* or *justificationism* is sought in the other direction (Stout, 1981). Here moral (as opposed to scientific) rationality is justified or given foundation by an autonomous realm of moral imperatives that exists objectively from factual premises, an idea that is captured by the is–ought dualism. The positivist desire, then, in the case of science and ethics is to provide rational foundation or justification for our scientific and moral commitments, and this to ward off the specter of skepticism (in the case of science) and relativism (in the case of morality).

Yet the fact-theory distinction of positivist epistemology has been widely discredited (e.g., Lakatos, 1978; Suppe, 1977). Similarly, the logical coherence of the is–ought distinction, is now also under furious assault (Stout, 1981; Hampshire, 1949; MacIntyre, 1959, 1984; Hudson, 1969), as is the related distinction between form and content (Döbert, 1990; Noam, 1990; Levine, 1979a). One option that might have seemed available to Kohlberg, then, at least in hindsight, was simply not to fuss too much about whether he was conflating is–ought claims in the study of moral development, since there are now grounds for thinking that this dualism is not the formidable logical barrier that it was once widely assumed to be. Yet this latter view is still controversial, and we must respect Kohlberg's attempt to walk the fine line between asserting the Piagetian view of development while avoiding what seemed like an imposing logical fallacy. Let's examine Kohlberg's instructive solution to his dilemma.

How to Commit the Naturalistic Fallacy and Get Away with It

In 1971 Kohlberg wrote an important paper entitled "From Is to Ought: How to Commit the Naturalistic Fallacy and Get Away With It in the Study of Moral Development." He made the following claims: (1) He claimed that his research demonstrated the *fact* that a "universal moral form emerges in development and centers on principles of justice." (2) This moral form is Kantian in the sense that the moral ideal is defined not by content but by formal criteria for judging the sophistication of a moral judgment, such as impersonality, universalizability, prescriptiveness, and so on. In Kohlberg's words, "The moral man assumes that his moral judgment is based on conformity to an ideal norm, not on conformity to fact" (p. 223). The fact-value distinction, then, is asserted. (3) Moral development research can test whether this Kantian, formalist view of the moral ideal fits the psychological facts. That is, do people actually reason the way Kantians envisioned? Is Kantian moral deliberation a real psychological option? Do individuals come anywhere close to the moral ideal when they reflect on moral issues? This research cannot, however, show that Kant's moral ideal is the "right" way to think about morality, that is, it cannot tell us what morality ought to be. After all, "moral autonomy is king, and values are different from facts for moral discourse" (p. 223). (4) However, ethics or logic can tell us which morality is to be preferred, what morality ought to be based on an internal logical analysis. That is, ethics and logic can tell us why one morality (Stage 5) is better than another (Stage 4) according to formal, ethical criteria. But scientific investigations have a role to play, too. Scientific investigations of factual moral beliefs should be able to support this internal, logical analysis by showing why "the developmentally higher philosophy [Stage 5] can handle problems not handled by the lower ones [e.g., Stage 4]" (Kohlberg 1971, p. 223). How can science do this? By means of the Piagetian criteria of development.

The key assertion is this: "The scientific theory as to why people factually *do* move upward from stage to stage, and why they factually *do* prefer a higher stage to a lower, is broadly the same as a [normative] moral theory as to why people *should* prefer [on formalist grounds] a higher stage to a lower stage" (Kohlberg, 1971, p. 223).

What does this mean? Kohlberg is claiming that although psychological theory (is) and normative ethical theory (ought) are not identical, there is, nonetheless, an important relationship between them. The formal ethical criteria about what constitutes a good *moral* judgment (or philosophy) is "broadly the same" as the (Piagetian) psychological (developmental) criteria as to what constitutes a good moral *judgment*. For example, the Piagetian developmental criteria for what constitutes a stable equilibrium (differentiation, integration) is parallel to, maps onto, or is broadly the same as the formalist philosophical criteria as to what makes a good moral theory (prescriptiveness, universality). What makes Stage 6 a completely adequate ideal equilibrium in a psychological sense is much the same as whatever makes Stage 6 a moral ideal, in an ethical sense. The formal criteria of psychological adequacy map onto the formal criteria of ethical adequacy in a parallel way. The formal criteria of prescriptiveness and universality are isomorphic with the developmental criteria of differentiation and hierarchical integration. Hence, by this maneuver, Kohlberg commits the naturalistic fallacy (since he draws an isomorphic connection between the psychological "is" and the normative "ought"), but he gets away with it because he only draws a parallel or mapping relationship between the two realms and does not reduce one to the other.

On the basis of this argument Kohlberg could claim that upward movement through his stage sequence yielded judgments that were progressively better on both psychological and moral grounds insofar as upward movement (development) gradually approximates the ideal equilibrium and the moral ideal described by Stage 6. Kohlberg also used this argument to justify his efforts at moral education. What justifies the effort is the fact that gains in development improve moral reflection. Yet Kohlberg's isomorphism argument proved to be controversial (Siegel, 1981; Locke, 1986; Rosen, 1980). One critique in particular prompted Kohlberg to reinterpret the nature of his is-ought claims. Jürgen Habermas (1983, 1990) urged that Kohlberg's (1971) isomorphism argument (which he termed the "identity thesis") be abandoned in favor of a "complementarity thesis" and that the stage theory itself be thought of as a *rational reconstruction* of the development of moral reasoning. Kohlberg accepted this interpretation of his theory (Kohlberg, Levine, & Hewer, 1983), so we must now attempt to consider what it amounts to.

Rational Reconstructions and the Complementarity Thesis

Let's begin by examining what is meant by a rational reconstruction. According to Kohlberg (following Habermas), an interviewer must enter into an empathic dialogue, a sensitive two-way communication, with a subject. The point of entering such a conversation in this way is to come to some understanding of what the subject is trying to communicate regarding her vision of the moral world. The meanings that subjects bring to bear on moral issues matter, and the interviewer must attempt to phenomenologically grasp these meanings from their perspective. Hence, interviewing requires an interpretive stance. It requires one to adopt a hermeneutical attitude that is not unlike the stance taken when one attempts to interpret a text. For example, when one approaches a text, one is trying to understand the author's point of view. One is trying to understand the author's intentions in a given act of communication. What does the author mean? What vision is the author attempting to communicate? One would not dream of trying to understand an utterance apart from some grasp of the overall meaning-intention of the author. In an interview one is not attempting to explain a behavior in isolation from the subject's own judgment about what the behavior means. One is not merely recording an observation—this would be to adopt a positivistic stance. Rather, insofar as the subject is the author of her moral perspective, insofar as she is trying to communicate some aspect of her moral vision, the interviewer must give up the privileged position as observer and participate in the dialogue. The interpreter must get involved and negotiate the meaning and validity of truth claims, get a handle on the standards by which the rightness and wrongness of actions can be evaluated. In other words, the interviewer must actively assume the perspective of the Other in order to see things, phenomenologically, from her point of view. There is no other way to capture the meaning of a moral utterance. A subject's reasoning about justice cannot be faithfully grasped without adopting this interpretive stance.

But now the task of the developmental psychologist is to make sense of the subject's moral intuitions, that is, to render some developmental account of them in order to relate them to some propositional truth claims (a theory). To do so the researcher must have recourse to explanatory concepts that are external to the interview-dialogue. In a sense the interviewer, who initially attempted to grasp the perspective of the subject's moral vision, must now adopt the stance of the scientist by relating this vision to the validity claims of a normative ethical theory. The researcher must adopt an objectivating, or third-person, attitude, one that seeks to explain the data in light of some normative standard. According to Dwight Boyd (1986, p. 58), "The psychologist must adopt a perspective and utilize concepts and truthfulness checks which are 'external' to the interpretive stance [and these concepts] facilitate the reconstruction of qualitative changes in how. . . justice reasoning is manifested [in the dialogic interview]." The stage theory, then, armed as it is with external normative standards of adequacy (instantiated as Stage 6), is a reconstruction of justice reasoning.

In what sense, then, is the relationship between the psychological theory and the normative ethical theory one of complementarity (but not of isomorphism or identity)? The normative ethical theory is required in order to define the domain of psychological inquiry (e.g., what is to count as justice reasoning). This definition provides categories that are then used to reconstruct the moral intuitions of participants into ontogenetic stages of justice reasoning. In this way, the normative theory has a role to play in the explanation of psychological stage development. "For instance, the normative theoretical claim that a higher stage is philosophically a better stage is one necessary part of a psychological explanation of sequential stage movement (Kohlberg et al., 1983, p. 16). Of course, psychological explanation requires many other things besides, say, some account of transition mechanisms, such as cognitive conflict, some specification of prerequisite attainments in logical or social-cognitive development, some view on the importance of sociomoral atmosphere or of role-taking opportunities, and the like. But at least part of the explanation for why subjects prefer the moral perspective of a higher stage is that the higher stage is seen to yield a better perspective, and the normative ethical theory tells us why it is better. In this sense the ethical theory functions as one part of the explanation of stage development.

What if the empirical claims of the psychological theory are vindicated, supported by research—what does this tell us about the adequacy of the normative ethical theory? Although the adequacy of the ethical theory must be established on philosophical grounds, empirical evidence is not irrelevant to its assessment. For example, if the empirical claims of the psychological theory were falsified, the normative character of the ethical theory might reasonably be doubted. As Habermas (1983, p. 266) puts it, "The success of an empirical theory. . . may function as a check on the normative validity of hypothetically reconstructed moral intuitions." In other words, the philosophical adequacy of some normative ethical theory is given credibility if it "works empirically" (Boyd, 1986).

A complementary division of labor appears to exist, then, between philosophy and moral psychology. As Habermas (1990, p. 39) puts it, "The empirical theory [e.g., Kohlberg] presupposes the validity of the normative theory it uses. Yet the validity of the normative theory is cast into doubt if the philosophical reconstructions prove to be unusable in the context of application within the empirical theory." In other words, the psychological theory requires the ethical theory in order to define the domain of inquiry and to provide an adequate conception of the *telos* of moral reasoning, the moral ideal. This conception provides a guidepost that allows one to reconstruct the moral intuitions of subjects into stages of justice reasoning. The empirical theory, in turn, contributes to the assessment of the adequacy of the ethical theory. If the psychological theory is successful, we are entitled to greater confidence in the normative claims of the ethical theory (although the ethical theory also requires philosophical justification). If the empirical claims are falsified, however, then we would have reason to rethink our normative ethical commitments (since they do not work empirically).

The complementarity thesis suggests that the empirical status of the psychological theory has a bearing on what we are to think of the normative ethical theory. That is, the adequacy of "is" claims are relevant for the assessment of "ought" claims. Empirical data do contribute to our assessment of its normative claims. But the reader may well wonder just how far complementarity goes. Does it extend in the other direction? That is, if the normative ethical theory is found wanting on strictly philosophical grounds, should this state of affairs have any bearing on how we appraise the psychological theory? Does the incoherence of the moral ideal transfer to the psychological claims of the stage theory insofar as the philosophically discredited ethical theory defines the domain of inquiry and generates concepts used in the reconstruction of data into justice stages? It is entirely possible, for example, for the psychological claims of the stage theory to be well attested but for grave doubts to exist regarding the philosophical adequacy of the moral ideal. In this case, should the incoherence of "ought" claims breed suspicions about the developmental explanation of "is" claims?

To my knowledge no one has taken up this particular issue in any formal way, although some philosophers, notably Owen Flanagan (1991), have insisted that ethical theories show a measure of psychological realism. Presumably, it would count against the moral ideal of Stage 6 if it could be shown to violate even minimal standards of psychological realism. There are, to be sure, numerous philosophical critiques of Kohlberg's conception of the ethical ideal that Stage 6 is thought to represent (e.g., Locke, 1976; Senchuk, 1982; Aron, 1977; May, 1985; Trainer, 1977; Flanagan, 1982; Reed & Hanna, 1982; Meilaender, 1984). Some of these leave the impression that Kohlberg's stage theory is sadly corrupted because of (alleged) deficiencies in the philosophical grounding of the last stage. Matters are further complicated by the fact that the empirical grounding of Stage 6 has not yet been satisfactorily demonstrated. Indeed, the Kohlberg group has long struggled with how best to conceptualize the moral ideal (Kohlberg, Boyd, & Levine, 1990) as if to underscore the importance of staking Stage 6 to a defensible moral philosophic position. Yet there is the temptation for critics to invoke the complementarity thesis: If there are no useful empirical data on the psychological reality of Stage 6, then perhaps doubt is to be cast on the validity claims of the normative ethical theory. Or if the developmental telos is not yet nailed down, then perhaps the moral domain is insufficiently specified with the unhappy consequence that the rational reconstruction of the development of justice reasoning is ill defined and may be doubted. In contrast, some scholars appear frustrated with the undue influence that philosophical criteria are apparently having for how Kohlberg's stage theory is being evaluated. Some suggest that the more controversial philosophical notions simply be jettisoned from Kohlberg's theory (Puka, 1990a, 1990b) or else that attention be directed away from philosophical matters toward the considerable empirical strengths of the stage theory (Blasi, 1990).

The reader will recall that we entered this thicket precisely because Kohlberg's ontogenetic studies of justice reasoning were conducted under the aegis of a Piagetian understanding of development. As we have seen, development has its own internal standard of adequacy. Further, the telos of development functions as a normative standard and is the basis of a developmental explanation. When this understanding of development is applied to the study of morality, however, one is immediately confronted with a raft of contentious philosophical issues. The problem of how to relate normative standards of developmental adequacy and normative ethical standards becomes particularly acute when one is also committed to maintaining the autonomy and objectivity of ethics and when one is impressed with the putative dangers of the naturalistic fallacy.

Kohlberg embraced not only the Piagetian conception of development but also Piaget's genetic epistemological project, extending it into the moral domain.

Just as Piaget had investigated, in children's thinking, the development of cognitive concepts (e.g., space, time, logic, causality) that are of central importance to epistemology, so did Kohlberg take up the developmental study of concepts that are of central importance to moral philosophy. Kohlberg intended his genetic studies to be of some use to ethicists. He was convinced, perhaps more so early in his career, that "empirical developmental study might contribute to the solution of distinctly philosophical problems in both normative ethics and metaethics" (Kohlberg, 1971, p. 152). The former claim proved to be very controversial, as we have seen. About a decade later Kohlberg attenuated his claims about what his theory might be able to contribute to normative ethics, at least to some extent. He suggested, for example, that other researchers need not accept his philosophical adequacy claims in order to "begin the psychological study of moral development as we have done" (Kohlberg et al., 1983, p. 65). Whether one endorses Kohlberg's normative-ethical claims or follows him in his genetic epistemological aspirations for the moral domain is left to the personal choice of the researcher. One can still find the moral-stage framework a congenial and useful research tool even if one rejects Kohlberg's arguments for normative adequacy. Kohlberg's willingness to tolerate a separation of normative-ethical claims from the stage theory proper, at least as an option for other researchers, comes at a time when Stage 6 was dropped from the scoring manual and when strong claims for Stage 6 were otherwise being attenuated. Clearly, Kohlberg, in light of these attenuated claims for normative adequacy and for Stage 6, did not appear to think that the status of his normative-ethical claims should have any untoward consequences for the moral-stage theory. That is, if the normative arguments are, in fact, incoherent, then nothing necessarily follows as far as the stage theory is concerned. More recently, however, Stage 6 has made a "return" (Kohlberg et al., 1990), and one wonders if the neglect of normative-ethical claims is still an option for using the moral-stage framework. In any event, Kohlberg still insisted that researchers endorse his metaethical assumptions (but not, as we have seen, his normative-ethical claims) if they were to have recourse to the moral-stage approach. I will consider these metaethical assumptions in the next section.

Kohlberg's Metaethical Assumptions

For the logical positivist, to say that something is unscientific is to say that it is meaningless, that it is metaphysical and therefore beyond the pale of truth claims. As A. J. Ayer (1952, p. 31) puts it, "I require of an empirical hypothesis . . . that some possible experience should be relevant to the determination of its truth or falsehood. If a putative proposition fails to satisfy this principle, and is not a tautology, then I hold that it is metaphysical, and that, being metaphysical, it is neither true nor false but literally senseless." To qualify as meaningful with a claim to truth, a statement regarding a theoretical entity must be capable of translation into observational terms by means of correspondence rules (Suppe, 1977). As Kohlberg sees it, most modern psychologists approach the study of morality in this positivistic way. Hence, they tend to view ordinary moral language as unscientific (with all that entails). In order to talk about morality in a scientific (read "positivistic") way, one must translate moral terms (good, right, ought) into the language of science, into, say, operational definitions. The value relevance of moral terms is then stripped away in the translation, yielding operational terms that are themselves value neutral (and presumably more scientific). So when it is said, to use Kohlberg's favorite example, that "moral values are evaluations of actions that members of a given society believe to be right" (L. Berkowitz, 1964), this looks like an objective, value-neutral account of what moral values really amount to. Or when the behaviorist says that morality is better thought of as instances that evoke positive reinforcement, then we get a sense that vague, fuzzy metaphysical terms like "good" are nothing but events that happen to be contingently reinforced. For the positivist the language of morality and the language of science are incompatible. The former must be translated into the latter if we are to make any sense at all.

Kohlberg rejected this view. He argued that the language (e.g., correspondence rules) we use to describe morality is not value neutral after all. Indeed, when Leonard Berkowitz (1964) says that moral values are whatever a given society thinks is right, he is endorsing a moral stance—that of ethical relativism. This moral stance is unwittingly smuggled into the operational definition in the guise of presenting a coldly objective, value-free analysis of values. The operational definition takes a stand on morality without justification without admitting it, and it is the stance of moral relativism. No wonder positivists find nothing but relative moral values!

The conception of morality held out by positivist social science, then, is not value neutral, even in its operational form, but rather presupposes the truth of moral relativism. Hence, Kohlberg concluded that conceptions of morality cannot be value neutral, and that, indeed, one cannot study moral values in a way that neglects the value relevance of ordinary moral language. Perhaps another way of putting this is to say that scientific research is not possible without a theoretical framework. The difference between Kohlberg and the positivists is that Kohlberg is up front about his ethical framework and his ethical commitments and, indeed, argues strenuously for their adequacy. In contrast, the positivists pretend that theory-free observation is possible, that they are simply recording naked observations (hard facts) when in fact they are operating from a conceptual framework that assumes moral relativism. Their ethical commitments are hidden behind the jargon of positivist epistemology.

Kohlberg's conception of morality is value relevant in the sense that he believes moral options can be ordered developmentally (and development has an internal standard of adequacy) and in such a way as to satisfy formal philosophical criteria as to what constitutes an adequate moral judgment. One cannot hope to avoid invoking these normative, value-relevant standards when studying moral development. So Kohlberg's first assumption concerns the value relevance of ordinary moral language. His second assumption (phenomenalism) is that one must attend to the conscious motives and intentions of the actor in order to assess the moral relevance of a behavior. This contrasts with the psychoanalytic view, according to which moral motivation springs from unconscious guilt or from a desire to avoid the harsh actions of the punitive superego (Gilligan, 1976; Lapsley, 1994).

Because many of our irrational atavistic impulses are unconscious and because the functioning of the "moral arm" of the personality (the superego) is also unconscious, the human person is "not only far more immoral than he believes but also far more moral than he knows" (Freud, 1923/1961, p. 52).

Kohlberg's position also contrasts with behavioral views, according to which morality is judged by reference to overt behaviors and the consequences of behaviors. In his view the moral status of an action is indeterminate without some understanding of the phenomenological perspective of the agent. An action is moral if it is motivated by a moral judgment. A judgment is moral if it is informed by a moral principle or by moral reasons. And what is moral reasoning? Moral reasoning is "the *conscious* process of using ordinary moral language" (Kohlberg et al., 1983, p. 69). Moral activity is motivated by conscious moral deliberation guided by principles (contra Freud) and by phenomenologically relevant considerations expressed in ordinary moral language (contra behaviorists).

Kohlberg also assumed, following R. M. Hare (1952), that making moral judgments has a "universalizable intent." That is, when one asserts a moral principle, one asserts it not just for oneself only (or for another only). Rather one is asserting its universal applicability to everyone who might be in the identical situation in the relevant way. Kohlberg also assumed that moral principles have a prescriptive quality. That is, moral principles do not simply summarize general features of a problematic situation; they also command certain courses of action (One ought to do X). We are simply obliged to perform the relevant action if we judge our case to fall under the prescriptive authority of a moral principle—not just for ourselves but for everyone else whose case is subsumed by the principle. Hence the universal and prescriptive quality of moral judgments goes hand in hand (Hare, 1981). Prescriptive judgments, or actions motivated by prescriptive judgments, are derived from moral principles that have a universal intent. Moral rules, then, are universalizable prescriptions. Kohlberg derives this view from one reading of Kant's categorical imperative: Let the maxim of your conduct be the universal rule. It also follows, in his view, from a linguistic analysis of the meaning of moral terms.

According to Hare (1981), for example, prescriptivity and universalizability are formal, logical properties bound up with the meaning of moral terms. Knowing the meaning of moral terms obliges one to heed the demands of prescriptivity and universalizability, on pain of contradiction and incoherence. Hence, regarding universalizability, if I acknowledge that different situations are identical in relevant ways yet fail to reach the same moral judgment for each situation, I contradict myself. I am abusing the word "moral." Similarly, regarding prescriptivity, if I assent to the judgment that it is better to do X and then fail to do X when the opportunity arises, I have assented insincerely. Otherwise, I would have yielded to do the imperative (do X) that attaches to moral terms. And as noted previously, it follows from this linguistic analysis that anyone who commits to a prescriptive moral judgment ("I ought to help Jones in this situation X") also commits to a universal rule, on pain of incoherence. For example, if I conclude that Jones ought to be helped when he is in situation X, I am making this judgment not just for Jones but for anybody else (including myself) who might be found in the identical situation.

Kohlberg assumes, then, that it is possible to describe moral principles in a formal way. This assumption has both psychological and ethical sources. The psychological source is Piaget (or at least the received view of Piaget) and asserts that forms of reasoning, identified as cognitive structures, can be distinguished from the various contents of reasoning. Psychological formalism, then, focuses on the structural organization of judgments without necessarily implicating the content of the judgments themselves.

But moral reasoning, given its value relevance, is both a psychological matter and an ethical matter. Kohlberg derives his ethical formalism from the deontological tradition associated with Kant and his intellectual successors (and Hare, as we have seen). Moral conceptions, in Kohlberg's view, are best defined by general formal criteria, and it is the formal character of a moral judgment, its point of view, that is the focus of Kohlberg's stage theory. What are the formal characteristics of a moral judgment? Kohlberg (1971) mentions impersonality, ideality, universalizability, and preemptiveness. "Moral judgments," he writes, "tend to be universal, inclusive, consistent, and grounded on objective, impersonal or ideal grounds" (Kohlberg, 1971, p. 215). Judgments take on a moral character when they are fashioned in light of this moral point of view. In other words, formal criteria make judgments *moral* judgments. Kohlberg's developmental hypothesis is that individuals at the highest stages are better able to involve formal criteria in their deliberations; that is, they are better able to assume the moral point of view, and, consequently, their judgments are more morally adequate, in a formalist sense, than are the judgments of lower-stage reasoners. "Thus, the development of moral reasoning is a movement toward constructing the formal characteristics of a moral point of view" (Kohlberg et al., 1983, p. 83).

Finally, Kohlberg's theory assumes, following Rawls (1971), that justice is the core of principled morality and the first virtue of a person or of society. What are the concerns of justice? Justice is concerned with how best to adjudicate interpersonal conflicts, with how to fairly balance competing interests, and with how to distribute goods and rights in a principled way judged fair by the canons of impartiality, in short, with how to fairly distribute the "benefits and burdens" of cooperation (Rest, 1983). Justice must be our first concern, or else it must be the minimal core to morality, because we live in interpersonal settings where conflict is a real possibility. We live in pluralistic societies where there are competing conceptions of the good life and, indeed, within individual lives, competing goods that claim our attention. Justice, as seen from the moral point of view, is the "structure of conflict resolution for a dilemma of competing claims between or among persons" (Kohlberg et al., 1983, p. 37). To focus on justice, then, is to focus on that core of morality that presents the best claim to universal status given the centrality and ubiquity of conflict in human social life.

Justice is also that aspect of morality whose development is most amenable to description in terms of hard structural stages. The structure of justice, the nature of its operations, is similar to the operational structures of logical thought: "The justice operations of reciprocity and equality in social interaction parallel the logical and mathematical operations of reciprocity and equality in science and mathematics. In both the logical and justice domains, the use of operations implies equilibrated or reversible systems which we call hard structures" (Kohlberg et al., 1983, p. 37). With that we are now in a position to see how the hard structural analysis of justice operations yields the six stages of development. I take up this question in Chapter 4.

4

Kohlberg's Stage Theory

Stage Assumptions

I have already noted that Kohlberg adopted Piagetian stage criteria for his description of the justice stages. To justify a stage description, ontogenetic variation must follow an invariant sequence. The sequence must reflect recurring hierarchical integrations of lower-order stages into higher-order stages such that qualitative differences in the mode of organization are evident. Finally, stages must reflect structured wholeness (*structures d'ensemble*) in their range or scope of applicability. I will revisit these criteria when examining the empirical status of Kohlberg's theory. However, a few words regarding the structured-whole assumption would not be out of place here if only to clarify Kohlberg's position on the matter.

How inclusive must stage functioning be in order to satisfy the structured-whole assumption? Are structures content-specific or are they more general, more global—unifying performances across a range of diverse contents? In Chapter 1, I presented a version of Piaget's structured-whole assumption that is at variance with what I take to be the received view. The received view tends to interpret *structures d'ensemble* as requiring functional globality in the range of contents to be unified by a stage structure. I think this view is mistaken. In contrast, I presented a view insisting that Piaget favored the position that structures necessarily maintain an element of content specificity (Chapman, 1987, 1988).

There is, nonetheless, a diversity of opinion on the matter among developmental researchers (Sternberg, 1989). Some researchers (Loevinger, 1976; Kegan, 1982) endorse a rather totalizing view of global stages along the lines of the received view. Others (Chapman, 1987, 1988) hold out for the content-specificity view. This diversity is reflected in the moral-development domain as well. William Damon (1977b), for example, argues that the moral domain is characterized by discrete dimensions or issues (e.g., distributive justice, social rules, authority relations), each of which is organized by unique structures. These partial structures do not extend beyond the moral domain in question. Hence, Damon's view tends toward the notion of content specificity (see also Rest, 1979). What is Kohlberg's view?

Kohlberg takes an intermediate position (Colby & Kohlberg, 1987). Unlike Damon, for example, he argues the case for global structures within the moral domain. That is, justice structures unify judgments across a range of moral contents (i.e., across dilemmas, across various justice issues, across content practices, beliefs, and customs in other cultures, etc.). Unlike the received view, however, he argues that various cognitive and social-cognitive domains are marked by internally coherent structures that unify and integrate concepts within their respective domains. Hence, within domains one can identify internally coherent structural systems, each of which may follow its own stage sequence, and this is because structures cohere around a given function and each domain can be said to reflect a different function. According to Colby and Kohlberg (1987, p. 13), for example, "The specific structures of thought within a domain are determined in part by the nature of the function they serve, and each domain can be said to represent a different function." Hence, global structures organize diverse contents within a given domain but not between domains. So, for example, Piaget identifies a global structure whose function is to integrate logicomathematical concepts. Robert Selman (1980) identifies global structures whose function is to unify interpersonal concepts. And Kohlberg identifies global structures that unify justice concepts. But *structures d'ensemble* are not so global as to reflect a single coherent system that organizes performances *across* logical, interpersonal, and moral domains. The *structure d'ensemble* is lord of its own domain.

For Kohlberg, then, content specificity is limited to *domains* of content. Global structures are domain-specific. Kohlberg is required to maintain some version of the content–free structure view even in this domain-specificity version in order to justify his claim that the ontogenesis of justice reasoning is a universal phenomenon, to be found in all cultures regardless of the content of their respective moral practices or the particularities of their moral experience. That is, the campaign against cultural relativism (in moral matters) cannot countenance too much content specificity. Justice structures must show some measure of content-free globality in order to show that the seeming relativity in cultural practices, beliefs, and customs is only apparent, reflecting mere content differences among societies, differences that are ultimately structured by a deep appreciation of universalizable and prescriptive moral norms, that is, by the moral point of view (Lapsley, 1992b).

Kohlberg's intermediate endorsement of domain-specific global stages is not without its complications. It would appear that he attributes global structures to the domain of logicomathematical concepts, but this is problematic, as we have seen. Content specificity is immanent in the cognitive structures of logical development (Chapman, 1987, 1988). If this is correct, then it would appear that even Kohlberg's intermediate position is a stricter reading of *structures d'ensemble* than was perhaps intended by Piaget.

Kohlberg's position is nuanced in other ways as well. For example, although his stage model calls for within-domain global structures, the justice operations are not so general and integrative as to accommodate the comprehension of moral judgments made by others or their moral preferences or evaluations (Colby & Kohlberg, 1987; Rest, 1979), although this appears to be a retreat from an earlier view (Rest, Turiel, & Kohlberg, 1969). The justice operations are said to best describe the spontaneous production of moral judgments. Although Kohlberg also argued that cognitive and social-cognitive development can be delineated into a number of conceptually distinct domains, each characterized by internally coherent structures uniquely suited for particular domain-specific functions, he does posit isomorphisms and interdependencies among the domains. This position was hinted at previously with Kohlberg's assertion that the justice operations of reciprocity and equality parallel the reciprocity and equality operations in the logico-mathematical domain.

The interdependency among domains has been traditionally asserted by means of the necessary-but-not-sufficient formula: Logical operations are necessary but not sufficient for certain developments in social perspective-taking, which in turn are necessary but not sufficient for certain developments in the moral domain. This interdependency formula shakes out into a number of specific claims (e.g., Kohlberg & Gilligan, 1971): (1) Piaget's concrete operations are required for functioning at Stage 2 in Selman's sequence, which in turn is required for Stage 2 moral reasoning. (2) Early formal operations are necessary for Stage 3 social perspective-taking, which in turn is a necessary prerequisite for Stage 3 moral reasoning. (3) Consolidated formal operations are required for both Stage 4 perspective-taking and Stage 4 moral reasoning. Hypotheses 2 and 3 are revised versions of an earlier claim that formal operations are a prerequisite for principled (Stages 5–6) reasoning (Colby, 1973). The earlier claim was abandoned with a change in the way moral stages were scored (as we will see in the next section). What was once considered principled reasoning (and linked to formal operations) was redefined by the scoring change as an advanced form of conventional reasoning. Hence, as a result of changes in moral-stage scoring rules, it is now conventional reasoning that is thought to require early and consolidated formal operations as a prerequisite.

There is both a loose and a strict reading of what the interdependency formula entails. The loose reading suggests that the interdependency formula is merely making a claim as to what prescriptive reasoning entails—it necessarily entails certain competencies in logical and social-cognitive development. Judgments made at the highest levels of justice reasoning invariably reflect a great deal of cognitive and social-cognitive sophistication. Hence, under the loose interpretation, the interdependency formula is just a way of talking about moral judging—logical and social-cognitive competencies are built into the definition of moral structures—as opposed to a set of testable claims about the empirical relations among conceptually independent domains (Colby & Kohlberg, 1987). But since logical and social-cognitive development follow their own domain-specific sequences, it is also true that sophisticated logical and social-cognitive reasoning need not implicate sophistication in the moral domain. Consequently, any empirical claims that the loose reading may entail are directed toward the developmental hypotheses associated with justice reasoning.

A stricter reading treats the interdependency formula as an empirical hypothesis about dependent relations among the logical, social-cognitive, and moral domains. "In this view, it is claimed that the operations in question will necessarily be exhibited first in response to logicomathematical or physical problems, next in response to social problems, and last in response to moral problems" (Colby & Kohlberg, 1987, p. 13). In other words, there is a kind of *decalage* in the applicability of cognitive operations to the three domains. There appears to be empirical support for this view. Walker and Richards (1979) showed, for example, that subjects could be moved to moral Stage 4 only if they possessed "early basic" formal operations as a prerequisite. Even "beginning" formal operations were ineffective for motivating moral-stage advance. Similarly, Walker (1980) showed that subjects could be moved to moral Stage 3 only if they possessed beginning formal operations and were at Stage 3 perspective-taking (see also Kuhn, Langer, & Kohlberg, 1977; Selman, 1971; Krebs & Gilmore, 1982). However, there are also disconfirming studies (Broughton, 1983) and general doubts about the interdependency formula for domains (Turiel, 1983b; Loevinger, 1986) and about the hard-stage models that interdependency research assumes (Rest, 1979). I will examine at least some of these arguments a bit later.

Evolution of Stage Scoring

We are now in a position to examine the six stages of justice reasoning. The assessment of moral stages begins when a subject is asked to reflect on a number of moral issues that are suggested by one or more hypothetical dilemmas. The most famous Kohlbergian dilemma concerns Heinz, who must decide whether to break into the pharmacy of an ostensibly greedy druggist in order to steal a drug that would save Heinz's wife from certain death by cancer. The competing issues in this dilemma are life and law. Other dilemmas are presented to subjects in order to probe their understanding of authority relations, the importance of promise-keeping and contracts, the nature of punishment, and the role of conscience in morality. A subject is asked to reflect on these and other moral issues during the course of clinical interviews. Interview material is then transcribed for stage scoring.

Over the years the methodology of stage assessment has been revised in important ways in order to account for certain anomalies that appeared to violate the strict reading of Piagetian stage criteria. As a result of the sweeping changes in scoring methodology, there have been concomitant changes in how the six stages have been described (Colby, 1978; Colby & Kohlberg, 1987). Unfortunately, the pace of these changes has made it difficult for researchers, and many textbook authors, to stay on top of the most current version of the theory. So it would be useful to briefly recount some of this history before I describe the stages proper.

Kohlberg's (1958) doctoral dissertation introduced two scoring systems: Global Story Rating and Sentence Rating. Both systems were designed to analyze subject protocols for value contents thought to reflect a developmentally ordered series of moral types (stages). A manual was constructed that consisted of prototypical sentences thought to reflect (as probabalistic signs) the various moral types. With sentence scoring, every statement made by a subject was referred to the manual for a match and then stage-scored as appropriate. A stage profile was then generated based on the percentage of stage matches. In this system the sentence was the unit of analysis. With Global Story Rating the subject's total response to the dilemma was stage-scored. If the subject's global response seemed to point to more than one moral type, then major (dominant) and minor stage scores were assigned on intuitive grounds.

These scoring systems were content analyses in the sense that a subject's content concerns (e.g., fear of punishment, obeying the law, loving one's wife) served as a probabalistic sign of a moral stage (Colby & Kohlberg, 1987). If a subject mentioned fear of punishment, this was a probabalistic sign of Stage 1; if obeying the law, Stage 4 was indicated. The 1958 Sentence and Global Story Rating systems were used in moral-development research until 1971, when they were supplanted by Structural Issue Scoring.

The 1958 scoring systems were abandoned because they generated anomalous data. One study, for example, found that interviews were not sufficiently coalescing into internally consistent stages (Kramer, 1968). This seemed contrary to the structured-whole assumption (or one reading of it). Kramer also reported instances of stage regression. Many high school subjects who were classified at Stage 5 (or 6) were later classified at Stage 2 when they were in college. This contradiction appeared to violate expectations bound up with the notions of hierarchical integration and invariant sequence. This state of affairs was originally thought to represent a failure of the stage sequence for young adults in college (Kohlberg & Kramer, 1969). In other words, the integrity of the scoring methodology was not originally questioned. What was questioned was the applicability of the sequence for particular kinds of subjects.

Kohlberg (1973b) later revised this interpretation. He argued that subjects who enter college find the experience such that they are momentarily convulsed with relativistic reasoning—a condition that Dwight Boyd (1976, 1981) has dubbed "sophomoritis." One feature of this transition is that adolescents and young adults begin to seriously question conventional standards and moral authority. The focus on questioning itself gives these subjects a moral stance (relativity) that mimics the reasoning of a lower stage (Stage 2). However, the difference between the "regressed" college students and actual Stage 2 thinking is that the former attempted to articulate a relativistic *moral theory*. In fact, the structure of their thought seemed more advanced than even conventional reasoners. Hence, Kohlberg suggested that these ersatz instances of regression were actually evidence of a transitional Stage 4 ½.

But even this interpretation did not account for all of the anomalies (e.g., instances of stage skipping, regressions from Stage 4 to Stage 3, and the fact that movement from Stage 5 to Stage 4 ½ is still a regression), and deep suspicions grew about the adequacy of the 1958 scoring systems for generating data appropriate for hard-stage assumptions (Colby & Kohlberg, 1987); enter Structural Issue Scoring.

One problem with the 1958 scoring systems was that they tended to conflate structure and content. Probabalistic signs were now seen as an imperfect guide for detecting underlying thought organization. It was determined, for example, that a subject who mentions law and order could be reasoning at Stage 4, but not necessarily, since a concern with legal considerations could be evident at other stages as well. Issues of affiliation are not strictly the concern of Stage 3; of punishment and authority, not strictly the concern of Stage 1. Rather, the typological orientations are better thought of as contents that are, in fact, organized by a deeper underlying structure. Hence, there are different construals of what, say, law and order amounts to at the different stages with the nature of the differing construals being determined by the perspective that a subject brings to bear on the issues at hand. Each stage, then, can be characterized by a particular sociomoral perspective that unifies specific content concerns (law, life, punishment, affiliation, etc.). And this sociomoral perspective is just what defines the moral structure of the stage; namely, it is the principle that structures a subject's understanding of moral concepts (Colby & Kohlberg, 1987).

Consequently, the shift to Structural Issue Scoring entailed a redefinition of what was content and what was structure. Stage scores were no longer assigned globally to stories; nor were content concerns taken as signs for particular moral types. Rather, scores were assigned within content—at what level of discourse did the subject construe a given moral concept? In order to score case material, nine basic moral concepts were identified in a reference manual, accompanied by fairly abstract accounts of how these concepts were exemplified at each stage. The unit of analysis was now something large and general (a level of discourse, a sociomoral perspective), and its relation to moral concepts was correspondingly abstract. The abstractness of the manual, however, proved to be the undoing of Structural Issue Scoring. Oftentimes scoring decisions were subjective and hence, unreliable (Colby & Kohlberg, 1987). The current system, Standard Issue Scoring, was designed "to achieve greater objectivity and reliability in scoring by specifying clear and concrete stage criteria and to define the developmental sequence of the specific 'moral concepts' within each stage as well as the sequence of the global or general stage structure" (Colby & Kohlberg, 1987, p. 40).

Two important and related developments accompanied the transition to Structural Issue and Standard Issue Scoring. One was that Stage 6 was dropped from the scoring manual. With the new scoring system, none of Kohlberg's longitudinal subjects exemplified this advanced stage. That is, subjects who were classified as Stage 6 in the ideal-typical manuals of 1958 are now classified at lower stages (perhaps as low as Stage 3). Nonetheless, Stage 6 is still retained as a hypothetical end point of development.

One may well ask why Stage 6 is retained in this way if it does not appear to be an empirical possibility. It is retained as a hypothetical end point because of the nature of developmental explanation in the (Piagetian) cognitive structural tradition. As we have seen, the very coherence of the stage sequence hinges on the requirement that the sequence be closed by a kind of reasoning that is denoted by Stage 6, even if this reasoning is nowhere descriptive of actual moral agents. Development has its own internal standard of adequacy. This standard allows us to determine when change moves from less adequate to more adequate forms, where adequacy is defined by the functioning of the last stage in the sequence. Development proceeds toward a state of optimum complexity and adaptation, of which the last stage, the telos of development, serves as the normative standard. Hence the transition from earlier to later stages is made sensible by understanding how the transitions function as a means for reaching the final stage. Stage 5, in Kohlberg's sequence, cannot serve this function because it is not the most equilibrated form of reasoning and therefore cannot resolve certain problems in a way that is most adequate (the ideal equilibrium). Further, a Stage 5 reasoner cannot be expected to resolve moral dilemmas in a way that is completely adequate in a moral sense (the moral ideal) or in a way that secures agreement and consensus, which is the main point of moral deliberation (for the antirelativist). And it is just this desire to describe how it is possible to generate agreement and consensus on rationally justifiable solutions to moral dilemmas that is at the heart of the Kohlbergian project, a project that requires Stage 6 as the telos, since it is here that the desire for rational agreement is more ideally satisfied (Lapsley, 1992b; Kohlberg, 1973a).

I should add that it was not entirely correct of me to say that Stage 6 does not describe actual moral reasoners. It appears to describe an elite set of individuals who have had formal training in ethics (Kohlberg et al., 1983). This raises the intriguing possibility that it was their specialized content knowledge, acquired through formal education, that allowed them to articulate the moral point of view described as Stage 6. That is, perhaps it was *content* that made *structure* possible. This is an intriguing notion because it appears to reverse the common assumption in many quarters that schemas and strategies (i.e., structures) make the acquisition of content knowledge possible. However, there is growing recognition, which is most acute in the area of memory development, that content knowledge may well facilitate the acquisition of structures, cognitive schemas, and strategies (Chi & Ceci, 1987). If this latter point is true, and if it is true that content knowledge acquired through formal academic training made it possible for an elite group of subjects to articulate the moral point of view of Stage 6, then one may well wonder about the strategy that seeks to define content-free structures at lower stages. The importance of content is underscored by the research of James Rest, which I take up later in the text. He finds that formal education is positively correlated with principled moral reasoning, as measured by his Defining Issues Test (Rest, 1979; Rest & Thoma, 1985; Rest & Narvaez, 1991). There are also substantial correlations between formal college experience and reasoning on Kohlberg's interview (Colby et al., 1983), though this is interpreted as congruent with Kohlberg's claim that formal education provides "role-taking opportunities" that stimulate structural development.

Moral Substages and How Stage 6 Got Lost

One consequence, then, of the transition to Standard Issue Scoring was the reduction of Stage 6 to the status of a hypothetical end point. A second development was that Kohlberg identified A and B substages within the remaining stages. This development was one outcome of trying to come to grips with the regression problem and can be reconstructed in the following way (following Gibbs, 1979).

Recall that formerly principled high school students (according to the 1958 manuals) apparently regressed to a Stage 2 kind of relativism. But when Kohlberg examined their protocols, he noted that their relativism seemed to be of a different order altogether—it appeared more sophisticated, more theoretical, than one would expect of Stage 2 reasoners. Kohlberg suggested that this reasoning could not really be principled (since it embraced relativism) but that it was more sophisticated than even conventional reasoning (since it was theory-defining)—hence the transitional Stage 4 ½. But if this transitional stage was theoretical, if the transitional college subjects were struggling with a moral theory of sorts, should not principled reasoning be similarly theoretical in nature?

Kohlberg resolved the problem in the following way. The principled stages were indeed defined in a very philosophic-theoretical way (with the consequence that Stage 6 receded from empirical view). And the theoretical discourse of transitional subjects was downsized into a species of conventional reasoning. It was judged to be universalizing tendencies of the member-of-society perspective. This meant that theoretical room needed to be carved out for this sophisticated kind of reasoning at the conventional level, and this was accomplished by the distinction between A and B substages. The traditional description of the stages (according to the 1958 manuals) was relegated to the A substage. The more theoretical discourse was denoted the B substage (Gibbs, 1979).

Kohlberg believed that the B substage would better account for moral action. That is, subjects at the B substage would have a keener appreciation of the prescriptive and universalizable nature of moral judgments (even if their reasoning was otherwise conventional) and would hence be more likely to engage in moral action they believed to be just (Kohlberg et al., 1983). The substages were also thought to reflect the two moral orientations that seemed to be described by Piaget's two stages of moral judgment. The A substage reflects a heteronomous orientation to rules and authority; the B substage reflects the autonomous orientation to fairness, equality, and reciprocity.

When subjects are asked to make a moral decision about what should be done to resolve a dilemma, some of them make content choices that reflect the heteronomous orientation; others make choices that are compatible with the autonomous position—regardless of their stage classification. Insofar as the autonomous choice is associated with higher-stage reasoning (Colby et al., 1983), it must be possible to detect some features of moral reasoning that are indicative of the highest stages (e.g., prescriptivity, universality) in the reasoning of subjects who make the autonomous choice. Hence, some subjects at Stage 3, for example, could make a heteronomous choice (A substage), and others at Stage 3 could make an autonomous choice (B substage), the latter being imbued with some of the formal (Kantian) features of a mature judgment. The substages, then, are defined by a mixture of content (choice) and structure (formal features such as prescriptivity, universalizability, and intrinsicalness). Reasoners at substage B tacitly use justice operations that satisfy formal criteria of adequacy better than do reasoners at the A substage. Consequently, the B substage is said to be more equilibrated than the A substage, which suggests that development can occur within stages (movement from substage A to B) as well as between stages. It is also possible for subjects to retain their A or B status when they advance to the next stage. One implication of this view is that Piaget got it wrong when he argued that there were two moralities in childhood, two moral orientations. In fact, there is one, and it runs a developmental course from less equilibrated (A substage) to more equilibrated (B substage).

The introduction of substages certainly complicates Kohlberg's reading of the form-content distinction. Kohlberg believed that hard stages would be revealed only if structure was thoroughly purged of content. Yet the more effectively his scoring methodology was able to accomplish this, the more Stage 6, the moral ideal, faded from view as an empirical possibility. As Gibbs (1979) put it, Stage 6 became "stranded" in an ethereal philosophical realm that made it difficult to see how it could be described in terms of Piagetian structures. Indeed, even Stage 5 is vanishingly rare in extant longitudinal samples. But the existence of the B substage provides a way of reintroducing formalist criteria of moral adequacy into a sequence that has seemingly lost its moral ideal, and the fact that this process entails the reintroduction of content is a matter of some interest. Stages are defined in terms of structure (the sociomoral perspective), but substages are defined by both content and structure.

It is hard not to see the attenuation of Stage 6 and the emergence of the B substage as an unrelated development. Whereas Kantian moral adequacy is lost as an empirical possibility with the reduction of Stage 6 to a hypothetical end point, it is regained with the discovery of the B substage. Although Stage 6 seems beyond the pale of most reasoners, some of its properties seep down to the B substages of lower stages. In this way some semblance of ideal moral rationality is retained; indeed, it is made more generally available even at conventional levels of justice reasoning. The more Stage 6 receded from view, stranded in an ethereal hypothetical realm, the more its formalist notions became a real possibility in the B substages of conventional morality. Curiously, then, principled reasoning, or some semblance of it, is at once exceedingly rare and common.

Levels and Stages

The six-stage sequence of justice reasoning is demarcated into three levels: preconventional, conventional, postconventional (principled). The structure of reasoning characteristic of each level is defined as the sociomoral perspective. As such the sociomoral perspective structures one's construal of moral concepts and unifies them into an integrated and coherent moral judgment. According to Colby and Kohlberg (1987), the three levels can be thought of as three ways of relating the self to the moral expectations of society. In the preconventional level, moral rules and norms are external to persons; that is, they are imposed from the outside by authority figures. At the conventional level, the self internalizes the expectations of authority. At the postconventional level, what is outside (expectations of authority and of society) and what is inside (self-chosen principles) are clearly distinguished, with emphasis placed on the latter for defining moral options.

Within each level there are two stages. The second stage within a level is a more equilibrated form of the structure, that is, a better articulation of the structuring sociomoral perspective. For example, the sociomoral perspective of the preconventional level (Stages 1 and 2) is the *concrete individualistic perspective*. This perspective focuses on the concrete needs, values, and desires of persons with subjectivity who have different, and potentially conflicting, psychological preferences. Stage 1 is an unstable construal of this perspective, however, since the psychological preferences of others are obscured by the agent's egocentrism (among other failings). The sociomoral perspective of the conventional level (Stages 3 and 4) is the *member-of-society* perspective. It is the perspective that construes justice as that which best advances the values, interests, and desires of "us" members of society, where society is an interpersonal community of those who are in close relationship (Stage 3), that is, a society of friends, or else a more societal community of impersonal citizens (Stage 4). At the postconventional level the sociomoral perspective is the *prior-to-society* perspective of a rational moral agent who has a partly (Stage 5) or fully (Stage 6) self-conscious grasp of universalizable principles that *anyone* would want to see instantiated in *any* ideally moral society.

Reasoning about justice is further described by reference to justice operations. The justice operation of *equality* is defined by one or more of the following: (1) identical quantities of goods for all or for all relevant persons, (2) equal consideration of claims, and (3) the assertion that all persons are equal in some relevant sense. The justice operation of *equity* adjusts or corrects the application of equality given (1) extenuating circumstances or (2) the existence of inequality prior to distribution of goods. Consider this example: Two girls, Cara and Katie, are to compete in a 100-yard dash. But Cara is partly debilitated by a foot injury. How should the race be run fairly? Equality bids us to ignore Cara's infirmity by treating the runners equally—both shall begin the race at the starting line. Equity bids us to compensate for the infirmity, say, by giving Cara a 20-yard head start. In this way equality is "corrected" in the interest of fairness. Hence, equity recognizes that sometimes fairness demands unequal treatment. Modern affirmative action programs are premised on this notion of equitable treatment of opportunity claims, but such treatment is also evident in less contentious areas, such as the handicap system of scoring in golf and bowling.

The justice operation of *reciprocity* exchanges or distributes honors, goods, punishments, and so on on the basis of just deserts—effort, talent, and the like. Two additional justice operations, *prescriptive role-taking* and *universalizability*, are pegged to the desire for fair procedures (procedural justice) for adjudicating competing justice claims and for procedural checks on the validity of one's justice reasoning.

Prescriptive role-taking is an attempt to balance the perspectives of those who have a claim to justice, typically by adopting a set of procedures that ensures a fair, impartial consideration of claims. Kohlberg suggested that "moral musical chairs" might be a good way to describe one formalized procedure. Here one systematically determines if a candidate solution to a moral dilemma is still acceptable when seen from the perspective of each claimant. Everyone who has a claim to justice must systematically (and often imaginatively) evaluate matters from all sides. One indication that the solution is inadequate is just when the solution cannot be reversed, that is, when it cannot be maintained when claimants exchange their perspectives. Universalizability asks, "Is it right for *anyone* to do X?" It is a way of expressing one form of Kant's categorial imperative: Let the maxim of thy conduct be the universal will. It is also implied (following Hare) in the very meaning of moral terms. At the principled stages these procedural justice operations are deliberately and self-consciously used as validity checks on the application of equality, equity, and reciprocity operations.

Table 4.1 summarizes some key features of the six-stage, three-level sequence. Within each stage are brief descriptions of its social perspective and the way justice operations are applied. One way of getting a feel for the developmental features of the sequence is to focus on one or more of the justice operations (e.g., reciprocity or universalizability), then to chart its development through the six stages. I will leave this as an exercise for the interested reader. What concerns us now is a general description of each stage.

Stage 1: Heteronomous Morality

This stage has much in common with Piaget's morality of constraint. Reasoning at this stage is characterized by moral realism, egocentrism, physicalism, and heteronomy. Moral realism is reflected in the conviction that moral qualities attach to actions just as surely as physical qualities (mass, size, color) attach to objects. Certain actions are just good or bad in themselves in an absolute and literal way. No justification, no consideration of motives, is required. Because the child is egocentric, she cannot differentiate her perspective from the perspective of others, particularly those magnificent others who have authority or social power. Hence, a perspective that differs from that of authority is not recognized. And what gives authority its special status? The moral significance of authority figures is defined physicalistically. Sanjam, who is rich, Jason, who is big, and Schick, who is famous, have greater moral authority and more valid claims to justice than Vikram, who is poor, Roy, who is small, or Zane, who is infamous. Finally, morality is heteronomous. That is, what is right or wrong is defined by those who have authority and power. It is not a product of the collaboration of equals joined in solidarity. Moral rules are something we are given from the outside or from above, not something that is constructed from the inside or chosen in a free act of moral autonomy.

Stage 2: Individualistic, Instrumental Morality

With the decline of egocentrism the subject is now able to accurately infer the social perspective of other individuals. The child now sees that others have their own interests and desires, all of which are reasonable and justified. A kind of moral relativity emerges that sees all interests as equally valid. The problem that emerges is how to secure one's own interests in the face of the potentially competing or conflicting interests of other claimants. One way to ensure that one's own needs are gratified is to establish pragmatic agreements with others ("if you scratch my back, I'll scratch yours"). Justice is thus seen as an instrumental exchange of favors,

TABLE 4.1   Levels and Stages of Justice Reasoning

Level 1. Preconventional Morality: Concrete Individualistic Perspective

Stage 1. Heteronomous Morality

Sociomoral perspective Egocentric point of view and moral realism.

Norms   Concrete rules are categories of right and wrong behavior that are defined "realistically" and that are not associated with the psychological perspective or expectations of self or of others.

Justice operations

Equality   Strict equality is mandated for those who fall into relevant categories (e.g., for good sons, important persons, thieves). Unequal distribution is tolerated if it falls upon members of a less valued category (bad sons, not so important persons, people with less social power).

Reciprocity   Goods or actions are exchanged according to the rule "same for same" without establishing a psychological hierarchy of values for the goods or actions (e.g., hunters kill animals, so animals should kill humans).

Equity   Absent.

Prescriptive
role-taking   Absent.

Universalizability   A rule is generalized barring exceptions unless they are for authorities who create and enforce the rule or norm.

Stage 2. Individualistic, Instrumental Morality

Sociomoral perspective Concrete-individualistic.

Norms   Psychological standards exist for regulating actions thought to satisfy the psychological needs and interests of other selves. Self-other expectations balance through concrete exchanges.

Justice operations

Equality   The self and other are persons with psychological needs and interests that can be satisfied by an exchange of goods or actions. Good and bad have no intrinsic value other than as a way to describe the needs, desires and interests of individual psychological persons.

Reciprocity   Concrete exchanges of equal goods (values) meet the needs of self and other(s).

Equity   Strict exchange is compensated for by focusing on special needs (e.g., the poor may steal because of their special need).

Prescriptive
role-taking   It is acknowledged that the self has needs, just as others do.

Universalizability   There is concern for limiting deviation from the norm lest it upset the system of exchange (e.g., if one person gets away with it, others may try to).

Level 2. Conventional Morality: Member-of-Society Perspective

Stage 3. Interpersonal Normative Morality

Sociomoral perspective Coordination of individual perspectives into a third-party perspective characterized by shared norms held in common.

(continued)

TABLE 4.1   Levels and Stages of Justice Reasoning (continued)

Norms	*Shared expectations are held by persons in the relationship. These norms function to support and maintain relationships.*
Justice operations	
Reciprocity	Obligation is seen as a kind of debt that cannot be repaid by some concrete equal exchange (as at Stage 2). Rather, the desire to reciprocate must be accompanied by the appropriate sentiments (loyalty, gratitude). Relations are maintained not only by equal exchange of concrete goods but also by a reciprocation of loyalty, obligation, fellow feeling, debt.
Equality	Persons who are good role occupants or have good motives or sentiments are to be treated equally.
Equity	Deviations from the norm are tolerated for extenuating circumstances or for good intentions.
Prescriptive role-taking	Golden Rule: "X is right or fair from my point of view if I can accept it as right or fair from your point of view."
Universalizability	There is a concern for limiting deviations from the norm lest they upset the community of selves who have good motives, intentions, or moral sentiments (vs. system of concrete exchange among self-interested selves, as at Stage 2).

Stage 4. Social System Morality

Sociomoral perspective	The individual takes on the perspective of a generalized member of society. The perspective one takes is stepped up to consider not just the interests of those with whom one is in immediate relationship, but also the general societal perspective.
Norms	Regulation (e.g., laws) are designed to limit general disorder and disagreement.
Justice operations	
Equality	Rights and obligations of citizens are equal before the law.
Equity	The system (vs. an individual, as at Stage 3) grants exceptions for an application of social standards that otherwise are insensitive to special needs or extenuating circumstances.
Reciprocity	The sentiments of duty, loyalty, obligation, link individuals in relationships not only to each other (as at Stage 3) but also to society. There is also a debt to society owed by virtue of participating in social institutions and receiving the benefits of participation.
Prescriptive role-taking	Individual actions are balanced with societal standards. One may still do X if illegal; but X is still wrong by societal standards, and one will have to accept the consequences.
Universalizability	Deviations must be limited lest they breed disrespect for social institutions and societal standards (vs. the interpersonal community of well-disposed individuals, as at Stage 3).

Level 3. Principled Morality: Prior-to-Society Perspective

Stage 5. Human Rights and Social Welfare Morality

Sociomoral perspective	That of a rational moral agent who has an intuitive prior-to-society awareness of universalizable values that anyone would want to see reflected in a moral society.

(continued)

TABLE 4.1   Levels and Stages of Justice Reasoning (continued)

Norms	Standards that maximize and protect individual human rights are established by free persons through special procedures designed to secure agreement and consensus.
Justice operations	
Equality	The ultimate value of human life and liberty conveys the recognition that individuals have equal rights, worth, and dignity.
Equity	In earlier stages the notions of equality were derived from norms, laws, etc. These norms and laws were then used to justify the notion of equality. That is, the "target" of compensation was the notion of equality itself—one is equitable so that some notion of equality can be maintained. At Stage 5, the target of compensation is reversed. Now the target is the equity norm itself. Equality of life and liberty are not justified by equity norms but are assumed by them as the foundation of justice reasoning. Hence, when respect for human life is lessened or is abridged because of the insensitivity of norms, procedures, or laws, the equity operation reasserts the foundational assumptions of equality of life and liberty.
Reciprocity	Concrete, symbolic equivalents are exchanged between freely contracting persons with emphasis on notion of free agreement on contracts.
Prescriptive role-taking	The need to account for the perspective of each party in a social situation is stressed.
Universalizability	Moral norms are to be generalized to all human persons living in any society whatever.

Stage 6. Morality of Universalizable, Reversible, and Prescriptive General Ethical Principles

Sociomoral perspective	The moral point of view, prior-to-society.
Norms	The justice operations of equality, reciprocity, equity, prescriptive role-taking, and universalizability become self-conscious principles and procedural justice checks on the validity of reasoning.

Source: Adapted from Kohlberg (1986).

goods, or sanctions. Stage 2 thinking is incapable, however, of settling disagreements and conflicts when they invariably do arise.

Stage 3: Interpersonal Normative Morality

The pragmatic, tit-for-tat reciprocity of Stage 2 gives way to a more ideal form of reciprocity at Stage 3. Here the concrete, individualistic perspectives of others are coordinated into a relational perspective. Consider this analogy: When boy meets girl, two individuals are conjoined in a relationship for the sake of which certain actions and values are expected. That is, two perspectives are integrated into a third (the "coupleship") that relates them. The two individuals are expected to abide by shared expectations and shared norms that did not exist prior to the relationship. For example, individuals who marry are expected to be a good occupant of the role "married person" and to commit to all the norms and expectations the role entails. A similar notion is at work at Stage 3. The separate perspectives (of Stage 2) are now coordinated into a third-party perspective that stresses relational values and shared moral norms. Hence, being a good role occupant (loving wife, dutiful son, loyal friend); being altruistic, faithful, prosocial; being "good"; having praise-worthy motives or the appropriate relationship-supporting sentiments and disposi-tions—these are all seen as the foundation of shared moral norms. This is also the stage when a mature understanding of the Golden Rule emerges. At Stage 2 the Golden Rule is understood in terms of pragmatic reciprocity: Do unto others *so that* they will do unto you; or Do unto others *what* they have done unto you. At Stage 3, reciprocity is stated in more ideal terms: Do unto others *as if* the others *were the self*. One limitation of this kind of reasoning is the lack of awareness that even good role occupants sometimes come into conflict. How to adjudicate con-flicts even among individuals who are good role occupants, how to prioritize their claims, and how to relate to the broader society are intractable issues from the per-spective of Stage 3.

Stage 4: Social System Morality

At Stage 3 the moral reasoner takes the perspective of "us" members of society, where society is the collection of friends who are in close relationship. At Stage 4 the notion of society is expanded to include the impersonal collectivity of citizens who share general social institutions. What regulates conduct is not shared rela-tional expectations (as at Stage 3) but rather a consistent set of legal codes that is applied impartially. Sometimes it is unfair to distribute honors, goods, or favors to our friends or to give those with whom we have some special relationship greater moral consideration. Justice that was applied in a partial way such that our friends (or good role occupants) were excused or rewarded but others were held account-able or punished would make a mockery of the claim that we are all equal before the law. Impartiality, then, is a way of ensuring the equal consideration of justice claims. The norms that were so important at Stage 3 now serve the cause of main-taining impartiality and consistency, of maintaining the law or the integrity of social institutions (vs. the relationships themselves). That is, the sentiments of duty, loyalty, and obligation attach not only to persons within the society of close rela-tionships (Stage 3) but to the larger society as well. We have our interpersonal debts, to be sure, but we also owe a debt to society for the benefits we enjoy by virtue of our relationship to the formal institutions of society. Conflicts that are problematic within the confines of interpersonal community are referred to the system of laws and institutionalized practices for resolution. The needs, interests, and values of the social system and the desire to support societal institutions are important moral considerations at Stage 4.

Stage 5: Human Rights and Social Welfare Morality

At this first principled stage the ethical perspective of the ideal rational moral agent comes into clearer focus. The rational moral agent, from a prior-to-society perspec-tive, identifies liberty and human dignity as universalizable values that anyone would want to build into an ideally just society. We do not, of course, live in ideally just soci-eties. Systems of law and government are often insensitive to fundamental rights and values. Consequently, it is now possible, from this moral vantage point, to criticize existing legal frameworks and existing institutional practices for their failure to protect or extend fundamental human rights. Whereas Stage 4 can be described as a society-maintaining perspective, Stage 5 takes on a society-creating perspective. At Stage 4 one could justly consider a claim by asking, Is it legal? But at Stage 5 one can now challenge the law by asking, Is it moral?. By posing this question in this way the Stage 5 moral agent is staking out the position that some rights and values are so fundamental that no legally constituted authority can abridge them.

The ideal society is conceived along the lines of the social contract: Society is a system into which autonomous individuals freely enter in order to promote fundamental values and general human welfare. Exactly how to maximize individual rights and social welfare is established procedurally, that is, through procedures of agreement engaged in by free individuals. The distinguishing feature of this stage (and Stage 6) is the fact that reasoners are expected to articulate the difficult notions of social contract and natural rights in a quasi-philosophic moral *theory*. Principled thinking is self-reflexive philosophic discourse in the sense that principles are self-consciously articulated and appealed to in order to ground moral reflection. In addition, the principled reasoner is concerned with formalized procedures for checking the validity of one's deliberations. This is more perfectly accomplished at Stage 6.

Stage 6: Morality of Universalizable, Reversible, and Prescriptive General Ethical Principles

The structuring principle at Stage 6 is the moral point of view. What is the moral point of view? It is the view that integrates the various justice operations into a self-reflective mode of justice reasoning. The operations themselves become principles that guide reflection and elements that govern the stance that one should take toward all others. There is, first, a commitment to equality; namely, all persons affected by a moral decision must be heard. Their claims must be equally and honestly considered. Prescriptive role-taking is used as a deliberate procedural justice check on the validity of decision-making. One such agreement procedure is formalized as moral musical chairs, where all parties to a decision systematically and mutually attempt to reverse their perspectives in order to see if a candidate judgment is still considered fair from the perspective of the others. Heinz must determine if his desire to steal the drug is fair from the perspective of the druggist; the druggist must determine if his desire to secure his property rights is reasonable from the perspective of Heinz. (Kohlberg has determined that whereas Heinz can reverse his judgment, the druggist cannot. Consequently, stealing the drug is an ethically permitted option for Heinz, since the value of human life takes precedence over commercial rights).

Kohlberg has also formalized Stage 6 prescriptive role-taking in terms of John Rawls's (1971) notion of the original position. The technique works this way: When confronted with moral options one must imaginatively place oneself (and other claimants) in a hypothetical situation that exists prior to society. That is, one must assume the original position of one who exists just prior to entering human society. Imagine now a dialogue among other claimants who have also assumed this position. The purpose of the dialogue is to choose the principles that will inform the just society into which the claimants will enter. The dialogue is constrained by two conditions. (1) One must don the veil of ignorance. That is, one must be divested of all knowledge of who one will be. One must be blind to one's self-interest and therefore blind to one's identity and the sort of markers (gender, race, religious commitments, education, social class, etc.) that convey identity. (2) One must assert the self's prerogatives even though one is ignorant of the particularities of who the self will be. These conditions ensure impartiality while at the same time forcing claimants to consider the possibility that, since they do not know who they will be when they enter society, they must design a society that is so just that whoever they turn out to be (rich, disabled, visible minority), they will find arrangements to be fair and equitable. Engaging in moral musical chairs and conducting a thought experiment from the original position after donning the veil of ignorance, then, are ways of formalizing the ideal prescriptive role-taking characteristics of Stage 6.

The moral point of view also endorses the intrinsic worth, value, and dignity of all human persons. This view is summarized by the Kantian injunction to respect persons: Treat others as ends in themselves and not as means to an end. Indeed, whereas Stage 5 attempts to secure trust, dignity, and community by free agreement and social contract, there is an appreciation at Stage 6 that social contracts presuppose trust, dignity, and community. That is, trust and community are not derived from agreements but are rather inviolable aspects of personhood that precede, precondition, and make possible whatever social contracts are consented to.

The moral point of view also embraces the criterion of universalizability (Let the maxim of thy conduct be the universal will). Hence, not only should Heinz steal the drug but everyone else in Heinz's predicament should steal the drug too. And presumably, Heinz is enjoined to steal the drug not only for his wife but for anyone else in her position as well. Finally, the moral point of view operates from articulated general principles, which may include the principle of justice (respect persons), the principle of utility (greatest good for the greatest number), and the attitude of universal caring (*agape*).

The Return of Stage 6

In her recent book Iris Murdoch (1992) notes that justice and compassion are the two cardinal virtues upon which all the other virtues depended (p. 63). "The quality of attachments," she writes, "is the quality of our understanding. Being dutiful involves being just, justice must make a pact with mercy" (p. 295). In her view, the sense of moral duty cannot be dispensed with, yet it is not the whole of morality. Justice must not be eclipsed, but compassion is also part of the moral fabric of our lives. Will and duty must be joined to "Eros"—"justice must make a pact with mercy" (Murdoch, 1992). It would appear that some such pact was attempted in a recent reformulation of Stage 6.

It was noted earlier that Stage 6 is not currently an empirical possibility, and this entails difficulties for giving coherence to the stage sequence. Kohlberg was keenly aware of this problem. In his last theoretical paper he noted that the sequence requires a clearly articulated end point in order to (1) identify the data that are to be counted as an instance of the moral domain and (2) provide a normative criterion of adequacy (Kohlberg et al., 1990). This paper heralds the return of Stage 6 and provides Kohlberg's last statement on its characteristics.

In this last testament the moral point of view of Stage 6 is described as being fundamentally "respect for persons." But respect for persons is not simply a matter of justice with its attendant notions of rights, reciprocal duties, and equality. It is also a matter of benevolence with its attendant notions of sympathizing, making empathic connections, and identifying with others; promoting good and limiting harm; and the like. Justice and benevolence are both necessary in human relationships, and therefore, the two attitudes must be coordinated in any moral deliberation.

According to Kohlberg and others (1990) benevolence is logically prior to justice. It provides a lens that focuses on the intention to promote good. It is an expression of one's psychological attachment and empathic connection to others. Justice, however, provides a different focus. Whereas benevolence is motivated by the desire to promote good and limit harm, justice is oriented toward the adjudication of competing claims in the interest of fairness. Empathy (benevolence) and justice are both ways of respecting persons, but they require different operations in order to achieve their ends. Whereas benevolence is oriented toward empathic connections with others, justice requires the momentary separation of individual wills so that claims can be impartially and equally considered through the operations of ideal role-taking. Benevolence constrains justice through its focus on promoting the general good. Justice constrains benevolence by insisting that benevolent solutions respect individual rights.

Put this way, benevolence and justice appear to be in tension. But Kohlberg and others (1990) argue that they are mutually supportive attitudes that are coordinated by the deep structure of the moral point of view. They write: "The aim of the autonomous Stage 6 moral agent is to seek resolution of moral problems in such a way that promoting good for some does not fail to respect the rights of others, and respecting the rights of individuals does not fail to seek promotion of the best for all" (p. 158). In this formulation, then, justice is not the first principle of morality but is rather an attitude that coexists alongside the allied attitude of benevolence; both are examples of respect for persons, which now assumes the dignity of being the single principle of principled morality.

Kohlberg and others (1990) further note that respect for persons (justice, benevolence) is present in the earlier stages but that it takes a principled form only at Stage 6. As such, it is a perspective that guides deliberations when moral norms come into conflict. Stage 6 continues its concern with fair procedures. It is also marked by a disposition to enter into agreement-seeking dialogue. The original-position methodology and moral musical chairs are affirmed as useful thought experiments that operationalize the ideal prescriptive role-taking that is characteristic of consensus-seeking at Stage 6. Ideal reciprocal role-taking is formalized as a three-step process: (1) One must take the perspective of others in order to truly understand their claims and interests. (2) One must assume that others are making the same attempt. (3) One must temporarily separate the actual identities of persons from their claims in order to appraise the claims impartially on the basis of their merits, that is, on the basis of the claims themselves, and not on who presses the claim. The procedural justice checks bound up with universalizability are also retained as an element of Stage 6 deliberations.

What is strikingly novel about this account of Stage 6 is the addition of "sympathy" operations to the consensus-seeking procedures characteristic of this stage. Sympathy is described as the cognitive organization of the attitude of benevolence with its emphasis on empathy, connection, and identification with others. Sympathy is the active interpretation of empathic connections, and it works through two kinds of understandings: (1) understanding persons and (2) understanding general facts of the human condition. To understand persons is to understand that individuals are self-determining agents who quite rightly pursue their own interests, and these interests derive from a life plan or from significant projects to which one makes a commitment. To understand general facts of the human condition is to understand that life projects are contingent on a host of things such as psychological, social, historical, and cultural factors.

Hence, when actual consensus is unavailing, the Stage 6 reasoner attempts to claim an ideal consensus through imaginative, agreement-seeking thought experiments. And one enters these thought experiments with a full grasp of the person in all of her complexity (sympathy) while at the same time coordinating this understanding with the requirements of impartiality and universalizability (justice). Kohlberg and others (1990) claim that this conception of Stage 6 more clearly anchors this last stage on the internal developmental logic of the prior stages, the sequence of which unfolds with ever increasing complexity of prescriptive role-taking. Their claim contrasts with the view of John Gibbs (1979), who argues that revisions to the moral-stage theory stranded the principled stages in a philosophical realm with the consequence that they could no longer be considered natural stages in the Piagetian sense. Time will tell, of course, if this theoretical return of Stage 6 will also occasion its return to the scoring manual, and possible empirical demonstration.

The Empirical Status of the Stage Theory

Kohlberg was devoted to the task of delineating hard stages of justice reasoning. Hence, in empirically validating the stage theory, he sought evidence of structural development characterized by invariant sequence, hierarchical integration, and structured wholeness. Since 1958 there have been many hundreds of studies of Kohlberg's stage theory. However, relatively fewer studies have used the newer Standard Issue Scoring rules. The first major study using Kohlberg's longitudinal sample was reported in an important monograph by Colby and others (1983). As one commentator put it, the results were "spectacular" (Rest, 1983).

The authors pursued the structured-whole assumption by looking for evidence that subjects tend to reason at a single modal stage, that stage scores are reliable and show strong internal consistency, and that moral judgment would cut across the various contents that are reflected in the dilemmas and issues. What did the results show? Estimates of internal consistency were quite strong, easily in the .90s range. Other forms of reliability (test-retest, alternate form, interrater) were also in the same range and were similarly impressive. Subjects indeed tended to use a single modal stage in their reasoning. About two-thirds of all scores were assigned at the subject's modal stage, with a lesser number scored as stages adjacent to the mode. Only 9 percent of the interviews showed evidence of a third stage. When correlations among stage scores (across dilemmas and issues) were examined in a series of factor analyses, only one interpretable factor emerged, suggesting that moral judgment is a single general domain. Hence the strong internal consistency, the high degree of alternate form and test-retest reliability, the emergence of just a single factor of moral judgment that cuts across issues and dilemmas, and the tendency of subjects to use a single modal stage; all of these findings were interpreted as evidence in favor of the structured-whole assumption.

What about the sequential properties of the stage sequence? The evidence here is unambiguous. Developmental analyses showed that 56–58 subjects showed upward stage movement. There was no evidence of stage skipping. No subject reached a particular stage without having gone through the previous stage. There was no evidence of stage regression that could not reasonably be attributed to measurement error. There was, of course, no evidence for Stage 6, and Stage 5 was only slightly in evidence. This means that stage development (over a 30-year period) is largely limited to Level 1 and Level 2. But the developmental trends are clear. As the authors put it, "Perhaps most noteworthy is the orderliness and regularity of the developmental curves, with earlier stages dropping out as later stages enter such that the subject seems to be always in transition from one stage to the next" (Colby et al., 1983, p. 49).

There were other findings of interest. Although moral judgment was not related to general intelligence (IQ), it was related to educational experiences and to social class. Subjects did not appear to consolidate Stage 4 without attending college, and none attained Stage 4/5 without completing college. Further, middle-class subjects had better access to Stage 4 and Stage 4–5 than did working-class subjects (although these stages were accessible to college-educated subjects who had working-class origins). These latter findings are not incongruent with Kohlberg's theory. He has argued that social experiences that promote role-taking, responsibility, and participation in the secondary institutions of society provide socioenvironmental conditions for moral stage growth. Colby and others (1983) concluded that this evidence strongly supports a Piagetian stage model for capturing the nature of moral development

Lawrence Walker (1982, 1983, 1989; Walker, de Vries, & Bichard, 1984; Walker & Taylor, 1991) has also provided strong evidence in favor of the moral-stage theory. In one study evidence was provided on the hierarchical nature of moral stages (Walker et al., 1984). Hierarchicality is typically shown by examining the pattern of preferences subjects show toward moral reasoning above and below their current stage. If they understand but reject lower-stage reasoning, prefer and use current-stage reasoning, and/or prefer but do not use higher-stage reasoning (indicating either preference but not understanding or understanding but not production), then one is entitled to greater confidence in the hierarchical integration assumption of the stage theory. Using Guttman scaling techniques, Walker and others (1984) showed that moral understanding is cumulative. Subjects understand lower-stage reasoning and reasoning at their current stage, but understanding tends to decline thereafter. Indeed, understanding is limited to one stage (+1) above the current stage. The fact that subjects understand but do not use +1 reasoning suggests that understanding precedes production. Additional evidence in favor of the hierarchical nature of moral reasoning is provided by James Rest and his colleagues (Rest, 1973; Rest, Turiel, & Kohlberg, 1969).

In a longitudinal study Walker (1989) reported strong evidence in favor of the sequentiality claims of the stage theory. Only 6 percent of the sample showed minor stage regressions, and there was no stage skipping over the two-year longitudinal interval. In a more recent study Walker and Taylor (1991b) report that subjects tend to reason at a single modal stage, with lesser amounts at immediately adjacent stages. Hence, subjects are either in a stage or in transition. They also report that stage transition is predicted by a particular pattern of reasoning characterized by a greater percentage of reasoning above the modal stage than below it. Stage transition and sequentiality can also be investigated experimentally. This is done by attempting to induce cognitive conflict, which is presumed to be a disequilibrating factor that motivates development to the next stage. How does one induce cognitive conflict? The typical research strategy is to use the +1 convention, that is, to pitch moral arguments one stage above the subject's current stage.

In one study Walker (1982) found that +1 and +2 stage reasoning induced movement toward the next stage. Although +2 reasoning was effective in motivating stage movement, it was apparently understood (assimilated) in +1 terms. There was no evidence for stage skipping or stage regression at posttest, indicating support for the invariant sequence assumption.

In another study Walker (1983) attempted to specify with more precision the kinds of conflict most conducive to stage transition. He exposed children to the moral reasoning of adults that varied in the following important ways:

1. Adults conflicted with each other at a stage +1 the child's current stage (pro/con +1).
2. Adults agreed with each other (at +1) but disagreed with the child's position (con +1).
3. Adults agreed with each other (at +1) and also with the child's position (pro +1).
4. Adults conflicted with each other at the child's current stage (pro/con 0).
5. Adults agreed with each other at the child's current stage (pro 0)—a control condition.
6. No treatment control was used.

Cognitive developmental theory would generally predict that conditions 1, 2, and 3 would stimulate stage development, since these conditions all involve some measure of cognitive conflict. There is conflict in the *stage* of reasoning (+1) in all three conditions, with an additional source of conflict coming from whether *opinions* are consonant. What did Walker (1983) find? The results showed that conditions 5 and 6 did not induce development. This was expected in light of the fact that no conflict was present in these two conditions. The greatest development was induced by conditions 1 and 2. Indeed, optimal development is stimulated by a combination of conflicting opinions pitched at higher-stage reasoning. Moderate development was induced by condition 3. This suggests that simple exposure to +stage reasoning is sufficient to stimulate development and that conflicting opinions are not necessary. Condition 4 also showed moderate stage growth, indicating that exposure to +stage reasoning may not even be necessary. Rather, simply hearing the pros and cons of one's own stage of reasoning may make one aware of the inadequacies of one's position and thereby motivate movement to the next stage. This may be particularly true of subjects who already possess the logical and social-cognitive prerequisites for stage growth.

In his studies, then, Walker provided strong evidence for the sequential and hierarchical properties of Kohlberg's stage theory, and he clarified the role of cognitive conflict in motivating stage transition. Kohlberg's theory also predicts that the moral-stage sequence will be found in other cultures. It assumes, for example, that the great variability that is evident in cultural beliefs, customs, and practices are merely content differences that are nonetheless organized by the sort of deep structures that his theory describes. The claim that moral development tends toward the same understanding of moral adequacy in all cultures and societies is certainly a controversial feature of Kohlberg's theory. And it has drawn significant fire (Buck-Morss, 1975; Simpson, 1974; Sullivan, 1977; Shweder, 1982). But Kohlberg's claim could not be more clear. He writes: "All individuals in all cultures use the same thirty basic moral categories, concepts or principles, and all individuals in all cultures go through the same order or sequence of gross stage development, though they vary in rate and terminal point of development" (Kohlberg, 1971, p. 175). Is this claim well founded?

One longitudinal study (Nisan & Kohlberg, 1982) examined samples of males from three locations in Turkey: Ankara, the national capital; a provincial capital; and a small traditional village. Four interview sessions were conducted between 1964 and 1976 on dilemmas that were adapted to reflect the Turkish setting. The results were straightforward. There was substantial evidence of sequential development in stage scores. Indeed, out of 35 changes in stage, only 4 showed a longitudinal reversal. There was no evidence of stage skipping. The authors also reported variations in rate and terminus of development between village and urban subjects. In general, the rate of development was slower in the village than in the city. The preconventional stages (in pure form) were largely absent in urban subjects under age 15 and in village subjects under age 18. Further, village subjects tended to stabilize at Stage 3, a finding also reported by Carolyn Edwards (1975) in her Kenyan study.

The authors suggested that perhaps Stage 3, with it relational perspective, is functionally adaptive in traditional societies that place a premium on communal consensus and face-to-face interactions.

A second study (Snarey, Reimer, & Kohlberg, 1984) examined longitudinal development in a sample of kibbutz-born Israeli adolescents. The results here are strikingly similar to the findings of Colby and others (1983). For example, strong psychometric properties were reported for the moral-judgment interview. Interrater agreement in stage assignments fell on the same stage or within one-half of a stage about 93 percent of the time across three scorers. Internal consistency was similarly impressive, with 83 percent of all reasoning classified at the same major stage or at immediately adjacent stages (indicating transition). Internal consistency, the extent to which subjects are stage-consistent in their moral judgments, is thought to speak to the issue of structured wholeness. There was no stage skipping in evidence, and only 6 percent of observed longitudinal stage changes were contrary to invariant sequence predictions.

Numerous other studies have been reported over the years. In an important paper John Snarey (1985) examined 45 studies (including the two just noted) that were conducted across 27 countries. He drew the following conclusions:

1. The moral-judgment interview is "reasonably culture fair," especially when dilemmas reflect the local culture and subjects are interviewed in their native language.
2. Stage skipping and stage regression are rare, suggesting that the invariant sequence claim is "well supported."
3. Stage 1 to Stage 3/4 or Stage 4 is in evidence "virtually universally."
4. Stage 4/5 and Stage 5 were "extremely rare" in all samples.
5. However, some cultural groups and social classes did show trace amounts of principled reasoning. "Folk groups" in traditional societies do not, but some urban middle-class subjects do show some evidence of postconventional reasoning.

Although Snarey worried about the relative absence of postconventional reasoning in many of the cross-cultural samples and although he did suggest that the stage model (and scoring manual) should accommodate a "wider range of cultural world views" in addition to its current grounding in Western philosophic notions (of Rawls, Kant, Hare), he nonetheless concluded that these 45 studies provided "striking support for the underlying assumptions" (p. 202) of Kohlberg's stage theory and its universality claims (see also Walker & Moran, 1991).

It would appear, then, that Kohlberg's stage developmental theory of moral judgment, and his assessment of moral structures, enjoy considerable empirical support. Indeed, as Rest (1986b, pp. 464, 466) puts it, "The findings are without parallel in all of social cognitive development. For no other measurement procedure in the field have such strong confirmatory trends been reported. . . . If one is not favorably impressed with these findings, it is difficult to know what would be impressive in all of the social development literature." There are, to be sure, important reservations about the theory as well. This is to be expected with a research program as provocative as his. Before we consider at least some of these criticisms, we need to focus on three final aspects of Kohlberg's theory: moral action, moral education, and the possibility of a "soft" seventh stage.

Moral Action

As we have seen, Kohlberg's stage theory describes developmental transformations in the understanding of justice. Moral-reasoning structures are progressively elaborated until the principled moral point of view comes into clear focus, and these progressive elaborations of moral structures can be demarcated into a hierarchically organized series of six stages. One must now ask just what the relationship is between the stages of moral reasoning and moral behavior. There is a well-founded, commonsense notion that moral functioning should ideally be united in thought and deed. But it is also true that knowing the right thing to do and actually doing it are often very different matters. No one is terribly impressed by a moral reasoner who talks a good game but fails to put his moral sophistication into practice. Insofar as Kohlberg's theory is a developmental account of how different forms of moral knowledge are constructed from social experience, one would expect the theory to have some implication for how we are to understand the relation between moral thought and action. Can the stage theory help us understand whatever consistency there is to be found between moral reasoning and moral conduct?

I noted earlier that Kohlberg (among many others) defined distinctly moral action as any action that is motivated by a moral judgment. An action, no matter how beneficial, no matter how salutory its consequences, is nonetheless morally neutral unless it is done for moral reasons, that is, unless it is performed in light of moral principles or values that the agent constructs or accepts as binding. Yet Kohlberg's embrace of the form-content distinction is a seeming obstacle to any straightforward relationship between thought and action. Our moral choices (content) seem only loosely related to forms (stages) of moral knowledge.

One famous example is the study by Haan, Smith, and Block (1968) of Berkeley students who participated in the free-speech demonstrations of the early 1960s. The student demonstrators were clustered at both the principled and preconventional levels. Indeed, the general structural perspective that defines each stage seems to leave ample room for very different moral options. As Blasi (1980) pointed out, the same moral perspective (stage) can lead to different moral options, and the same moral option can be justified by any of the stages. The fact that the structure of moral reasoning is compatible with a variety of contrasting decisions and actions is well attested by a table that invariably appears in most textbook accounts of Kohlberg's theory. The table typically presents the Heinz dilemma and then lists, stage by stage, the sort of reasons that one could invoke for why Heinz should, and should not steal the drug. Here it is seen that the same structure of reasoning (e.g., Stage 3) can justify both options.

Yet Kohlberg (1987; Kohlberg et al., 1983) has more recently argued that moral stages serve as a lens or screen through which an individual appraises social situations. As one moves higher up the stage hierarchy, one's appraisal of dilemmas and social situations is conditioned by a keener appreciation of the fact that moral judgments are prescriptive—they imply an obligation (I ought to do X) to fulfill the command imposed by the moral imperative. Hence, one should expect judgment and action to more closely interpenetrate with advances in moral reasoning. One begins to see more clearly, as one moves up the stages, that *reasons are motives* for action.

Consequently, one might expect higher-stage reasoning to be incompatible with certain kinds of conduct. There is, indeed, some evidence for this view. One study showed, for example, that cheating was less likely with more advanced moral reasoning (Malinowski & Smith, 1985). Furthermore, Augusto Blasi (1980) concluded on the basis of his review of the moral judgment-action literature that there is "considerable support" for the idea that judgment and action are related, however modestly. He found, for example, that moral reasoning distinguishes delinquents from nondelinquents (but see Jurkovic, 1980, for a contrary assessment). In addition, higher-stage reasoners tended to be more altruistic, prosocial, and honest and better able to resist conforming to another's view than lower-stage reasoners. In another study McNamee (1978) found that a large majority of Stage 3 and Stage 4 subjects agreed that it was proper to come to the aid of a victim. Here, subjects agreed on the deontic choice (aid the victim) irrespective of stage. However, Stage 4 subjects were more likely to actually help the victim than were Stage 3 subjects, and Stage 5 subjects more likely than Stage 4 subjects. Once again this suggests that the tendency to perform the action suggested by deontic choice is progressively more likely as one moves up the stage hierarchy.

But what is it about higher-stage reasoning that conveys this consistency between thought and action? One clue was provided by Daniel Candee, whose 1976 study linked moral structure and moral choice on Kohlbergian dilemmas. Kohlberg's dilemmas were originally constructed to contrast two broad (Piagetian) moral orientations: a heteronomous respect for authority and rules and an autonomous (Kantian) concern for human rights and social welfare. Candee found that higher-stage subjects tended to choose alternatives consistent with the autonomous orientation. The heteronomous orientation, you will recall, was instantiated as the A substage, and the autonomous orientation was denoted the B substage. Type B reasoning reflects an intuitive grasp of those formal elements of principled reasoning (prescriptivity, universality) that Stage 5 subjects articulate in an explicit way. In other words, at substage B, conventional subjects make judgments of rights and responsibility in a way similar to the judgments made at the principled level. But at Stage 5, the embrace of prescriptivity and universality is self-conscious and explicit, and the Type B reasoning of lower stages embraces these principles in a tacit, intuitive way.

Two hypotheses follow. (1) As research has indicated, there is a monotonic relationship between thought and action; that is, the higher the stage, the more likely one will perform an action consistent with deontic choice. (2) This consistency results from the fact that higher-stage individuals are more likely to judge that the self is responsible for putting the deontic judgment into action. But why? Why should higher-stage reasoners better appreciate the self's responsibility for acting upon a judgment? Because at higher stages subjects realize that moral judgments leave them no other choice. At higher stages subjects realize that moral principles are prescriptive and that corresponding moral judgments are obligatory and binding. Hence, Stage 5 subjects should not only agree on the action to be taken (i.e., make the autonomous choice), but they should also be expected to follow through with whatever action this choice obligates them to take. Once again, moral obligation and moral responsibility flow from the fact than one has made a moral judgment based on principles that are prescriptive. And this is true not just at Stage 5 but often at the B substage of lower stages, where the prescriptive and universal character of moral judgments is grasped in a tacit way through intuition.

This latter point suggests that the consistency between thought and action is not simply a matter of stage sophistication; if it were, only Stage 5 subjects would show the desired consistency. Given the relative rarity of Stage 5 even in "advanced" societies, this conclusion would be very depressing indeed. Fortunately, such consistency can also come about through an intuition of prescriptivity that is evident at the B substages. "Accordingly, if we are going to look for a relationship between moral thought and moral action, we should look to those persons who judge that it is right to perform the more moral behavior, either by virtue of their Stage 5 reasoning, or by virtue of their B substage intuitions" (Kohlberg et al., 1983, p. 51).

The available evidence would appear to support the claims for Type B reasoning. For example, although most conventional reasoners (Stages 3, 3/4, 4) were of the judgment that one should not administer electric shock to a "learner" in the Milgram experiment, only those at the B substage acted consistently with this judgment, presumably because they also made the *responsibility judgment* that it was the self, not the experimenter, who was ultimately responsible for the learner's welfare (Candee & Kohlberg, 1983). There also appears to be age-developmental shifts from substage A to B. That is, persons who move from A to B remain at B even when they change stages (Colby et al., 1983). Type B appears earlier in democratic cultures than in authoritarian cultures, among popular children (vs. isolates), and among students who attend democratic alternative high schools (Kohlberg, 1987). Gibbs, Clark, Joseph, Goodrick, and Makowski (1986) also report that Type B reasoning is related not only to situational moral courage but also to the tendency to appraise complex social situations in terms of moral significance, attesting to the lens or screen function of moral stages.

As we have seen, Kohlberg argued that thought-action consistency comes about when subjects make a responsibility judgment, that is, when they perceive the self as responsible for acting upon a deontic judgment. And responsibility judgments are more likely to be made by Stage 5 and Type B reasoners, who more keenly appreciate the prescriptive, obligatory nature of moral principles. In Kohlberg's model, then, self-responsibility is derived from the clear (Stage 5) or intuitive (Type B) grasp of prescriptivity. This formulation of the responsible self was largely informed (with an important caveat) by Augusto Blasi's (1983a) Self Model of moral action. The Self Model entails seven formal propositions, which are described in Table 4.2.

According to Blasi (1983a), moral structures are only indirectly related to moral action. They serve to appraise the moral landscape but do not directly generate action. This is due to the fact that just because an agent appraises the social situation through the lens of sophisticated moral criteria does not guarantee that she will also see the personal relevance of the situation, or even its relevance for morality. Consequently, the place to begin looking for consistency in thought-action is not the sophistication of moral structures (contra Kohlberg). Rather, the relationship between thought and action hinges on the concrete decision to act or not act. Consistency flows not from structure but from choices.

Indeed, as we have seen, general moral perspectives and particular action choices are rather independent of one another. Action does not directly follow from judgment. Instead, when one makes a moral judgment one must next filter this judgment through a second set of parameters that speaks to the issue of whether the self is responsible (in contrast to Kohlberg's view, which suggests that self-responsibility directly follows from a prescriptive moral judgment). Is that which is morally good also strictly necessary for the self? Is acting in this way so necessary for my understanding of who I am that not to act is to lose the self? Are moral notions so central to my identity, so foundational for my self-understanding, that failing to act or indulging in excusing rationalizations is to undermine what is so core to my personhood? Blasi suggests that the cognitive motivation for moral action springs from this sense of fidelity to oneself in action. It springs from a

TABLE 4.2   Blasi's Self Model of Moral Action: Seven Propositions

Proposition 1	Moral actions are responses to situations that are defined by and interpreted according to moral-reasoning structures.
Proposition 2	Moral action directly depends on the moral choice and only indirectly on the structure of moral reasoning.
Proposition 3	Moral judgments are processed through a second set of rules regarding responsibility. The function of responsibility judgments is to determine the extent to which the morally good action is also strictly necessary for the self.
Proposition 4	The criteria used to arrive at responsibility judgments vary from person to person and are related to one's self-definition.
Proposition 5	The transition from judgment of responsibility to action is supported by the tendency toward self-consistency, which is a cognitive motive for objectivity and truth.
Proposition 6	Consistency between moral judgment and moral action will be higher if an agent has attitudes or strategies for dealing with interferences from conflicting needs and motives.
Proposition 7	To act inconsistently with one's judgment of responsibility is to induce guilt. Guilt is an emotional response to inconsistency within the self.

Source: Adapted from Blasi (1983a).

moral identity that is deeply rooted in moral commitments—commitments so deeply rooted, in fact, that to betray these commitments is also to betray the self. Blasi further suggests that moral identity may be a dimension of individual differences. That is, being moral may or may not be part of one's essential self. Or, different people may have defined their core, essential selves according to different moral characteristics.

Kohlberg's model is similar to Blasi's in that both appeal to responsibility judgments of the self as what motivates moral action. But there is an important difference. For Kohlberg, moral motivation to act comes from one's fidelity to the prescriptive nature of moral principles. Responsibility is entailed by the formal, categorical character of a moral structure and flows directly from it. Hence not to act is to betray a principle. For Blasi, in contrast, moral motivation to act is a consequence of one's moral identity, and not to act is to betray the self. Perhaps Kohlberg was unwilling to implicate the self more directly in this sort of moral deliberation lest he open the door to aretaic evaluations of personal selves. As I noted earlier, for Kohlberg, only principles and actions are open to moral appraisal (judgments of adequacy) as a consequence of his stage theory. We will have occasion to revisit Blasi's work on the moral personality in Chapter 12.

Moral Education

In the late 1960s Kohlberg's attention was increasingly drawn to educational matters. His renewed interest in education was sparked by the findings of one his graduate students, Moshe Blatt. In an early study Elliot Turiel (1966) found that stage change could be experimentally induced by presenting subjects with moral arguments that conflicted with their current stage of moral reasoning. As we have seen, experimental induction of stage change was a way of testing the sequentiality assumptions of the stage theory. But Blatt pressed this finding into the service of an educational intervention with sixth-grade students in a Jewish Sunday school. For 12 weeks he met with these students to discuss a series of hypothetical moral dilemmas. He assumed that a variety of stage responses would emerge during the course of these discussions and that children would suggest a variety of stage-dependent moral solutions. His task was to recast these solutions at the stage one above (+1) the student's current stage usage. After 12 weeks Blatt found that 64 percent of the students gained one full stage in their moral reasoning.

The "Blatt effect" showed that moral discussion groups could be an effective classroom intervention (Blatt & Kohlberg, 1975). Scores of interventions have since been attempted (for reviews, Lockwood, 1978; Enright, Lapsley, Harris, & Shauver, 1983; Enright, Lapsley, & Levy, 1983; Lapsley, Enright, & Serlin, 1989; Schlafli, Rest, & Thoma, 1985). The general finding is that group discussion of moral dilemmas works, although effectiveness is often more modest than was initially reported by Blatt. What is not so clear is why or how it works (Berkowitz, 1981; Lapsley et al., 1989).

It was presumed that the plus-one convention works because it introduces disequilibrating elements into a child's moral reasoning, that is, it induces cognitive conflict, which is then thought to motivate the child to adopt the moral stance represented by the better-equilibrated, next-higher stage. Yet it is not always clear just what cognitive conflict amounts to. For example, Norma Haan (1985) argued that moral reasoning results not from (private, internal) cognitive disequilibrium but from social disequilibrium, that is, from the attempt to equalize mutual social relationships and interactions. She found that playing moral games was more effective in stimulating moral reasoning than was discussion of moral dilemmas and that when cognitive disequilibrium was pronounced, it had little effect on moral reasoning (Haan, 1985). Similarly, Damon and Killen (1982; Killen, 1991) found that conflict tended to retard, not promote, stage growth in justice reasoning. In this study stage change was associated with a style of peer interaction that was "characterized by a reciprocal quality of acceptance of transformation of one another's ideas" (p. 365).

This would appear to direct our attention to communicative-dialogic styles within peer interactions, a line of research taken up by Marvin Berkowitz and his colleagues (Berkowitz, Gibbs, & Broughton, 1980; Berkowitz & Gibbs, 1983; also Kruger, 1992). They found that optimal stage disparity within moral-discussion groups can be as little as one-third of a stage, which is easily represented within a sufficiently heterogenous classroom (Berkowitz et al., 1980). But they reported as well that *transactive discussion* is also a powerful predictor of moral stage change (Berkowitz & Gibbs, 1983).

What is transactive discussion? It is a mode of dialogue that *operates* on the reasoning of another (e.g., clarification, comparative critique, contradiction, competitive extension) rather than simply representing it (e.g., paraphrase, feedback or justification request). They argued that "moral stage development results from discussion in which each member engages in the reasoning of his/her discussion partners with his/her own reasoning. Rather than merely providing consecutive assertions, discussants 'operate' on each other's reasoning. In a very dialectical sense one's own reasoning confronts the other's antithetical reasoning in an ongoing dialogic dynamic" (Berkowitz & Gibbs, 1983, p. 402). This might suggest that the effectiveness of moral-discussion groups may well hinge on students' experience with operational dialogue, on their vocabulary, on their ability to communicate or to lead good discussions more generally (Lapsley et al., 1989; Berkowitz, 1981), as well as on the introduction of plus-stage moral arguments. Along the same lines, Walker and Taylor (1991a) provided evidence that moral education in the family operates similarly. In this study, moral development was more likely when parents adopted a Socratic discussion style in the context of higher-level moral reasoning and otherwise supportive interactions.

The plus-one convention, then, is a prototypic Kohlbergian intervention. Yet Kohlberg was dissatisfied with educational efforts that were simply restricted to the stimulation of individual moral development, particularly if discussions revolved around abstract, hypothetical dilemmas. In his view moral decisions are rarely made in splendid isolation. Rather, they are more typically made in the context of collective norms and group processes that could well inhibit adequate reflection, or else prevent moral action (e.g., Kohlberg, Hickley, & Scharf, 1972; Power, Higgins, & Kohlberg, 1989; Higgins, 1991). Moral education, then, is incomplete unless one addresses the justice of the entire structure and functioning of the school. Teachers, students, and administrators confront problems of rights, duties, and responsibilities on a daily basis. How these issues are handled affects the "moral atmosphere" of the school (Power & Reimer, 1978). Hence if one is going to "teach justice," one must also examine how authority is used, how decisions are made, how conflicts are resolved, and how responsibility is taken or shirked within the context of the school as a whole. Justice must pervade the entire context in which the teaching and the learning of justice is to take place. Consequently, Kohlberg began to see that rational discussion of these sorts of moral issues "should be part of a broader, more enduring involvement of students in the social and moral functioning of the school" (Kohlberg & Turiel, 1971, p. 456). And this means a commitment to *educational democracy*.

Educational democracy implies a cooperative endeavor on the part of students and teachers for constructing a just educational environment. Practically, it means that students and teachers have a formally equal say in how the school is to be structured and operated. Through community meetings students learn the habits of democratic participation, and they develop skills for dealing with issues in a fair, just way. In this way, students come to see how fundamental democratic values are constructed and how these values allow us to live constructively, and in community, in a pluralistic, free society (Power, 1991b).

Educational democracy was instituted in a small number of alternative high schools as a means of examining the effects of moral atmosphere on moral reasoning and conduct. According to Power and others (1989), participatory democracy within a school provides six advantages: (1) It more effectively promotes moral development insofar as community meetings deal with real-life, rather than hypothetical, dilemmas. (2) It encourages students to think for themselves rather than rely on imposed solutions by external authorities (teachers, administrators). (3) Following Dewey, it provides students with an opportunity to learn democrative values by actually practicing them. (4) It increases the probability that better decisions will be made, since the views of teachers, administrators, *and* students will be taken into account. (5) Democratic participation breaches the chasm between peer and adult cultures within the school by creating a sense of communal solidarity and a sense of shared ownership and responsibility for school rules. (6) It promotes discipline and rule-following, since there is social pressure to uphold democratically approved rules.

The moral-atmosphere approach is influenced by Durkheim's (1925/1973) view that individuals develop attachments (to the group) and that collective norms evolve from group activity itself. Thus, one could characterize development within just communities in terms of how advanced are the collective norms of sharing, of trust, of valuing the community, and the like, and these aspects of communitarian development could be described in stage terms that are independent of the moral stage theory. Table 4.3 presents two such sequences.

Research indicates that the just-community intervention dramatically alters the moral culture of the school (Power et al., 1989). Students who attend democratic alternative schools have a high degree of collective prosocial norms and a strong sense of community. They rate their schools higher than do peers at traditional schools. They make more judgments of prosocial responsiblity at higher stages of development. They are more likely to report violators of school rules and to endorse collective restitution. Furthermore, just-community interventions

TABLE 4.3   Stages of Collective Normative Values and the Sense of Valuing the Community

---

Stage 2

Collective normative values

No explicit awareness of collective normative values. But there is a generalized expectation that individuals should recognize individual rights and resolve conflicts through exchange. *Examples:* Do not rat on one another; live and let live; help others when you want to.

Sense of valuing the community

No sense of community apart from individual exchanges among group members. Community is valued insofar as it meets the concrete needs of its members. Community denotes a collection of individuals who do favors for one another or upon whom one relies for protection. *Examples:* The community is like a bank. Members meet to exchange favors, but you cannot take out more than you put in.

Stage 3

Collective normative values

Refers to relationships among group members. Membership in a group implies living up to shared expectations. Conflicts should be resolved by appeal to mutually accepted collective values. *Examples:* Members of a group should be able to trust one another with their possessions. Members of a group should care about other members of a group.

Sense of valuing the community

Refers to a set of relationships and things shared among group members. The group is valued for the friendliness of its members. The value of the group is equated with the value of its collective expectations. *Examples:* The community is a family in which members care for one another. The community is honorable because it helps others.

Stage 4

Collective normative values

Stresses the community as an entity distinct from its individual members. Members are obligated to act out of concern for the welfare and harmony of the group. *Examples:* Individuals share responsibility for the whole group. Individuals should participate in the political life of the group.

Sense of valuing the community

The school is explicitly valued as an entity distinct from the relationships among its members. Group commitments and ideals are valued. The community is perceived as an organic whole composed of interrelated systems that carry on the functioning of the group. *Examples:* Stealing affects the community more than the individual because we are the community. We are not just a group of individuals.

Source: Adapted from Power, Higgins, & Kohlberg (1989).

developmentally advance more lower-stage children than is the case with moral-discussion programs (Power, 1979). Although overall moral-stage growth is typically modest, Power and others (1989) note that there is an upward limit on how much stage growth can be realized by any intervention and that democratic values and communitarian solidarity are indeed valid educational goals in their own right (see also Lickona, 1980, 1991).

Is There a Seventh Stage?

Finally, Kohlberg has speculated about the existence of a "soft" seventh stage that is oriented toward metaethical, metaphysical, or religious frameworks as sources of existential meaning (Power & Kohlberg, 1980; Kohlberg et al., 1983). At Stage 7 one attempts to answer the "limit questions": Why be moral? Why act morally? These questions are directed toward the limits of our understanding (Power & Kohlberg, 1980), and when our pre-reflective confidence that we should be moral is thereby shaken by a demand for ultimate justification of our moral commitments, we are taken beyond the domain of justice into domains that address ultimate concerns such as religion. Stage 6 can tell us what is moral, but it cannot tell us why we should act morally. It cannot tell us why justice makes sense in a corrupted world full of injustice, evil, and suffering. Working out the ultimate justifications for our moral commitments may well entail an appeal to theistic or other appropriately cosmic considerations. Identifying with God or with the vast rhythms of nature or seeing the self as one with being or with the universe—seeing oneself in union with a cause larger than oneself—might be a way of grounding the ultimate significance of one's life. According to Kohlberg and colleagues (1983, p. 41), "Ethical and religious soft stage development culminates in a synthetic, non-dualistic [e.g., self-other, subject-object] sense of participation in and identity with a cosmic order. The self is understood as a component of this order, and its meaning is understood as being contingent upon participation in this order." As such, Stage 7 reasoning presupposes postconventional justice reasoning. From this high perspective, principles of justice are seen as being in harmony with the broader cosmic order rather than as arbitrary human constructions.

A Critical Appraisal of Kohlberg's Stage Theory

Assessment of Kohlberg's theory is made difficult by its very richness and complexity. In some sense, my evaluation of his cognitive developmental approach will unfold over the next few chapters. But the first approach at critical appraisal can be attempted here. Kohlberg's stage theory has attracted many different kinds of criticism over the years. Some have doubted the evidential claims and psychometric properties of an earlier scoring system (Kurtines & Greif, 1974), although these claims have been defended as well (Broughton, 1978; Kuhn, 1976). Standard Issue Scoring has also been faulted (Cortese, 1984), although the strong empirical evidence reviewed here would seem to blunt much of this criticism. Some have concluded that the various theoretical and methodological revisions are ad hoc strategems that indicate a degenerating research program (Phillips & Nicolayev, 1978), although this assessment has been disputed (Lapsley & Serlin, 1984). I have already had occasion to note the vigorous philosophical debates that have swirled around Kohlberg's ethical-universalist claims, although it is uncertain just what role this criticism should play in the evaluation of the psychological theory.

Carol Gilligan (1977, 1982) argued that Kohlberg's emphasis on justice ignores or degrades a uniquely feminine approach to moral issues, an approach that emphasizes benevolence and caring as a legitimate moral orientation. Elliot Turiel (1983a) argued that Kohlberg's theory conflates two independent domains of social knowledge, the moral domain and the domain of social conventional knowledge. Hence, Gilligan wants to expand what is taken to be the moral domain in order to include benevolence and caring; Turiel wants to restrict the moral domain by excluding social convention from its purview. James Rest (1979) attempts to expand moral-judgment research in another direction as well, namely, to include alternative stage models and modes of assessment. These three attempts to expand or restrict moral developmental research will be considered in subsequent chapters. What I will consider more fully here are criticisms of Kohlberg's structured-whole assumption.

Kohlberg's research program was devoted to showing that moral structures are structured wholes that unify reasoning across a range of justice concepts. I have reviewed evidence to suggest that he has succeeded in identifying global moral structures in the hard, Piagetian sense. The Kohlberg group takes evidence of strong internal consistency of stage-responding as an indication that the structured-whole assumption of hard Piagetian stages has been vindicated. Yet these internal-consistency data, and their interpretation, have been challenged (Fischer, 1983; Rest, 1983, 1986).

Rest (1986b) argues, for example, that the evidence for strong internal consistency in Kohlberg's data may be an artifact of Standard Issue Scoring rules that forbids the recording of lower-stage responses in the interview protocols. For example, Standard Issue Scoring attempts to assess competence by using probes that elicit the upper limits of a subject's understanding of a moral issue. The upper-stage inclusion rule bids the interview scorer to ignore lower-stage responses if higher-stage responses are evident elsewhere in the protocol. This is justified by an appeal to the hierarchical integration assumption (i.e., the higher-stage response includes the lower-stage response; hence the latter can be ignored). Yet one effect of this scoring rule is to ignore evidence of stage heterogeneity. Rest suggests that this scoring rule generates strong internal consistency and interrater reliability but otherwise makes a test of the structured-whole assumption unfalsifiable.

Krebs, Denton, Vermeulen, Carpendale, and Bush (1991) note a number of additional ways that stage heterogeneity can be masked by Standard Issue Scoring rules. For example, when the stage assignment of particular judgments is combined to generate stage scores for issues, the major stage is designated as that stage which garners the highest percentage of judgments, regardless of what that percentage turns out to be. Anomolous scores are ignored for purposes of stage assignment of issues unless they constitute at least 25 percent of the case material. When issue scores are combined to generate a global-stage score, issue scores that fail to represent 25 percent of the total are ignored. Finally, although lower-stage scores are retained in the calculation of the continuous index of moral reasoning (moral maturity scores), Krebs, Denton, and others (1991) note the following anomaly: It is possible for a subject to get a score of 300 moral-maturity points (indicating Stage 3) by either (1) making all of one's judgments at Stage 3 or (2) by making half of one's judgments at Stage 2 and half at Stage 4.

It is suggested, then, that Standard Issue Scoring rules exert a homogenizing effect on interview data and that this effect leads to overestimating internal consistency and underestimating stage heterogeneity. Dennis Krebs and his colleagues (Krebs, Denton, et al., 1991; Krebs, Vermuelen, Carpendale, & Denton, 1991; Carpendale & Krebs, 1992) and others (Leming, 1978) have reported substantial stage variation as a function of dilemma type. Indeed, stage variation is sometimes observed on the (same dilemma type) when one is asked to reason from both sides of the issue. In one study, for example, nearly 25 percent of the subjects showed changes in stage of reasoning depending on whether they argued in favor of capital punishment or in opposition. In this study, opposition to capital punishment was associated with higher stages of moral reasoning (de Vries & Walker, 1986).

Hence, many researchers suggest that any strong reading of the structured-whole assumption is not justified. According to this view, subjects have a variety of stage structures available to them, lower structures are not displaced in favor of higher structures, and what structures do get used is a function of the pull exerted by the nature of dilemma issues (Levine, 1979b; Rest, 1979; Krebs, Denton, et al., 1991). But perhaps this just means that Kohlberg's reading of what the structured-whole assumption entailed was an overly strict appropriation of Piaget's *structures d'ensemble* in the first place and that moral structures show the same *décalage* as is evident in the logicomathematical domains. That is, perhaps the flexibility of moral structures and evidence of stage heterogeneity violate the received view only on Piagetian *structures d'ensemble* and are compatible with Piaget's own views on the matter after all.

5

Moral Components and the Defining Issues Test: Enlarging and Constricting the Moral Domain

In the next few chapters I will review the work of James Rest, Carol Gilligan, Elliot Turiel, and their respective colleagues. These scholars were all Kohlberg's friends and collaborators, but they nonetheless developed prominent research programs in reaction to certain features of Kohlberg's stage theory. James Rest developed the Defining Issues Test, which is an objective, standardized method of assessing moral reasoning. He has also argued for a more complex stage model that is at variance with Kohlberg's own view of the matter and has situated justice reasoning within an integrative, four-component model of moral functioning. In his view moral behavior involves (1) interpreting the situation in terms of possible courses of action and their consequences, (2) balancing and integrating competing views and determining which alternative satisfies a moral ideal, (3) deciding which plan to put into action, and (4) implementing the plan of action. Justice reasoning of the Kohlbergian sort is an element of the second component. Rest attempts to enlarge the moral domain by considering alternative stage models that adequately capture the complexity of moral development and by considering additional components that adequately capture the complexity of moral functioning. I examine his important research program in this chapter.

Carol Gilligan attempts to enlarge the moral domain in a different way. She argues that traditional developmental theory overlooks or else misclassifies a line of development that is uniquely feminine. In her view, Kohlberg's concern with justice and its attendant emphasis on rights, duties, and free contractual agreements of autonomous agents, although perhaps compatible with developmental themes that stress the masculine concerns with separation, autonomy, and independence, is nonetheless at variance with an alternative moral voice that emphasizes the relational and socially encumbered values of caring, benevolence, and personal responsibility. Gilligan claims that the relational themes of the ethic of care are more faithful to feminine sensitivities than is Kohlberg's rights orientation and that, for this reason, the moral voice of women has not been heard in Kohlberg's interview data. I will examine Gilligan's views in Chapter 7.

Finally, if Rest and Gilligan attempt to enlarge the moral domain in various ways, Elliot Turiel wishes to restrict it to its proper dimensions. Turiel argues that social knowledge can be delineated into separate categories or domains. The moral domain is concerned with prescriptive and universal moral rules. The domain of conventional knowledge is concerned with arbitrary, parochial societal conventions that regulate behavior within organizations. The personal domain consists of those issues that apply only to the self and that the self claims as its own preserve. Each of these domains exists as a separate category of thought in the mind of the child. Unfortunately, to the extent that Kohlberg views moral development as the progressive differentiation of postconventional moral concerns from Level 2 conventional concerns, that is, to the extent that Kohlberg views conventional reasoning as an inferior form of moral reasoning, he conflates moral and conventional knowledge and fails to see that conventional knowledge is a separate domain characterized by its own line of development. The domains approach to social knowledge, which was first covered in Chapter 2, will be examined in more detail in Chapter 6. I begin here with Rest's development of the Defining Issues Test and his componential model of moral behavior. This will require us to revisit the issue of *structures d'ensemble*.

Structures d'Ensemble Revisited

In Chapter 2, I examined two readings of the structured-whole assumption. One reading, which I dubbed the received view, argues the case for content-free structures that globally unify intellectual functioning across a range of contents. Another reading argues for content-specific structures. Both readings are ostensibly Piagetian, although I argued that the latter reading is probably closer to Piaget's own intentions. We saw in Chapter 4 that Kohlberg embraced the stricter reading of the structured-whole assumption. He felt that justice reasoning could be made to conform to the received view on structural development if justice structures could be stringently purged of content. Indeed, Standard Issue Scoring was so designed with this aim in mind—to distinguish structural form from content, thereby increasing the chances that justice reasoning would reveal the desired hard-stage properties.

In Chapter 4 we also saw that strong evidence exists in favor of important features of Kohlberg's stage theory, indicating that confidence in Standard Issue Scoring is not misplaced. For example, the sequentiality assumption of the stage theory appears to be well supported. Individuals tend to move through the stages in an invariant order. Stage skipping has never been observed, and stage regressions are rare and are otherwise compatible with measurement error. There is also compelling evidence that progressive developments in moral reasoning are hierarchical in nature. Each succeeding stage is a progressive elaboration of previous stages in the sense that lower-stage elements are integrated within the emergent stage structure.

I also reviewed evidence that seemed to support the received view on the structured-whole assumption. In many studies subjects appeared to coalesce around a single modal stage in their thinking about various justice issues. Kohlberg and his colleagues interpreted this evidence of internal consistency in stage responding as a vindication of their claim that content-free structures of justice reasoning can indeed be delineated and that global justice structures unify thinking across a range of content issues within the moral domain. In Kohlberg's view subjects are either in a stage or in transition to the next stage.

Although the sequential and hierarchical claims of the stage theory appear to be well attested, claims for the structured-whole assumption have proven to be more controversial. Critics charge that Standard Issue Scoring rules tend to homogenize stage responding, with the effect that stage heterogeneity is unreported or underestimated, and that stage consistency is thereby overestimated. Critics also charge that Kohlberg's stage model is too simple to capture the complexities of moral development. It is too simple, for example, to think that subjects are at or in a stage and that this stage mediates the totality of their responding in the moral domain. In support of this view there is evidence of substantial intrapersonal and situational variation in moral reasoning. Further, different kinds of dilemmas appear to "pull" for different stage structures, and certain contents resist easy assimilation by extant justice structures.

In light of this evidence of variation in stage use, Charles Levine (1979b) has argued for an additive-inclusive stage model as opposed to Kohlberg's transformational-displacement model. Under the additive-inclusive stage model, earlier stages are not displaced by later stages but remain available for use depending on the nature of dilemmas, person variables, and social context. That is, the hierarchical transformation of lower stages is not so inclusive or integrative as to eliminate the functioning of earlier structures. Later integrations do not deform earlier structures so completely that they are lost or unavailable. Earlier stages reflect independently working structures that are "on line" even when more sophisticated structures are acquired. This sort of model seems to be required, in Levine's view, in order to account for variation in stage *use* as a function of person and situation variables: "This hybrid theoretical orientation encourages one to investigate the relationship between respondent characteristics, stage use, and the specific characteristics of social situations" (p. 161). This perspective further encourages researchers to "measure the separate use of each stage of reasoning" and to ask "how often any particular stage is used, given the impact of certain variables on reasoning" (p. 160). I reviewed evidence compatible with this model in Chapter 4 (e.g., Krebs, Denton, et al., 1991; Krebs, Vermuelen, et al., 1991).

James Rest (1975) has a similar view of the stage concept in moral-development research. Although it is proper, in his view, to characterize a sequence of stages as an ordered series of logically distinct and qualitatively different patterns of thinking, one still requires quantitative descriptors in order to capture the degree to which the various thought organizations are manifested in a subject's responses. What is difficult for a simple stage model to account for is the sheer variability of responding *within* subjects *across* dilemmas, testing conditions, and response modes. With this in mind, Rest argues that Kohlberg's simple stage model is burdened with a number of empirical problems.

For example, there is evidence, even in the new scoring manuals, of stage mixture in moral judgments. About 30 percent of Kohlberg's subjects show fluctuations of one-third of a stage (up or down) over a two-week period, indicating that sub-jects cannot be easily characterized as in a stage (Rest, 1983). Further, different response modes and testing characteristics yield different estimates of moral sophis-tication. As we will see shortly, recognition and preference-rating tasks typically reveal more sophistication than Kohlberg's verbal-production task. "That different tasks and response modes [make] a difference in stage scoring is another empirical disconfirmation of a simple stage model" (Rest, 1983, p. 587).

There are also stage inconsistencies that result from the kinds of dilemmas that subjects are asked to consider. That is, certain stories "pull" for particular stages (Rest, n.d.). In Chapter 4, I noted one study finding that over 23 percent of subjects showed a stage disparity of one stage or greater on capital punishment dilemmas, calling into question the strict reading of the structured whole assumption (de Vries & Walker, 1986; but see Walker, de Vries, & Treviathan, 1987; Bush, Krebs, & Carpendale, 1993).

Consider the Krebs (Krebs, Denton, et al., 1991) data. These researchers pre-sented adult subjects with three kinds of moral dilemmas. One set consisted of two Kohlberg dilemmas from the standard interview assessment. In addition, a proso-cial dilemma (fulfill a contract or help another) and an impaired-driving dilemma were used. A strong claim for structured wholeness would be vindicated if global stage assignments across the four dilemmas were highly consistent. But this was not the case. Although subjects (N = 60) were fairly consistent in their responses to the two Kohlberg dilemmas—73 percent scored at the same major stage, 98 percent within adjacent major stages, 87 percent within adjacent substages—there was much less consistency between these stage assignments and stage assignments to the other dilemmas. For example, only 28 percent of subjects scored at the same substage on both the Kohlberg and prosocial dilemmas (with lower stage assign-ments for the prosocial dilemma), and only 9 percent scored at the same substage on both the Kohlberg and the impaired-driving dilemma (with most impaired-driving scores at a lower stage).

Another way to assess stage consistency, in addition to comparing global scores across dilemmas, is to examine the distribution of an individual's stage judg-ments within dilemmas. Colby et al. (1983) established the following criteria for stage consistency: At least 90 percent of a subject's judgments must fall within adja-cent stages. What do the Krebs data (Krebs, Denton, et al., 1991) show? On the Kohlberg dilemmas, 88 percent of the subjects satisfied this criterion on adjacent major stages, but only 27 percent of subjects satisfied the criterion on adjacent substages. Krebs concluded that these findings constituted only weak support at best for the structured-whole assumption, even on Kohlberg's test.

What happens when the other dilemmas are included? Stage consistency fails the criterion. Only 68 percent of the subjects satisfied the criterion on the five major stages, and only two subjects satisfied it on the nine-point scale of substages. In fact, 87 percent of the sample displayed a range of four or more substages across the four dilemmas (Krebs, Denton, et al., 1991). There is hence clear evidence of stage fluctuation within, and stage inconsistency across, dilemmas, indicating that moral structures are quite flexible and that adults base their moral judgments on *several* stage structures, depending on dilemma type, a conclusion that is compatible with Levine's (1979b) additive-inclusion stage model.

In Rest's view, this evidence of stage heterogeneity discredits Kohlberg's simple (displacement) model. Instead, he argues for

> . a more complex conception of the stage model of development that recognizes that subjects are not completely "in" one stage or another but manifest a range of organizational structures depending on the difficulty of the task and stimulus characteristics, testing conditions, response modes, stringency of scoring criteria and other factors. Therefore, directional change is not viewed as proceeding step by step, one stage at a time, but rather as a shifting distribution of responses whereby the "lower" stages decrease while the "higher" stages increase (Rest, Davison, & Robbins, 1978, p. 264).

Consequently, it would appear that simply assigning qualitative stage scores to subjects may well mask important sources of variation and may well be misleading given the evidence for stage heterogeneity, subject fluctuations, the availability of multiple-stage structures, and the apparent content and situational dependencies evident in moral assessment. What seems to be required is a quantitative measure that yields a more probabalistic index of stage preference or stage use insofar as multiple stages may well be reflected in the data. The Defining Issues Test (DIT) is one such measure, and it appears to satisfy Levine's (1979b, p. 160) desire for an index that measures "the separate use of each stage" and "how often any particular stage is used." Let us now have a closer look at this important research tool.

The Defining Issues Test

The DIT consists of six moral dilemmas, one of which is an adaptation of the classic Heinz dilemma. After a subject reads a dilemma, she is asked to make a choice as to how to resolve a dilemma (e.g., steal or not steal a drug). Next, the subject is asked to rate the importance of 12 issue statements. That is, on a five-point scale ranging from "great importance" to "no importance," the subject is asked to rate how important each of 12 issues are in helping the subject think through the dilemma. These issue statements are prototypic statements that reflect Kohlberg's stages of moral development. One issue statement regarding the Heinz story concerns "whether a community's laws are going to be upheld." This is a prototypic Stage 4 issue. Another issue is "whether Heinz is stealing for himself or doing this solely to help someone else." This is a prototypic Stage 3 issue. A prototypic issue for Stage 6 is "What values are going to be the basis for governing how people act towards each other?" and for Stage 5, "whether the law in this case is getting in the way of the most basic claim of any member of society."

After subjects rate each issue statement on importance, they are then required to rank order their top four important issue statements (out of the 12) from "most important" to "fourth most important." If the "most important" issue statement reflects a principled stage (Stage 5 or 6), four points are awarded. Three points are awarded if a principled stage is denoted "second most important," two points if a principled stage is "third most important," and so on. The raw principled morality score (P-score) is simply the addition of the weighted preference scores across the six dilemmas. The P-score is most usefully expressed as a percentage of principled reasoning. The DIT assumes, of course, that moral issues will be construed differently by people at different moral stages and that only subjects who have some moral sophistication will find the principled-stage statements to be attractive or important considerations (Rest, Turiel, & Kohlberg, 1969; Rest, 1973).

The DIT also includes procedural checks for response sets and idiosyncratic responding. For example, three issue statements (across the six dilemmas) attempt to catch subjects who appear to be responding to extravagant, high-sounding language. Consider this issue item from the Heinz battery: "whether the essence of living is more encompassing than the termination of dying, socially or individually." The language, though impressive, is meaningless. Other items are meant to catch inattentive responding. Consider this item: "whether Heinz is a professional wrestler, or has considerable influence on professional wrestlers." If a subject attached "great importance" to this item, we would have grounds for doubting the reliability or seriousness of his responding.

Research on the DIT began in the early 1970s. In 1973 Rest published the results of his doctoral dissertation (Rest, 1973). Although this paper was ostensibly concerned with providing evidence on the hierarchical nature of moral reasoning, it also established the grounds for pursuing the DIT's preference-ranking technique (see also Rest et al., 1969). Three hypotheses were put to the test. (1) Stage statements that are one stage above (+1) a subject's current stage will be difficult to comprehend. Statements below a subject's own stage will be comprehended but not spontaneously produced. (2) Subjects will comprehend various stages of moral reasoning but will prefer the highest stage they can comprehend (i.e., view the highest comprehended stage as "more adequate"). (3) There should be a match between a subject's stage and the highest stage comprehended.

What Rest needed to do was construct a measure of comprehension, and a measure of preference. Prototypic statements were then generated for each stage. Comprehension was assessed by how well subjects could recapitulate and evaluate the ideas reflected in each statement. Preference was indexed by rating and ranking each statement on a scale of "convincingness." What did he find? Regarding comprehension, Rest noted four findings: (1) Subjects tended to either fully understand the statements of a given stage or not understand them. (2) If a subject comprehended the statements of a given stage, he or she understood the statements of all preceding stages. This suggests that comprehension is cumulative. (3) There was a close relationship between a subject's own spontaneous stage and comprehension scores. That is, comprehension scores were high up to the subject's own predominant stage but declined thereafter. Subjects were increasingly unable to comprehend statements that were higher than their own stage of reasoning. (4) The best predictor of comprehension was not the predominant stage but the highest stage comprehended. When a subject is scored for moral stage, she normally produces spontaneous judgments that range across a number of stages.

However, her stage assignment is based on the one stage that seems to predominate. But this means that some subjects will spontaneously produce judgments that are above their predominant stage. Consequently, predominant stage and highest stage comprehended are not necessarily the same stage. Indeed, "subjects tend to produce spontaneously a substantial amount of the highest stage they comprehend" (Rest, 1973, pp. 102–103). What about preference? Rest (1973) showed that (1) subjects prefer the highest stage comprehended and (2) subjects prefer the higher-stage statements in their development order (i.e., Stage 2 statements are preferred over Stage 1, Stage 3 over Stage 2, etc.).

Rest (1973) drew a number of conclusions. First, moral judgment is hierarchical in nature. The stages represent a cumulative order of difficulty. Second, each succeeding stage is progressively more adequate, as revealed by the preference rankings. Third, subjects do not necessarily prefer their own stage but rather the highest stage they comprehend— "There is no particular preference for either one's own stage or for the next stage towards which one is moving; there is an ordered preference for the highest stage one can comprehend, regardless of one's own spontaneous stage" (p. 196).

Fourth, the three tasks, spontaneous production, comprehension, and preference, are a kind of Piagetian *decalage*. The spontaneous production of moral reasons is much harder, since it requires one to articulate a moral theory of sorts. Elaborating statements made by others in the comprehension task is simpler than spontaneously generating one's own moral statements, and indicating preference is much simpler still, since one does not even have to demonstrate the sort of comparative elaboration that the comprehension task requires. Hence the three tasks (preference, comprehension, spontaneous production) could well mark phases in the acquisition of a new stage. The first sign that a new stage is within reach is when a subject indicates preference for its prototypic judgments. Comprehension and spontaneous production would then mark additional phases in the subsequent consolidation of the new stage.

This study is often cited as strong support for the hierarchical integration assumption of moral-stage theory, but it is also easy to see here the rudiments of the DIT methodology. The DIT also presents subjects with stage prototypic statements, to which preference rankings are solicited. By 1974, 16 studies using the DIT were completed, and the measure was formally introduced into the literature (Rest, Cooper, Coder, Masanz, & Anderson, 1974). In the following year the first longitudinal study (to my knowledge) was published (Rest, 1975). This study showed that the DIT could detect developmental change over a two-year period. High school and junior high students showed greater preference for principled reasoning during this period, but the younger subjects also showed preconventional to conventional shifts in their reasoning. There was no evidence of step-by-step movement through the stage and no evidence of sex differences. Some of the older subjects were attending college when they were retested. These subjects gained twice as much as their peers who were not attending college, although these groups were not significantly different when they were still in high school.

Indeed, formal education is more highly correlated with principled reasoning than is chronological age.

The reader would have noticed that this study identifies a much greater incidence of principled reasoning in the thinking of adolescents and young adults than is the case with the Kohlberg assessment. If one simply looked at Kohlberg's results, one would have to conclude that principled reasoning is exceedingly rare, even in samples of adults. Yet the DIT shows that even junior high students show some incidence of principled reasoning. But the explanation is straightforward. The DIT is a recognition-preference task, which is easier than Kohlberg's spontaneous verbal-production task. Hence, the DIT is likely to detect higher forms of thinking earlier than is possible with the moral-judgment interview.

Since these groundbreaking studies over 500 studies have been conducted using the DIT, necessitating a number of scholarly reviews of the literature (Rest, Davison, & Robbins, 1978; Rest, 1979, 1983, 1986a). The DIT has fared exceedingly well in these studies. Indeed, few research instruments command as much confirmatory evidence as does the DIT. It has strong psychometric properties (e.g., Davison & Robbins, 1978). It is sensitive to sequential development. It is not contaminated by cohort or generational effects. It can be discriminated from other variables (e.g., IQ, personality variables, attitudes, other measures of cognitive development). And there are pragmatic benefits as well, namely, the DIT is standardized, easily administered, and objectively scored (see also Gibbs & Widaman, 1982, for an objective, standardized version of the Kohlberg interview).

Rest's characterization of stage development departs from Kohlberg's. He does not assume that subjects are in a stage. Or, alternatively, he assumes that stage assignment will always be affected by content, method of assessment, task difficulty, testing conditions, and other factors. He prefers to define each stage not in terms of an abstract analysis of logical (justice) operations but rather in terms of schemes of cooperation. That is, the six moral stages describe six schemes of cooperation. A scheme of cooperation is a generalized view of how people should cooperate in social relationships. Each stage (or each scheme of cooperation) can be described in terms of two dimensions: (1) a conceptualization of shared expectations, that is, how rules are known and shared for coordinating goals and plans; and (2) how interests can be balanced to achieve a stable social organization. Table 5.1 describes the form that these dimensions take at each stage. The third column of Table 5.1 summarizes the stage prototypic conception of rights and duties that these twin dimensions entail.

What is seen to develop in this sequence is "the progressive understanding of the various possibilities of cooperative relationships, how rights and duties are balanced, and the conditions that sustain the cooperative schemes" (Rest, 1983, p. 587). Rest suggests that these stage descriptions, in addition to methodological differences in assessment, make it possible to identify many more instances of principled reasoning than is possible with Kohlberg's assessment, "in which a subject must deliver a philosophical lecture in response to the Heinz story to be credited with higher stage thinking" (Rest, 1983, p. 589). Nonetheless, the DIT stage

TABLE 5.1 Rest's Conceptualization of Moral-Stage Development

Stage	Shared Expectations	Balancing Interests	Central Concept
1	Adult makes demands on child's behavior.	Rules made by adults. Child knows that obedience will bring freedom from punishment.	Obedience: "Do what you're told."
2	Exchange of favors can be mutually decided.	Each party reciprocates if self-interest gains in the exchange.	Instrumental egoism: "Let's make a deal."
3	Individuals attain mutual understanding through reciprocal role taking.	Cooperation stabilized through friendships. Each party anticipates needs, wants, and feelings of the other and acts to advance the other's welfare.	Interpersonal concordance: "Be nice and kind and you'll get along with others."
4	Public law informs us of what is expected.	Rule-following, with the, expectation that others will also obey the law and live up to their jobs and responsibilities, is the basis of society's system of cooperation. We can make plans because of our confidence in the stability of this system.	Law and duty to the social order: "Everyone is obligated and protected by the law."
5	Formal procedures for making laws are designed. We think rational people will accept these procedures.	Law-making procedures are devised to reflect the general will and protect basic rights. Democratic participation gives us confidence that our interests will be duly considered and is the basis of whatever claims we make on others.	Social consensus: "One is obliged accept what is decided in accordance with due process."
6	Cooperation among rational, impartial, and equal individuals is a logical requirement of social organization.	A scheme of cooperation annuls arbitrary distribution of rights and responsibilities. The social system is "equilibrated."	Nonarbitrary cooperation: "How rational people would organize cooperation is moral."

Source: Adapted from Rest (1983). Used by permission of John Wiley.

descriptions and Kohlberg's are broadly similar. Indeed, Rest often interprets evidence of DIT principled reasoning as evidence in favor of Kohlberg's conceptualization of postconventional reasoning.

We are now in a position to revisit the moral action issue. As noted at the outset of this chapter, Rest has a more complicated model of how moral behavior is made possible (or is inhibited), and he has recently provided some encouraging evidence in its favor.

The Componential Model of Moral Behavior: Moral Action Revisited

In Chapter 4, I examined Blasi's Self Model of moral action. This model suggests that moral behavior is more likely to follow moral judgment if those considerations are deemed essential and core to one's personal identity. One must not only discern what the moral law requires; one must also conclude that the moral law is applicable to the self and that the self is responsible for enacting its requirements. Reasons are sufficient motives for action just because the integrity of the self is at stake. Blasi goes on to suggest that there may well be individual differences in the way people come to identify their essential selves with moral considerations. People may differ in how deeply moral notions penetrate their self-understanding, or they may differ in the kinds of moral considerations that are judged constitutive of the self. One then imagines that under some conditions, moral action and inaction implicate the self in important ways. Lynn McFall (1987, p. 12) puts the matter well: "We all have things we think we would never do, under any imaginable circumstances; some part of ourselves beyond which we will never retreat, some weakness however prevalent in others that we will not tolerate in ourselves. And if we do that thing, betray that weakness, we are not the persons we thought: there is nothing left that we may even in spite refer to as I." Unconditional moral commitments that are core, deep, and essential to our self-understanding contribute to our sense of personal integrity in action. These are the "deepest most serious convictions we have; they define what we would not do, what we regard as outrageous and horrible; they are the fundamental conditions for being ourselves, for the integrity of our characters depends upon them" (Kekes, 1989, p. 167).

Kohlberg has also embraced some notion of the responsible self in his account of how moral judgment gets translated into moral action. The bridge between knowing the right thing to do and doing it is the understanding that the self is responsible. Yet there is also the impression that moral action is still mostly a matter of having sufficient knowledge of what the moral law requires. That is, moral action flows from moral judgment just because a moral principle is prescriptive. What determines moral conduct is "knowledge of the good" (Grover, 1980). The moral self is one who appreciates the moral point of view or is one who has a keen appreciation of the fact that the strictly formal properties of a moral judgment (prescriptivity, universality) necessarily entail a commitment to action. I suggested that there is probably a limit to how thoroughly Kohlberg can allow the responsible self to be implicated in moral action lest how we evaluate the moral status of an *action* transfer too easily to an evaluation of the moral *agent*, thereby opening the door to an aretaic use of the stage theory, a prospect that Kohlberg has always resisted.

The componential model of James Rest (1983) complicates matters further. In his view there is much more to moral cognition than simply deciding what the moral law requires or even that the self is accountable to the moral law. He argues that there are four broad components to moral functioning, only one of which is the sort of moral reasoning described by Kohlberg and Piaget. Let us now see what these four components amount to.

Component 1

Moral deliberation begins when one attempts to interpret the situation. Real moral quandaries are rarely structured quite as neatly as hypothetical dilemmas. Real moral quandaries are usually shrouded in a fog of moral ambiguity. There is typically more uncertainty about the facts of the matter, more uncertainty about realistic options, courses of action, and their consequences. There is uncertainty about intentions, motives, and interests. Our perception of problematic situations may be keen or blunted. We may be sensitive or insensitive to salient cues that define situations as problematic and as requiring a response. "Egoistic anxiety veils the world" (Murdoch, 1992, p. 175). Visual metaphors are required. We must see, look about, interpret events.

Component 1 processes involve the cognitive processes of perception, appraisal, and interpretation (see also Pekarsky, 1983). In addition, our own affective arousal (e.g., anger, anxiety, envy, empathy, apathy, revulsion) may well be part of what needs to be interpreted in a compelling situation. Kohlberg has suggested that the moral stage serves as a lens or screen that guides this sort of moral perception and that role-taking is the social-cognitive process that takes these factors into account, although this would probably be disputed by Rest (1983) and others (Blum, 1991; Pekarsky, 1983).

Component 2

Component 2 processes begin once we have settled on an appraisal of the problem situation. When possible courses of action are identified, one must now evaluate them in light of a moral ideal "Many things I *can* do, but what *ought* I to do, what does the moral law require?" This second component requires us to incorporate social norms and moral principles into our moral deliberations. Kohlberg's stage theory (and Piaget's) falls under this heading; that is, it describes the second component of moral deliberation. In the Kohlbergian tradition the "derivation of a moral course of action in a specific situation follows from a generalized structure that defines obligations and rights" (Rest, 1983, p. 563). But as we have seen, a given stage structure could conceivably generate multiple options (and the same option might be justified by any number of stage perspectives). Consequently, reasoning about the justice of various options cannot be the end of moral deliberation. One must also *make a decision*. This is the province of Component 3.

Component 3

Component 3 is concerned with decision-making and with moral motivation. Although the moral ideal may indicate one possible course of action, it is also the case that alternative options may well be suggested by competing (prudential, aethestic, self-protective) values. "Therefore, parallel to formulating a *moral* course of action, a person may be formulating courses of action oriented towards other values. Oftentimes, other values are so important to a person that they preempt or compromise moral values" (Rest, 1983, p. 564). Models of human decision-making and reflections on the sources of moral motivation, then, are the prototypic concerns of Component 3. Blasi's Self Model would seem to focus on this third component of moral deliberation.

Component 4

Let's say that one has adequately appraised the problem situation (Component 1), has identified its moral elements (Component 2), has worked through competing values, settling on the action that conforms to the moral law; let us say further that one is also sufficiently motivated to pursue the moral action (Component 3). Is the matter settled? Does moral action follow directly from the motivated decision to do the right thing? No, for as everyone knows, the road to hell is paved with good intentions. What is now required is for the plan of action to be implemented. But implementation will require courage, perseverance, resolve, and competence. It will require one to keep the goal in sight, not to lose heart, not to give in to temptations of various kinds. It will require ego strength and character. It will require inner strength, determination, and a willingness to keep one's eye on the prize. These characterological dispositions are the domain of Component 4.

Each of these domains is associated with important research traditions. The componential model rightly suggests that there are many kinds of cognitions that contribute to moral deliberation and that moral behavior is not a straightforward deduction from any one kind of cognitive process. Moral judgment of the Kohlbergian sort cannot be expected to carry the burden of explaining the totality of what goes into moral behavior. This was attested in a recent study by Thoma, Rest, and Davison, (1991; Thoma & Rest, 1986). These authors argue that the moral judgment-action relationship is moderated by a *utilizer dimension*. The utilizer dimension describes a subject's tendency to allow justice-based considerations to influence his or her moral decision-making. The relationship between moral judgment and action increases as utilization increases. Let's examine this line of argument in more detail.

Recall that each story on the DIT lists 12 issue statements that subjects are to rate as to their importance for resolving the dilemma. These issue statements are keyed to Kohlberg's stages. Thoma and others (1991) report evidence that these stage-prototypic issue statements are related to action choices. That is, individual DIT items seem to favor one course of action (e.g., steal the drug) over alternatives (don't steal the drug). Further, there is evidence that subjects typically have action choices in mind before they begin rating and ranking the issue statements and that this action preference constrains the sort of issues that are judged important or not important. It would appear, then, that story-specific information, as reflected in the DIT issue statements, is logically related to action choice. If this is true, one should be able to predict moral action by knowing two things: (1) how important an issue statement is judged to be, that is, its "moral merit," and (2) the degree to which the issue statement favors one action choice over another, that is, story-specific information. To test this hypothesis, an algorithm was constructed that related these two pieces of information. As it turns out this algorithm score was a more robust predictor of moral-action choices than was the total DIT score alone. Hence, moral-judgment scores alone are not the best predictor of moral-action choices. Rather, story-specific information, in addition to moral-judgment scores, leads to a better prediction of moral action.

Yet some subjects did not relate story-item information to action choices in the expected way. For example, some subjects would endorse "don't steal the drug" as an action choice and yet rate and rank issue statements in a way that favored the "steal the drug" alternative. Enter the utilizer dimension. Subjects whose action choice was highly related to their ratings and rankings of issue statements were said to be "high utilizers." That is, they appeared to utilize the same Component 2 considerations when making the action choice and when rating and ranking the importance of issue statements. Low utilizers, in contrast, appeared to be using a very different (and unspecified) Component 2 process in the action-choice and ranking phases of the assessment. Consequently, knowing the moral-judgment scores of low utilizers is not helpful in predicting their moral action. Prediction should improve, however, as utilization increases, and this was indeed shown to be the case by Thoma and colleagues (1991).

This study suggests that moral judgment alone does not produce moral action and that multiprocess models such as the four-component model may well be necessary to improve our understanding of moral functioning. Let us bring this discussion to a close by examining the Kohlbergian reaction to the DIT research program.

A Kohlbergian Appraisal

I have been contrasting two stage models of moral development, namely, the "simple" Kohlbergian displacement model, which suggests that lower stages are transformed and displaced by higher stages, and the more complex additive model, which suggests that multiple stages are available depending on a host of personal and situational factors. The simple model takes a strong stand on the structured-whole assumption and is favored by evidence of stage homogeneity. The complex, additive model is associated with evidence of stage heterogeneity.

Colby and Kohlberg (1987) argue that both stage models are necessary for capturing the complexity of moral development. Their general argument runs like this. Moral judgment is a complex thing and can be described in a number of ways. One can focus, for example, on the spontaneous production of moral judgments in an interview situation. That is, when I ask you an open-ended question about a moral issue, you are required to produce a free, unencumbered verbal response. This is quite different from asking you to simply comprehend the moral statement produced by another. This, in turn, is quite different from asking you to state a preference for one judgment or another made by another. Kohlberg's interview focuses on the production of moral statements; Rest's DIT focuses on comprehension and preference. Further, the two assessments pull for different kinds of moral judgments. The Kohlberg interview pulls for the upper level of a subject's thinking, that is, it pulls for the subject's moral competence. One has greater confidence that competence is being assessed when one takes the opportunity to probe and clarify the subject's responses. This can happen only in the give-and-take of an interview format. In contrast, the DIT does not pull for competence. Subjects cannot elaborate or clarify why they endorsed (or did not endorse) issue statements produced by others. Consequently, it is difficult to know how a subject really understands an issue statement.

These considerations lead Colby and Kohlberg to conclude that spontaneous productions of moral judgments can be characterized by hard stages, with hierarchical transformation and displacement, but that hard stages do not characterize comprehension and preference. That is, the *structures d'ensemble* of justice reasoning are not so structured, or so holistic, as to encompass the sort of judgments that are assessed by the DIT. For these latter judgments, the additive-inclusion model is more appropriate. The production of moral judgments, reflecting competence, are stagelike in the hard Piagetian sense, but the comprehension of moral judgments made by others is not. Indeed, there is little reason to expect comprehension to be stagelike insofar as one comprehends arguments at a variety of stages—all of the arguments at lower stages and some of the arguments at the stage one or two above one's current modal stage. This would not explain, of course, the evidence of stage heterogeneity that was evident in the production tasks used in the Krebs (Krebs, Denton, et al., 1991) study.

What about preference judgments? Is it a problem for the simple stage model if subjects endorse (prefer, find convincing) a lower-stage argument? On the one hand, this does seem to be a problem, since, presumably, the lower stage has been transformed and displaced by the higher stage. Consequently, lower-stage arguments should be judged inadequate from the perspective of the higher, more equilibrated stage and therefore rejected (Turiel, 1974). But here Colby and Kohlberg (1987) appear to tilt toward the additive-inclusion model. Hierarchical transformation is not so radical and thoroughgoing as to totally deform the lower-stage structure. Some of the insights of the lower stage are retained. Hence, "although the stage as a whole may undergo transformation as the individual develops, many of the insights achieved at the lower stages remain valid from the higher stage perspective though they are now embedded in a more complex and sophisticated position" (Colby & Kohlberg, 1987, p. 116). They give this example: A Stage 4 or Stage 5 subject can endorse the Stage 3 judgment that "you ought to keep a promise because the person you promised trusts you," although the reason one should keep promises, the understanding of trust, will show more sophistication than is possible at Stage 3.

Finally, Colby and Kohlberg (1987) reject the suggestion that their strong evidence of internal consistency is an artifact of Standard Issue Scoring rules or the notion that these rules unduly homogenize what is essentially heterogeneous data. Although these rules do forbid the assigning of more than one stage (or substage) score at the level of norms and elements, multiple scores can be assigned at the level of issue and dilemma if there are multiple matches to the manual. But, they argue, this has just never happened, and the Piagetian hard-stage model is indeed vindicated for the case of prescriptive moral judgments spontaneously produced and scored for moral competence. These and other arguments will surely characterize moral-judgment research for some time to come. Let us now turn to the issue of gender bias and the alternative ethic of care.

6

Domains of Social Knowledge

Partial Structures and the Received View

The view that social knowledge is usefully delineated into various domains follows from Turiel's (1975, 1983a) understanding of Piaget's genetic epistemological project and also from the Piagetian conception of cognitive structures. As we saw in Chapter 1, Piaget wanted to find out how different forms of knowledge developed. What sort of knowledge was Piaget interested in? Piaget's interest in epistemology directed him to the developmental study of those domains that were of central concern to epistemologists. Hence his research focused principally on children's logical, mathematical, and physical knowledge. Note that the study of epistemology fell neatly into a number of categories—logic, mathematics, and physics. Hence, to ask how different forms of knowledge develop is to ask a domain-specific question (Chapman, 1988). Scientific and philosophic knowledge is conceptually confined in domains. Knowledge of physics and knowledge of mathematics or of logic are not the same kinds of knowledge. Hence there is every expectation that the development of knowledge in each of these broad domains requires different sorts of explanations.

It also follows that Piaget's description of the forms of knowledge, that is, his description of how knowledge within each domain is structured, will also be content-specific. That is, development within domains will reflect the emergence of *partial structures*. This is in contrast to what I have been calling the received view of Piagetian structures. The received view insists that global structures organize the totality of one's understandings across a range of contents and domains of activity. The received view concerning global structures is plausible only if one reads Piaget to say that form (structure) and content are independent. In this case, the same structure can be applied to different contents. One would then expect to see synchrony in development across a broad range of content domains. However, the finding that children do not appear to master the conservation tasks (e.g., of quantity, weight, volume) at the same time—that is, the application of structures does not seem to be content-free after all but tied to particular domains of knowledge—is thought to undermine the Piagetian structured-whole assumption.

But I have suggested that the received view is not an accurate description of Piaget's understanding of cognitive structure. There is not one general organization of thought that structures knowledge in general. Instead, understanding is conceptually bounded by categories of thought, each of which is organized by partial structures that arise distinctively within each domain. Piaget did not believe that form and content could be radically distinguished. Instead, cognitive structures always maintain an element of content specificity. A defense of this view will set the stage for Turiel's approach to social knowledge.

Consider, by way of example, the stage of concrete operations. This stage characterizes most of the grade school years and can be defined by reference to eight logical forms (the grouping structures). How do grouping structures arise? First, physical operations are applied to different contents. The demands that contents impose will therefore require different operations. When these operations become interiorized and grouped into an organized form, the grouping structures (i.e., the forms of organization) will necessarily retain their content specificity. As Chapman (1988) puts it:

> Different areas of content can involve different physical operations, and there is no *a priori* reason why the different physical operations should be grouped at the same time, even though the groupings may be formally analogous once they have been formed. In short, Piaget did not make a radical ontological distinction between form and content. . . . The logical forms (i.e., the groupings) are forms of organization among the content-bound physical operations. *This organization cannot exist apart from their respective contents, because without the latter there is nothing to be organized.* (p. 166, emphasis added)

This reprise of the Piagetian project helps us understand Turiel's argument. Just as epistemological knowledge is necessarily domain-specific, so too is social knowledge. If it makes sense to distinguish among logical, mathematical, and physical domains of knowledge, it also makes sense to distinguish among moral, social-conventional, and personal-psychological domains of social knowledge. Just as knowledge of mathematics, logic, and physics is not one kind of epistemological knowledge, so too knowledge of morality, social convention, and personal-psychological concepts is not one kind of social knowledge. Similarly, if structures maintain an element of content specificity, it follows that the structures of knowledge in the various social domains (e.g., morality, social convention) arise from domain-specific kinds of activities and experiences. Different social experiences are structured differently, leading to conceptually bounded domains of social knowledge. Hence, according to Turiel (1983a, p. 20), "Cognitive structures are partial in that they encompass delimited domains of knowledge; thinking is organized within the boundaries of fundamental categories (e.g., logical-mathematical thinking, moral judgment). Development within a domain entails reorganizations of thought, so that separate developmental sequences can be identified for each domain."

This suggests that moral and conventional knowledge have different developmental sources. Different forms of social knowledge develop because children experience different kinds of social interactions. From these social interactions children draw different inferences that are organized in domain-specific ways. And these organizations of knowledge follow separate developmental trajectories. Let's look at this argument in more detail.

Morality and Social Convention

What is the difference between morality and social convention? Turiel follows many contemporary philosophers (e.g., Dworkin, 1978; Gewirth, 1978) in the way he characterizes the conceptual difference between the two domains. Moral judgments are characterized by a number of formal properties. A moral judgment is binding and obligatory for agents. One is not permitted to evade a moral judgment by appealing to one's personal inclinations. In this sense moral judgments are impersonal. Impersonal moral judgments are also universally applicable. Hence, they apply to anyone in the relevant situation, and they have force independently of social context.

Furthermore, moral injunctions do not derive from institutional practices, and they are not established by agreement or consensus. For example, it offends our moral sensibilities to suggest that the injunction "don't kill innocent children" has moral force only because we all agree that this is a bad thing. The source of a moral injunction cannot be derived from social agreement and consensus. If this were true, we would have to stand silent if some social system thought that it was a good thing to kill innocent children from time to time. If this were true, it might be possible to raise "cheat your neighbors" and "steal what you need" to the status of high moral obligations if there were sufficient agreement that these injunctions would further our social ends.

We also recognize that certain actions can be judged wrong from the moral point of view even though the actions are widely practiced. Moral obligation and institutional practices are hardly the same. No one is permitted to appeal to law, etiquette, or custom in order to sidestep the obligations imposed by a moral prescription. As Gewirth (1978, p. 24) puts it: "Judgments of moral obligation are categorical in that what persons ought to do sets requirements for them that they cannot rightly evade by consulting their own self-interested desires or variable opinions, ideals, or institutional practices." The fact that morality has force and validity apart from social ideals or institutional practices allows us to criticize societal institutions. Some institutional practices are unjust. Some desires, opinions, and ideals are unworthy of us. And no amount of social agreement can make what is unjust, just or what is immoral, moral.

Hence, morality is a set of prescriptive requirements that are categorical, obligatory, impersonal, and universally applicable. Moral principles are phrased independently of social structures and institutions and, indeed, are the basis for evaluating them. In contrast, social conventions are those procedures generated by social organizations that produce behavioral uniformities among members. Social conventions serve a social function—to coordinate the activities and interactions of individuals who belong to the social organization. Unlike moral rules, social conventions are established by consensus and agreement. They are binding just because we agree to abide by them. And because they follow from the accepted institutional practices of social organizations, conventions are contextually relative and arbitrary in the sense that alternative conventions could have been instituted to achieve the same social ends and different social systems can institute different conventional practices.

Turiel (1983a) argues that social conventions are part of the definition of social organizations. He draws a distinction between two kinds of rules: regulative rules and constitutive rules (see Searle, 1969). Regulative rules are logically independent of some preexisting activity that the rules are invoked to regulate. I might regulate classroom activity by insisting that students address me with a formal title, that they raise their hand before speaking, and that they take notes with only Berol Boldliner pens. But classroom activities don't have to be regulated in this way. Indeed, classroom activities undoubtedly existed prior to these rules and can be regulated by any number of other rules or by no rules at all.

Constitutive rules, in contrast, do more than merely regulate behavior. They constitute the very grounds for participating in the activities in the first place. They create the behaviors that they are to designed to regulate. The rules that govern chess, baseball, and the Canadian Football League bring into existence behaviors that constitute the activity in question. These behaviors did not exist prior to the rules. Rather, these behaviors are constituted by the rules themselves. If you wanted to know why Birge stole second base, you will have to refer to the institutional context defined by the rules of baseball. If you want to know why the Pittsburgh Steelers usually punt on fourth down but the Winnipeg Blue Bombers usually punt on third down (or what it means to punt and what a down is) you will have to refer to the constitutive rules that define the activities of the National Football League and the Canadian Football League, respectively. Indeed, the number of downs allowed for an offensive series in football is one of the distinguishing marks of the two football leagues. The two social organizations (NFL, CFL) are constituted by two sets of defining rules. These sets of rules give rise to behaviors that define the two social organizations.

In Turiel's (1983a) view, social conventions are constitutive rules. Conventions produce the behavioral uniformities that make the social system possible:

> Conventions. . . are aspects of the social organization of social systems that are designed to specify behaviors that contribute to the definition of a social system. The reasons for those behaviors are in the makeup of the social system and not in other considerations. It is in this sense that conventional acts are arbitrary. . . . Outside of the context of the constituted system, the acts are arbitrary in that there are no compelling reasons for behaving one way or the other. . . From the viewpoint of a constituted system, conventions are relative to the context in which they exist. In a differently constituted system, a particular convention may not exist or may exist in another form. (Turiel, 1983a, p. 38)

The punting rules of football, to continue our example, are relative to organizational context. The "four-down" rule makes perfect sense in the social-organizational context of the NFL, but not the CFL. In turn, the "three-down" rule is a defining attribute of the CFL but is considered a strange practice from the perspective of American football. (Indeed, the practices of both social organizations can seem quite odd from the perspective of a devotee of the Australian Football League, who may think it quite arbitrary whether one punts on third down or fourth down.) Of course, the CFL could change its constitutive punting rule to align more with accepted practice in the NFL, but this would also entail a redefinition of the Canadian game.

Moral principles are not constitutive rules in this sense just because moral rules are not arbitrary, contextually relative, or alterable by consensus. "Thus, the notion of a constitutive system of social organization is not applicable to the moral domain. Moral prescriptions are not arbitrary acts that become definitional types of social interactions. Moral prescriptions. . . are analytically independent of systems of social organization that coordinate interactions" (Turiel, 1983a, p. 39).

Let us summarize the distinction between the moral and social-conventional domains. Social conventions establish behavioral uniformities and coordinate social interaction. In addition to having this regulative function, social conventions are constitutive rules that define the social organization. They have force through common agreement. Hence, social conventions are contextually relative and arbitrary. Moral rules, in contrast, are not arbitrary, and they are not established by social consensus. Rather, moral rules are categorical, obligatory, impersonal, and universally applicable. This suggests that moral transgressions are to be judged wrong regardless of social norms or institutional practices. No one is entitled to pummel vulnerable children, not even if sanctioned by institutional practice or common consent. In contrast, conventional violations are judged wrong only if a social norm or rule exists prohibiting the action. For example, I will be heavily penalized if I try to punt on fourth down in the CFL but will be greatly encouraged to make the same play in the NFL.

It should be clear that Turiel's understanding of the moral domain accords well with the formalist tradition in ethics. This tradition informed Kohlberg's understanding of the moral domain as well. Turiel departs from Kohlberg with his claim that conventional knowledge is an independent conceptual domain. Social knowledge is not, in Turiel's view, a jumble of moral and conventional considerations that only later become increasingly differentiated with development. Instead, conventional and moral knowledge are distinguishable at an early age and follow independent lines of development. This is because moral and social-conventional understanding are constructed from different kinds of social experiences. In Turiel's (1983a) view, moral judgments are inferences that are constructed from social events that have intrinsic consequences. The meaning of these events does not depend upon social norms or group standards. In contrast, social-conventional judgments are constructed from social events that take their meaning from an institutional context. Let's flesh this out by considering the following examples.

1. Joey sees a classmate across the room. He walks over to this classmate and pushes him to the ground. As the boy attempts to stand up, Joey punches him three times in the face.
2. It is time for Joey's class to go to the washroom. Two lines form. One line is for girls waiting to use the girls' washroom; the other line is for boys waiting to use the boys' washroom. When it is Joey's turn, he walks right past the boys' washroom and enters the girls' room instead.

There is clearly something very different about the two transgressions illustrated by these examples. In the first example, Joey is committing a moral transgression. In the second, Joey is violating the conventional expectation that boys are not to use the girls' bathroom. In the first example, one is drawn to the intrinsic consequence of Joey's action, namely, harm and suffering visited upon the classmate-victim. We do not bother to ask, in this case, whether the school has a rule about such matters before we are entitled to evaluate Joey's conduct. It is not the institutional regulations or system of laws that motivates our evaluation of Joey's actions as a moral transgression. Rather, our moral evaluation is bound up with the intrinsic "brute fact" that Joey has caused pain and suffering by his actions. Although most schools do indeed have rules that forbid assault, these rules do not convey our moral evaluation, and we need not refer to them. Indeed, Joey's actions would still be a moral transgression even if no such rule existed or even if Joey's school actually permitted assaults.

What must a child do in order to structure this first event in terms of a moral judgment? Turiel (1983a) suggests that it might go something like this: First, the child must abstract from the event the understanding that pushing and punching inflict pain and suffering. Perhaps the child will connect her own experience of pain with the pain experienced by the victim. The child then will attend to Joey's rationale for visiting pain upon the victim and judge its validity. The child might imagine what the state of affairs might be if Joey did not assault the classmate. That is, by comparing the negation of the event, that is, its nonoccurrence, with what actually happened, perhaps the child could come to some inference as to what would be desirable in a social interaction. It is usually desirable that social interactions do not lead to pain and suffering. From this understanding, the following moral prescription might follow: One ought not to inflict pain. Hence, a child generates a moral prescription by a social-inference process that is grounded by intrinsic elements of the experience itself. Not once did the child need to consult the school handbook in order to help her understand the nature of Joey's transgression.

The social event described by the second example leads to a very different appraisal. Did Joey commit a transgression here? To judge that he did requires one to understand something about the social organization of the school and the kinds of behavioral uniformities that the regulations of the school promote. In the absence of any institutional regulation, there is no reason Joey should not use any bathroom he chooses. That it is judged wrong for Joey to use the girls' bathroom follows from an inference that he violated an explicit regulation or an implied conventional uniformity. Hence, rather than referring to features intrinsic to the experience, as was the case for moral judgments, one must refer here to the social context, to the demands imposed by social organizations, in order to evaluate possible conventional violations. "It is social organizational factors, such as consensus, rules, and authority that provide meaning to the act. It is by starting to conceptualize the social context in which they are embedded that the child forms an understanding of conventions" (Turiel, 1983a, p. 44). Conventional judgments, then, are structured by conceptions of social organization. Moral judgments, in turn, are structured by conceptions of justice.

Because moral and conventional judgments are structured by different sorts of understandings and have their sources in different developmental experiences, it is reasonable to expect social-conventional reasoning to follow a line of development independent of the moral domain. This follows from Turiel's embrace of the "partial structures" view. Partial structures are content-specific to domain. Moral structures organize conceptions of justice and are constructed from social experiences that have moral features. Social-conventional structures organize conceptions of social organizations and arise from social interactions that point toward features of the institutional setting.

The Development of Social-Conventional Reasoning

Social-conventional reasoning is thought to undergo a seven-stage sequence of development (Turiel, 1983a). This sequence is summarized in Table 6.1. Each stage in this sequence describes a twofold understanding of social systems and the role of conventions in coordinating interactions within the social systems. Hence, one's understanding of social conventions is strongly tied to how one construes the nature of social systems more generally, and these understandings are expected to show structural development through seven stages. The stage concept that Turiel embraces is often called the *transformational model.* It is a Piagetian model that Kohlberg also endorsed (Colby & Kohlberg, 1987), although Turiel's stages are quite distinctive in one important respect. Look at the stage descriptions in Table 6.1. Stages 2, 4, and 6 are described as "negations of convention." Stage 2 is a negation of the Stage 1 understanding of convention. Stage 4 is a negation of the Stage 3 understanding, and so on. In other words, in order to get from Stage 1 to Stage 3, one has to pass through a stage of thinking (Stage 2) that rejects Stage 1 thinking. Similarly, to get from Stage 3 to Stage 5, one must first come to reject the thinking of Stage 3, and the organized reflection on its inadequacies is denoted as Stage 4. The development of social-conventional reasoning, then, is characterized by successive periods of affirmation and negation. The negation levels are periods of disequilibrium that mark the transition from a lower to a higher stage (Turiel, 1974, 1977).

Disequilibrium is induced when an individual notices contradictions, discrepancies, and conflicts in the application of one's current mode of thinking about social organization and social conventions. This conflict leads to a reevaluation of the adequacy of one's thinking and a rejection of specific conventions. The disequilibrium of the negation phase will give rise to a new affirmation of social convention as elements of the lower stage are transformed and integrated into a new stage of thinking. Turiel (1974, 1983a) suggests that the negation levels have their own defining characteristics and that the dialectical shifting between periods of affirmation and negation reflect the continuous construction and reconstruction of social-conventional concepts across development.

Perhaps we can get a handle on this stage sequence by focusing on the four affirmation stages (see Table 6.1). Recall that each stage reflects a particular understanding of social organization and of social convention. At Stage 1 the child (age six to seven) has no systematic understanding of social organization. She is aware of

TABLE 6.1   Stages of Social-Conventional Reasoning

Stage 1	Convention describes uniform behavior (age 6–7).
Stage 2	Negation of Stage 1 understanding of convention as mere social uniformities. Conventional acts are arbitrary, and the fact that "everybody does it" is not sufficient to maintain the convention (age 8–9).
Stage 3	Conventions affirm the rule system. Although the rules are arbitrary and changeable, we follow conventions because that is what is expected by those in authority (age 10–11).
Stage 4	Negation of Stage 3 understanding that conventions are part of the rules. Conventions are nothing but social expectations (age 12–13).
Stage 5	Conventions are norms in social systems characterized by fixed roles and static hierarchical organization (age 14–16).
Stage 6	Negation of Stage 5 view that norms serve to maintain social systems. Conventions are nothing but societal standards that have become codified through habitual use (age 17–18).
Stage 7	Conventions are shared knowledge among members of a group that has the function of facilitating social interactions (age 18–25).

Source: Adapted from Turiel (1983a). Used by permission of Cambridge University Press.

status and power differences between people (e.g., doctors and nurses, teachers and students), but these differences are not connected to the functioning of institutions. She is also aware of certain social uniformities, for example, doctors are usually men and nurses are usually women, but the existence of these uniformities is thought to be part of the natural order of things. As such, they should be maintained just because they exist. This idea also shows up in the child's understanding of social conventions. Conventions are established by people who have authority, status, and power, usually because they know more and have greater expertise. Although the child views the conventions as binding, certain persons (e.g., the authorities) may be excepted. The purpose of conventions in social life is also dimly understood. It is their mere existence that gives conventional rules the authority they have. Hence, conventions, and the social uniformities that they induce, are considered binding just because they exist, not because they have some role to play in coordinating social interaction. In other words, a conventional rule (e.g., kids should address teachers by a formal title) is justified just because everyone does it. But what if some kids don't address teachers by their formal titles, wouldn't this undermine the justification for the convention? If it is behavioral uniformity itself that justifies the conventional rule, shouldn't violations of uniformity undermine the rule? This is not well understood by Stage 1 children. Deviations from social uniformity do not seem to undermine the binding authority of the conventional rule. This inconsistency, and the fact that authorities can depart from the rule that is otherwise considered binding by the child, prepare the child for the Stage 2 negation of Stage 1. At Stage 2 the child rejects the idea that mere uniformity is the basis of social conventions, and also the idea that conventional rules attach to the personal authority of specific adults.

A new affirmation of social convention emerges at Stage 3. Whereas the Stage 1 child has no understanding of social organization and tends to view convention as mere behavioral uniformity to the individual authority of powerful others, the Stage 3 child is now aware of social systems. What is more, conventions are seen to follow from social structures. Unlike the child at Stage 1, at Stage 3 child attempts to explicitly connect social-conventional rules to the functioning of social organizations. Here rules attach not to persons (as at Stage 1) but to persons who have *roles* within the authority structure of the social system. One is obliged to obey conventional rules not because everyone seems to be doing so, that is, not on the basis of mere social uniformity (as at Stage 1) but rather because conventional expectations are part of a rule system. Rules can be changed, certainly, and specific acts are considered arbitrary unless otherwise covered by a social convention within a particular social system. It is the rule system that coordinates social relations, and it is the system itself that provides a basis for uniformity. Hence, departures from behavioral uniformity do not undermine the legitimacy of social conventions (as at Stage 2). But what is missing at Stage 3? What is missing is a clear understanding of the function of conventional rules. The child certainly understands that social systems have a certain structure that produces behavioral uniformities; that is, the child understands that social conventions are connected to elements of social systems, but why must conventional rules take exactly this form? The child understands that the social system coordinates social relations and thereby affirms its authority and rules, but what is not understood is how these social relations are coordinated for particular functions. Because the child does not see the broader function of conventional rules within social systems, that is, does not see that rules coordinate social relations for particular functions, the child comes to see, at Stage 4, that conventions serve no real purpose at all. They are nothing but social expectations that do not have the force of rules that have to be obeyed. Hence, social conventions are completely arbitrary and one is not obliged to conform to them. This does not mean that Stage 4 children do not understand that social organizations have general aims. Social interactions are not aimless. There is a point to what happens within a classroom or a business office. But what is not understood is how social conventional rules contribute to these aims. Hence, the functions of social groups and social-conventional expectations are not understood at Stage 4. This negation of Stage 3 is followed by another reaffirmation of social convention at Stage 5.

At Stage 5 one appreciates the fact that one is part of a hierarchically organized collective, often referred to as society. The society is a complex organization of different role statuses. Tenured professors have more status and authority than untenured professors. Professors, whether tenured or not, have more status and authority than students. Teachers have more status than children. Physicians have more status than patients, lawyers more status than clients. Society controls and guides interactions within the same group and social status and between groups of different status by a system of conventions, appropriate to status and role, that is codified. That is, behavioral uniformity is maintained among members of a group by a codified system of conventions. If I want to join the firm of Howard, Fine, and Howard, I must adopt the conventions of this firm, that is, I must dress and act in the "company way." By wearing a suit and tie, I affirm the social organization of this firm, and my place within it. Similarly, students must adopt the conventions that regulate how students are to address teachers, since the social context of the school demands that behavioral uniformity be maintained in just this way. Using the proper titles affirms the relationships and organization structure of the society called school. Hence, social conventions regulate and symbolically affirm the relations that exist within the social organization. Why should social conventions be affirmed? Because uniform behavior maintains the social group. What if one violates the social convention? Then one must be excluded from the group (e.g., expelled from school). If the violations are widespread, the very functioning or existence of the group might be threatened.

Hence, at Stage 5, conventions are seen as codified standards of conduct that maintain the structure and very definition of the social system. There is also the view, however, that social conventions are context-specific. That is, conventions are unique to a given social context and are appropriate for specific functions. This view is denied at Stage 6. At this stage, one is certainly aware that social conventions are codified standards of the social system, but one denies that these conventional standards are really necessary for carrying out the functions of the group. Social systems are not maintained by behavioral uniformity—there is no reason for professionals to wear the appropriate office uniform, or for teachers to be addressed with titles. Lawyers will still do what they do regardless of how they dress at the office. Teachers and students will still teach and learn regardless of whether titles or first names are used in the classroom. Conventions do not serve any particular function and are not necessary for the successful completion of any social task or for the maintenance of the social system. Instead, we resort to them only out of habit and tradition. Hence, whereas social conventions were thought to be nothing but the expectations of certain other people at Stage 4 (a negation of Stage 3), at Stage 6 social convention is thought to be nothing but the expectations of the social system (a negation of Stage 5). Social systems have certain functions, to be sure, but mandating uniform behavior within the system through codified social conventions has nothing to do with them.

Social convention is reaffirmed at the Stage 7, the final stage of social-conventional reasoning. At Stage 5, one views social convention as a societal code that defines the social group. Indeed, conventions affirm the status hierarchy and make possible whatever it is the social group sets out to do. At Stage 6, one doubts that these codified conventions have any useful function at all. They are nothing but behavioral expectations based on tradition and habit. At Stage 7, however, one understands that social conventions are not societal codes; they do not define the social group and are not a way of maintaining the distribution of status within the organization. Rather, conventions are shared, agreed-upon uniformities of behavior. As in Stage 6, one understands these social conventions to be behavioral uniformities that are born of tradition and habit. But one additionally sees the functional utility of these habitual modes of behavior. Their function is to coordinate social interaction and to facilitate the workings of the social system. They serve the needs of efficiency and coordination. Why should one adhere to social conventions? Because one assumes that others are aware of the same norms and will conduct themselves accordingly. Hence, one conforms because one expects others to do so.

What is the empirical status of this complicated stage sequence? The correlation of Stages with age appears to be quite strong, ranging from .80 to .90 (Turiel, 1978). In a longitudinal study Turiel (1983a) presents evidence to suggest that the direction of change is upward to higher stages. Mean stage scores were uniformly higher on a second testing (vs. the first testing) with stronger developmental differences being evident over longer testing intervals. Only 6 percent of the sample showed a stage regression over the longitudinal testing intervals (one-, two-, or three-year intervals). In addition, "some subjects who had been at affirmation levels during the first testing were at negation levels during the second testing; similarly, some subjects originally at negation levels shifted to affirmation levels" (Turiel, 1983, p. 104), which was viewed as support for the equilibration model assumed by the stage sequence. Whether subjects moved through the stage sequence in a stepwise fashion could not be addressed by these data.

Although the extant evidence on the developmental features of the sequence of social-conventional reasoning is favorable, whether movement through the stages progresses in a stepwise fashion has not been a question. Rather, most of the research has been devoted to the question of domain distinctions in social knowledge, and here the empirical evidence is remarkably clear. Let's have a closer look at this line of research.

Empirical Evidence

Suppose you interview children who have just witnessed two kinds of transgressions at school. In one case, a child hits a classmate. In the other, a child is observed to be playing during a designated work period. How would children evaluate the two transgressions? In one study of this sort, Nucci and Turiel (1978) found that children (and teachers) made sharp distinctions between the two kinds of transgressions. For example, most students and teachers denied that hitting would be permissible if there were no rule to prohibit it, whereas conventional transgressions (e.g., playing while one is supposed to be working) could be permitted in the absence of a rule. What is more, the responses of both teachers and pupils to moral transgressions focused on the intrinsic consequences of the act for the victim (e.g., harm, personal loss, violation of rights). Although preschool children rarely responded to conventional violations (unlike older children; see Nucci & Nucci, 1982b), teachers did so, and they tended to focus on the need to obey school rules in order to maintain order.

Numerous other studies have produced similar results (e.g., Nucci & Nucci, 1982a; Weston & Turiel, 1980; Smetana, 1981). Judith Smetana (1981), for example, asked young children to evaluate five moral and five conventional transgressions. The moral transgressions included the following: hitting another, not sharing, shoving, throwing water on another, and taking another's apple. The social-conventional violations included a child not participating in show-and-tell, not sitting in a designated place during story time, not saying grace before a snack, not putting toys away correctly, and not placing belongings in the designated place.

These moral and conventional violations were judged by children using a number of criteria. The *rule contingency* criterion asked, in effect: "Would this act be permitted if there were no rule to prohibit it?" The *rule relativity* criterion asked: "Would this act be permitted at home or in another school?" Children were also asked to evaluate the seriousness of the transgression and the deserved punishment. The results were quite clear. Moral transgressions are more serious rule violations than are conventional transgressions, and they deserve more punishment. Conventional transgressions are more permissible in the absence of a rule and are held to be relative to social context. Moral transgressions are prohibited regardless of social context and regardless of whether an explicit school rule is in force.

Since conventional and moral rules are not treated similarly by children, Smetana (1981) concluded that Piaget's claim that young children have a heteronomous respect for rules in general may not be correct and that children's differential understanding of moral and conventional rules may spring from different kinds of social interactions in infancy. "Rudimentary notions of social convention may arise from the infant's earliest communication games and interactions with a caretaker. Moral concepts may develop from early social interactions involving harm to persons and sharing" (Smetana, 1981, p. 1336; also, Smetana, 1985) Indeed, in a later study, Smetana (1989) found that mothers responded in different ways to the moral and conventional transgressions of their toddlers. Whereas conventional violations were often met with undifferentiated commands that the behavior cease or that the child mind the rules, moral transgressions were responded to with requests that the child attend to the victim's perspective and the consequences of his or her action or with an evaluation of rights. This suggests that moral and conventional understandings are constructed very early in life from different kinds of social interactions both at home and in school.

Smetana's (1981) study nicely illustrates the general research strategy in this tradition. Children (and adults) are presented with either naturally occurring events or events in a story format. The event is typically a rule violation. In an interview children are asked to make a number of criterion judgments. Is the behavior right or wrong? How serious is the transgression? Would the proscribed behavior be permitted in another school or country or at home? Could we change the rule regarding X? Would the action be permitted if there were no rule to prohibit it? Over 30 studies (see Turiel, Killen, & Helwig, 1987; Killen, 1991; Smetana, 1983, for reviews) have provided convincing evidence that children do indeed make conceptual distinctions between morality and social convention. Moral rules are directed to aspects of social interactions that involve intrinsic harm (injury, loss, violation of rights, etc.). They are prescriptive and universalizable. They cannot be altered by consensus. It is always wrong to hit or cause injury, always wrong to steal, and no school authority can make these actions permissible. No one is entitled to weaken or to eliminate moral rules. We just can't decide among ourselves that on Tuesdays it will be permissible to hit our neighbors, break their pencils, or take things from them. Conventional rules, in contrast, are directed to features of social organization. They are binding because they make organizations work better. But they are relative to social context. Other social organizations can have different rules or no rules at all regarding some class of behavior. And social-conventional rules can be changed by the relevant authority or by consensus. If there were no rules to the contrary, students could address teachers by their first names, boys could use the girls' bathroom, one could speak without first raising one's hand, one could go up the down staircase, or eat with one's fingers, and the like.

Although very young children distinguish between moral and social-conventional events, this is not to suggest that children acquire or utilize all of the criterion judgments at once or that the domain distinction is evident across the full range of transgressions that might be evident on the playground, in school, or at home. There are, in fact, interesting sources of variation. Siegal and Storey (1985) found, for example, that newly enrolled day-care children do not make the moral-conventional domain distinction as readily as do "veterans" of day care. The application of criterion judgments for making domain distinction shows greater stability and generality with age (Tisak & Turiel, 1988) and appears to be acquired in an orderly fashion (Smetana & Braeges, 1990). Under some conditions, children will recommend that one should violate a moral rule rather than commit a serious, highly deviant social-conventional transgression, particularly if peer approval is at stake (Tisak & Turiel, 1988). Although abused and neglected youngsters are sensitive to the domain distinction between morality and convention, they do give variable ratings of moral transgressions. Abused children consider psychological distress more universally wrong than do neglected children. Neglected children regard unfair access to resources more universally wrong than do abused children; both results reflect the character of their respective rearing and socialization experiences (Smetana, Kelly, & Twentyman, 1984).

Is the moral-conventional domain distinction unique to American samples, or is it a universal feature of social cognition? A number of studies have shown that children in other societies also distinguish between morality and social convention in much the same way as do North American samples (Song, Smetana, & Kim, 1987; Nucci, Turiel, & Encarnacion-Gawrych, 1983; Hollos, Leis, & Turiel, 1986), although the cross-cultural generality of this domain distinction has also been contested (Nisan, 1987, 1988; Shweder, Mahapatra, & Miller, 1987; Gabennesch, 1990; see Turiel, Killen, & Helwig, 1987; Turiel, Nucci, & Smetana, 1988; Turiel, Hildebrandt, & Wainryb, 1991, for commentary).

Does the domains approach to social knowledge have any educational implications? Larry Nucci (1982, 1991; Nucci & Weber, 1991) has been most keen to draw out the implications of this research tradition for values education. In his view values education should be sensitive to the domain distinction between morality and social convention. He argues that contemporary moral education strategies are quite limited because the teaching of social values is not coordinated with students' differentiated understanding of morality and convention. Too often moral issues are conflated with social conventional issues with the unhappy result that social issues of great complexity are simply reduced to the moral component. It is domain inappropriate, for example, to treat violations of social convention as if they were moral issues. Similarly, one would not want to promote social-conventional knowledge by considering moral issues. The moral and conventional domains are distinct, each follows its own line of development, and values education should be sensitive to this fact.

Indeed, even contentious issues such as premarital sexuality or drug usage by adolescents may not be obvious moral issues insofar as these may well be considered personal matters that fall outside the purview of moral or even conventional regulation (Nucci, 1991). Consequently, values education should be coordinated with domains, since the child's own "natural epistemology" differentiates among different categories of social knowledge. Hence, in Nucci's view, the aim of a social-conventional intervention is

> to move students through the progression of stages in conceptions of convention toward a coordinated understanding of the importance of convention for the organization and coordination of social interactions within social systems. As a result students should be able to comprehend the function of these arbitrarily designated traditions and customs for the maintenance of cultural organization and cultural continuity, while appreciating the ways in which variations in convention serve to define differing cultural patterns. (Nucci, 1982, p. 107)

One implication, then, is that students should be encouraged to develop their thinking about the role of social conventions in the functioning of societal organizations, and in a way that disentangles conventional issues from moral issues.

A second implication concerns disciplinary practices in the schools. Teachers who make domain-inappropriate responses to student transgressions are not viewed as legitimate socialization agents (Nucci, 1984, 1985). A teacher loses credibility with students if he moralizes about, say, violating the dress code, chewing gum in class, or other matters of social convention. Teachers who are sensitive to the domain distinction in their disciplinary practices are more positively evaluated by students and are seen as more credible sources of authority.

A third implication concerns what to make of disruptive students. In a longitudinal study Geiger and Turiel (1983) found that most disruptive junior high students, that is, adolescents who defy school authority and who violate classroom regulations, were scored at Stage 4 in the social-conventional stage sequence. Recall that Stage 4 describes a period of negation of social convention as an aspect of a rule system. Virtually all of the nondisruptive students were scored at Stage 5, a stage that affirms convention as part of the rule system. When 20 disruptive students were retested a year later, 13 were considered nondisruptive. Twelve of these 13 students had acquired Stage 5 as a major or minor stage. Of the 7 students who were still disruptive a year later, 4 showed no stage change, and 3 had acquired Stage 5 as a minor stage. These results suggest that Stage 5 is clearly associated with good conduct, whereas Stage 4, with some exceptions, is associated with disruptive behavior. Hence, many of the ordinary conduct problems often seen in youngsters who make the transition to junior highschool may well represent developmental changes in students' understanding of social-conventional rules.

Are there other domains of social knowledge in addition to the moral and social-conventional domains? I have alluded to a third domain that implicates a realm of personal prerogatives that are understood to be conceptually distinct from both moral prescription and conventional regulation. Private aspects of one's life, behaviors that affect no one else but the self or are considered one's own business, are thought not to invoke considerations of moral obligation or of societal convention. What friends to choose, what recreational activities to engage in, what books to read, how to groom or dress, whether to masturbate—these are private matters that reflect upon the actor and are not subject to moral evaluation or regulation by the conventions of society.

In one study Nucci (1981) found that subjects readily sorted various behaviors into moral, conventional, and personal domains, indicating that individuals make clear distinctions about how to categorize many kinds of social behavior. Furthermore, subjects judged moral violations (e.g., stealing, hitting, lying) to be more serious than violations of social convention (e.g., addressing a teacher by her first name, chewing gum in class, talking without raising one's hand). In turn, conventional violations were judged to be more serious than personal violations (boy wearing long hair, playing with a forbidden friend, keeping correspondence private). If a behavior has an impact on others, it is generally subsumed under a moral heading. If the behavior has an implication for the effective functioning of organizations, it is judged to be a matter of etiquette, custom, or social convention. If the behavior appears to affect only the self, if it is seen as a matter of personal preference and autonomy or an expression of personal identity, then it is a matter not subject to moral prescription or societal regulation. Indeed, as I noted previously, many adolescents may well consider drug use and premarital sexuality as personal matters (Nucci, Guerra, & Lee, 1989) rather than as matters that should entail moral or societal regulation. Consequently, it is ill advised, in Nucci's (1991) view, to treat all troublesome adolescent behaviors as if they are amenable to moral education or as evidence of weak moral character. Morality is not implicated unless adolescents view their conduct in terms of its consequences for the welfare of others. Once again, values education should be coordinated with domains of social knowledge.

Finally, the domains approach also provides an interesting perspective of the nature of religious prescription. In one study Nucci (1985) asked Roman Catholics to evaluate a long list of sins in light of two criterion judgments: (1) Would it be all right for the pope and cardinals to drop the ban against this sin?

(2) Would it be permissible for another religion to engage in these proscribed activities if this religion had no rules or laws condemning them? The list included such sins as rape, stealing, slander, murder, ridiculing a cripple, betraying secrets, kidnapping, and other moral offenses. The list also included sins against church conventions, such as not attending Sunday mass, ordaining women, receiving communion without confession, and not attending mass on Easter or Christmas. The two questions were also applied to a number of sexual conventions, including masturbation, birth control, divorce, premarital sex, and homosexuality.

Nucci (1985) found that Catholic high school and college students rated the moral offenses to be significantly greater transgressions than the conventional transgressions. This finding is similar to what is typically reported in this literature, namely that moral and conventional transgressions are not evaluated in the same way; moral transgressions are more serious rule violations than are conventional transgressions and merit greater punishment. Hence these Catholics are clearly drawing a distinction between morality, which is "serious," and conventional church and sexual rules, which are less serious.

Could the pope and cardinals change the rules regarding these transgressions? The Catholics in this sample were almost universally agreed that church authorities could not alter the ban against the moral offenses, that is, rape, murder, and stealing are always wrong, and no authority can alter this fact. The church has no authority to remove rules regarding moral transgressions. In a sense, these activities are condemnable regardless of what is taught by the church, which suggests that morality enjoys a measure of autonomy with respect to religious beliefs.

What about church and sexual conventions? On this score a majority of Catholics thought it was permissible for the church to change its position on such matters as birth control, the ordination of women, and premarital sex. Clearly, for many Catholics, these behaviors are matters of church convention and have force in light of organizational commitment and not on moral grounds. Would it be permissible for members of other religions to engage in these practices if their denomination had no rule banning them? Most Catholics were willing to relativize transgressions against church and sexual conventions, but not moral transgressions. Hence, whereas it would not be wrong for other religions to ordain women or to permit masturbation or premarital sex, it would still be wrong for other religions to permit moral offenses. Moral rules have a universalizable intent and are binding regardless of social context or religious commitment. This universalizable element does not seem to be present in the evaluation of church conventions or sexual practices, suggesting that these latter activities are imbued with a conventional value system, not a moral one. One implication of these findings is that whereas official church teaching may view birth control as a moral issue, most American Catholics view it as a conventional issue; herein may lie the source of resistance to this official teaching on the part of many American Catholics. Whether dissenting Catholics are correct in their appraisal of birth control as a conventional (or personal) issue is not, of course, addressed by this research.

These findings have been replicated with other samples of Catholics (Turiel et al., 1991, Study 2), as well as with samples of Amish Mennonites, orthodox Jews, and fundamentalist Christians (Nucci, 1985, 1991). For example, children were asked if God's command could make some act, such as stealing, morally permissible. Most children denied that this was possible. As one Calvinist child put it, "If God said to steal, and the Devil said 'don't steal,' we would worship the Devil" (cited in Nucci, 1991, p. 32).

These intriguing findings support the notion that religious believers are also sensitive to domain distinctions between moral and conventional rules, even when it comes to religious prescriptions. It also suggests that it is not religious belief that under girds morality. In one of Plato's dialogues Socrates puts this question: "Is the pious loved by the gods because it is pious, or is it pious because it is loved by the gods?" (*Euthyphro*, in Grube, trans., 1975). In modern idiom this might read: "Is something moral because God approves it, or does God approve it because it is moral?" If God approves of it because it is moral (and it is not moral simply because God approves of it), then morality is distinct from piety and rests on a foundation independent of religious commitments, or even belief in God. This way of answering the question is compatible with Nucci's research on domain distinctions between morality and religious convention (Nucci, 1991).

We are now in a position to consider a number of critical reactions to this provocative research program, which I will take up in the next section.

Critical Appraisal

Turiel's research program is often viewed as an attempt to shrink the moral domain to its proper dimensions. That is, the moral domain should not include matters of social convention or matters of personal prerogatives, since these are conceptually distinct domains, and even young children know it. Furthermore, moral and conventional judgments follow independent lines of development, since they are constructed from qualitatively different kinds of social interactions and social experiences. If different domains of social knowledge are constructed from different kinds of social experiences and therefore follow independent lines of development, one would not expect to find interdependencies among these domains (Turiel, 1983b). There would be no theoretical reason, for example, to expect one domain of reasoning to be necessary but not sufficient for reasoning in another domain.

Turiel's work is viewed as a strong challenge to Kohlberg's theory. Kohlberg's theory describes, for example, a conventional level of moral development (Stages 3 and 4), implying that morality and social conventions are not clearly distinguishable, at least not until one reaches the principled level of moral reasoning (Stages 5 and 6). In addition, as noted in Chapter 4, Kohlberg did indeed view the relationship among domains of reasoning as a series of interdependencies: Cognitive development is necessary but not sufficient for social-cognitive development (perspective-taking); social-cognitive development is necessary but not sufficient for moral development. What, then, is the Kohlbergian response to the challenge posed by the domains approach?

Kohlberg suggests that claims regarding the scope of the moral domain must be grounded by a philosophical analysis that is corroborated by empirical evidence (Kohlberg et al., 1983). The domains approach is faulted on both counts. A philosophical justification for shrinking the moral domain is absent, and empirical evidence regarding the hard structural characteristics of the social-conventional stage sequence is not yet available. Are these reasonable criticisms?

Although there is some evidence that speaks favorably to the sequential properties of the social-conventional stage sequence, it is fair to say that the range of evidence that is typically adduced in support of a stage theory in the social-cognitive domain does not seem to be available (Lapsley et al., 1989). But it is not entirely accurate to say that a philosophical specification of the domain distinction is lacking. Turiel (1983a) does indeed appeal to an ethical tradition that draws a distinction between morality and convention (e.g., Dworkin, 1978; Gewirth, 1978). In fact, Turiel and Kohlberg share this tradition. It is a distinctive feature of the Kantian deontological tradition that a sharp demarcation be made between what is moral and what is nonmoral, with "morality" being defined in terms of certain formal criteria. Hence, both Kohlberg and Turiel share the same definition of the moral, and they share the idea that not all value concerns are distinctly moral concerns. They would appear to differ on other matters, such as when psychological subjects make the domain distinction and the nature of structural development.

In a later paper Colby and Kohlberg (1987) acknowledged the impressive evidence that even young children make domain distinctions between morality and conventions. When Kohlberg uses the term "conventional" to describe the second level of moral development, he does not mean that children fail to make domain distinctions. Rather, he implies "a focus on socially shared moral norms and roles as the basis for making *morally* prescriptive judgments of rights, responsibilities and so on" (Colby & Kohlberg, 1987, p. 11). Colby and Kohlberg (1987) also suggests that just because the domains appear to be distinct, this does not mean that the domains are independent. There is no reason to give up the notion that there are interdependencies among domains just because children seem to distinguish morality and conventions:

> The fact that children from the beginning can tell moral concerns apart from conventional concerns does not imply that the two sets of concerns do not inform and influence one another. Conventional and moral concerns, in fact, are so closely intertwined that one frequently becomes the other in the course of development, as when, certain issues of sexual propriety are transformed from moral into conventional issues in an individual's thinking. (p. 15)

The notion that moral and conventional concerns are "closely intertwined" is not necessarily a lethal criticism. Indeed, the domains approach readily acknowledges that complex social events may involve both moral and conventional considerations and that the same event may be construed differently by different individuals. But the "closely intertwined" argument is sometimes thought to point to a more telling criticism, namely that there are perhaps many cases where "conventional" activities have profound moral implications.

Along this line James Rest (1983) does not think that the conceptual distinction between morality and social convention makes much sense. This is because morality does not exist in the abstract but is instead embedded in social organizations. Indeed, both social convention and morality logically implicate concepts of social organization. As Rest (1983, p. 609) puts it, "How could there be justice or morality *without* social organization?" What is more, moral reasoning presupposes social organizations and provides criteria for evaluating social practices and arrangements. I take this to mean (in part) that the fact that children and adults discriminate between the conventional and the moral does not mean that they ought to make such discriminations. Adolescents may well view drug usage or premarital sex as mere conventional regulations or as personal prerogatives; that is, they may deny the moral aspects of these behaviors, but this does not necessarily mean that they are right to do so.

Rest (1983) is particularly troubled by Turiel's narrow understanding of what gives an act a distinctly moral status. For Turiel, an act takes on moral implications only if it has direct and intrinsic consequences for the welfare of another. This definition of the moral is too narrow, in Rest's view, because a person's welfare can also be affected by social arrangements or by certain societal practices that may well be conventional in the defining sense that the particular arrangement or practice is arbitrary or relative to a particular society or historical context. Rest (1983) lists the following examples: driving on the right hand of the street, paying taxes on April 15, having presidential elections every four years in November. Although these practices are relative to American society and are arbitrary in the sense that other practices could be substituted in their stead, they nonetheless have moral implications in the sense that they bear on human welfare. "Therefore, we cannot relegate these social practices to a domain separate and independent of morality" (Rest, 1983, p. 609). Furthermore, one can think of examples whereby violations of social convention would have moral implications (e.g., wearing a bikini to a funeral) and where instances of "intrinsic harm" would not necessarily be judged immoral (female circumcision). Hence social convention and morality are related to each other in complex ways that defy their categorization into independent domains (Rest, 1983).

How might Turiel respond to this sort of criticism? In a recent paper Turiel (1989) reiterates his view that there are indeed "hard" or "marginal" cases where there appears to be considerable overlap between domains (Turiel & Davidson, 1986). But he insists that evidence of domain ambiguity, overlap, or mixture does not invalidate the conceptual distinction between morality and social convention. If exceptional cases invalidate a category distinction, then the gender categories male and female would be invalidated by the existence of hermaphrodites. Indeed, Rest's (1983) counter examples have force, Turiel (1989) suggests, just because Rest has a prior theoretical commitment to the view that morality is global and cannot, therefore, be distinguished from social organization. When Rest looks at ambiguous cases, he concludes that morality and convention cannot be independent domains and that category distinctions are illegitimate; he is committed to the view that moral judgments cannot be confined to a specific domain. When Turiel looks at ambiguous cases, he sees them as complex examples where moral and conventional considerations have to be disentangled and coordinated; that is, complex, exceptional cases do not invalidate the general category distinctions.

In a recent monograph Turiel and his colleagues take up this issue more directly by investigating how individuals make judgments about hard case nonprototypical social issues such as abortion, homosexuality, pornography, and incest (Turiel et al., 1991). They refer to these as nonprototypical issues because they are quite unlike the typical exemplars of moral and conventional problems identified by their research program. A typical moral issue involves considerations of intrinsic harm, rights, welfare, and justice and has universalizable implications. A moral rule is not contingent on common practice, consensus, or agreement. Immoral conduct must be proscribed. Moral rules, then, are generalizable, prescriptive, and context-free or noncontingent. A prototypical moral issue would be something like killing, rape, or theft.

In contrast, conventional and personal issues do not revolve around issues of intrinsic harm or justice. Conventional rules are directed toward bringing about efficient social organization, can be altered by consensus, and have force by virtue of common agreement or practice. Unlike moral rules, personal-conventional rules are therefore contingent, nongeneralizable, and nonprescriptive. Prototypical issues in this domain include such things as the propriety of eating horsemeat, going nude at a public beach, men's wearing makeup, or smoking marijuana.

Insofar as the two domains (moral vs. personal-conventional) are to be differentiated in accordance with these criteria (rule contingency, generalizability, prescriptivity), it should be clear that our hard cases are not at all typical of either domain. The status of abortion, pornography, and homosexuality is contentious, and public discourse has taken a variety of positions with respect to their legal and moral implications. It may well be the case, for example, that one may evaluate abortion as killing or as doing intrinsic harm to a person who bears significant human rights but may nonetheless retreat from generalizing this judgment to others or condone abortion as a private matter. Abortion (for example) is nonprototypical because it has criteria features of both domains.

In one study, two groups of individuals were identified. In one group, subjects indicated that they thought these issues (e.g., abortion, pornography, homosexuality) were moral issues and that it was "not all right" to sanction their practice (or "it depends"). Another group thought that these were nonmoral issues and that it was "all right" to sanction their practice (or "it depends"). They were then asked to evaluate one issue from each domain, that is, a prototypical moral issue (rape, killing), a prototypical personal-conventional issue (see previous examples), and a nonprototypical issue (see previous examples). How did the two groups approach these issues?

The results with respect to the prototypic moral and conventional issues were in accordance with prior research—killing and rape are wrong (negative evaluation), it is always wrong to engage in these practices (universalizability), it should be wrong everywhere (generalizability) and in spite of common practice or agreement (rule contingency), and they should be legally proscribed. A consideration of rights and justice compels this evaluation. In contrast, the personal-conventional practices are a matter of personal choice, are contingent on local practice, are positively evaluated, and are not subject to legal prohibition.

A greater diversity of opinion was evident, however, in the evaluation of the nonprototypical issues. Even subjects (Group 1) who had negative evaluations of abortion, pornography, and homosexuality and who were convinced that these issues were indeed moral issues reasoned about these putative moral issues differently than they did about killing and rape. In brief, these subjects condemned the nonprototypical practices, viewing them as morally wrong (just as they did killing and rape), yet they were unwilling to endorse their legal regulation, leaving their practice up to personal choice (just as with prototypic personal-conventional issues). Hence, unlike when judging prototypical moral issues such as killing and rape, subjects allowed notions of choice and personal jurisdiction to influence their judgment of nonprototypic issues.

According to the authors this shows that social reasoning is "heterogeneous" (Turiel et al., 1991). Different kinds of judgments are possible depending on the social domain in question. Sometimes judgments, evaluations, and justifications are similar and consistent; sometimes not. For example, consistent judgments were evident for the clear-cut, prototypic issues in the moral and personal domains. For prototypic moral issues, individuals make prescriptive judgments, grounded by considerations of rights, justice and welfare, that are noncontingent and generalizable. But this way of moral judging coexists with judgments about personal issues, which are grounded by considerations of personal choice, context, and contingency. And these moral and personal-conventional ways of judging coexist as well with reasoning about nonprototypical issues—issues that do not fall cleanly into either domain. "Accordingly, the results demonstrate that each subject maintains noncontingent, generalizable prescriptive judgments about clear-cut moral issues alongside judgments about the validity of personal choice and jurisdiction with regard to some socially meaningful issues" (Turiel et al., 1991, p. 79).

To say that social reasoning is heterogeneous and is structured by different social domains is thought to count against those sociological (Gabbennesch, 1990) and anthropological (Shweder et al., 1987) perspectives that argue that moral rationality can be reduced to conventional social practice or is otherwise a reflection of a homogenous, single cultural orientation (e.g., individualism). It perhaps counts against the sort of criticism mounted by Rest (1983) as well—that moral concerns are invariably embedded in social organizations and therefore cannot be cleanly segregated from putatively nonmoral (conventional) issues.

According to Turiel, however, context is not unitary. Society, culture, and social organization are not one homogenous thing. Morality is not global. Individuals do not simply assimilate issues of great complexity to the moral domain. Individuals make differentiated judgments that are coordinated with different domains. They apply domain-appropriate criteria to social issues. Even when confronted with complex (nonprototypical) issues that overlap domains, individuals attempt some sort of integration or coordination (Killen, 1990). There are many kinds of social interactions, some of which are made problematic by varying construals and assumptions about social reality—and domains of social reasoning reflect this fact.

Definitional Issues and the Unity of the Moral Self

Another type of criticism is possible. Some critics point out that the various domain distinctions simply follow from Turiel's definitional preferences. That is, Turiel begins with a particular definition of the moral and, armed with this definition, proceeds to carve up social knowledge into domains. For example, following the Kantian tradition, moral considerations are just those that are deontic, universalizable, nonarbitrary, and prescriptive and that have intrinsic, interpersonal consequences. If some instance does not meet this definition, it is not a moral consideration. If some rule is contextually relative, arbitrary, and alterable by consensus and has implications for social organization, it is conventional, not moral. Similarly, if an instance is not moral, that is, is not universally obligatory, and is not conventional, that is, has no implications for social organization and indeed has relevance only for the actor, it is personal. Actions that are judged to be one's own business and have implications only for the agent fall outside of the moral and conventional domains into a domain of personal prerogatives.

Clearly, if these distinctions follow from a particular definitional preference, it is also possible that others may indeed quarrel with the various domain distinctions from the perspective of an alternative set of definitions. In other words, it may be that the domain distinctions make sense only if we buy into a particular definition of the moral. As Blasi (1990, p. 44) puts it, "While Turiel gives the impression that his definition of morality is in fact so universally used as to constitute genuine common understanding, in reality it is the result of an a priori philosophical choice that he and his colleagues have made."

In Chapter 5, I noted that one criticism of Kohlberg's theory is that he endorsed a narrow and minimalist conception of the moral life. What is neglected in Kohlbergian theory is the notion of virtuous character, or a "thick" conception of the moral self (Punzo & Meara, 1993). Perhaps a similar criticism can be mounted here against the domains distinction, particularly as it relates to the personal domain. The personal domain includes those choices that are neither demanded by moral obligation nor suggested by custom, etiquette, or convention. How to dress, what books to read, what friends to choose, whether to masturbate, whether to use drugs, these may well fall beyond the purview of morality and convention into a domain of personal prerogative.

But to define the moral domain in such a way as to exclude notions of virtue and character, indeed, to limit the moral domain to simply those hard cases that require impartial conflict resolution (Kohlberg) or to those cases that involve intrinsic consequences for the welfare of others (Turiel), would seem very odd from the perspective of virtue ethics. It is not morality as such that is demarcated from social convention, but rather a particular conception of morality as defined by a particular ethical tradition. The domain distinctions would not make much sense from the perspective of other ethical traditions.

From the perspective of virtue ethics, for example, the personal domain is indeed a moral domain. From the standpoint of virtue, the personal domain cannot be considered a refuge from our ethical concerns about the moral agent in his or her personhood (Blasi, 1990). The domain of moral choice cannot be compartmentalized in this way, for individual choices, even those that deal with private matters, even those that affect the agent alone, even those that one would not dream of universalizing, can be subjectively obligatory in ethically relevant ways given our conception of what it means to live a good life with integrity (Witherell & Edwards, 1991; Lapsley, 1992b). For choices of vocation, friends to cultivate, books to read, recreations to pursue, and more, all have a bearing on the development of moral character (Norton, 1988), on the sort of person one claims oneself to be—to such an extent that certain courses of action, certain options, are prescribed given the particularities of our moral identity. Many personal choices, both public and private, implicate the moral status of the self just because they are reflections of our identity and character (Lapsley, 1992b).

In short, those who criticize the domains distinction worry about two related things. First, they worry about the unity of the moral self given the compartmentalization of social knowledge into domains. Compartmentalization, a hallmark of modernity, usually breeds concerns about fragmentation and unity (Habermas, 1990). Second, they worry about the marginalization of morality, that the purview of morality has been diminished, shrunk into a corner—that large and expanding areas of our common and private life have become shielded from the demands of moral evaluation. And they worry about the impression that morality is "an occasional part-time activity," some "specialized isolated moment appearing in a continuum of non-moral activity," that it is the product of some ethical faculty that can be switched on and off on separate occasions of moral choice (Murdoch, 1992, pp. 297, 303).

Critics who worry about fragmentation and marginalization are tempted to resort to what Turiel calls global perspectives on morality. Indeed, we can now identify the common theme in the criticism of the psychologist (Rest), the sociologist (Gabbenesch), and the anthropologist (Shweder). These critics, each in their own way, attempt to assert the priority of the ethical life in human affairs. Each attempts to assert its unity and centrality. Each reflects a general reluctance to see the ethical component of human life whittled away into a neat conceptual box.

The novelist-philosopher Iris Murdoch (1992) might also be said to have a global perspective on morality. In her view, moral evaluation is thoroughly infused throughout the fabric of human life. There is an "immanent morality" in all of human consciousness (Murdoch, 1992) just because construal, evaluation, and interpretation—the effort to see clearly and truthfully no matter what the issue—already presuppose a commitment to values, already presuppose a particular character. Even our simplest decisions are "haunted" by moral discrimination (Murdoch, 1992, p. 26). What we see often depends on who we are. There is a moral consideration that is prior even to the sorting of issues into domains. Indeed, the "omnipresence of morality" (Murdoch, 1992, p. 39) is implicated in all our acts of perceiving, of surveying the social landscape, of discriminating, of making judgments of all kinds.

The domains approach does not, of course, endorse the marginalization of morality or the fragmentation of the moral self. The domains approach would probably locate the unity of the self in cognitive acts of domain coordination. Morality is not marginalized but simply accorded its proper place among the differentiated judgments of which human reason is capable. However, the domains approach is hostile to what it regards as global perspectives on morality, largely because these perspectives are unwilling to acknowledge the differentiated judgments that individuals do make in response to a messy and complicated social reality. Is common ground possible? Can the "omnipresence of morality" perspective be reconciled with the notion of domain-centered rationality? Are so-called global views of morality committed to the notion that social reality is homogeneous? These are questions that I leave with the reader.

7

Moral Orientations: Gender, Benevolence, Caring

Overview of the Great Gender Debate

In 1976 Constance Holstein published the results of a longitudinal study that was to have far-reaching implications. Holstein appeared to discover a gender bias in the Kohlberg scoring rules (Structural Issue Scoring). Although Holstein's data do not unambiguously support such a charge (as we will see), they were widely taken to suggest that female respondents to the Kohlberg interview are typically scored at Stage 3, whereas male respondents are typically scored at Stage 4. Insofar as higher stages are more adequate in both a moral and psychological sense, it would appear that the moral judgments of women are outpaced by the more mature judgments of men. Holstein argued that the relational themes of Stage 3, with its emphasis on compassion, sympathy, and love, are congruent with the communal, expressive feminine sex role in American society, in contrast to the agentic, instrumental sex role for men. Yet as one moves up the Kohlbergian stages, the moral reasons adduced from the feminine perspective are increasingly devalued as a lower form of moral reasoning. Kohlberg's scoring rules are insensitive to feminine moral sensibilities, Holstein argues, largely because they were derived from a sample of "young white males": "Emotional response to moral conflict which is exemplified by females more than males results in adult female reasoning being *categorized with children*" (Holstein, 1976, p. 61, emphasis added).

In the following year Carol Gilligan (1977) began a systematic exploration of gender themes in developmental theory, which culminated in her landmark book *In a Different Voice* (Gilligan, 1982). This book sparked a stimulating, and sometimes contentious, debate that was not at all confined to the narrow halls of academic developmental psychology. Gilligan argues that developmental theory has traditionally associated ideal development with the masculine ideal, with the consequence that the uniquely feminine line of development is either ignored or misinterpreted. Her argument applies to Kohlberg's theory as well.

Kohlberg's description of the moral ideal reflects the themes of separation, autonomy, and independence, but these themes are bound up with masculine sensibilities and devolve from male socialization experiences. The moral problem, for Kohlberg, is one of opponents who clash over rights. Opponents are free and autonomous agents whose rights-claims are to be equally and impartially considered, and it is suggested that there are winners and losers. Moral deliberation begins with the assumption that moral claims are best considered from an ideal perspective that is prior to society, where free-standing claimants are unencumbered by relational commitments. The need for friendships and social ties is not automatically assumed. Indeed, the calculus of conflict resolution demands that persons be stripped of identifying characteristics and treated impersonally. Fairness is a matter of contract. Just agreements must be judged fair from the perspective of anyone and must be applied universally without illegitimate and partial considera- tion of those with whom we may have special ties.

Gilligan argues that these themes are foreign to the experiences of women. Instead, women approach moral problems assuming the priority of relationships, assuming that the self is encumbered with social commitments. Their focus is on caring and benevolence and on the personal self, who is responsible for nurturing the web of relationships within which one is defined. To puzzle about hypothetical dilemmas, to reason from an idealized "perspective of eternity" (Stout, 1981), to treat persons as logical abstractions in formalized procedures that are no more than an "arithmetic problem with persons"—all of these approaches are at odds with the feminine ethic. Hence

> the moral judgments of women differ from those of men in the greater extent to which women's judgment's are tied to feelings of empathy and compassion and are concerned with the resolution of real as opposed to hypothetical dilemmas. However, as long as the categories by which development is assessed are derived from research on men, divergence from the masculine standard can be seen only as a failure of development. *As a result, the thinking of women is often classified with that of children.* (Gilligan, 1982, p. 70, emphasis added)

Gilligan repeats, then, Holstein's (1976) claim that the moral reasoning of females is inappropriately calibrated on a scale that is more suited to the develop- mental themes of men. But here, the perspective of women and their unique ethic is devalued, and "classified with that of children."

Since 1982 the terms of the gender debate have noticeably shifted, as we will see. The charge of gender bias in Kohlberg's theory has shifted to the claim that although men and women are more similar in Kohlbergian justice reasoning than previously supposed, there is, nonetheless, an alternative moral orientation (a "dif- ferent voice") that is friendlier to the developmental experiences of females, and it is one that Kohlberg's theory is ill suited to assess. In turn, Kohlberg attempted to incorporate some of Gilligan's insights into his most recently revised conception of the Stage 6 moral ideal (Kohlberg et al., 1990). Before considering these develop- ments, we need to look at the ethic of care and responsibility in more detail (see also, Noddings, 1984).

Moral Voices and Their Sources

The moral voices of men and women spring from different developmental sources. According to Nancy Chodorow (1989), whose views Gilligan (1982) endorses, boys and girls are confronted with two different tracks of personality development, one that emphasizes separation and individuation and another that emphasizes connection and ongoing symbiotic attachments (see also Josselson,

1988). One track emphasizes agentic differentiation and the other, communal embeddedness. These developmental tracks arise from the fact that women are almost universally the primary caretakers of young children and the masculine gender role usually draws the father away from private, domestic matters to more public social roles in society and culture.

Let's consider the case with boys (following Chodorow, 1989). Masculine gender identification is a matter of the boy coming to replace his primary identification with his mother with an identification with the male gender role, represented by father. Mothers typically assist by emphasizing the boy's masculinity in opposition to their own femininity. Yet the father is a more remote figure. His social role is typically exercised outside of the family, in the "big world" of work and culture. The inaccessibility of masculine social activities means that the boy is required to imagine or fantasize about males' roles. Consequently, his gender identification is said to be positional rather than personal. That is, the boy identifies with aspects of the male *role*, with the *position* of the father rather than with the "personal father," who is more inaccessible in the early rearing environment. However, this serves to sever male role-learning and masculine gender identification from emotional attachments. As Chodorow (1989, p. 51) puts it, "In all societies characterized by some sex segregation, much of the boy's masculine identification must be of this sort, that is, with aspects of his father's role, or what he fantasizes to be the male role, rather than with his father as a person involved in a relationship to him."

Masculine gender identification is thus a complicated affair for the boy. The boy must come to identify the masculine role with the activities of father, yet the father's role is inaccessible and elusive. This difficulty leads to an important development. Since it is difficult to imagine just what the male role entails given the relative distance of the positional father from domestic family life, it becomes necessary for the boy to define the masculine role in negative terms, that is, by defining it in terms of what it is not: It is not feminine, not like mother, not like women. Femininity is therefore devalued. In Chodorow's view, this repudiation of femininity takes two forms. First, the boy denies his attachment to his mother and with it his strong sense of dependency on a woman. Second, the boy rejects his infantile identification with the mother by repressing his own feminine sensitivities and by identifying instead with the social world outside of the family, that is, with work, society, culture, where he imagines the masculine position of his father to be located. By shifting his identification away from his mother and domestic life to imagined activities in the masculine world of society and culture, the boy attempts to denigrate femininity both within himself and in the larger society. This psychological dynamic helps explain, in Chodorow's view, "the universal social and cultural devaluation and subordination of women" (1989, p. 51). It is also clear that masculine gender identification must take place in the absence of satisfactory affective relational experiences. The attachment to the mother is devalued, but an authentic personal relationship with the father does not compensate for this devaluation. Instead, identification with the father is limited to the narrow learning of masculine roles vaguely perceived.

In contrast, gender identification is a more continuous affair for the girl. Role-learning for the girl is bound up with the activities of the "personal" mother, who is constantly available in the early rearing environment. The feminine role is bound up with a mother who is loved and with whom the child identifies. Consequently, feminine role-learning requires neither the repression of attachment nor the repudiation of identification, as is the case for boys. Mothers also identify more with daughters than with sons, making differentiation between mother and child even less an issue for girls than for boys. Indeed, the similarity between mother and daughter in terms of gender, role, and values is accentuated. The sense of connectedness is nurtured in an ongoing attachment relationship. According to Chodorow (1989, p. 52), the girl's "identification with her mother is not positional—the narrow learning of particular role behaviors—but rather a personal identification with her mother's general traits of character and values."

The structure of the family, then, leads to different experiences of separation and differentiation for boys and girls. This, in turn, leads to different trajectories of gender personality development. For the boy the masculine personality must be formed apart from the maternal relationship and independently of affective relational experiences more generally, in a world that is external to domestic family life. For the girl the feminine personality emerges in the context of continuing attachments and identifications with the mother. David Bakan (1966) suggests that this sex-typed pattern of gender socialization leads to different gender personalities. The masculine personality, he says, is oriented toward "agency," whereas the feminine personality is oriented toward "communion":

> Agency manifests itself in self-protection, self-assertion, and self-expansion; communion manifests itself in the sense of being at one with other organisms. Agency manifests itself in the formation of separations; communion in the lack of separations. Agency manifests itself in isolation, alienation, and aloneness; communion in contact, openness and union. Agency manifests itself in the urge to master; communion in noncontractual cooperation. (p. 15)

The two moral voices identified by Gilligan (1982) appear to cut along the agency-communion dimension. Because masculine development resonates to the agentic themes of separation, independence, and autonomy, the boy is oriented toward the impartial demands of justice. Because feminine development resonates to the relational themes of attachment, communion, and bonding, the female is oriented toward the felt need to care and to be responsible to other selves.

For men the moral self is an independent agent, standing alone, encumbered only by rights and rightful claims. For women, the moral self is embedded within social networks and is encumbered by responsibilities. Whereas men define the self in terms of separation, women define the self in terms of connections. Men assess the self in terms of an ideal standard of perfection, women in terms of particular activities of care. Men are concerned about the clashing rights of autonomous selves; women are concerned about the clashing responsibilities of mutually connected selves. Men attempt to resolve conflict by formatting separations: by detaching persons from their claims, by dissolving relational commitments into a hierarchy of rights, by juridically appraising claims according to the abstract conventions of logic and law. Women attempt to resolve conflict with dialogue and communication, by finding inclusive solutions that maintain connections, and by avoiding judgments that threaten the web of relationships. Men seek solutions that are fair, where fairness involves an equitable application of rules or a free contractual agreement. Women seek solutions that are benevolent, where benevolence is a matter of responsible caring. For men moral fault is linked to aggression and the violation of rights and justice. For women, moral fault is a failure to respond. For men the moral life takes place in the big world of society and culture, among fellow citizen-strangers whose activity must be coordinated by impersonal laws impartially applied. Consequently, community life demands the establishment of rules and laws so that autonomy may be protected. Indeed, formal regulations are required in order to limit aggression, confrontation, and the violation of individual rights. For women the moral life takes place within the context of personal relationships and is governed by standards of care. Images of violence and aggression are replaced with images of love, nurturance, and responsible benevolence.

The feminine ethic, then, is characterized by the impulse to care, to nurture relationships, to shoulder responsibilities. It is marked both by a sensitivity to contextual complexity and by a reluctance to pass judgment. But these notions are seen to "fall through the sieve of Kohlberg's scoring system," with the result that they are devalued as utterly conventional notions that fall outside the moral domain (Gilligan, 1982, p. 31). From the masculine perspective of rights and justice, the feminine ethic can be viewed only as an inadequate moral stance (but see Friedman, 1985, 1991).

Levels of Care

Gilligan heard the moral voice of responsibility and care in interviews of women who were facing imposing personal dilemmas (Gilligan, 1982; Gilligan & Belenky, 1980). On the basis of these interviews she suggested that the feminine ethic can be charted through three broad levels of development. At Level 1 the focus is on the needs of the self. The survival of the self is the sole object of concern. Moral conflict is a matter of the self having conflicting needs, and self-discipline, imposing sanctions on the self, is a proper moral response. When this perspective is criticized for its self-preoccupation, one enters a transitional phase. During this transition the self begins to appreciate the importance of attachments and connections, and the notion that one has a responsibility to one's relationships comes into clearer focus. Yet there is conflict between what is owed the self and what is owed to others. There is conflict between one's own wishes and needs and the responsibilities that one has for others.

At Level 2 the conflict is resolved in terms of the conventional notion of feminine goodness. The self adopts the maternal morality of self-sacrifice, where the good is equated with caring for others. Since the only legitimate target of caring is others, one's own needs are devalued. The self is excluded from the possible targets of caring. When the illogic of this position leads to problems in relationships, a second transitional phase is entered. Here there is an attempt to sort out the confusions between self-sacrifice and caring for others. The self must also be a target of caring. One attempts to be responsible to the needs of both self and other, to be sensitive to situational complexity and the consequences of one's actions in an honest and "real" way.

These tensions are further resolved at Level 3, where the injunction to care is raised to a universal obligation. Here care is a self-chosen principle that condemns exploitation and violence and enjoins one to respond.

What is seen to develop in this sequence is a progressively richer understanding of relationships. Each of the three levels reflects a particular understanding of how the self and other are related. "This ethic," Gilligan writes, "evolves around a central insight, that self and other are interdependent. . . In this sequence, the fact of interconnection informs the central, recurring recognition that just as the incidence of violence is in the end destructive to all, so the activity of care enhances both others and self" (Gilligan, 1982, p. 74).

We are now in a position to consider the empirical status of Gilligan's theory. Three research questions are of interest. (1) Is there is gender bias in Kohlberg's scoring system? A gender bias is implicated if women are habitually classified at lower stages than are men. There is the additional expectation that women will be scored at Stage 3 (given its relational perspective) and that men will be scored at higher stages. (2) Are there two moral orientations, one of justice, the other of care, and do men and women differentially prefer one to the other? If Gilligan's theory is to be sustained, then the use of moral orientation should be clearly gender related: Men should be predominantly oriented to justice issues; women should be predominantly oriented to issues of care and responsiblity. (3) Does the feminine ethic conform to the developmental sequence identified by Gilligan? This third question can be answered here. There does not appear to be sufficient evidence at the present time to evaluate the developmental features of the care-and-response orientation.

An Empirical Appraisal

Let's take up the first question. Is there a gender bias in Kohlberg's scoring system such that women are routinely classified at lower stages of moral reasoning than are men? As noted earlier, Holstein's (1976) longitudinal study was one of the first to raise the gender-bias issue (see also Haan et al., 1968). She interviewed 53 adolescents and their parents on two occasions over a three-year interval. The issue of gender bias arose twice in her study. At one point Holstein wanted to determine if the moral stages could be aligned along the liberal-conservative political dimension. She asked subjects to indicate their position on various sociopolitical issues (e.g., gun control, wiretapping, fair housing). Stage 5 subjects held more liberal attitudes on these issues than did conventional Stage 3 and Stage 4 subjects. But there were no sex differences (i.e., men and women were equally liberal at Stage

5). Stage 4 subjects were relatively conservative in their political attitudes, but again, there were no sex differences. However, Stage 3 females were significantly more liberal than were Stage 3 males. When asked to justify their political choices, females more often cited "compassion for another's suffering" (the justification of males was not indicated). Holstein suggested that this sort of justification is not only prototypic of Stage 3 with its emphasis on compassion, sympathy, or love but is also congruent with the stereotypic female role. When subjects were asked for their views on that part of Kohlberg's interview that focuses on the affectional system (i.e., on relationships, welfare concerns, role stereotypes, love, sex, intimacy), females scored at Stage 3, males at Stage 4.

The possibility of gender bias was also raised when Holstein considered evidence of stage skipping. Some young males appeared to skip from Stage 2 to Stage 4. Some young females appeared to skip from Stage 3 to Stage 5. Why would some boys skip stage 3? According to Holstein, because Stage 3 is incompatible with the traditionally instrumental male role. Why would some girls skip Stage 4? Because Stage 4 is incompatible with the traditionally expressive female role. Holstein did acknowledge, however, that the three-year interval may have been too long and that subjects may not have skipped these stages after all.

Yet other aspects of Holstein's data do not support the charge of sex bias. Although boys appeared to reason at modal Stage 4 at Time 2 and girls at modal Stage 3(4), there were no significant differences at either testing time when the continuous index of moral reasoning (moral-maturity scores) was considered. Although fathers had higher moral-maturity scores than mothers at Time 1, there were no significant differences between mothers and fathers at Time 2. What is more, the modal stage of both mothers and fathers was Stage 4 at both testing times. This would not appear to be strong evidence that the moral reasoning of women is "categorized with children's" (Holstein, 1976, p. 61).

Even though Holstein's (1976) data do not provide unequivocal evidence to sustain the gender-bias charge, perhaps an analysis of the moral-development literature as a whole would reveal such a bias. Walker (1984) conducted the most thorough review of the literature on this question. In 41 studies of children (age 5–17) only 6 reported sex differences. Of these 6, one difference was not statistically significant, and 5 favored girls. In 46 studies of adolescents and youth, only 10 reported sex differences. Of these 10, 3 were discounted on statistical or methodological grounds. Two found no overall sex difference but did report an interaction effect with sex-role identity or dilemma type. One found women more advanced than men. Two found men more advanced than women, but in ethnic groups where the status of women is low. Two final studies reported higher stage scores for men, but the difference was less than half a stage. What about adults? In 21 studies of adults, 4 reported sex differences favoring men. The modal stage score of women, however, was Stage 4.

Walker (1984) concluded that gender differences in moral reasoning are exceedingly rare. In 108 studies, only 8 clearly indicated significant sex effects, and many of these were confounded by educational level or occupational status or were scored with outdated manuals. In any event, the magnitude of difference was quite small (less than half a stage). Walker (1984, p. 688) suggested that "rather than arguing over the extent to which sex bias is inherent in Kohlberg's theory of moral development, it might be more appropriate to ask why the myth that males are more advanced than females persists in light of so little evidence."

Although Walker's (1984) review did not entirely settle the matter (Baumrind, 1986; Walker, 1986, 1991), it is fair to say that the weight of the evidence makes it difficult to sustain the charge of sex bias in Kohlberg's scoring system. Sex differences are also very rare in the DIT literature (Rest, 1979, 1983). Further, many recent studies published since these reviews typically report nonsignificant gender differences (e.g., Walker et al., 1987; Walker, 1989). Indeed, even the expectation that females are more caring, altruistic, or empathic than males may not be entirely self-evident (Brabeck, 1983; Krebs, 1970).

Although men and women appear to reason similarly within the constraints of the Kohlberg interview, perhaps it is the case that women would prefer an alternative care orientation if such an orientation was actively elicited. Are there two moral orientations, one of justice-rights and one of care-responsibility, and do women and men gravitate toward one or the other?

In a recent paper Gilligan and Wiggins (1987) suggested that it is most problematic to conclude that there are no sex differences in morality. After all, men are more likely to be deviant, antisocial, and aggressive, and women are more likely to be nurturant and empathic: "The overwhelming male composition of the prison population and the extent to which women take care of young children cannot readily be dismissed as irrelevant to theories of morality or excluded from accounts of moral development. *If there are no sex differences in empathy or moral reasoning, why are there sex differences in moral and immoral behavior?*" (p. 279, emphasis added). In their view, these sociological facts (e.g., that men are more immoral than women and woman are more nurturing than men), in addition to morally relevant differences in how boys and girls are socialized, must be woven into a new theoretical framework. This frame once again draws our attention to the developmental origins of moral orientations (see also Thomas, 1993; Calhoun, 1988).

Developmental Sources of Moral Orientations

According to Gilligan and Wiggins (1987) the dynamics of early childhood revolve around the themes of inequality and attachment. These themes give rise to different understandings of the self in relationship, which in turn lay the groundwork for two moral visions, one of justice, and one of care. Inequality is reflected in the child's awareness of dependence on powerful adults. The child is aware of being smaller, less powerful, and less capable. The experience of inequality sensitizes the child to issues of justice ("it's not fair!"), since the possibility of oppression is ever present.

Yet the parent-child relation is also experienced as an attachment-love relationship. Within this relationship the child learns important lessons about how to be in relationship: how to care, how to treat others, how to manage feelings, how to sustain connections with others, how to avoid hurt, and so on. The experience of attachment sensitizes the child to issues of care ("I don't love you anymore!"; "You don't care about me!"), since one is vulnerable to the possibility of abandonment.

The experiences of the self in relationships of inequality and attachment are universal features of childhood, equally applicable to boys and girls. These experiences sensitize the child to two sets of moral standards: the standard of justice (don't treat others unfairly) and the standard of care (help others). Boys and girls know and understand each standard. However, subsequent gender-role socialization may tend to emphasize one or the other orientation. For example, the experience of inequality may not be pronounced for girls if they identify with their mothers, to whom they are strongly attached. In this case the girl's self-understanding will probably coalesce around the dynamic of attachment, the formation of connections, and the standard of care.

In contrast, the experience of inequality is likely to be more pronounced for the boy, who is required to identify with a more distant father while maintaining an attachment with the mother. In contrast to girls' self-understanding, that of boys is likely to coalesce around the dynamic of independence (overcoming the inequality), separation, and the standard of justice. But if the boy's feelings of inequality are not mitigated by ongoing attachments and if the boy also taps into cultural patterns of male dominance, the prospect for aggression and violence is much greater, which perhaps accounts for the unpleasant sociological facts noted earlier.

According to Gilligan and Wiggins (1987), both developmental lines are myopic in their own way: Girls may lose sight of the problems that arise through inequality; boys may be insensitive to the problems that arise from detachment. Yet in many cases these two moral perspectives interact in the lives of men and women, leading to ambiguity and conflict in how real dilemmas are to be resolved. Put this way, the sex difference issue is recast. It is not a matter of which perspective is superior or better or which is the more moral gender. Rather, the issue concerns how the two moral perspectives interact in situations of moral choice and the gender-typed pattern of preference exhibited by men and women. Let's look at the research.

Empirical Status of Moral Orientations

Nona Lyons (1983) started from the assumption that men and women have different understandings of the self in relationship. The separate and objective self characteristic of men experiences relationships in terms of reciprocity among separate individuals. Others are treated with objectivity, and fairness is a matter of treating others the way one wants to be treated. Objectivity, reciprocity, and fairness are most usefully maintained by a system of rules that highlights one's obligations, duties, and commitments. Interpersonal issues are recast in terms of conflicting rights that are to be adjudicated according to impersonal procedures and objective rules. In contrast, the feminine connected self experiences relationships as a response to others. The connected self is concerned with shouldering burdens, alleviating distress, and minimizing suffering. These activities are carried out through caring which sustains relationships; and maintaining caring relationships is thought to be important because of the very fact that people are interconnected.

Thirty-six individuals, ranging from age 8 to 60 were interviewed about real-life dilemmas. A coding scheme was devised to identify the "rights" and "response" orientations in the case material. The results were as expected. The response ethic predominated in 75 percent of the female respondents but in only 14 percent of the males. In contrast, the rights orientation predominated in 79 percent of the male respondents, but in only 25 percent of the females (the percentages are, of course, yoked).

Although all females gave evidence of the response orientation in their interviews and all males considered the rights orientation, 36 percent of the males gave no indication of the response orientation in their case material and 37 percent of the females gave no hint of the rights approach. When subjects were asked, "How would you describe yourself to yourself?" 63 percent of the females were rated "predominantly connected," and 79 percent of the males were rated "predominantly separate/objective." Lyons (1983) concluded that a strong relationship exists between sex-typed patterns of self-definition and moral choice. The morality of care, she argued, is a lifelong concern of individuals and one that should not be assimilated to Kohlberg's morality of justice.

Gilligan and Attanucci (1988b) asked 34 women and 46 men about their personal experience of moral conflict and choice. The Lyons (1983) coding scheme was adapted to reveal the extent to which justice and care considerations were evident in the case material and in what combinations. About 65 percent of the men revealed a "justice only" orientation or a "justice focus" in their stories. About 32 percent of the men showed a mixture of care and justice. None had a "care only" orientation and only a single male had a "care focus." In contrast, 35 percent of the females showed a "care only" or "care focus"; 35 percent showed a combination of care and justice; 29 percent showed a "justice focus" or "justice only" orientation. The authors concluded that men *and* women appeal to *both* care and justice in their moral deliberations but that men gravitate toward the justice orientation and women gravitate toward the care orientation (see also, Vasudev, 1988; Gilligan & Attanucci, 1988a). It would also appear that many more women are willing to utilize the justice orientation than are men the care orientation. In any event, this evidence was taken to support the idea that the two moral orientations (care, justice) serve as a framework by which men (justice) and women (care) organize their thinking about moral conflict and choice.

Two other studies, however, appear to undermine a strong reading of Gilligan's moral-orientations argument. Ford and Lowery (1986) found that men and women considered both justice and care "fairly equally" in their descriptions of self-generated personal dilemmas. This counts against the view that moral orientations are gender related. Nonetheless, it was also true that the justice orientation was deemed more masculine and the care orientation more feminine: Men who scored high on a measure of femininity (i.e., were nurturing, affiliative, self-subordinating) rated care considerations more highly; care ratings were more stable over time for women, whereas justice ratings were more stable over time for men.

Walker and colleagues (1987) conducted the most extensive study to date on the issue of moral stages and moral orientations. They interviewed 10 boys and 10 girls from each of grades 1, 4, 7, and 10, and their parents (N = 240) on both standard and personal real-life dilemmas. They sought answers to the following questions: (1) Do hypothetical and real-life dilemmas pull for different stages of moral reasoning? (2) Are there sex differences in stage of moral reasoning within or across dilemma type? (3) Are the two moral orientations in evidence as individuals think about these dilemmas, and do the orientations pull for one gender or the other? (4) Is the care-and-response orientation scored at lower stages of moral reasoning? (5) Are there developmental trends in the use of moral orientations?

Regarding the first question, the authors found that hypothetical dilemmas elicited a slightly higher stage of moral reasoning than did the real-life dilemmas. But the degree of structural unity was quite high, at least on the nine-point continuum of stages and substages. About 91 percent of the subjects scored at the same stage or adjacent moral stage on the two dilemmas. There was no sex difference in the stage assignments to hypothetical or real-life dilemmas.

Do the two moral orientations pull for one gender or the other? Apparently not. Only 16.7 percent of the subjects were consistent in the use of a single orientation. For the most part, women did not use care considerations more than males, and males did not use justice more than females. If the care orientation was consistently used by anyone, it was by 10th-grade *boys*.

Do real-life dilemmas pull for care responses? Not very much, and not consistently. Dilemma type (real vs. hypothetical) did not pull for one orientation over the other at grades 4, 7, and 10. However, first-grade children gave more care responses to hypothetical dilemmas, and adults gave more care responses to real-life dilemmas.

Does the personal or impersonal nature of the content of the dilemma pull for one orientation or the other? This appears to be true. Dilemmas that focus on a personal relationship tend to elicit care responses. Dilemmas that focus on impersonal relationships tend to elicit justice-rights responses. But there were no sex differences. That is, when the dilemmas focused on personal relationships, men were as likely as women to use the care orientation. When the dilemma was impersonal, women were as likely as men to use a justice approach.

Is there a relationship between moral development and preference for moral orientation? And is this better shown with real or with hypothetical dilemmas? Preference for justice or care did not vary by stage of moral development when reasoning on hypothetical dilemmas was examined. But an interesting pattern did develop when real-life dilemmas were considered. First, individuals with a care orientation or a split (care-justice) orientation showed higher levels of moral reasoning. Second, individuals at the preconventional stages (Stages 1 and 2) preferred a rights orientation, subjects at the conventional levels (Stages 3 and 4) were about evenly distributed between orientations, and Stage 5 subjects used both orientations. The authors concluded that the two orientations are not disjunctive and are not gender typed. Hence it is inappropriate to consider the two moral orientations as either/or options. Indeed, it may be the case that one who has mature moral judgment attempts to integrate or coordinate issues of justice-rights and care-responsibility.

This latter suggestion accords with Kohlberg's view of the matter. I noted in Chapter 4 that the most recent theoretical revision of Stage 6 appears to leave room for the concerns identified by Gilligan. The emphasis on respect for persons entails an attitude of empathic connectedness and identification with the other and a willingness to enter into dialogue in order to secure agreement. Alongside justice operations, at Stage 6, are operations of sympathy, which orient the moral reasoner to the concrete concerns and life projects of the other. Justice and sympathy are dual concerns that the principled reasoner attempts to coordinate. I will simply refer the reader to that discussion. Kohlberg has more formally responded to the challenge that Gilligan mounted to his stage theory; I close my look at this issue by considering his response.

Kohlberg's Response

Kohlberg and others (1983) argued that the word "moral" can have two meanings. One sense of the word "moral" is captured by what they take to be the moral point of view. The moral point of view is concerned with the formal properties of a moral judgment: Is it impartial? Can it be universalized? Is it prescriptive? Is it motivated by a desire to settle conflicts and reach agreement?

The second sense of the word "moral" accords better with the domain of concern to Gilligan: What does it mean to care and to be responsible in special relationships with family and friends? This is a moral orientation for three reasons: (1) it exhibits a concern for the welfare of another; (2) it is motivated by feelings of obligation and responsibility; and (3) it emphasizes the need for dialogue and communication. It may be the case that different kinds of moral dilemmas evoke one or the other moral orientation. For example, personal moral dilemmas that arise in the context of special relationships may indeed evoke the impulse to care and to be responsible. Hypothetical dilemmas may pull for the justice orientation. Although this may be true, Kohlberg and others (1983) are adamant that these are not *alternative* moral options. The two orientations do not define two kinds of morality. They are better thought of as end points along a continuum. Indeed, the postconventional reasoner recognizes the distinction between the two approaches and attempts to coordinate them. "Reasoning at this post-conventional level leads to a tolerance about the resolution of personal dilemmas of personal obligation, while at the same time upholding a general framework of non-relative justice which provides the context within which individually varying personal moral decision-making may take place" (Kohlberg et al., 1983, p. 25). The universalistic ethic of justice with its injunction to respect persons can indeed handle dilemmas that involve special relationships. Although focused on rights and duties, justice also elicits considerations of relational ties and the importance of dialogue and communication.

Consider the Heinz dilemma. The fact that Heinz loves his wife, cares for her, and is otherwise obligated to be responsible to her by virtue of the special relationship of marriage serves to deepen his obligation to respect her right to life. Feelings of empathy, caring, benevolence, the attitude of sympathy, deepen our commitment to justice. Moral deliberation about justice is necessarily consensus-seeking with an emphasis on dialogue and prescriptive role-taking. In contrast, the ethic of care is ill suited to resolve conflicting claims, since it does not include the notions of impartiality and universalizability. It is ill suited to deal with those situations where all of the claimants are people we should care about. In this case, justice operations are required to sort out just what our obligations ought to be among those with whom we have special relationships. (This is probably milder than Kohlberg would have put it. There is a sense in which he would claim that we are obliged to care for *anyone* who is entitled to a consideration of justice, not just those with whom we share a special relationship. But this caveat does not alter the main point.)

A More General Debate

The debate between Gilligan and Kohlberg is one part of a more general debate in ethics concerning the fundamental nature of moral functioning (e.g., Blum, 1988; Williams, 1981; Becker, 1991; Pincoffs, 1971; French, Uehling, & Wettstein, 1984). Some have complained that the Kantian moral domain is exceedingly minimalist in its range of applicability. To focus on hard-case moral quandaries is to suggest that the point of ethics, or the point of moral psychology, for that matter, is juridical puzzle-solving—solving highly problematic dilemmas in rulelike ways. Apart from the fact that few of us routinely encounter the sort of dilemmas puzzle-solving is designed to adjudicate, what quandary ethics leaves out is a consideration of virtuous character and what it means to live a good life with integrity (Pincoffs, 1971; Norton, 1988). Analyzing virtue and accounting for characterological dispositions to virtue and vice have long been principle foci of ethics, at least until the Enlightenment (Schneewind, 1990). These activities also accord well with lay, commonsense understandings of the moral life of persons. Hence, defining the moral domain in such a way as to exclude notions of virtue and character, indeed, limiting the moral domain to simply those hard cases that require conflict resolution, segregates much of our lives from the purview of ethics and results in a moral psychology that is narrowly conceived.

Doubts have also surfaced among some ethicists about whether the Kantian understanding of the moral domain is a real psychological option for most individuals (Williams, 1981; Taylor, 1989). And others have doubted the propriety of insisting on dilemma-solving procedures that require us to adopt an ideal standpoint that effectively separates us from our own personalities and interests. The latter two doubts are related, of course. Adopting the standpoint of an ideal spectator is a procedural device that motivates impartiality and it ensures that the moral law is applied impersonally and universally. But such a stance seems to require that we become abstract persons, free from contaminating personal relationships, life projects, and significant identifications. It seems to ask that we adopt a point of view not our own (Becker, 1991). It seems to ask us to give up those goods that make our lives distinctive, meaningful, and worth living (Williams, 1981). Is it realistic to ask us to give these things up for the sake of some impartial, objective good? To the extent that one is required to be socially disembodied into impartiality, to the extent that one must stand outside of social structures and relationships, above history, in order to become the universal, impartial agent, to the extent that principled reasoning requires this, then perhaps we are left with an account of the moral agent that is, at best, psychologically suspicious (Lapsley, 1992a).

The moral voice identified by Gilligan is thought to represent a corrective to the impartialist, Kantian tendencies evident in Kohlberg's theory (Blum, 1988). Although her theory does not specifically focus on virtues and character, it does seem to construe the self in more realistic ways (Thomas, 1993). Indeed, the real object of Stage 6 is not so much "people like us" but rather the abstract rational moral agent who is divested or "thinned" of every characteristic that ordinarily makes one distinctive. In contrast, for Gilligan, the self is "thickly" constituted by identity-defining relationships that make a special claim on us. In her view we have a *partial*, special obligation to ourselves, to family, and to friends (see Kapur, 1991, for a defense of this view). It would be most implausible, for example, under the requirement of universalizability, to insist that Heinz is obliged to steal the drug not just for his wife but for any stranger in similar need. It is implausible to take the injunction "respect persons" to mean that we owe as much to strangers as to our special relationships. It is unrealistic, and not a little repugnant, to adopt a rules-and-duty approach to our life with friends and family (Stocker, 1976). It seems odd to expect us to act "with perfect impartiality in every aspect of our lives and with perfect Kantian attention to universalizable principles" (Becker, 1991, p. 699). Let's explore this a little further.

According to Stocker (1976) modern ethical theories tend to divorce moral reasoning from the motivation to be moral, a condition he called (somewhat inaccurately) moral schizophrenia. For example, any authentic human life lived well will necessarily require friendship, fellow feeling, love, community. These goods require that the other be treated as part of what is valued in one's life, and valued for the sake of the other. Yet the juridical decision-making procedures of deontic moral deliberation treat these goods as irrelevant to the requirement to submit to the impartialist obligations imposed by moral prescriptions. To achieve friendship, one must treat the other as a person who is loved and valued for his or her own sake, and not as an abstract, external, replaceable figure devoid of defining attributes in a round of moral musical chairs. Seeking the goods of community, affection, and friendship seems at odds with trying to live a rule-bound life imbued with obligations and duties. Indeed, behaving in certain ways only out of a sense of moral duty and obligation seems to miss the point of what an ethical life should amount to. I would be suitably astonished, for example, to realize that my friend Himes has come to my aid only out of a sense of moral duty.

Gilligan's other moral voice is a useful reminder that some aspects of our moral life are poorly described by impartialist conceptions of universal justice. What deontological rule ethics is said to leave out is a sufficiently warm-blooded account of moral agents. Whereas rule ethics is concerned with good and bad actions, virtue ethics embraces aretaic reflections on good and bad persons. Agents, not acts, are the principle object of ethical reflection. Whereas rule ethics asks, What ought I to do?, virtue ethics asks What sort of person ought I to be? Whereas rule ethics is keen to describe decision-making procedures for resolving concrete moral dilemmas, virtue ethics is keen to describe aspects of moral character that sustain individuals for living the good life. Rule ethics orients one to the obligations of the universal moral law. Virtue ethics orients one to the cultivation of virtuous dispositions. Whereas rule ethics attempts to describe a universal morality that transcends community and tradition, virtue ethics directs our attention to the communitarian foundations of our moral identity. Although Gilligan's theory is not a virtue ethic, I think it is fair to say that part of its attraction stems from a widespread impatience with the tendency of rule ethics to appropriate the entirety of the moral domain to itself.

Impartialism does have its defenders, of course. Don Adams (1993) argues, for example, that impartiality does not mean avoiding information or making ourselves ignorant of important facts about ourselves or somehow taking everyone's point of view simultaneously. Impartial decision-making simply involves correct and proper weighing of relevant factors. If the image of detachment is relevant at all to the notion of moral impartiality, it simply points to the need to be wary of biasing, prejudicial factors and to be attentive to relevant factors. Indeed, contrary to the popular image of detachment, impartiality sometimes requires that we become more attached, or more properly attached, to the concerns, interests, and perspectives of others in order to reach fair and proper judgments. As Adams (1993) puts it, whereas it is important to detach ourselves from "distorting lenses," we must also "attach" ourselves to "focusing" lenses. "Judges must learn to focus carefully on certain things and to become almost oblivious to certain other things. Requiring us to be impartial is nothing more or less than requiring us to view the situation *correctly*" (p. 228).

Along similar lines it is argued that impartiality does not mean impersonality (Rawls, 1971); that acting from duty is compatible with "thick" moral personhood (Baron, 1984); that under some circumstances showing partial consideration to family and friends either is patently unfair (Grunebaum, 1993; Rest, 1983) or can otherwise be justified by universalist ethics (Gewirth, 1988); that impartial moral criteria should not always give way to personal projects (Flanagan, 1991), since some personal commitments are just unworthy of us, or evil; and that a commitment to the detached perspectives of the moral point of view is not alienating in any important respect (Piper, 1987) and is compatible, in any event, with a thickly constituted "communitarian" self (Alejandro, 1993). Others argue that virtue ethics is ill equipped to give a rational account of morality; that it is of little help to applied ethics (what should I *do*?); and that Kantian ethics is, in fact, an ethics of virtue (e.g., Louden, 1984, 1986; but see McDowell, 1979).

Clearly, the debate between rule ethics and virtue ethics has often taken on an either/or quality within moral philosophy. Such a position is often necessary in academic discourse in order to sharply delineate the important issues at stake. The point of raising these issues here is simply to note that these debates are not irrelevant to empirical research in moral psychology insofar as moral philosophic criteria are often the starting point for conceptualizing the moral domain. Indeed, we will have occasion to revisit this debate in a later chapter. Suffice it to say here that Kohlberg's revision of the moral ideal to include both justice and sympathy operations is a useful, suggestive accommodation that one hopes will break down the barrier between "either" and "or" and point the way to broader, more integrative conceptions of the moral domain.

8

Positive Justice and Prosocial Reasoning

In the remaining chapters of this text I take up a number of topics that seem to res-onate with the moral agenda and priorities of the general lay public. Most parents and concerned citizens are not really interested, it seems to me, in how adolescents and adults reason about hard-case moral dilemmas. I suspect that the Kohlbergian project would leave most people cold, especially when it is pointed out that most people never reach the principled stages of reasoning, that the best we can do is move development along to better forms of conventional reasoning, and that the relationship between this kind of moral reasoning and moral behavior is uncertain or modest at best.

.I think that when most nonacademics get together and talk about moral issues, they talk about the crisis of values in contemporary society. They worry that children no longer seem to be socialized the way they used to be. Society has got-ten more coarse, life is cheaper than it used to be, standards of right and wrong no longer seem to be taught in families or in the schools. Somehow the whole process of moral socialization has gone awry. When lay individuals talk about morality, they are less interested in how hypothetical dilemmas are resolved and more concerned with how to teach certain values. They are not interested so much in defeating moral relativism as they are in inculcating honesty, generosity, altruism, how to share, how to be kind, and more. The most pressing moral problem facing most parents is how to develop better kinds of individuals, not how to develop better modes of reasoning.

In Chapter 9, I take up a number of research traditions that address the issue of moral socialization more directly. In Chapters 10–12 I examine some important work on moral character, moral identity, and the moral personality. I begin to look at these issues, however, with an examination of positive aspects of moral reasoning.

Positive Justice Reasoning

In approaching the moral domain, Kohlberg focused on qualities of reasoning that involve considerations of rules, laws, authorities, and formal obligations. This is sometimes called prohibition moral reasoning (Eisenberg-Berg, 1979a; Eisenberg, 1982) in order to distinguish it from those moral concerns that tend to minimize formal principles and obligation. Typically these latter concerns focus on sharing, helping, and responding to distress and on being kind, empathic, charitable, coop-erative, and altruistic. These "positive" behaviors are called prosocial because they

148

are intended to be of benefit to others when external criteria for doing so are absent or minimal, especially when the cost of performance is high and the self does not benefit (Eisenberg & Mussen, 1989). This is not to suggest that prosocial behaviors are done for no reason, just that the reasons invoked by the Kohlbergian moral reasoner need not be implicated in prosocial behavior (Mussen & Eisenberg-Berg, 1977). For example, prosocial behavior need not be motivated by a concern for justice, that is, for how rights and duties are to be fairly apportioned when there are conflicting claims. Prosocial behavior is not primarily concerned with conflict resolution. Acts of kindness, compassion, and altruistic self-sacrifice need not always be motivated by principles of fairness. Indeed, one can even imagine prosocial behaviors being motivated by egoistic, pragmatic, and other distinctly nonmoral considerations.

Yet there are situations when conflicts do arise within the prosocial domain. Although sharing is a prototypic prosocial behavior, it is sometimes unclear as to how best to share when there are many claimants and limited resources. How does one fairly distribute the goods (e.g., wealth, status, power, economic opportunity) of a society? Children are often enjoined to share their toys and belongings, and parents must allocate rewards and allowances; but what criteria do the child or parent use to guide prosocial inclinations? Prosocial behavior is traditionally defined as "voluntary behavior designed to benefit another" (Radke-Yarrow, Zahn-Waxler, & Chapman, 1983), yet how best to go about benefiting others may not be clear when there are so many to benefit and resources are few. To develop a scheme of sharing that is fair, then, is a problem of *distributive justice*. And it would appear that distributive justice is a domain that blends a concern for prosocial behavior with a concern for fairness.

Distributive Justice Reasoning

In short, distributive justice is a domain that is concerned with fair sharing. What do children know about fair sharing? If one examined the dominant theories of moral development, those of Piaget and Kohlberg, one would have to conclude "not very much." Kohlberg's theory is silent on the moral abilities of young children. His stages pick up in late childhood (age 10) and focus on issues (e.g., should I steal a drug to save a life?) that are foreign to the daily experiences of children. One would have to assume, on the basis of Kohlberg's theory, that young children are egocentric, that their moral sensitivities are dominated by a punishment and obedience orientation, and that real progress to the next stage is not possible until early adolescence.

More light is shed on the problem by Piaget's (1932) work that did focus on the moral judgments of young children (see Chapter 2). For Piaget (1932/1965) distributive justice is a matter of equal treatment, and children do not insist on equalitarian treatment much before middle childhood. In the heteronomous phase of moral judgment, which Piaget describes as the morality of constraint, judgments about what is fair are confused with whatever it is the adult commands. Hence justice is not distinguished from authority or law. When the child comes to appreciate the morality of cooperation and does so as a result of more equalitarian social interactions with peers, she insists on more nearly equal treatment, or on what Piaget calls distributive justice. Later still, the child's concern with strict equality becomes attenuated by her concern with the concrete situation of particular claimants. In other words, in her concern with equity, she corrects the application of strict equality by taking into account extenuating circumstances.

Yet Piaget's work was not so much focused on prosocial concerns but on the fair distribution of punishment. Distributive justice is a moral sense that stresses the notion of equality in social relationships; it is the "idea of equality" (Piaget, 1932/1965, p. 232), and it yields a concern for punishments and retributions that are equally applied, reciprocal, or equitable. Presumably, the "idea of equality" should be applicable as well to the more prosocial behaviors like sharing.

Much of what we know about children's understanding of fair sharing (distributive justice) is the result of William Damon's pioneering research. In his view "positive justice" is "that aspect of justice that is concerned with problems generated in prosocial interactions: for example, problems of how to distribute property fairly, of ownership and property rights, of responsibility for another's welfare, and of what constitutes a good response to another's actions" (Damon, 1975). In his graduate work Damon (1971, 1973) articulated a stage sequence that described children's progressive understanding of what constitutes fair sharing ("how to distribute property fairly"). This sequence was revealed on the basis of *methodè clinique* interviews of children who ranged in age from 4 to 10. The interviews centered around various sharing dilemmas that children were asked to resolve. Here is one of them (from Damon, 1975):

> All of these boys and girls are in the same class together. One day their teacher let them spend the whole afternoon making paintings and crayon drawings. The teacher thought that these pictures were so good that the class could sell them at the fair. They sold the pictures to their parents, and together the class made a whole lot of money. Now all the children gathered the next day and tried to decide how to split up the money. What do you think they should do with it? Why?

The interview went on to pose a number of solutions: Should the kids who made the most pictures get more money? Should the child who made the best pictures get more? Should the lazy kids get less? How about the best-behaved children or the child who is poor? It was the teacher's idea to make pictures in the first place, so maybe the teacher should get more of the money?

Children are confronted, of course, with a number of distributive criteria: Should our sharing be governed by *equality* (everyone gets the same), by *merit* or *desert* (whoever makes the most or the best gets the most), by *equity* (the poorer child or the youngest child gets more than the others), by *self-interest* (whoever wants the most should get it), or by other behavioral (best-behaved) or physicalistic (girls should get more, or the biggest child) criteria? Children's endorsement of the various distributive criteria was shown to undergo a six-stage sequence. The stages of distributive justice reasoning:

0-A: How much to share is governed by the child's wishes. If a child simply asserts a wish for more of the goods, these wishes should be respected ("I should get more because that is what I want").

0-B: There is an intuitive understanding that some criteria apart from naked self-interest, as was the case in the previous stage, must govern sharing. But the criteria endorsed at this stage are external, physicalistic, observable realities such as size, age, gender, and so on. These criteria are applied, however, in a post hoc way, usually to justify a decision that favored self-interest ("all of us boys should get more").

1-A: Sharing is now governed by a notion of strict equality. Everybody must get the same. This is Piaget's notion of distributive justice.

1-B: The notion of strict equality is replaced by a consideration of reciprocity in action, that is, there should be just paybacks for appropriate and inappropriate behavior. This consideration typically emerges in the form of concern with merit and just deserts. If you made the most pictures or the best pictures, you should get more of the rewards. If you were lazy or made lousy pictures, you should get less.

2-A: What do we do if one child made the best picture but another worked harder, yet a third has a greater need of money, and a fourth is disadvantaged because of her age or handicap? At this stage the distributive decision is no longer simply one of merit, since many individuals may merit special consideration. Here there is recognition that there can be many different but otherwise equally valid claims to the goods to be shared, and therefore the best one can do is work out equitable compromises. There appears to be no a priori way of excluding certain claims, since many claims can be considered equally valid. One has to carefully consider each party's perspective, then work out some quantitative compromise. Maybe the one who excelled should get the most but the one who is disadvantaged (say, by age, ability, or poverty) should get some small reward for the effort.

2-B: By late childhood, children attempt to coordinate equality and reciprocity with the demands of the situation or the goals and purposes of the social organization. If the larger purpose of the group is to increase the production of pictures, then the compromises between equality and reciprocity (merit, desert) should be tilted toward this end. If the overall purpose is to increase group solidarity, perhaps other compromises are possible. A goal-oriented solution provides a basis for excluding certain claims as irrelevant. For example, "We can't give Henry more just because he is older, since favoring age wouldn't increase group cohesion."

It should be clear that in this stage sequence young children are being credited with far more sophisticated understandings about justice than Kohlberg's theory suggested. By middle childhood, and certainly by the time they enter Kohlberg's first stage, children are already coordinating claims based on equality and merit in their distributive decisions. Let's now examine this sequence in light of the research literature.

Mèthode Clinique Research

In one of the first empirical studies on this sequence Damon (1975) attempted to show how distributive justice reasoning was related to reasoning in the Piagetian, logical domain. Children who ranged in age from four to eight were administered a distributive justice interview and asked to solve five operational tasks that involved mathematical and physical logic. Two of the operational tasks (multiple classification and class inclusion) were designed to assess the child's understanding of classification. A third task (multiple seriations) assessed the child's understanding of logical compensation. A fourth assessed the child's ability to coordinate spatial perspectives, and the fifth task assessed the child's understanding of ratios and proportionality.

In accordance with Piaget's theory, performance on each of the logical operations tasks was expected to show stage development. These tasks were included in the study to test the claim that there are structural similarities (isomorphisms) evident in positive justice and logical reasoning. For example, in order to group persons with their justice claims, children would need classification skills. In order to coordinate sharing with notions of desert and merit, the child would need logical compensation skills. In order to assess the positive justice claims of each claimant, children need perspective-taking skills. It was hypothesized that Level 2-B would be associated with the most advanced form of classification, compensation, and perspective-taking (characteristic of Piaget's stage of concrete operations). Level 0-B would be associated with the least-sophisticated understanding of classification, compensation and perspective-taking (characteristic of preoperational thought); Level 1-B would be associated with intermediate forms.

Let's examine the results by considering three questions. First, what is the relation between age and both positive justice and logical reasoning? The correlation of age and positive justice was very strong ($r = .85$). Level 0-A was characteristic of four-year olds; Level 0-B had a mixture of four-and five-year olds; 1-A had a mixture of five- and six-year olds; 1-B a mixture of six- and seven-year olds, while 2-A and 2-B were characteristic of eight-year olds. Once again, sophisticated understandings of moral concepts are clearly evident at a rather young age (e.g., by third grade), an idea that is supported by other research (Wellman, Larkey, & Somerville, 1979). Age was also strongly correlated with reasoning on the logical operations tasks (mean correlation $r = .63$). Obviously, older children perform better on the operational reasoning tasks than do younger children.

Was performance on the positive justice and operational tasks correlated? Positive justice reasoning was strongly correlated with all of the operational reasoning tasks, but especially with the spatial perspective-taking task, which suggests that moral decision-making may place a premium on assuming the perspective of others. When the relationship was examined age by age, the following results were obtained: Justice reasoning and logical reasoning were uncorrelated at age four; justice reasoning was correlated with two-fifths of the logical tasks at age five, with three-fifths of those tasks at age six, and with four-fifths of those tasks at ages seven and eight.

What if the relationship between justice and logical reasoning is examined stage by stage? Here Damon (1975) showed that Levels 0-A and 0-B were associated with preoperational thought, 2-A and 2-B with concrete operational thought, and 1-A and 1-B with transitional forms of operational reasoning. On the basis of these results Damon (1975) concluded that there are indeed structural similarities evident in positive justice and logical reasoning. The two domains interpenetrate; they inform and support each other, especially at the higher levels. But this does not mean that reasoning in one domain causes or makes possible reasoning in the other. That is, there is no evidence that performance in one domain (logical reasoning) is strictly necessary for performance in the other (positive justice), a view that is widely assumed in the social-cognitive developmental literature. This view shows up, for example, in Kohlberg's claim that reasoning in the Piagetian domains is necessary but not sufficient for reasoning in the moral domain. But Damon's results suggest otherwise (see also Broughton, 1983; Lapsley, 1990). Hence, although logical and moral reasoning are strongly associated, "the priority of logical to moral reasoning does not appear to be necessary in development: even among normal subjects, the pattern may be quite the reverse" (Damon, 1975, p. 312; Damon, 1979, 1981). Indeed, "quite the reverse" was also reported by Kurdek (1980), using a modified assessment of positive justice reasoning.

It should be pointed out, however, that although the necessary-but-not-sufficient formula does not appear to describe the relationship between logical and moral (positive justice) reasoning, it is invoked to describe the relationship between social perspective-taking and positive justice reasoning. Selman and Damon (1975), for example, link the levels of positive justice reasoning with the stages of perspective-taking identified by Robert Selman (1971, 1980; Selman & Byrne, 1975). In Level 0 of this sequence, for example, the young child is dimly aware that different people may have different points of view, yet the child is unable to assume the perspective of the other without contaminating it with her own perspective. This egocentric feature of perspective-taking is necessary for reasoning at Damon's Level 0-B. Here the child is dimly aware that some criteria other than naked self-interest must govern her sharing, yet she settles on "objective" criteria that nonetheless favor the self. Similarly, Level 1 in the perspective-taking sequence is said to underwrite positive justice reasoning in Level 1-B, and Level 2 perspective-taking is thought necessary for Level 2-B positive justice reasoning.

In another early study Enright and Sutterfield (1980) found that positive justice reasoning was associated with different qualities of peer interaction. Using interviews and naturalistic observations, they found that children who showed higher forms of positive justice reasoning also seemed to be socially competent and the targets of positive social interactions by others. The authors suggested that perhaps the kinds of reciprocity that are coordinated in judgments about sharing (viz., balancing notions of equality, merit, and desert) are played out in actual social situations in terms of greater social sensitivity to the needs of others and that this sensitivity is associated with greater social competence. Hence, in their view, positive justice reasoning is "ecologically valid" insofar as it is related to actual social interactions in the child's natural environment.

These two studies, then, show that advanced levels of distributive justice reasoning are associated with advanced forms of logical reasoning and with competent social behavior. What about the developmental properties of the stage sequence? In one longitudinal study Damon (1977b) found that children who showed change after one year tended to move upward to the next level. Some children, however, tended to move down to the next lower stage, and many children showed no change at all after one year. Consequently, Damon (1977b) was cautious in ascribing the traditional features of stagelike development to the positive justice stage sequence. But what might account for the turgid pace of development (such that so many children showed no change) and the instances of apparent stage regression (some children "reversed" to lower levels of reasoning)?

One explanation is straightforward: A one-year interval was simply not sufficient to capture social-cognitive development in middle childhood. Further, perhaps there was a difficulty in how level scores were assigned to subjects. Damon (1975) assigned an overall level score on the basis of the "predominantly used" level across the various dilemmas. So, for example, if a child uses Level 2-A on three dilemmas and 1-B on one dilemma, the child is assigned an overall level score of 2-A. Parenthetically, Enright and Sutterfield (1980) assigned level scores somewhat differently. Rather than base them on modal "predominantly used" level preference, they assigned quantitative scores to each level (e.g., 0-A = 0; 0-B = 0.5; 1-A = 1.0; 1-B = 1.5, etc.) and then calculated an arithmetic average. But perhaps any method that assigns a single, global score based on (modal or arithmetic) averages across dilemmas misses important information—the spread of scores across the various positive justice dilemmas.

The spread of scores is an interesting variable, since it has been linked to the very nature of stagelike development. There are a number of models of stage development. According to one model, if there is extensive spread of scores across a number of stages, this may indicate a child's readiness to move to the next stage. For example, Turiel (1974) suggested that *stage mixture* is an indication of a readiness to develop, a sign of cognitive conflict, especially if the spread of scores is tilted in favor of the next higher level. A second model suggests, however, that stage transition is indicated not so much by stage mixture but by a *consolidation* of reasoning at one's current stage (Flavell & Wohlwill, 1969). In this case it is the consistency of responding, not spread or mixture, that is the best predictor of stage transition.

These issues were taken up by Damon (1980) in another longitudinal study. In addition to calculating a global stage score, he also devised a measure of spread. Spread above the mode was simply the sum of the percentage of use of all stages above the predominant, modal stage. Spread below the mode was the sum of the percentage of use of all stages below the predominant, modal stage. In addition to being interested in mechanism of stage transition, Damon (1980) also wanted to examine, of course, the pattern of longitudinal change over a two-year interval. Hence he looked at three testing times: (1) the initial sampling, (2) the first longitudinal testing after one year, and (3) the second longitudinal testing after two years.

What did he find? The stagelike nature of positive justice development was in better focus after a two-year interval. Indeed, children who showed an initial downward reversal after one year corrected themselves by the second year. By the end of year 1 (the second testing), 71 percent of the children who changed showed progressive development. From year 1 to the second longitudinal testing (year 2), 71 percent showed progressive development. But from the initial testing to year 2, nearly 86 percent of the children who changed showed progressive development. What is more, the children who changed the most after two years were the ones who initially had the lowest modal scores for their age. These children appeared to catch up after a two-year interval. Which model of stage transition appeared to account for progressive development? Damon (1980) found that spread above the mode was the best predictor of stage transition ($r = .43$). Indeed, spread below the mode was negatively correlated ($r = -.38$) with progressive development.

Damon (1980) concluded that positive justice reasoning does indeed show stepwise progressive development as indicated by the stage sequence but that stage transition is marked by continuity. In his view, "even stagelike development proceeds gradually with considerable continuity in the child," and development is "gradual, mixed, and uneven" even if the stages themselves describe qualitatively different modes of reasoning (Damon, 1980, p. 1017). This is compatible with Heinz Werner's (1957, p. 137) claim that "development, insofar as it is defined as increase in differentiation and hierarchization is, ideally, continuous." The next round of empirical studies was undertaken by Robert Enright and his colleagues, who used quite a different methodology. After examining this literature, we will have occasion to wonder if differences in methodology are a telling consideration in our understanding of the distributive justice sequence.

Robert Enright and the Distributive Justice Scale

Scholars in the structural developmental tradition are interested in gauging the organizational properties of intelligence. They seek to identify the structure of thought. They assume that pattern of organization (structure) and what gets organized (content) are separable. Indeed, the content of intelligence is to be explained in terms of structure. It is the structure of thought that explains why certain content is possible or evident in a child's protocol. They further assume that childrens' understanding of some concept undergoes development and that this development is the result of transformations in the pattern, organization, and structure of reasoning. Since the desire is to describe structural organization, and not the contents to be organized, some means must be found of identify the underlying structure in a process that is not contaminated by content. How should this be done? We have seen that the structural tradition insists on the clinical interview as the only reliable way to gauge the underlying structural properties of intelligence (Damon, 1977b).

In the context of an interview one can carefully probe a child's answers in order to capture the formal aspects of her reasoning. Any other approach, such as the use of questionnaires, leads to the danger of settling on mere content choices without revealing the child's formal understanding of the issue at stake. This approach focuses on the surface appearance of things without tapping the underlying structural, organizational realities.

Although the clinical method yields a rich data source, it is also said to have certain disadvantages (but see Turiel, 1983a, for a stiff defense). A premium is placed, for example, on the child's verbal facility. Each interview is potentially idiosyncratic, since there can be no question of a standardized assessment across all children. Replication is made difficult not only because every child potentially takes a different "test" but also because many interviewers are typically involved. Clinical assessment is also costly and labor intensive, since interviews have to be transcribed and the written record carefully combed for structural clues.

In order to address some of these potential disadvantages Robert Enright (1981; Enright, Franklin, & Manheim, 1980) devised an objective, standardized assessment of distributive justice reasoning, called the Distributive Justice Scale (see Kurdek, 1980, for yet another methodology). Although the DJS strays from Damon's clinical method, it nonetheless trades on some of its key features. In Damon's (1977b) clinical assessment, for example, the child's initial resolution of a distributive dilemma is carefully confronted with alternative solutions. These solutions represent the distributive criteria representative of other levels of reasoning. In a sense, then, the clinical method (as used by Damon) is an elaborate paired-comparison assessment. The child's response to a sharing dilemma is progressively paired with other stage-related justifications for sharing, and the interviewer then determines which criteria seem preferred. The DJS incorporates this in a standardized format.

The DJS consists of two sharing dilemmas similar to the kind used by Damon (1977b). In one story, children are making pictures at a summer camp. A man comes along and buys the pictures with a lot of nickels. How, then, should the children distribute the money? In the DJS each of Damon's stages is represented pictorially. Each picture shows four children. One child is bigger, one is poor, one made the most pictures, and one simply wants more of the nickels. Beside each child are pictures he or she drew and the nickels each is to be awarded. The picture for Level 0-A, for example, shows a girl who wants more of the nickels actually getting more. The picture for Level 1-A shows all the children getting exactly the same number of nickels. The picture for Level 2 shows a compromise struck between the most deserving child (who made the most pictures) and the child who has the greatest need.

After a child has made an initial attempt at resolving the sharing dilemma, pairs of pictures are then presented to the subject such that each stage-picture is paired with every other stage-picture. With each presentation the subject is asked to state a preference as to which picture represents the more fair way of distributing the money. Note that this assessment is completely standardized. It is objective in the sense that the interviewer is not required to make a judgment as to whether a child's oral response is indeed a structural clue. The child's verbal skills are not taxed, since only pointing is required to state a preference. The DJS has built-in consistency checks and is equipped to detect idiosyncratic or careless responding.

Across three studies Enright, Franklin, and Manheim (1980) found strong age trends using the DJS. No sex effects were evident, and performance on the DJS was discriminated from verbal abilities. In addition, distributive justice reasoning was associated with reasoning on logical reciprocity (conservation) tasks. Indeed, they found, unlike Damon (1975), that logical reciprocity preceded or developed synchronously with distributive justice reasoning, and only rarely did social reciprocity develop first. This finding is compatible with the necessary-but-not-sufficient account of the relation between logical and social reasoning. Finally, the authors found cross-cultural generality for the stage sequence in a sample of children tested in Zaire.

Later studies expanded upon these findings while extending the research in other directions. For example, the finding that Piagetian logical reciprocity tends to precede the development of distributive justice reasoning was replicated in both an American and a Swedish sample (Enright et al., 1984, Study 1). When distributive decisions involve family members rather than peers, reasoning is typically at higher levels (Enright et al., 1984, Study 2), probably because the distributive norm within the family is centered more on need than on equality. This finding suggests that distributive justice reasoning is sensitive to contextual factors, although there are developmental constraints as well (Sigelman & Waitzman, 1991).

Along the same lines, it is interesting that Damon (1977b) also reported variation in stage use as a function of context. He found, for example, that distributive justice reasoning is typically higher when hypothetical dilemmas are used as opposed to real-life sharing dilemmas. This is because there is a greater temptation to reward oneself with more of the treats to be shared under conditions of actual sharing, and this applies more to younger than to older children. This regard for self-interest exerts a downward press on the level of reasoning, although there is a developmental constraint evident here as well. Rarely did distributive justice reasoning drop more than one stage when the child was confronted with an actual sharing dilemma as opposed to a hypothetical dilemma. Hence this finding, and the one reported by Enright and others (1984), suggest that stage and context interact in distributive justice reasoning. As these authors point out, "One cannot describe a child as advanced or delayed without specifying the context" (p. 1749).

Social class is an important contextual marker, and three studies were devoted to exploring its relation to distributive justice reasoning (Enright, Enright, Manheim, & Harris, 1980; Enright, Enright, & Lapsley, 1981). These studies found that lower-class children lag behind their middle-class peers, and this is true regardless of race. One reason this might be the case is linked to the fact that social relations among children from different social classes are decidedly nonreciprocal. In these studies middle-class children were often the targets of peer nominations and positive attributions even from lower-class children. Middle-class children were invariably "nice," "fair," and "good friends." In contrast, lower-class children were poorly thought of even by lower-class children. They were invariably "not nice" and "not fair." Insofar as Piaget (1932/1965) had speculated that reciprocal peer relations are the engine that drives moral development, social class integration did not appear to be fostering social reciprocity across class lines, which may have influenced the developmental lags that were evident in distributive justice reasoning among lower-class children (Enright, et al., 1981).

A final study examined the possibility that distributive justice reasoning is sensitive to cohort effects (Enright et al., 1984, Study 3). A complex sequential design was used to examine the longitudinal development of four groups of kindergartners and fourth-graders. One group of kindergarten students was assessed on the DJS in 1978, then retested in 1979. Another group was initially tested in 1979, then retested in 1980. Similarly, a sample of fourth-graders was initially assessed in 1978, then retested in 1979. A new sample of fourth-graders was assessed in 1979, then retested in 1980.

The results showed that developmental progressions in these groups were not due to cohort effects (although time-of-testing effects cannot be controlled in this design). Development was rapid at the youngest ages, averaging half a stage, but slower in middle childhood (a quarter-stage). Note that fairly rapid development was evident among 5- and 6- year-olds even after one year, which contrasts with the turgid development noted by Damon (1975) after the same interval. The authors also noted that 17 percent of the 9- and 10-year-olds apparently regressed from Level 2 to Level 1 reasoning. Although measurement error cannot be discounted, perhaps this regression is due to the fact that the transition to adolescence induces a greater concern with equality (Level 1), particularly given the strong peer-conformity needs often expressed by young adolescents (Berndt, 1979; Costanzo & Shaw, 1966). If this is true, distributive justice reasoning may fluctuate not only in response to contextual factors but also in response to major developmental transitions.

Summary of Positive Justice Reasoning

It is now time to summarize our look at positive justice and to examine some collateral issues. Clearly the stage sequence enjoys considerable empirical support. Strong longitudinal age trends are evident. The sequence is related to various measures of cognitive development and is observed in at least two other cultures, attesting to the universality claims often made in this tradition. Performance is not associated with verbal facility or with cohort effects and appears to show interesting contextual variations.

What is striking about this literature is the degree of convergence between the set of findings revealed by the clinical method and the findings yielded by the Distributive Justice Scale. Although the two methods come to different conclusions about the priority of logical reasoning for justice reasoning and the pace of development, one is struck more by the similarity of findings than by the differences. As a result one is tempted to conclude that perhaps much of the quarreling that is induced because of theoretical commitments and the concomitant desire for methodological purity is overdone, at least as far as the distributive justice domain is concerned.

Damon (1977b) is sometimes criticized for not taking a firmer stand on the stage issue (Rest, 1983). A firm stand would entail a commitment to the view that each stage is a structured whole, or a general stage that organizes diverse content. This received view is often taken to be the orthodox Piagetian position on what "stage" amounts to (see the discussion in Chapter 1). In contrast, Damon (1977) endorses a "partial structures" view, which holds that different domains or concepts may be variably organized or that structures always maintain an element of content specificity. This "agnostic position" on global stages seems problematic, according to Rest (1983), because it pays insufficient attention to the systemic qualities of thinking. Thought is not a jumble of disconnected concepts. Rather, the various concepts take their meaning from their relationship to more encompassing organizations of thought, the *structures d'ensemble*:

> If Damon's levels indicate nothing more general and fundamental than solutions to the specific problems of positive justice. . . then we do not have any information about children's moral thinking regarding lying, promise-keeping, fighting and self-defense, punishment, cheating on games or school tests, being disruptive and unruly, special responsibilities to family and kin, performing assigned chores, and all the other situations in a child's life that involve moral issues. (Rest, 1983, p. 604).

This criticism would also be directed at the domains approach to social knowledge. We saw in Chapter 6 that the domains approach also endorses the more delimited understanding of partial structure. As Turiel (1983a, p. 21) points out, "Interactions with fundamentally different types of objects and events should result in the formation of distinct concepts. From the perspective of partial structures, therefore, stages or levels of development are not autonomous, self-contained units manifested across tasks and situations."

The reader will recall, too, the discussion of Piaget (see Chapter 1) suggesting that a partial-structures understanding of stage may actually be closer to the Piagetian mark than the ostensible Piagetian orthodoxy that has grown up around the received view. Hence, whether Damon's embrace of partial structures is a weakness or a strength depends largely on how one reads Piaget and what a notion of *structures d'ensemble* can be reasonably expected to explain. I see no reason to indict Damon's stage theory for failing to also explain how children come to understand authority, punishment, lying, or the many other specific topics noted by Rest (1983). As Turiel (1983a) points out, the partial-structures position is not committed to the view that thought is a messy jumble of disconnected domains. Rather, the system of organization has to be demonstrated by research. "The proposition is that there is neither a general structure of mind as a whole to be identified nor are there so many domains of knowledge that we are left with a series of elements but no system of organization" (Turiel, 1983, p. 21). Perhaps Rest (1983) is calling for as much effort to go into specifying the system of organization as is being expended in the specification of partial domains.

Perhaps a more telling criticism is that the positive justice stage sequence seems absent any clear notion of hierarchical integration. The sequence represents a taxonomy of various sharing criteria with little indication of why one criterion (e.g., equity) is better than another (e.g., equality) or how it is than one perspective is transformed to yield the next. Why should a Level 2 compromise override considerations of merit (Level 1-B) or equality (Level 1-A)? In other words, why is Level 2 more sophisticated and "better" than the sort of distributive decisions that are made at lower levels (and in what sense are they lower)?

While noting this difficulty, Rest (1983) does suggest that there is a rationale for ordering the levels nonetheless. In his view each successive level in the stage sequence describes a better scheme of cooperation in the sense that children gradually come to endorse distributive criteria that are more likely to draw social support and consensus. The sequence describes how children struggle with fair resolutions to sharing dilemmas, where fairness is linked the widest possible consensus or cooperation or to the broader aims of the social organization.

This brings to a close our look at distributive justice reasoning. The distributive justice sequence was identified on the basis of sharing dilemmas that children were asked to reflect upon. In these dilemmas the goods to be shared belonged to no one in particular, and the decision was essentially one of how to share among the group what was given to the group as a whole. But what if the sharing dilemmas were altered so that what was to be shared was property that one actually owned? What if the dilemmas focused not so much on sharing but on other prosocial behaviors such as helping? What if the decision to share or help involved some direct cost to the self in terms of the self's needs, desires, and goods? This was the problem undertaken by Nancy Eisenberg and her colleagues. Their work has led to another important research tradition within the moral domain: the domain of prosocial reasoning. I take up her work in the next section.

Prosocial Reasoning

Prosocial reasoning is said to be another aspect of positive justice (Eisenberg-Berg, 1979a). It emerges in those conflicts where one must decide whether to satisfy one's own needs, wishes, and preferences or those of others when there is no clear formal obligation to help others. Should a poor farming community, Circleville, give up much of its harvest to a neighboring community whose farmlands have been flooded even though the residents of Circleville might go hungry themselves? Should I donate blood even though I am physically weak or even if it might disrupt my studies or cost me my job? Should we come to the aid of a woman being mugged even if there is some danger to ourselves? Is it right that I should develop my special talents, compete for prizes and honors, when my time could also be spent, or better spent, helping people with special needs?

When children are presented with these prosocial dilemmas, they typically produce a wide variety of responses. Indeed, in an early study childrens' responses were coded into over two dozen "moral consideration categories" (Eisenberg-Berg, 1979a). Table 8.1 provides examples of most of these categories. These categories

TABLE 8.1 Moral-Consideration Categories in Prosocial Reasoning

---

1. *Punishment and obedience*
   "If I don't help, someone will find out and punish me."

2. *Hedonistic reasoning*
   "I wouldn't help because I might be hungry" (pragmatic self-gain).
   "She'd help because they'd give her food the next time" (direct reciprocity).
   "She'd help because she has friends in town" (affectional relationship).
   "He wouldn't help because then he could go to college and help more people some day" (socially accepted rationalization).

3. *Nonhedonistic pragmatism*
   "I'd help because I'm brave."

4. *Needs-oriented*
   "He needs blood" (concern for physical-material needs).
   "They'd be happy if they had food" (concern for psychological needs).

5. *Reference to humanness*
   "You'd share because they're people."

6. *Stereotyped reasoning*
   "It's nice to help" (stereotyped image of good or bad persons).
   "I'd help because crippled children are nice" (stereotyped view of others and their roles).
   "It's only natural to help" (stereotyped image of majority behavior).

7. *Empathic orientation*
   "He would feel sorry for them" (sympathetic caring).
   "I'm trying to put myself in her shoes" (role-taking).

8. *Approval and social acceptance*
   "His parents would be proud of him if he helped."

9. *Internalized affect*
   "She'd help because seeing the villagers fed would make her feel good" (positive affect related to consequences).
   "I'd feel good knowing that I lived up to my principles (positive affect from self-respect).
   "She would feel guilty if they were hungry" (negative affect related to consequences).
   "He'd think badly of himself if he didn't do the right thing" (negative affect, lack of self-respect).

10. *Abstract reasoning*
    "She has a duty to help others" (internalized norms, laws, values).
    "I'd help because she has a right to walk down the street and not get mugged" (rights of others).
    "If everybody helps one another, we'd all be better off" (generalized reciprocity).
    "If everybody helps, society would be a lot better" (condition of society).

Source: Adapted from Eisenberg-Berg (1979a).

describe a central theme in a child's prosocial moral judgment about what ought to be done by the protagonist in the dilemma. For example, when presented with one of the just-mentioned dilemmas, a child might express a desire to help if she thinks she may avoid punishment by doing so or if helping is somehow expected by those in authority. Alternatively, a child might want to help for strictly hedonistic reasons, namely, helping the self might gain friends, esteem, or help in return. Maybe one should help because one is concerned for the material or psychological needs of the other or because the other is a person like everybody else. Having stereotyped views about what good people do in these situations or what is naturally done or what people who need help are generally like may dominate prosocial reasoning. Perhaps we are prosocial in order to gain approval or because we take the others' perspective or because acting in a prosocial way makes us feel good and helps us avoid guilty feelings. Perhaps there are abstract reasons for acting prosocially. Hence, one might appeal to a sense of duty, to the needs of society, to the rights and dignity of those in need, or to general laws and norms in order to justify a prosocial response.

These moral-consideration categories represent a taxonomy of possible content responses that are not ordered developmentally. Yet preference for some of these categories appears to related to age (Eisenberg-Berg, 1979a). Categories that reflect greater empathic awareness and awareness of abstract, internalized moral norms increase with age, whereas hedonistic, needs-oriented, and stereotypic considerations, and the desire for interpersonal acceptance and approval, decrease with age. Interestingly, young children rarely appealed to punishment and obedience as a rationale for acting prosocially, a finding that has been often replicated (Eisenberg-Berg & Hand, 1979; Eisenberg-Berg & Neal, 1979). This calls into question, of course, the generality of Kohlberg's first stage of justice reasoning.

The developmental nature of prosocial reasoning was clarified in a series of sophisticated longitudinal studies. In the first study 4- to 5-year-olds were reinterviewed 18 months later on how they would resolve prosocial dilemmas (Eisenberg-Berg & Roth, 1980). During this interval there was a significant decline in the use of hedonistic reasoning and increases in the use of needs-oriented and approval-oriented reasoning. These developments were unrelated to role-taking ability. In a second longitudinal study, Eisenberg, Lennon, & Roth (1983) reinterviewed this sample of children 18 months later, when the children were age 7–8 (Cohort 1). Note that this testing was the third time these children were interviewed. The reader might wonder if perhaps these children would now be "test-wise," since they had responded to the interview twice before. Maybe the results obtained would be due not to developmental considerations but simply to the effects of repeated testing. To examine this, the authors added a second group of 7- to 8-year-olds that was tested for the first time. If its results were broadly similar to the results of Cohort 1 (the original longitudinal group), then the effects of repeated testing could be ruled out. In addition, yet another group (Cohort 2) of 5- to 6-year-olds was reinterviewed after a one-year interval.

No repeated-testing effects were evident. But the results again showed the steady decline of hedonistic reasoning from age 5–6 to age 7–8. And once again, needs-oriented reasoning increase until age 7–8. When these samples were followed two years later (Eisenberg et al., 1987), hedonistic reasoning was rarely seen between ages 7–8 and 9–10. The steady increase in needs-oriented reasoning leveled off. What is more, additional prosocial categories were in greater evidence in middle childhood. For example, pragmatic, approval–interpersonally oriented, stereotypic, affectional-relational, role-taking, and positive-affect reasoning categories began to dominate the protocols of 9- to 10-year-olds. This study also reported a gender difference. Older girls showed more evidence of sympathetic role-taking than did boys. The authors also demonstrated a relationship between prosocial reasoning and prosocial behavior. The more hedonistic a child was, the less likely the child was to share when sharing involved some cost. When helping was not costly, however, there was no relationship between prosocial behavior and prosocial reasoning. Finally, this study also showed that empathy was positively related to needs-oriented reasoning and to higher levels of prosocial reasoning but was negatively correlated with hedonistic reasoning. Empathy also predicted prosocial behavior at older (11–12) but not younger (9–10) ages. As Hoffman (1984, 1987) points out, empathy may mediate altruistic behavior only at older ages, when one is in a better position to appreciate the life circumstances of others.

What is known about the prosocial reasoning of adolescents? Many of the trends noted in middle childhood continue into adolescence (Eisenberg, 1990). For example, Eisenberg Miller, Shell, McNalley, & Shea (1991) report that higher modes of prosocial reasoning (e.g., internalized norms, laws, rules; generalized reciprocity) are in much greater use by mid-adolescence. A number of categories that peak in middle childhood begin to decrease in use. Hence, approval and stereotypic prosocial reasoning decline by mid-adolescence, as does direct reciprocity. Recall that in middle childhood, girls show a much greater use of sympathetic caring and perspective-taking than do boys. But by mid-adolescence, boys catch up. Boys also revert to slightly more hedonistic reasoning. Prosocial reasoning is also related to prosocial behavior and to empathy, although empathy is only an uncertain predictor of prosocial behavior.

On the basis of these studies Eisenberg (1986) formalized the development of prosocial reasoning into developmental levels. These levels are summarized in Table 8.2. The longitudinal evidence just reviewed makes clear that there are broad shifts with age in the kinds of motives children appeal to in their prosocial reasoning. But Eisenberg (1986) has avoided making strong hard-stage assumptions about this stage sequence. She is not committed to the notion of invariant sequence, and she is uninterested in whether each developmental level is a structured whole. Indeed, children may appeal to prosocial justifications from a variety of levels, even lower levels that they ordinarily would have passed through. Some subjects may not exhibit a particular level at all before showing evidence of a higher level. Although there is encouraging evidence that the sequence obtains in other cultures (e.g., Eisenberg, Boehnke, Schuhler, & Silbereisen, 1985; Eisenberg, 1986), no strong

TABLE 8.2   Levels of Prosocial Reasoning

Level 1: *Hedonistic, self-focused orientation*
The motive for helping or not helping is linked to possible consequences for the self.
Would helping lead to direct gain? If I help now, will the other person help me later, or
like me? Predominantly used by preschoolers and younger elementary school children.

Level 2: *Needs-oriented orientation*
A concern is expressed for the needs of others even when these needs might conflict with
one's own. This concern is expressed without clear evidence of sympathy, guilt, or self-
reflection. Predominantly used by many preschoolers and grade school children.

Level 3: *Approval and interpersonal orientation and/or stereotypic orientation*
Prosocial intentions are judged in light of stereotypic notions of good or bad persons—one
should help persons who are "nice" or "good," but one is not required to help persons who
are "not nice" or "bad." Prosocial behavior is also indicated if it wins approval or acceptance. Predominantly used by some elementary and high school students.

Level 4a: *Self-reflective empathic orientation*
Prosocial reasoning shows evidence of self-reflective perspective-taking or sympathy, an
empathic concern for the other's humanity, and whether one's actions will engender positive feelings or guilt. Predominantly used by some older elementary school children and
many high school children.

Level 4b: *Transitional level*
One appeals to internalized norms and values and a sense of duty and responsibility. There
is a concern for the welfare of the general society and a desire to protect the rights and
dignity of others. These "principled" motives, however, are not strongly or clearly articulated. A minority of high school students and late adolescents use this mode of reasoning.

Level 5: *Strongly internalized stage*
The appeal to internalized norms, duties, responsibilities, and rights is clearly stated.
Because these considerations are strongly internalized, the issues of self-respect and living
up to one's values are also characteristic of this stage. This stage is not evident among elementary school children and is evident among only a minority of high school students.

Source: Adapted from Eisenberg (1986). Used by permission of Lawrence Erlbaum.

commitment to the universality assumption is made. Eisenberg does appear to
endorse the additive-inclusive model of stages but deemphasizes the notion of
hierarchical integration (Eisenberg, 1986).

Is prosocial reasoning related to other capabilities? This question does not
appear to have attracted much interest over the years. Low to moderate correlations between prosocial reasoning and Kohlbergian assessments of justice reasoning
have been reported (Eisenberg et al., 1983), but nonsignificant correlations have
been reported as well (Kurdek, 1981). Prosocial reasoning appears to be positively
correlated with liberal–humanitarian political attitudes (Eisenberg-Berg, 1976),
especially among women (Eisenberg-Berg, 1979b). It is positively correlated with
religious participation (Eisenberg-Berg & Roth, 1980) and with scholastic abilities
in adolescent boys (Eisenberg-Berg, 1979b). Prosocial reasoning is positively correlated with cognitive role-taking among adolescent females (Kurdek, 1981). There

was no correlation, however, between role-taking and prosocial reasoning in young children in Eisenberg-Berg and Roth's, 1980 study. Hence, this relationship appears to be weak and inconsistent (Eisenberg, 1986).

Children's reasoning about their own spontaneous prosocial acts also seems to be similar to their reasoning when responding to hypothetical dilemmas (Eisenberg-Berg & Neal, 1979). Furthermore, the conditions that elicit prosocial reasoning may vary depending upon the nature of social relationships. For example, children appear to respond to peer requests with the various prosocial categories of reasoning but resort to authority, punishment, and obedience justifications when responding to the requests of adults (Eisenberg, Lundy, Shell, & Roth, 1985), probably because requests and commands are not clearly distinguished by children when coming from an adult and because what adults typically want usually requires obedience.

In sum the domain of prosocial reasoning is clearly one of the most impressive research programs in developmental psychology. The stage sequence describes a taxonomy of motives that children appeal to when they reason about prosocial conflicts. Prosocial reasoning begins in a fog of hedonism and egoistic considerations and is gradually oriented with development toward an ever widening social nexus that ultimately takes into account the welfare of the general society.

But the course of development moves prosocial reasoning in an internal direction as well. As one moves through the levels there is a shift away from a consideration of personal gains one might accrue as a consequence of helping toward a more principled desire to see that the *other person* gains; one's own self-respect comes to hinge on whether one lives up to strongly internalized prosocial values that respect the dignity and rights of other persons.

We have not, of course, exhausted our look at prosocial development. The stage sequence identified by Nancy Eisenberg's research program describes the sort of reasoning that is evoked in situations of prosocial moral conflict. Like Kohlberg's theory, then, it focuses on conflict resolution. Unlike Kohlberg's theory, it carves out a larger role for moral emotions such as empathy. This larger role for moral emotions is even more clear in those situations that do not involve moral conflict. Oftentimes our prosocial inclinations are evoked automatically, without much conscious deliberation and certainly without much conflict (Karniol, 1982). There is a presumption that it is our empathic and sympathetic response to the plight of others that motivates our acts of helping, sharing, donating, volunteering, consoling, and other prosocial behaviors. We will need to examine this claim. We may also wonder just how prosocial dispositions are socialized in children and when they emerge in development. If children are egoistic, do they ever engage in prosocial behavior? Under what conditions are children likely to display whatever prosocial dispositions they have? I will take up these issues in Chapter 9.

9

Prosocial Behavior

Are Children Prosocial?

I defined prosocial behavior as any behavior that is intended to benefit another. This definition suggests that any prosocial inclination must involve at least some awareness of the distress, plight, or need of the other. If children are egocentric, as Piagetian theory leads us to believe, this awareness is difficult for the child to come by. If children are also egoistic and hedonistic, as Eisenberg's work leads us to believe, then even if there is awareness, the tendency to help is factored through the calculations of naked self-interest. So we must ask if young children are indeed prosocial in spite of their many cognitive limitations, and one way to get started is simply to explore whether young infants and children are sensitive to the emotional cues of others.

Are young children attuned to the distress of others, or at least aware in a general way of the emotional displays of others? There is evidence that young children are indeed responsive to the emotional cues of adults and other children. Even young infants have shown evidence of emotional sensitivity to the distress of other infants (Hay, Nash, & Pedersen, 1981; Simner, 1971). Indeed, an infant as young as one day old will cry vigorously, spontaneously, and intensely, with real feeling, in response to the distress cry of another infant, but not in response to a tape recording of his or her own cry (Sagi & Hoffman, 1976; Simner, 1971; Martin & Clark, 1982). This phenomenon points to the possibility that empathic arousal may be a hardwired response tendency in humans, one that is evolutionarily selected and part of human nature (Hoffman, 1981; Plutchik, 1987).

After six months of age infants become adept at decoding various facial expressions of emotion (Ludemann, 1991; Ludemann & Nelson, 1988; Nelson, 1987; Schwartz, Izard, & Ansul, 1985; Nelson & Dolgrin, 1985; Oster, 1981). They echo the emotional displays of adults. Infants frown or cry, for example, when they see or hear a caretaker's negative emotional display. At nine months of age an infant shares and cooperates in toy play with her mother and shares also in her mother's visual exploration of a room. For example, an infant will often follow her mother's line of regard as the mother looks about a room (Scaife & Bruner, 1975). Infants begin to use the emotional expressions of others as cues by which to appraise uncertain or threatening situations, a phenomenon called *social referencing*. A toddler for example, will often stay in his mother's visual field in order to keep himself apprised of his mother's emotional reactions to what he is doing, since these reactions are cues for how the child should react (Feinman, 1982; 1992; Carr, Dabbs, & Carr, 1975). Oftentimes a child will have an accident, say, he falls down on his backside. How should he react? He quickly scans for his mother in order to appraise her reaction. She is alarmed, and it shows. The child, who sees the signals of alarm on his mother's face now has the information he needs to react to falling down—he, too, is alarmed (because Mom is), and he starts crying. To use other, more experienced individuals as a social reference for how one should react in these sorts of situations is no minor achievement, for what underlies social referencing is the tacit understanding that the emotional displays of others convey information (Bretherton, Fritz, Zahn-Waxler, & Ridgeway, 1986). And there appears to be ample evidence that infants will use a caretaker in this way in order to vicariously appraise some event or situation.

Play episodes between mothers and infants also show that infants can produce and comprehend emotional gestures and signals and can initiate and respond to intentional communications (Bretherton et al., 1986). The mutual and reciprocal exchange of positive affect, cooing, smiling, babbling, and the like often takes on the qualities of a behavioral dialogue replete with "turn-taking" (Beebe, Alson, Jaffe, Feldstein, & Crown, 1988; Kaye, 1982; Mayer & Tronick, 1985). First mothers will engage the infant with cooing, smiling, and touching; then infants respond with cooing, smiling, and physical movement. There is hence a kind of emotional sharing going on in these exchanges whereby mother and child achieve an interactional synchrony. Indeed, infants often take the initiative to provoke an emotional reaction from a mother who pretends she is sad or presents a "still face" (i.e., without expression). In these situations infants vocalize, point, or attend in order to engage their mother in an emotional exchange, almost as if they are trying to snap their mother out of it. If this doesn't work, infants often show signs of distress (Cohn & Tronick, 1983; Mayes & Carter, 1990). Infants of mothers who are actually depressed show many expressions of anger and sadness (Pickens & Field, 1993; Cohn, Campbell, Matias, & Hopkins, 1990), a more unfortunate kind of emotional sharing to be sure.

By the time of the first birthday, then, the infant can decode facial and vocal displays of emotion, can utilize the emotional expressions of others to regulate his or her own emotions, can initiate and respond to emotional gestures in a reciprocal, mutual way and as a means of regulating interpersonal behavior (Campos, Campos, & Barrett, 1989). Toward the end of the first year of life, then, the child becomes aware that the self and others are independently existing entities (Lewis & Brooks-Gunn, 1979) and that these entities have feelings, display emotions and execute intentions, just like "I" do. What is more, there is a dawning awareness that the chasm between "you and me" can be breached by attending to emotional displays and by generating and exchanging emotional cues and signals. The infant is tacitly aware that *"minds can be interfaced* or that *intersubjectivity can be deliberately generated"* (Bretherton et al., 1986, p. 531, my emphasis). By 20 months of age many infants can begin to verbally label at least some emotional states and, by 28 months, can make causal statements about emotions ("You sad, Mommy. What Daddy do?"). Indeed, there is evidence that preschool children have better emotional discernment than has traditionally be credited to them. Preschool children can correctly identify the emotional reactions of others and, more impressive, can correctly identify the causes of another person's emotional reactions, particularly the other's negative emotions (Fabes, Eisenberg, McCormick, & Wilson, 1988; Fabes, Eisenberg, Nyman, & Michealieu, 1991). Toddlers are empathically responsive to the mood states of others and often reproduce, share, or participate in the emotions of others. For example, when two-year-olds witnessed affection between adults, they responded in kind (Cummings, Zahn-Waxler, & Radke-Yarrow, 1981). When they witnessed conflict and anger, they responded with aggression during play periods with peers (Cummings, Iannotti, & Zahn-Waxler, 1985), which again points to a kind of sharing of affect (Thompson, 1987).

But are young children prosocial? Do they ever engage in behavior that is intended to benefit another? Indeed they do. Children under two often share their toys and give things away (Hay, 1979; Rheingold, Hay, & West, 1976), possibly to initiate or sustain social interaction (Eisenberg, Pasternak, Cameron, & Tryon, 1984). By the second birthday children verbalize their understanding of another's needs, wants, and intentions (Bretherton, McNew, & Beeghly-Smith, 1981), will comfort a younger sibling (Dunn & Kendrick, 1982), and will attempt to alleviate another's distress by expressing sympathy, showing concern, and offering help (Zahn-Waxler & Radke-Yarrow, 1982). In one study the percentage of children under 30 months of age who performed helping behaviors was broadly comparable to the rates of much older children—and half of these younger children did so on their own initiative, with 75 percent doing so with no promise of external reward (Bar-Tal, Raviv, & Goldberg, 1982). Hence, not only are young children empathically responsive to the emotional states of others (Strayer, 1980), there is also evidence of prosocial behavior (Denham, 1986; Dunn & Munn, 1986; Bridgeman, 1983; Grusec, 1991) .

And these prosocial inclinations continue to be observed throughout early childhood (Iannotti, 1985; Bridgeman, 1983; Payne, 1980; Radke-Yarrow, Zahn-Waxler, et al., 1976; Krebs, 1970; Bryan & London, 1970; Ugurel-Semin, 1952). In one study, for example, when young children heard infants cry, children as young as 4 and 5 years of age displayed signs of emotional arousal, made empathic statements, and offered to help, especially when the cries were not too intense and the baby's mother was present (Zahn-Waxler, Friedman, & Cummings, 1983). In a laboratory study, 50 percent of children from ages 7 to 9 left their room in order to come to the aid of a stricken child (Staub, 1970; 1971), a percentage that was also reported in a naturalistic study of 8- to 10-year-old children (Severy & Davis, 1971). What is more, even young children (1) have useful notions as to what makes one an effective helper (e.g., willingness, competence); (2) are aware that good intentions may fall short of the mark; (3) recognize that different problems may require different kinds of helping, and (4) are aware that the person being helped must cooperate (Barnett, Darcie, Holland, & Kobasigawa, 1982).   .

None of these prosocial inclinations on the part of toddlers and preschool-age children will come as a surprise to parents, teachers, or day-care workers. Parents, sometimes to their chagrin, are well aware of the "help" that their young children offer around the house. When mothers and fathers get busy on some household chore, such as vacuuming, sweeping, or dusting, they can be sure that the child will be right behind, rendering "assistance" that may not always be welcomed. As Harriet Rheingold (1982) points out, this participation in the work of adults is very much an early sign of prosocial behavior. In her study she observed three groups of young children (18, 24, and 30 months of age) and one or the other of their parents (and male and female strangers) in a laboratory that was decorated to look like a home. The "home" was apparently a bit disheveled, as there were nine tasks that clearly needed to be done. These tasks included such things as setting the table; placing magazines, cards, and books in their proper places; sweeping up bits of paper; folding laundry; making up a cot; and the like. The parent was instructed to begin working on a task much as he or she would at home but not to explicitly instruct the child to help.

Rheingold (1982) observed that the children in the three age groups showed a high degree of spontaneous "helping." Among the youngest children (18 months), 65 percent helped on at least half of the tasks, and nearly 100 percent of the older children participated. What is more, the children rendered assistance cheerfully, with alacrity, with minimal cues, and before the parent voiced an intention to do the chore. They helped not only the parent but also unfamiliar male and female strangers. They knew the goals of the task, performed behaviors appropriate to the goal (and hence, in a real way, assisted), and accompanied their help-giving with appropriate verbalizations ("I help you; I hold that little light bulb"). There is hence every reason to regard this behavior as prosocial. Children realize there is a job to do; they offer their assistance to see that the job gets done.

Although parents could undoubtedly finish the chore more efficiently, Rheingold (1982) suggests that the efficient execution of chores by parents makes for inefficient teaching of prosocial behavior. When parents allow the child to help, when the child is given the opportunity to be of assistance, the parent is capitalizing on a "teachable moment"; that is, the parent is taking the opportunity to introduce the child to the pleasures of prosocial helping, sharing, and cooperation. So when the child helps with the dusting or picks up the paper or puts the forks on the table, the child is gaining valuable training in prosocial development. This is a kind of moral socialization; this is how prosocial dispositions are developed in children. But there are other benefits as well. To be part of a collaborative activity with adults, especially parents, is a source of great pride to the child. It provides an opportunity to acquire knowledge and to hone skills. It gives the child a sense of competence and the mastery to complete a task, to participate in the big world of adults. Indeed, in Rheingold's (1982, p. 124) view, "To assist another is a positive social behavior not to be denied to the very young." The moral here for parents: Suffer the little children and let them help.

It would appear, then, that the young child presents a more complex developmental picture than the bare notions of egocentrism and egoism would otherwise suggest. Simply put, children are empathically sensitive and responsive to the distress of others, and they engage in prosocial behavior. What is more, these inclinations are evident at a very young age and long before sophisticated cognitive abilities are in place. This conclusion seems apt: "Children. . . are not only egocentric, selfish and aggressive; they are also exquisitely perceptive, have attachments to a wide range of others, and respond prosocially across a broad spectrum of interpersonal events in a wide variety of ways and with various motives" (Radke-Yarrow et al., 1983, p. 484). This last point bears further examination. Although young children have decided prosocial inclinations, this does not mean that their prosocial behavior is necessarily motivated by high-minded altruism. Indeed, we saw in Nancy Eisenberg's research program on prosocial reasoning that young children's motives for helping are often colored by hedonistic self-interest and other distinctly nonmoral considerations (e.g., approval, acceptance). Hence we need to distinguish between prosocial behavior and altruistic behavior. There is a view that prosocial behavior (i.e., behavior that benefits another) must meet certain conditions before it is properly called altruistic. It must (1) benefit another, (2) be performed voluntarily (3) and for its own end (4) with no expectation of personal gain and (5) perhaps at some cost to the self (Bar-Tal, 1976; Krebs, 1970). Hence, although altruistic behavior is necessarily prosocial (it is intended to benefit another), not all prosocial behavior is altruistic (since benefiting another could be done for self-serving, egoistic reasons).

Altruistic Motives

Daniel Bar-Tal and his colleagues (Bar-Tal, Raviv, & Leiser, 1980) have suggested that altruistic behavior may show stagelike development. In the first stage children help only when requested or commanded and when the request or command is accompanied by concrete rewards or explicit sanctions. In the second stage, a child helps in order to comply with the wishes of authorities. In the third stage children begin to take the initiative to help another in recognition of the other's needs but expecting some sort of reward in return. In the fourth stage, the child has a greater awareness of broad social norms and therefore helps in order to comply with these societal expectations and thereby gain approval. In the fifth stage, the child initiates help because she is aware that she is part of a social system where reciprocated helping (generalized reciprocity) is a norm. Hence, if the child helps another now, she can count on help when she needs it in the future. Finally, in the sixth stage, true altruism becomes a possibility.

One should notice two things about this sequence. First, as the child moves through the stages, he is required to take an increasingly more general social perspective, away from concrete rewards and sanctions of particular situations toward a consideration of what authorities and social systems are like and what they require of us; finally, the child adopts a more principled altruistic stance that requires genuine self-sacrifice. In this respect Bar-Tal's sequence is similar to the development of role-taking and of moral development more generally. And not surprisingly, advances in social-cognitive development are assumed to underwrite this advance in altruistic behavior. Indeed, this sequence was developed with these theoretical considerations in mind. Second, this sequence is broadly similar to Eisenberg's sequence of prosocial reasoning. Hence, it describes development of altruistic behavior as originating in pragmatic concerns about rewards and then progressing toward a concern for doing the stereotypic thing that might gain one approval and toward more principled self-sacrifice.

In an ingenious experiment Bar-Tal and his colleagues (1980) devised behavioral episodes that paralleled the altruism stages. Children were asked to play a "numbers-guessing" game. The "winners" (who won and lost was prearranged) were given seven pieces of candy as a prize. In the first condition, the experimenter simply left the room after the child was awarded the prize. If the child spontaneously shared with the "loser," the child was interviewed, debriefed, and dismissed from the study. This episode corresponds to the sixth stage and reflects altruism. If the child did not share, the second episode, which corresponds to the fourth (normative) stage commenced. Here the child was read a brief story where the norm of helping and sharing was the main theme. If the child did not share after hearing about the norm of sharing, the third episode began. This third episode was designed to parallel the third stage, which emphasizes internal initiative for sharing but with a promise of concrete rewards. The child was given the information that if any child chose to share, that child would get an important role in an upcoming play. If still the child did not share, she was simply told to share (Stage 2), and then told to share with the promise of a big prize (Stage 1).

This experimental manipulation of stages is really quite a novel way of determining, in a way that does not require a verbal interview, the motives that govern children's sharing behavior. What did the authors find? Only 7 percent of the kindergarten sample shared in the altruistic and normative conditions, compared to 23 percent of second-graders and 38 percent of fourth-graders. Hence, the older the child, the more likely sharing was spontaneous and the more likely it was initiated without promise of external reward or without being reminded of the social norm (in the case of the altruism condition).

At the other end of the spectrum, 24 percent of the kindergarten children shared under the Stage 1 condition, and just 2 percent of the fourth-graders did so. There were approximately equal amounts of sharing among the three grades in the Stage 2 and Stage 3 conditions. What is more, over half of the children who shared in the Stage 1 episode did so for rather low-level reasons (because a reward or prize was promised; because they were commanded). In contrast, 81 percent of the older children invoked higher-level motives, such as notions of normative obligation, generalized reciprocity, or altruism. These trends were replicated in a later study of 9- to 13-year-old boys using a similar methodology. In this study, older children tended to donate in the higher-stage experimental conditions and to explain their donation in terms of more advanced motivations (Raviv, Bar-Tal, & Lewis-Levin, 1980). Hence, it is clear that by middle childhood, most children have rather clear ideas about what is expected of them in those social situations where prosocial, altruistic opportunities present themselves.

Another motivation for performing prosocial actions may be the attribution that one is the sort of person who does prosocial things. Consider the following scenarios: (1) Watson tells children in one group that they are neat and tidy. He tells those in another group that they ought to be neat and tidy. Which children will actually become neater, refrain from littering, pick up after themselves? (2) Watson tells children in one group that they are cooperative. He tells those in another group that they are competitive. Do the groups behave accordingly? (3) Watson tells some children that they donated candy because they must really enjoy sharing. He tells others that they donated because sharing was expected of them. Which group is more likely to share in the future?

These are not entirely fanciful situations. Indeed, these scenarios were the principal manipulations in important research studies. Miller, Brickman, and Bolen (1975) found, for example, that directly telling children that they are neat and tidy was more effective for influencing their behavior than telling children that they ought to be neat and tidy. Telling children that they are cooperative will increase cooperative behavior. Telling them that they are competitive will increase competitive behavior (Jensen & Moore, 1977). Children who are told that they donated candy because they are the kinds of children who seem to like to share will more likely share in the future than children who are simply told to share because sharing is the expected thing to do (Grusec, Kuczynski, Simutis, & Rushton, 1978).

The common thread in these studies seems to be that if you "give a name, they'll play the game," as the expression goes. That is, when one produces for oneself or is given a certain attribution ("You are generous"; "You are neat and tidy"), this attribution serves to alter one's self-understanding. One is then more likely to act in ways that confirm this self-understanding (Lepper, 1983), probably because the attributions are now part of one's self-concept, and people are motivated to behave in self-consistent ways. An alternative explanation, however, is that the character attributions made in these studies are simply a form of positive reinforcement. That is, what makes the praise in these studies work is not the fact that a trait-character disposition is being imputed and self-concept is being influenced but rather the fact that some occasional neat, tidy, generous, and cooperative *behavior* is being positively reinforced by praise. So one might expect a child to improve on his generosity either when a generous *act* is praised ("It's nice that you shared") or when a positive trait attribution is imputed ("You must be the sort of boy who likes to share"). Both statements are simple forms of positive reinforcement. But is it true that either kind of statement would promote positive behavior?

This issue was teased out in a series of experiments by Joan Grusec and Erica Redler (Grusec & Redler, 1980). In one experiment seven- and eight-year-old children were given an opportunity on three different occasions to donate or share marbles and pencils, to help an adult fold cards, and to prepare drawings for sick children. On the first two occasions, some children who shared were given a positive character attribution, such as this one: "Gee, you shared. I guess you're the kind of person who likes to help others whenever you can. Yes, you are a very nice and helpful person." Other children were reinforced (praised) for donating or helping: "Gee, you shared. It was good that you gave some of your marbles to those poor children. Yes, that was a nice and helpful thing to do." Other children were told nothing about their sharing or helping (control condition). Note that the distinction between the attribution and the reinforcement conditions was whether the person (attribution) or the behavior (reinforcement) was praised. There is a difference between being a nice *person* (attribution) and doing a nice *thing* (reinforcement).

What did they find? When it came to donating marbles, the first test of these conditions, there was no difference between character attributions and reinforcement. Both conditions were effective (vs. control condition) in promoting donation. In subsequent situations, however, only the attribution condition facilitated prosocial behavior. Hence, more children folded cards, shared pencils, and returned drawings in the attribution condition than in the reinforcement condition. Indeed, praising behavior (reinforcement) and saying nothing at all (control) were equally ineffective on these later tasks. When children are told to do something, exhorted to do the right thing, or rewarded for doing so, their motivation for prosocial can always be attributed to an external source ("Dad made me") or to reinforcement ("Dad praises me when I do X"). But when the child is given character attribution ("You must be the sort of person who likes to be helpful and kind"), the child comes to see that she must be doing X not because of external pressure or rewards but rather because she is a kind and helpful person.

The authors came to two conclusions. First, since children who were given character attributions were likely to engage in subsequent prosocial behavior, it is likely that their self-concept, their understanding of themselves as kids who do nice and helpful things, affected their actual prosocial activities. "Children whose self-concept includes the view of themselves as helpful people will behave consistently with that self-concept" (Grusec & Redler, 1980, p. 529). Second, the effects of character attributions appear to generalize to new situations. These effects are more enduring, whereas the effects of praise and reinforcement of behavior are much more delimited and situation-specific.

This leads to an interesting conclusion. Simple moral exhortation, that is, telling children what they ought to do and praising what children actually do are both relatively ineffective for promoting prosocial dispositions in children (e.g., Grusec, Saas-Kortsaak, & Simutis, 1978), since neither approach is likely to influence the child's self-concept. Furthermore, there is evidence to suggest that rewards and reinforcement *undermine* prosocial motivation in the long run, especially when the prosocial behavior was something the child did out of intrinsic motivation, and especially in situations where rewards are no longer forthcoming (Fabes Fultz, Eisenberg, May-Plumlee, & Christopher, 1989)

The effectiveness of character attributions assumes, of course, that young children think of themselves as possessing enduring personality traits that are stable over time or that young children define their self-concepts in terms of stable psychological dispositions. For example, when Nicole's self-concept is bolstered by a particular character attribution ("You must be a kind and helpful person"), this attribution is incorporated into her self-concept. Because Nicole understands that her personality (self-concept) is composed of enduring traits (kind, helpful), she is now more likely to conform her behavior to this self-understanding.

But research suggests that young children do not have this understanding of personality much before age 8 (Livesley & Bromley, 1973). Hence, character attributions should be more effective with older children (say, age 8) than with younger children (e.g., kindergarten age). This was indeed shown in a second experiment by Grusec and Redler (1980). Using procedures similar to those in their first experiment, they showed that the effectiveness of character attributions hinges on whether the child understands that the self is composed of enduring and consistent trait dispositions. Yet a third experiment added nurses to this conclusion. In this study 8-year-old children made the distinction between what they did (their acts) and who they believed themselves to be (character attributions), as in the first two experiments, but not 10-year-old children. The older children were equally affected by attributions and reinforcement, as if both have an implication for prosocial situations (see also Smith, Gelfand, Hartmann, & Partlow, 1979). Perhaps as we get older we come to a better appreciation of the fact that what we do has a bearing on the sort of person we are.

These experiments are fascinating for two reasons. First, they lead to interesting conclusions about how to promote prosocial dispositions in children. There is an old bromide that says that when parents discipline a child, they should condemn the act but not the child. A parent should say: "I love you very much, and I don't object to you, but I do object to what you have done." In this case a distinction is appropriately drawn between statements about acts and statements about persons, with the condemnation falling on the act but not the person. But Grusec and Redler (1980) suggest that when it comes to socializing altruistic behavior, we should reverse matters and praise the child, not the behavior. At least for children under eight years of age, we should draw a distinction between acts and persons, since praising an act and praising the person appear to have very different effects. When we praise the child, when we make a character attribution, we have an effect on her self-concept, which probably motivates the child to conform her behavior accordingly across a range of prosocial situations. It would appear, then, that there is an asymmetry between praising and punishing. With praising, we focus on the person, not the act. With punishing, we focus on the act, not the person.

So one of the factors that may motivate altruism is simply the understanding that one is the sort of person who does altruistic things. The altruistic motive is tied to self-understanding, to one's conception of oneself and the kind of person one is. And we have seen that inducing character attributions is an effective way of promoting prosocial dispositions in children. The effectiveness of dispositional praise (character attributions) on altruistic behavior has been replicated in a more recent study by Mills and Grusec (1989). These authors also report, however, that girls may be less likely to attribute their altruistic behavior to internal sources (the self) and that other processes in addition to changes in self-perceptions may be responsible for motivating prosocial behavior. There is hence much more to be said about socialization of altruism. But before turning to this sprawling literature, I need to examine two mechanisms that are often said to mediate altruistic, prosocial behavior: perspective-taking and empathy.

Perspective-Taking, Empathy, and Altruism

It is widely presumed that a capacity for empathy and the development of perspective-taking abilities is what accounts for prosocial, altruistic behavior. This should be a familiar notion by now. I have already had occasion to mention the role of perspective-taking in moral development. We have seen, for example, that perspective-taking abilities are thought to be necessary but not sufficient for moral reasoning. What is more, we have seen that the development of prosocial reasoning (Eisenberg) and of altruistic motivation (Bar-Tal) entails that one assume an ever widening social perspective as one progresses through the respective stages. Similarly, and by implication, it is natural to assume that the ability to take the point of view of the other in distress, our ability to appraise the perspective of the other-in-need, is just what is behind our altruistic behavior. We cannot really take any action to benefit another until we see that the other needs to be benefited, and such may require that we see the world as the other sees it, that we put ourselves in the other guy's shoes. This is perspective-taking.

And studies have similarly implied that our empathic sensitivity to the plight of the other, or our emotional responsivity, is what motivates altruism. Empathy and perspective-taking are allied notions that have not always been clearly distinguished in the literature. Perspective-taking is usually described as the ability to infer something about the experience of another—what the other is thinking (cognitive role-taking), what the other can see from her visual perspective (spatial-visual-perceptual role-taking), or what the other's emotional experience must be (affective role-taking). Empathy has sometimes been defined as a cognitive awareness of another's emotional experience (Deutsch & Madle, 1975; Borke, 1971), but this definition makes empathy a species of affective role-taking, a confusion that is sometimes (Staub, 1987), but not always (Underwood & Moore, 1982), lamented. More typically, however, when one speaks of empathy, one is making reference not so much to comprehension or understanding of another's affective experience ("In my judgment, Fox is experiencing sorrow"). Rather, empathy is said to imply a vicarious sharing in the affective experience of the other ("I feel Fox's sorrow"). If one is empathically sensitive to the dire straits of the person in need, if the emotional distress of the other resonates within us, if the emotional experience of the other is somehow made our own, then we should be motivated to respond to the other's distress in an altruistic, prosocial way.

What does the research literature show regarding the relationship between perspective-taking, empathy, and prosocial, altruistic behavior? Let's first examine the case for perspective-taking.

Perspective-Taking

Perspective-taking is not a unidimensional ability. Indeed, many different kinds of processes are implicated by the label. We have already noted that perpective-taking comes in at least three forms: cognitive (what does the other think?), spatial (what does the other see?), and affective (what does the other feel?). The ability to veridically assume the perspective of the other is a skill that gets progressively better (in each of these domains) as a child develops. The child is initially egocentric, that is, embedded within his or her own perspective. The young child fails to differentiate her point of view from the point of view of others. So, when the child attempts to determine what another person thinks, sees, or feels, she attributes to the other her own perspective instead, that is, she attributes to the other what she is thinking, seeing, or feeling. The child does have some dim notion that the other person's perspective must be different, but she lacks the perspective-taking abilities to determine just what that perspective must be and so attributes to the other her own perspective instead. How to characterize perspective-taking abilities is still a matter of discussion.

Tory Higgins (1981) has provided the most insightful and compelling analysis of perspective-taking yet available in the literature. In his view perspective-taking has been conceptualized in a number of ways in the social-cognitive developmental literature. It involves, first, an ability to determine the attributes of others over and above what is suggested by a particular situation. If we learn something about Vanessa (she is happy) simply by looking at aspects of the situation (she is opening a present), our judgment is not independent of the stimulus input; indeed, we are simply describing the obvious characteristics of a situation, and we have not engaged in perpective-taking. Similarly, if we reach a judgment (Billy is sad) by projecting our own intuitions onto the other ("If that happened to me, I'd be sad"), then we have allowed the self to intrude upon our judgment, and we have not engaged in perspective-taking. In both of these situations there is no real need to assume the perspective of the other, no need to engage in role-taking, since in the first instance, we simply described the situation, and in the second, we simply projected our own feelings to the other.

So the first requirement for role-taking is that one must make an inference, and this inference must be independent of the stimulus situation and independent of one's own contaminating perspective. We must, quite literally, take the other's perspective, and to do this we need to disentangle it from situational cues and from our own perspective. But as Higgins (1981) points out, taking the other's perspective while controlling or inhibiting our own is no simple matter, and it varies in complexity. Put simply, there are many things that need to be kept in mind as one attempts to infer the perspective of the other.

Oftentimes when young children attempt to take the other's perspective they rarely get beyond simply describing the concrete, observable characteristics of the other. As they get older, however, children come to make inferences about the covert, internal psychological traits and dispositions of the other. Here, then, are two perspective-taking processes that appear to show developmental change: (1) With development children's inferences move away from observable, concrete characteristics of the other person (Billy is tall and has many toys, toward inferences about covert, internal, psychological traits and dispositions (Billy is honest). (2) With development, children's inferences coordinate and balance an increasing number of elements or pieces of information: "First I can think about me, then I can think about you, then I can think about you thinking about me, then I can think about you thinking about me thinking about you," and so on. This is called recursive role-taking (Miller, Kessel, & Flavell, 1970). Alternatively, this feature of role-taking development might be captured this way: "First I think about me and my thoughts, then I can think about you and your thoughts, then I can think about me from your perspective (reciprocal role-taking), then I can think about or monitor our interaction from a neutral third-party perspective (simultaneous role-taking), then I can take the point of view of many third parties, that is, of society itself" (Selman, 1971b; Selman & Byrne, 1974).

These perspective-taking processes involve, then, a progressive ability to take an ever widening social perspective. Clearly the number of elements that must be kept in mind increases linearly with age, from an egocentric concern with the self (one element) to an appreciation of the other's point of view (two) to the understanding that one can reflect upon the self from the other's point of view (three) to the point of view of a neutral observer who can monitor an ongoing self-other interaction (four) to the point of view of society itself (five elements).

In sum, it would appear that mature role-taking entails making an inference. This inference goes beyond situational cues and is absent the contaminating bias of one's own perspective. It is not based on a projection of one's own perspective onto the other. It is typically focused on the covert psychological aspects of the other's experience or, alternatively, involves balancing and coordinating numerous elements until the widest possible social perspective is within reach.

Numerous measuring instruments have been designed over the years to assess the various kinds of perspective-taking (e.g., Flavell et al., 1968; Enright & Lapsley, 1980). There is diversity in the varieties of role-taking that are assessed in this literature. There is diversity in the methodological procedures that are thought to reveal role-taking of any variety. Many of these task differences show wildly different estimates of when mature role-taking is possible. There are also a number of psychological processes that are invoked to account for performance on the various role-taking tasks. Role-taking is clearly a multidimensional construct that can be assessed with a dizzying array of techniques. I mention all of this just to prepare the reader for what must now seem an obvious conclusion: The relationship among the various measures of role-taking, both within and between domains, is often quite poor, and no wonder, given the diversity of constructs, measures, and processes (Shantz, 1983; Kurdek & Rodgon, 1975; Rubin, 1973, 1978; Ford, 1979; Enright & Lapsley, 1980; Lapsley & Quintana, 1989).

If the relationship among role-taking measures is inconsistent, or worse, then we should not be too confident that role-taking would predict prosocial, altruistic behavior. In fact, the empirical evidence on the relationship between perspective-taking and altruism was often judged to be inconclusive at best (Krebs & Russell, 1981; Mussen & Eisenberg-Berg, 1977). A positive relation is reported by some (Krebs & Sturrup, 1982; Buckley, Siegel, & Ness, 1979), a negative relationship by others (Lemare & Krebs, 1983), and both inconsistent (Barrett & Yarrow, 1977; Iannotti, 1978) and nonsignificant relationships (Eisenberg-Berg & Lennon; Emler

& Rushton, 1974; Zahn-Waxler, Radke-Yarrow, & Brady-Smith, 1977; Rushton & Wiener, 1975) have been reported as well.

An important paper by Bill Underwood and Bert Moore (1982) brought considerable clarity to this messy literature. They subjected the literature to a meta-analysis, which is a specialized quantitative technique for assessing and evaluating accumulated research findings. From the results of numerous empirical studies, one calculates a common estimate of the magnitude of the relationship between variables and effects (Hedges & Olkin, 1985; Glass, McGraw, & Smith, 1981). Hence, to use an analogy, what might look confusing and inconsistent at the level of trees (i.e., individual studies) takes on greater clarity at the level of the forest (effect magnitudes summarized across numerous studies).

When the relationship between perceptual role-taking and altruism was examined (across 4 studies), a mean correlation (M_r) of .28 was reported. When the effect of age was removed from the correlation, the magnitude of the relationship was much reduced, $M_r = .19$. These findings suggest that although there is a significant, positive relationship between spatial perspective-taking and prosocial behavior (helpfulness, comforting, and generosity), the correlation is quite modest, accounting for about 3–7 percent of the variance.

A similar relationship was reported for the altruism–social perspective-taking relationship. Across 10 studies, $M_r = .28$. When age was partialed from the correlation, it was reduced to $M_r = .19$. Again, the relationship between social perspective-taking and prosocial behavior (generosity, helpfulness, spontaneous acts in naturalistic settings, teacher ratings) is significant and positive but modest. That said, there is evidence that altruistic behavior can be increased when children are trained in social perspective-taking (Iannotti, 1978), which does suggest a greater role for perspective-taking than these modest correlations would otherwise lead us to believe.

Somewhat better results are reported for measures of moral development (treated here as a species of perspective-taking) and prosocial behavior. Indeed, the authors noted that "the data for moral reasoning are the most compelling we have seen, not for the magnitude of the relationship but for generality of the relationship" (Underwood & Moore, 1982, p. 158). Across 19 studies, the mean correlation coefficient among various measures of moral reasoning and prosocial behavior (generosity, bystander intervention, helpfulness, spontaneous prosocial behavior) was $M_r = .28$, which was reduced to $M_r = .21$ when age was partialed from the correlation. The relationship, then, is significant, positive, and consistent but modest, accounting for approximately 5 percent of the variance.

What about affective role-taking and altruism? What about empathy and altruism? The results here are disappointing indeed. The authors discerned a significant positive relationship between affective perspective-taking and prosocial behavior ($M_r = .28$), but this estimate was based on only two studies, one of which reported a nonsignificant relationship and the other reported a statistical relationship that is not easily computed into a correlational estimate. Some caution, therefore, is in order. The results for empathy were even worse. If empathy was related to prosocial behavior at all, the relationship applied mostly to adults. We will revisit this conclusion very shortly.

It would appear, then, that the various kinds of role-taking are related to at least some kinds of altruistic, prosocial behavior. The relationship, however, though apparently consistent and positive, is not very large. A significant amount of variation in the correlations is still left unaccounted for. However, given the diversity of role-taking constructs, the diversity of tasks and methodologies, and the diversity of processes that may well ground perspective-taking, I suppose we should be pleased or surprised that the correlations are as significant or as consistent as they are.

What are we to make of this? We have reviewed evidence that preschool children already have decided prosocial inclinations long before mature perspective-taking skills come on line. Apparently, young children are not so egocentric, not so embedded in their own perspective, not so "centrated" in their own point of view that they cannot help, comfort, share, cooperate. Furthermore, given the modest correlations just reviewed, there is apparently no guarantee that mature perspective-taking abilities will invariably motivate prosocial behavior (although they may increase one's tendency to benefit another). Indeed, mature perspective-taking can just as well be used to advance one's anti-social agenda of taking advantage of others through swindling, rationalization, sophistry, and manipulation (Lapsley, 1992b; Eisenberg, 1986).

So, young children, on the one hand, can be prosocial without the benefits of mature perspective-taking ability. Older children, on the other hand, need not be prosocial even when they can and do take the perspective of the other with great skill. Clearly, then, perspective-taking is neither necessary nor sufficient for prosocial behavior (Higgins, 1981; Eisenberg, 1986). It is not necessary to the extent that our prosocial behavior is an impulsive, automatic response in a crisis. It is not necessary to the extent that our information about the affairs of the other is based not on inferences but on projection or on our reading of the objective situation or on the categories, schemas, or scripts that are evoked by an event. It is not sufficient to the extent that other cognitive abilities in addition to perspective-taking must be available, say, to reconcile conflicting affective cues (Carlo, Knight, Eisenberg & Rotenberg, 1991). It is not sufficient to the extent that other cognitive processes or psychological dispositions must be on line to steer our perspective-taking knowledge into distinctly prosocial, moral directions and not elsewhere. Something else must intervene between understanding Jones and benefiting Jones. Perhaps it is our capacity for vicarious sharing of affect? Perhaps it is our capacity for empathy that motivates our prosocial altruism? If the Underwood and Moore (1982) review is any guide, we should not be holding out much hope on this score. But we need to revisit the whole issue of empathic affect and its role in moral psychology.

Empathy Revisited: Martin Hoffman's Theory

Martin Hoffman (1975b, 1987, 1991) has developed the most sophisticated account of empathy's role in our moral life. In his view moral action is motivated by the resonance of empathic affect. Indeed, empathy is implicated in nearly every moral encounter one can imagine: Should we cheat on our taxes? Should we inform on neighbors? Should we lie to keep our jobs? Should we end the life support of a stricken relative? Should we get a divorce? Should we end or continue the quarrel with our family? What are we to do about the hurtful gossip that comes our way? Under what conditions can I break a promise or favor a friend or relative at the expense of a stranger? What these issues, and undoubtedly countless others, have in common is the fact that they all involve potential victims. In human social life it invariably happens that we perform intentional actions that either are of benefit to others or do them harm. It seems odd that the great moral questions that we face always seem to involve potential harm, always seem to involve victims. No one seems to worry too much about the moral implications of actions that bring great benefits. It is the potential victimizing aspects of our conduct that typically give us moral pause.

But why do we worry so much about victims? In Hoffman's view, it is because we empathize with their plight. We have the capacity to share in the victim's emotional experience. The distress of the other is made our own. Because of this vicarious sharing of affect, we are motivated to come to the aid of victims, to relieve their distress, if only to relieve our own in the process. Hence, to say that empathy is a moral motive is to say that (1) most moral encounters involve victims and (2) empathic affect motivates us to come to their aid (Hoffman, 1991). Note that Hoffman does not say that moral motivation derives from moral *reasons*, is a product of a moral *judgment*, or becomes evident once one appreciates the fact that moral *principles* are *prescriptive*. This cognitivistic approach to moral motivation is, of course, more Kohlbergian than not. But unlike Kohlberg's theory, Hoffman's approach emphasizes the motivational properties of emotions. Moral action might well follow from a moral judging process replete with reasons and principles, but it need not evolve in this way.

One difference between Hoffman and Kohlberg lies in what they each take to be the typical moral encounter. For Kohlberg it is the dilemma where claims to justice must be evaluated. It requires moral deliberation and conflict resolution. It is approached through reasonable argument and the search for consensus through principled bargaining. The cognitive, rational character of this enterprise is clear. For Hoffman, in contrast, the typical moral encounter is not a moral dilemma that has to be thought through but a "bystander intervention" situation, where another person is in jeopardy, in distress, in danger, and we are in a position to come to his aid. Our response in this situation is probably more emotive than not and need not involve complex reasoning or appeals to principles. This emphasis on empathic motives and the emotional foundation of moral actions does not, however, mean that Hoffman therefore neglects cognitive factors, as we will see shortly (see Gibbs, 1991, for integrative possibilities with Kohlberg's theory).

Hoffman (1975b, 1981) has long argued that our capacity for empathy and the prosocial altruism that it motivates may well be a response tendency that is hardwired into human nature. Evolutionary biologists have long suspected that the notion of individual selection has given the process of natural selection an egoistic slant. That is, notions such as the struggle for survival, and the survival of the fittest appeared to emphasize the importance of individual survival—the individual selection of members of a species according to the criterion of fitness. So the strongest, fastest, smartest individuals survived and got to pass along their select genes to their offspring. Individuals who were weak, slow, and dumb did not survive and tended not to propagate their inferior "unfit" genes. The struggle for survival, then, implied that an individual had to look out for himself, be egoistic, in order to maximize the probability that his genes would be successfully passed along to the next generation. One imagines that our egoistic ancestors were strongly motivated to engage in self-preserving behavior.

Although evolutionary egoism is surely a possibility, it is now recognized that many species, including the human species, could not have survived outside of the workings of cooperative social life. What makes group life work is that, on occasion, one is required to engage in behaviors that benefit others even when by doing so one incurs great personal risk and high costs. Could there be an evolutionary basis for altruism and altruistic self-sacrifice? In Hoffman's (1981) view, biological altruism must have (also) been favored by natural selection. Altruism, like egoism, must have played a role in our evolutionary success as a species. It contributes to *group selection* (groups with more altruists tend to defeat groups with fewer altruists). It contributes to *kin selection*, that is, altruism contributed to the survival of kin and near relatives with whom we share our genes (and group life). What is more, there is evidence that altruistic behavior directed toward nonrelatives must also have been favored by natural selection, since rescuing others increased the probability that one would be rescued in return should the occasion arise (Trivers, 1971). Individuals who help each other, who engage in reciprocal altruism, tend to be more successful (e.g., in terms of propagating their genetic characteristics) than do individuals who face the danger on their own. Hence, Hoffman (1981, p. 124) concludes that "natural selection therefore favors a tendency to help others." In his view altruism and egoism are independent, genetically favored, naturally selected motives that are laid down in human nature during the course of our evolutionary history.

The cynic might argue, of course, that nothing we do is ever selfless. What passes for altruism is always, on some level, self-serving. Even when we engage in acts of heroic altruism, such behavior is really egoistic after all, the argument goes, since we are often applauded for our heroism, patted on the back, held up as an example. Our ego is massaged, we feel good about ourselves, and we bask in the warm glow of moral self-satisfaction of a good deed well done. Hoffman (1981) rejects this argument. Helping, he argues, is not ultimately self-serving, is not egoism in disguise. If altruistic behavior is really egoistic, that is, if we help only to gain approval, we will tend to help only when an audience is around to applaud our nobility or when our own need for friendship and affection requires satisfaction. Yet bystander-intervention research suggests that we tend to help, and help faster, when no one else is around and (Darley & Latane, 1968; Latane & Rodin, 1969).

Furthermore, we are most inclined to be prosocial when our own needs for approval and affection are already quite well satisfied (e.g., Staub & Sherk, 1970; Mussen, Harris, Rutherford, & Keasey, 1970). Indeed, Bryant and Crockenberg (1980) showed that children who experienced sensitive, responsive, and nurturant maternal caretaking, that is, who enjoyed the experience of having their own needs met, were more likely to engage in prosocial sharing and comforting.

A case is made, then, for a biological understanding of the altruistic motive. Altruism is part of human nature. It is part of the human genetic package, a response tendency that conveys "inclusive fitness." It is motivated by our hardwired capacity for experiencing empathic affect (Hoffman, 1975b). Empathic affect involves five modes of operation. In infancy empathic affect is evoked through *primary circular reactions*, as when an infant cries in response to the distress cries of other infants (Sagi & Hoffman, 1976). This term is not terribly apt. In Piaget's (1952b) theory, a primary circular reaction is a repetitive behavior (circular reaction) that is repeated in the attempt to reinstate a pleasurable event associated with the child's own body (which makes the behavior primary). By "primary circular reaction," Hoffman (1991) appears to be drawing attention to the fact that the distress of the other infant is not distinguished from self-distress, so that when distress cues are encountered, the child responds with his or her own cry of distress. It is almost as if the self and other are fused, as if the bodily discomfort of the one (signaled by distress cues) is experienced as discomfort by the other (signaled by empathic distress cues). This sort of emotional contagion appears to be eliminated from the behavioral repertoire as the child grows up, it being frowned upon by socialization agents.

A second mode of operation is *mimicry*, as when the child responds to the expressive cues (facial features, posture, vocal tone) of the other. A third mode is *classical conditioning*. Say that Sarah bangs her head against a door while crawling. It hurts; she cries. Later she observes her brother Billy hit his head on a door. Seeing his discomfort evokes associations with her own unfortunate encounter with the door, and she starts crying, too. Even young infants in the first weeks of life are capable of learning responses through classical conditioning, so this mode of empathic arousal is potentially operative quite early in life.

These first three empathic arousal modes (primary circular reactions, mimicry, conditioning) are rather automatic and involuntary. They are ways of experiencing empathic affect that seem part of our biological equipment, as it were, and they appear to be in place even before the infant is cognizant of the other, indeed, before self and other are clearly differentiated. What is more, these modes of empathic arousal require very minimal cognitive processing (Hoffman, 1991). Only sensory registration is required for primary circular reactions. Only simple pattern matching is required for mimicry. And even simple biological organisms can be classically conditioned. Again, all of this points out the fact that three of the five modes of empathic affect arousal appear to be innate in human nature, probably because of their survival value. As Hoffman (1975b, p. 614) puts it, it is part of our biological nature to "be built in such a way that our own feelings of distress will often be contingent not on our own but on someone else's misfortune."

The fourth mode of empathic arousal is verbal cues of the other's distress. The fifth mode is role-taking. These latter two modes clearly place a premium on advanced cognitive processes and symbolic capabilities.

So empathic affect is aroused through three involuntary, automatic mechanisms and through linguistic mediation and perspective-taking. The fact that there are five modes of empathic affect arousal suggests to Hoffman (1984) that our empathic reactions to distress are *over determined*. That is, there are multiple opportunities for empathy to be evoked, depending upon situational cues. If one mode of operation is not on line (say, mimicry) because of the nature of some situation (expressive cues cannot be seen), another mode of operation (conditioning) can step in to induce the appropriate empathic affect. Thus the arousal of empathic affect is a highly reliable response to another's distress. Hoffman (1991) also suggests that empathic affect is self-reinforcing. Every time Sarah empathizes with Billy's distress, the co-occurrence of Sarah's empathic affect and Billy's distress cues makes it more likely that distress cues will evoke the appropriate empathic affect in the future.

These five modes of empathic affect arousal simply point out the fact that the human organism has multiple systems available for responding to distress cues. Experiencing empathic affect, then, is a reliable human response; it is something you can count on human beings to do if there is reasonable attention to empathic cues. But to say that one must be reasonably attentive is to suggest a role for cognitive processes. Simple, involuntary mechanisms usually suffice to evoke empathic reactions, to be sure. But even here we need to attend to appropriate cues. The other person does, after all, signal distress. If our cognitive understanding of persons undergoes developmental transformations, such transformations should condition our experience of empathy as well (Burns & Cavey, 1957). Indeed, Hoffman (1975b) argues that the subjective experience of empathic affect is mediated by cognitive development, particularly our progressive understanding of persons. When cognitive development is factored into empathic arousal, we see that empathic development proceeds through four stages. Let's examine these stages of empathic development.

Stage 1: Global Empathy.   I have already had occasion to allude to this phenomenon. When self and other are not clearly distinguished, the distress cues of the other are confused with one's own empathically aroused distress. Consequently, and curiously, infants may be unsure of who is actually experiencing discomfort. For example, if Leda observes her brother fall and hurt himself, Leda may act as if she herself has been injured. She might then engage in those behaviors that she ordinarily finds comforting when she is distressed (e.g., sucking her thumb, clutching her blanket, running to her mother, or crying). Crying at the sound of the distress cries of other infants is another example of a global empathic reaction. Such emotional contagion is not, of course, an example of a mature empathic response, because the child may have little sense of the other's separate existence (Thompson, 1987). But global empathic reactions are clearly precursors to mature empathy.

Stage 2: Egocentric Empathy.   What is minimally required for true empathic responding is that the self and other be clearly differentiated. As Michael Lewis and Jeanne Brooks-Gunn (1979, p. 262) put it, "Being able to empathize means being able to place *oneself* in the role of the other, and this implies a notion of *oneself.*" By the first birthday the *existential self* is well in evidence. The existential self knows that "I" exist, "I" exist independently from others, and "I" can cause things to happen in the world. The existential self has a sense of independent existence and personal agency (Lewis & Brooks-Gunn, 1979). So by the first birthday something like a true empathic orientation is evident just because self and other are clearly differentiated—the independent, agentic self can now take action on behalf on another person who is not the self. But this does not mean that the action taken is entirely appropriate. One-year-old Leda knows that her brother Jesse is a separate person, and she knows that she can come to his aid; but she lacks the inferential abilities to gauge Jesse's subjective experience. Leda can only assume that Jesse's experience is similar to her own. So when Jesse is upset, Leda brings to him those objects (e.g., her doll, her blanket, her pacifier) that *she* finds comforting. Hoffman (1991) reports an incident whereby an 18-month-old boy took his own mother to comfort a peer who was crying even though the crying boy's mother was also nearby. In both examples the behavior is prosocial, the children are attempting to benefit another, and their prosocial behavior is motivated by appropriate empathic affect; but they are confused about internal states, and their response is invariably egocentric.

Stage 3: Empathy for Another's Feelings.   When role-taking skills are better developed, the child is able to infer another's subjective experience with greater accuracy and to tailor her responses more appropriately even if this means not helping when doing so would induce embarrassment, shame, and loss of face in the victim. Role-taking skills are helped along by improvements in language abilities. Indeed, empathic affect can be induced through symbolic means, that is, through information about the other who is absent.

Stage 4: Empathy for Another's Life Condition.   We noted earlier that perspective-taking development typically concludes with an ability to assume a general societal perspective—to take the point of view of the social system itself. Hence the young adolescent is now capable of empathizing with entire groups or categories of people (the poor, the oppressed, the sick). This ability may itself encourage the teen to develop a certain "ideology" or political posture. Because the adolescent can now take a more generalized perspective on someone's condition, he or she will now empathize with another's chronic condition or general state of deprivation.

This sequence illustrates the important role that cognitive processes play in mediating empathic affect. At Stage 4, for example, empathy is induced through complicated inferences about another's life condition. A "systems perspective" is required in order to comprehend the workings of, say, oppression or poverty or the formation of ideologies. These cognitive abilities bring into view a richer variety of targets with whom to empathize and a greater variety of conditions and situations within which these targets are embedded. Furthermore, we have seen how cognitive development makes it possible to construct moral principles and to understand moral argument. Moral judgments may well help us decide what to do in bystander-intervention situations. We often decide to intervene on the basis of sophisticated moral judgments, but empathic affect plays a role here, too. Indeed, in Hoffman's (1987, 1991) view, a comprehensive moral theory must establish a relationship between empathy and the construction and utilization of moral principles. It is readily assumed that empathy motivates bystander intervention. It is conceded that bystander intervention can also be motivated by moral reasoning. We have seen that empathic affect becomes better deployed with increases in social-cognitive development. So it is a short step from here to conclude that empathy plays a role in our selection and utilization of moral principles. Hoffman (1991) has attempted to carve out this relationship with more specificity in recent writings, particularly with respect to two moral principles, namely, the principle of benevolence and caring and the principle of fairness (distributive justice). I will focus here on the link between empathy and distributive justice, since it is perhaps less obvious and less direct than the relation between empathy and benevolent caring.

Empathy and Distributive Justice

Hoffman (1991) first takes note of three principles of distributive justice: need (allocate more resources to those who need more; those who need less should get less); equality (everyone should get the same); and equity (resources should be allocated according to merit or effort). Which distributive principle should we invoke? William Damon might suggest that this answer depends on the stage of social-cognitive development. For Hoffman, however, it may well depend on how empathic we are. If one empathizes with the plight of poor people, for example, the need criterion might be judged most fair. But if we can imagine how terrible it would feel to be deprived of the fruits of one's own labor, to be slighted after extraordinary effort, to have merit or desert frustrated, then perhaps we will find equity (or equality) to be more congenial. Apparently, then, when we think about moral principles, we think about victims. Our ability to foresee consequences, to imagine victims, to empathize with their condition, may well undergird our selection of distributive justice principles. Indeed, Hoffman (1991) suggests that individuals who are not empathic may well choose egoistic, self-serving distributive principles. For example, if I am a very productive, hardworking fellow but have rather impoverished empathic abilities, I might favor distributive decisions that favor equity, since I would thereby acquire more honors, rewards, and goods for my hard work and high production. Alternatively, if I am not at all productive and not terribly empathic, I will probably favor equality or need, since I will get just as much as anyone else regardless of my own sorry efforts, and perhaps more if my needs turn out to be great. In contrast, someone who is empathic might well choose equality or need even if he or she merits or deserves more (being very productive and hardworking). Alternatively, one might endorse some complicated compromise, namely, reward on the basis of equity for those who deserve or merit more, but forbid vast inequalities (equality) and make sure no one is severely neglected (need).

Hoffman (1987, 1991) notes one additional way that empathic affect and moral principles might be related. He argues that moral principles can become "hot cognitions." What are hot cognitions, and how do they come about? A moral principle becomes a hot cognition when it becomes yoked to some emotionally charged representation of victims, events, memories, culprits, actions, and more. That is, a "cold" moral principle, learned perhaps in the abstract, becomes "heated up" when associated with empathic affect, with emotion. During the course of development, empathic affect and moral principles are probably encountererd independently. Indeed, we have seen that very young children, infants and toddlers, are empathically responsive to the distress of others long before they acquire the cognitive abilities to articulate and understand moral principles. So during the long years of development, there are occasions that evoke empathic affect. There are occasions when we learn moral principles. When we encounter a "moral situation," it may activate emotionally charged memories but also relevant moral principles. When empathic affect and moral principle are evoked in this way, an association between them may form so that in the future, when the principle is invoked, so too is the affective reaction activated. In this way the cognition (a moral principle) becomes "hot" (emotionally charged with empathic affect). A moral principle, and its corresponding empathic affective reaction, may be jointly encoded in memory so that one or the other may be sufficient to activate a network of emotionally charged associations. We might become more committed to a moral principle if it is grounded on this sort of affective foundation, and having a principle may also modulate our emotional reaction to an event.

Hoffman's theory, then, carves out a large role for empathy in our moral life. He avoids any false distinction between moral cognition and moral emotion and has developed a plausible, comprehensive theoretical framework that carefully delineates their respective roles. Yet on the basis of Underwood and Moore's (1982) literature review, there appears to be little support for the otherwise plausible notion that empathy is an important moral emotion that mediates and promotes prosocial, altruistic behavior. If this conclusion were to stand, Hoffman's important theory would look much less appealing than it does. A more recent look at the empathy literature, however, has led to more encouraging conclusions.

Another Look at the Empirical Literature

Nancy Eisenberg and Paul Miller (1987) revisited the literature on empathy and its relationship to prosocial behavior. Whereas Underwood and Moore (1982) restricted their review to just one method of assessing empathy (picture and story methods). Eisenberg and Miller examined six additional methods, including questionnaires, experimental simulations, physiological indices, vocal, facial, and gestural measures, observer reports, and misattributions (e.g., if empathic arousal is misattributed to some cause other than a needy other, is one likely to help?). They also examined a considerably larger literature than was available to Underwood and Moore. Using metaanalytic techniques Eisenberg and Miller found generally positive associations between altruistic behavior and the various indices of empathy. The strength of the associations ranged from .10 to .36 and varied by method of assessment and by age of the sample. The relationship was weakest among children, for example, and strongest among adults. As the authors pointed out, the differences were probably due to the fact that emotional responses and behavioral reactions become better integrated with age. Young children may have more difficulty interpreting their empathic arousal and have more difficulty enacting their altruistic intentions (e.g., because of perceived lack of competence, not knowing how to help) than adults.

The empathy-altruism relationship also varied by method. As was also reported by Underwood and Moore (1982), picture-story methods of assessing empathy, such as the popular Affective Situations Test (Feshbach & Roe, 1968), were uncorrelated with altruistic behavior. Perhaps picture-story assessments are too artificial and not sufficiently evocative to arouse empathic affect. With the AST, for example, children are presented two story illustrations of each of four emotions: sadness, anger, fear, happiness. Each story is a very brief narrative portrayed on three slides and concerning a hypothetical event. After a child is presented with a scenario, the child is asked, "How do you feel?" or "How did the story make you feel?" But perhaps it is unreasonable to expect a brief three-slide story about some hypothetical event to arouse much emotion in a child. If the technique evokes any emotional reaction at all, it probably dissipates rather quickly after many trials (after eight stories and after being repeatedly asked, "How do you feel?").

Apart from picture-story ratings, however, virtually every assessment of empathy was associated with altruistic, prosocial behavior. Questionnaire measures of empathy (e.g., Bryant, 1982; Mehrabian & Epstein, 1972) are a popular form of assessment. They tended to correlate with altruistic behavior on the order of .17 (with a range of .14 to .20). As Eisenberg and Miller (1987) point out, questionnaires typically comprise many items and sample numerous kinds of situations and events and may consequently assess many factors other than empathy (e.g., personal distress, sympathy). However, this broader sampling across many kinds of situations improves the stability of the measures. Stronger correlations are also evident when (1) subjects are presented stimuli using evocative media (videotape, realistic enactments) and (2) when subjects believe that events are real and not hypothetical. In these simulated experimental situations the estimated correlation between empathy and prosocial behavior is .25 (range .19 to .30).

In general, then, the common correlations were consistent but not large. But Eisenberg and Miller (1987) insist that these correlations, although low, are an underestimate of the true relationship between empathy and altruism, and this for several reasons. First, the metaanalyses reported here included all known and available studies, even when measures used in some of them had weak or questionable psychometric properties or were clearly invalid. Second, in some studies the measure of empathy could have been confounded with allied constructs such as sympathy (e.g., feeling sorry for another vs. matching affect). Third, measures of altruism were sometimes suspect, confounding altruism, for example, with mere prosocial behavior that could have been motivated by egoistic considerations, by peer pressure, by social reinforcement, or by compliance. Yet for all of these difficulties, for all of these reservations, it does appear that empathy is a significant predictor of altruistic behavior, that the theoretical significance of empathy in our moral life has been vindicated, and that the more pessimistic conclusions of Underwood and Moore (1982) are therefore not warranted.

This said, there is clearly a significant amount of variation still left unaccounted for in these correlations, which again suggests that something else must be involved to mediate altruistic, prosocial behavior, in addition to (or instead of) empathy. One candidate is the sense of personal responsibility. In a recent study, helping behavior was predicted not by empathy but by attributions of guilt (Chapman, Zahn-Waxler, Cooperman, & Iannotti, 1987). The authors suggested that prosocial behavior may be motivated not so much by our tendency to "match affects," that is, by our tendency to feel the same emotions as another (trait empathy), but rather by our inclination to feel a personal responsibility for the other's well-being. Research also suggests that this sense of personal responsibility not only applies to helping but also leads to increases in other prosocial behaviors such as donating and sharing (Maruyama, Fraser, & Miller, 1982). Thus without an accompanying sense of personal responsibility, empathy may be ineffective for motivating altruism. Indeed, children who are socialized to feel responsible for persons in need tend to make reparations for transgressions and to respond with increased prosocial behavior to others in distress (Zahn-Waxler, Radke-Yarrow, & King, 1979).

Once again the responsible self emerges as an important notion in moral psychology. The responsible self was introduced in Chapter 4 when I examined the issue of moral action in the Kohlbergian research tradition. I examined Blasi's self model of moral action, which suggests that we are more likely to do what we know to be required of us when we come to understand that the integrity of the self is at stake in what we do or fail to do. And here we see the responsible, moral self in another guise we may be more likely to engage in prosocial behavior, engage in selfless altruism, precisely because we believe the self bears a responsibility toward the other. Perhaps what transforms moral principles into "hot cognitions" is not so much their association with emotionally charged affects but rather their association with self-understanding. Zahn-Waxler and others (1979) suggest that the responsible self, who is inclined toward prosocial behavior, is socialized by specific maternal child-rearing techniques. Hence I will close this chapter by examining the important issue of socialization. How can we nurture, evoke, train, and teach prosocial behaviors in our children?

Prosocial Behavior and Socialization

A number of suggestions have already been introduced regarding how parents can promote prosocial dispositions in their children. I noted, for example, that parents should provide opportunities for children to help around the house and make character attributions when they do help ("You're the kind of girl who likes to help"). In this final section I examine a number of additional proposals that are suggested by the socialization literature. This literature assumes that children come to learn moral standards from various adult authorities, or *socialization agents*, chiefly parents (Hoffman, 1975c). Hence, one line of research attempts to identify characteristics of parents and families that seem to be associated with moral behavior. A second line of research has tended to focus on mechanisms of learning. These mechanisms include modeling, imitation, and reinforcement, as well as those cognitive abilities that mediate the acquisition of moral standards communicated through the other mechanisms.

It should be clear that the two lines of research overlap, since moral teaching and moral learning take place in families (and in other contexts besides). Or to put it differently, the mechanisms of moral learning are implemented by parents of a particular kind. Families are distinguished by the kinds of models that are held forth for imitation, by differential patterns of reinforcement and discipline, by the sort of rational appeals that are made on behalf of moral standards, and so forth. Hence one can separate parenting and mechanisms of learning only in the abstract. Yet, this said, it is fair to say also that research on moral socialization has tended to emphasize different aspects of the parenting-learning relationship. Let's first examine certain key properties of families and parenting.

Families and Parenting

Somehow children have to learn what is, and what is not, appropriate behavior. They are exposed to various rules from an early age. Typically parents initially regulate the child's behavior around the issues of safety, respect for property, and respect for the rights of others. By the time their children are 30 months of age, parents are enforcing standards regarding family routines, self-care, and independence (Gralinski & Kopp, 1993). Children must come to obey certain regulations, to be sure, but they must also come to respect the social order itself and not simply the rules of the social order. This respect for social regulation is grounded in the child's respect for parents and the social organization of the family (Hoffman, 1975c). As Damon (1988, p. 52) puts it, "The child's respect for this authority is the most important moral legacy that comes out of a child's relations with his parents. The child's respect for parental authority sets the direction for civilized participation in the social order when the child later begins assuming the rights and responsibilities of full citizenship."

It seems rather obvious that children who are prosocial and altruistic are exposed to a regime of child-rearing that is somehow different from that of children who are antisocial and selfish. Just what this regime must be has attracted significant attention from researchers over the years. Martin Hoffman (1975a) has shown, for example, that altruistic children have at least one parent (typically the same-sex parent) who communicates altruistic values and at least one parent (typically the opposite-sex parent) who uses victim-centered discipline. Victim-centered discipline draws the child's attention to the feelings of the victim and emphasizes the need for reparation and apology. Indeed, for Hoffman, the disciplinary encounter between parent and child is the prime engine of moral socialization. It is the "teachable moment" par excellence for inculcating a prosocial moral orientation.

In a number of early studies Hoffman (1960, 1963; Hoffman & Saltzstein, 1967) found that a certain style of discipline was related to moral socialization. Parents who use *induction*, that is, who draw the child's attention to the consequences of his or her misconduct on others, accompanied by an appropriate rationale for the norm or standard in question tend to have children who internalize moral standards, who feel appropriate levels of guilt for misconduct and empathy for victims, and who accept responsibility for behavior. In short, parental inductions during disciplinary encounters promote moral development. But why? First, by drawing the child's attention to the consequences of his action on others, parents promote an other-centered perspective that encourages empathic identification with victims. Children are given a rationale, replete with cognitive elaboration, for why such behavior is forbidden. They are given instruction on alternative behaviors and more appropriate courses of action. But all of this must take place in the context of mild coercion. Parents must force behavioral compliance with the standard and then make the appropriate inductions. As Damon (1988) points out, the moral message—the cognitive elaborations, the rationale—does not stick unless behavioral compliance is enforced. Children must first comply; then the rationale underlying the compliance must be explained.

But parents can't overdo it. The iron hand must be concealed by the silken glove. If coercion is not mild but significant and salient, all the child remembers is the force and not the message. Induction works, then, because it combines mild control (to enforce behavioral compliance) and moral instruction on the rationale for the standard being socialized. This combination of control and instruction encourages the child to internalize the moral standard. The control inhibits misbehavior; the instruction provides the language and rationale that serve self-regulation in the absence of a monitoring authority (LaVoie, 1974; Parke, 1974; Sears, Maccoby, & Levin, 1957). Indeed, sanctions alone, or simply punishing a specific behavior, are unlikely to motivate a generalized self-regulatory capability in children (Bandura, 1991). Instead, explaining the rules, appealing to standards, and describing the consequences of a behavior on victims are much more likely to inculcate self-regulation and internal control (Hoffman, 1977). In fact, parents are better off not to draw attention to the negative things that might happen to the child as a result of misbehavior but rather to impose sanctions while drawing attention to the harmful effects on victims (Walters & Grusec, 1977). More will be said about self-regulation and moral agency further on.

Parents who use physical punishment, who use force or threaten force and are therefore *power assertive* in their discipline, tend to produce children who are angry, hostile, and aggressive (Eron, Walder, Huesmann, & Lefkowitz, 1974), who are not empathic, and who do not internalize moral values (Hoffman, 1975a, 1975c) or develop a coherent sense of conscience (Kochanska, 1991). Indeed, these children develop an external moral orientation that is based simply on the fear of getting caught or the fear of punishment.

Power assertion is, quite simply, a form of aggression against children. The child receives little moral instruction about rules, standards, norms, and the like, but plenty about power, threats, and coercion. Although power assertion is sometimes required in order to force a child to stop some injurious activity (e.g., running in the street, placing a finger in an electrical socket), it has few longer-term positive benefits. In fact, it appears to ensure compliance only when the threat of punishment is ever looming. It is controlling only when the iron hand is just a swing away. Yet the point of moral socialization is not to force children to adopt certain highly favored behavior just because not to do so is to risk severe sanctions. Rather, the point of moral socialization is to encourage children to take on the moral standards of adult society as their own, that is, to internalize these standards and to conform their behavior to them *just because* they believe in them. The goal of moral socialization is self-regulation and internal control (Mischel & Mischel, 1976; Bar-Tal, 1982; Peterson, 1982). Moral internalization is much less likely to occur with highly coercive, power-assertive disciplinary practices. Indeed, the more visible and salient the threat of force or the use of power, the less likely children will come to adopt adult standards (Lepper & Green, 1975).

A more subtle act of aggression against children is to withdraw love and affection from them, ignore them, refuse to speak with them, or say that they are no longer loved because of what they have done or failed to do. Love withdrawal manipulates a child's natural affection for his or her parents. It threatens to cut children off from what they crave the most, which is the love of parents and the security this love provides. Hence, considerable anxiety attaches to an action that is punished in this way. Naturally, children are quite responsive to love withdrawal as a disciplinary technique. It induces considerable anxiety. It induces considerable guilt. Children will inhibit misbehavior, exercise self-control, and respect others when consistently disciplined in this way in order to avoid feelings of anxiety and guilt. But they will do so not because they have internalized moral standards, not because they have come to respect the social organization and its moral system of regulation, and not because they understand and accept the rationale behind the standard but because they crave parental approval. Love withdrawal is more effective than is power assertion, but it is not as effective as induction.

Induction is closely related to the authoritative parenting style (Baumrind, 1971). If induction is a blend of control and rational elaboration, the authoritative parent is one who exerts firm control, but in the overall context of warmth, nurturance, and responsiveness. An authoritative parent sets clear, reasonable standards and makes consistent demands for maturity. The authoritative parent follows through with sanctions should the standards be violated, typically in an inductive manner. Such a parent is also responsive to the needs of the child and is warm, available, open to dialogue and communication. The child's point of view is duly considered. A certain amount of give-and-take is expected. This parenting style with its dual emphasis on firm standards and control on the one hand and clear communication, warmth, and nurturance on the other is most closely associated with a broad range of developmental competencies (Baumrind & Black, 1967; Baumrind, 1991; Denham, Renwick & Holt, 1991; Steinberg, Elman & Mounts, 1989; Dornbusch, Ritter, Liederman, Roberts, & Fraleigh, 1987; Steinberg, Mounts, Lamborn, & Dornbusch, 1991), including prosocial competencies, a sense of social responsibility (Baumrind, 1973a), and postconventional moral reasoning (Boyes & Allen, 1993). In fact, compliance is more likely among children whose parents are authoritative than among children whose parents are punitive and autocratic (Crockenberg & Litman, 1990).

Why does authoritative parenting work? It appears to work for the same sort of reasons that induction works. Damon (1988) points to the following factors: (1) The authoritative parent encourages the child's own empathic tendencies by confronting the child with the consequences of his or her behavior, particularly with respect to victims. (2) The authoritative parent not only sets clear standards but is committed to them, as evidenced by the fact that violations are consistently noted. (3) The authoritative parent communicates the general expectation that it is appropriate and "good" to obey legitimate authority. (4) The authoritative parent places realistic challenges in front of the child that are consistent with the child's capabilities. (5) The authoritative parent is a good role model of legitimate and effective authority.

In contrast, Damon (1988) argues that authoritarian and permissive parents make the same two mistakes, although they make them differently. These parents (1) fail either to confront their children with their transgressions or to do so consistently and (2) are overly intrusive. Authoritarian parents tend to praise or punish only when they are in the mood (Patterson, 1982), which means that prosocial behavior often goes unremarked and negative behavior goes unpunished. But when they are suitably aroused, authoritarian parents can be harsh, punitive, and arbitrary in their discipline (with perhaps the unhappy consequence that prosocial behavior is punished and negative behavior rewarded).

Permissive parents also fail to consistently confront their children with the results of their transgressions, but this is mostly because they are consistently averse to asserting their authority. They intrude into the lives of their children not in the form of arbitrary punitiveness, as with authoritarian parents, but with over protectiveness. As Damon (1988, p. 57) puts it: "The intrusion of permissive parents takes the form of a sentimental over protectiveness rather than coercion or punishment. The child is sheltered from experiencing unpleasantness of any type, even when this unpleasantness is simply a realistic consequence of the child's bad behavior." So it would appear that authoritative parenting and inductive discipline are the kinds of parenting practices that best favor mature moral socialization. These are, of course, rather broad aspects of family functioning, and there is some suggestion that the effect of these parenting styles on prosocial development may show subtle contextual variation. That is, the relation between parenting variables and prosocial development may not be universal across economic and ethnic lines (Bandura, 1991). There is evidence, for example, that Mexican American children are more cooperative than Anglo children, but they also perceive their parents to be more punishing and less supporting (Knight, Kagan, & Buriel, 1982; Knight & Kagan, 1977). Baumrind (1973b) also reports data on "harmonious" families, many of them Japanese American, where parents rarely exercise overt control over their children, probably because the children anticipate the wishes of parents and obey without being commanded. This is not the classic authoritative parenting style, yet children in harmonious families turn out just fine. They are just as socially competent and responsible as are children raised in authoritative households. Hence there are perhaps many ways to nourish prosocial dispositions in children, and authoritative parenting, though sufficient, may not be strictly necessary (Baumrind, 1989).

Recent research has focused on more particular aspects of socialization within families. Grusec (1991) reports, for example, that spontaneous prosocial behavior within the home is hardly ever rewarded with material reinforcement. Instead, social praise is more typical. That said, many prosocial behaviors (about one-third) are not responded to at all or are responded to minimally. What is more, children are rarely punished for not showing concern for others (Grusec, Dix, & Mills, 1982). Parents rarely make character attributions for positive behavior or engage in "empathy training" for spontaneous prosocial behavior (Grusec, 1991). When empathy training is used at all, it is used in the breach, that is, when children fail to be prosocial. As Grusec (1991) points out, the relatively infrequent use of character attributions and empathy training is surprising given their prominence in the research literature. What is more, recent research has shown that families that practice open discussion of feelings tend to have children who are good at making judgments about the emotions of others in affective perspective-taking situations (Dunn, Brown, & Beardsall, 1991). Presumably, family talks about emotions orient the child to a keener appreciation of the emotional states of others and provide valuable training in empathic sensitivity.

Social Learning and Social-Cognitive Theory

Any discussion of socialization must come to grips with the observational learning tradition (Rosenhan, 1972; Bryan & London, 1970; Krebs, 1970; Rushton, 1976), one important variant of which is now called social-cognitive theory (Bandura, 1986, 1991; Mischel & Mischel, 1976). This tradition has typically focused on the mechanisms of modeling, imitation, and social reinforcement. Informally, this tradition is known as "setting a good example." The literature leaves little question that observing prosocial models can have very powerful effects on children (Bandura, 1986; Rushton, 1976). Models have been shown to enhance altruistic behavior (Hartup & Coates, 1967; Grusec & Skubiski, 1970), generosity (Presbie & Coiteux, 1971; Lipscomb, Larrieu, McAllister, & Bregman, 1982), and resistance to temptation (Grusec, Kuczynski, Rushton, & Simutis, 1979). What is more, the effects of altruistic modeling appear to be quite durable over time (Rice & Grusec, 1975) and are enhanced when the model is powerful (Grusec, 1971) and when the child is given an opportunity to practice the modeled behavior (Rosenhan & White, 1967; White, 1972). Furthermore, models are much more effective when they match their words with deeds, that is, when they practice what they preach. Although simple preaching or moral exhortation can have an effect (Rice & Grusec, 1975; Rushton, 1975), the superiority of deeds compared to words is well established (McMains & Liebert, 1968; Hildesbrandt, Feldman, & Ditrichs, 1973; Rushton & Owen, 1975; Bryan & Walbek, 1970a, 1970b). The practical implication for parents seems clear.

The distinction between saying and doing, or the difference between preaching and practicing what one preaches, should now have a familiar ring to the reader. It is very similar to the problem we encountered with Kohlberg's theory, namely, how do we translate our moral reasoning into moral conduct? In this case, knowing the right thing to do and doing it are sometimes very different matters.

Perhaps what bridges the chasm between moral thought and moral action is the notion of the responsible self (Blasi, 1983a), that is, the notion that the self is responsible for enacting the moral law. In this case knowledge of a moral principle does not motivate action; rather what motivates action is the realization that the self is responsible for putting the principle into practice. The responsible self was also evident when I noted that prosocial behavior may not be motivated by our ability to "match affects," or by our "trait empathy," but by our inclination to feel a personal responsibility for the well-being of another (Chapman et al., 1987). Social-cognitive theory (Bandura, 1986, 1991) also has a take on the problem of moral thought and moral action, and it's solution will resonate with these other notions of the responsible self.

According to Bandura (1986), what bridges the chasm between thought and action is *moral agency*, where moral agency is governed by self-regulatory mechanisms. What motivates moral conduct is not so much external social sanctions, that is, the threat of punishment and social disapproval, but rather self-censure, self-condemnation, or what Bandura calls "self-reactive" processes. In his view self-reactive control has the more powerful influence in regulating moral conduct. With self-reactive control, we engage in prosocial behavior because to do so breeds self-respect and self-satisfaction. In turn we refrain from immoral conduct because to do so breeds self-reproach and self-condemnation (Bandura, 1991).

Self-regulatory mechanisms work through three major subsystems. We must first *monitor* our conduct. We must next *evaluate* our conduct in light of moral standards, and make *judgments* about the morally relevant features in the circumstances that confront us. Finally, our conduct so monitored and evaluated is subject to *self-reactive influence*. That is, we anticipate whether our behavior will do us credit and result in self-satisfaction and a stronger sense of self-worth or whether our behavior will do us no credit at all in light of our personal standards and result in self-contempt and a pervasive sense of shame. Furthermore, our ability to apply these self-regulatory mechanisms depends on our sense of *self-efficacy;* that is, the exercise of moral agency will hinge on our understanding of our own ability to control our motivations, to think through problems, and to implement a plan of action. In Bandura's view, "the stronger the perceived self-regulatory efficacy, the more perseverant people are in their self-controlling efforts and the greater is their success in resisting social pressures to behave in ways that violate their standards. A low sense of self-regulatory efficacy heightens vulnerability to social pressures for transgressive conduct" (Bandura, 1991, p. 69). Bandura's social-cognitive theory of morality is much richer than this brief synopsis can hope to convey. Bandura argues, for example, that self-regulatory mechanisms do not invariably exercise a controlling function within the individual. Self-regulatory mechanisms can be disengaged so that many kinds of behavior, some of them reprehensible, can be judged compatible with the moral standards we hold dear. We might distort or misconstrue our conduct in the monitoring process, judging our misconduct to be acceptable because it is being done for a "moral" cause or for some righteous purpose. We might use sanitizing euphemisms to disguise our culpability. We might ignore or misconstrue the consequences of our actions or displace our personal responsibility unto others or blame the victim. In short, much of Bandura's moral theory is an attempt to understand moral agency in all of its complexities.

It is fitting that I close this look at prosocial behavior with yet another account of the moral self. The moral self has been found lurking in a number of accounts of moral psychology. In the remaining chapters, I take up the issue more directly.

10
Moral Traits and the Moral Personality

In Chapter 9, I examined a number of research traditions that seemed to resonate more readily with a lay understanding of moral psychology. I suspect that when most people think about morality, the moral life, values, and the like, they have in mind certain prosocial dispositions to do the right thing, to be a person of a certain kind, namely, to be honest, fair, compassionate, sensitive to the needs of others, helpful, generous, large spirited, and more. I suspect that parents would rather their children be more prosocial than less. Parents would rather their children grow up to be persons of whom it could be said that these prosocial characteristics amply apply. How to raise children of good character is an important goal of most parents. Although the cognitive developmental approach may be reluctant to make aretaic judgments about the moral status of persons, the language of moral evaluation comes more easily to most everyone else.

We have seen that prosocial dispositions are indeed evident in children. According to Eisenberg and Mussen (1989), these "findings are consistent with the theoretical position that there are fundamental and lasting prosocial dispositions residing in individuals as general traits or states" (p. 18) and that the tendency to engage in prosocial action is "consistent, general, and enduring." In other words, prosocial dispositions coalesce in individuals. Prosocial dispositions are characteristic of persons to such an extent that one could invoke the language of traits to describe someone who is prone to prosocial action.

Although this may come as a surprise to the lay public, to say that moral dispositions coalesce in individuals as traits is to make a very controversial claim. The notion that human personality is constituted by traits strikes many researchers as a very peculiar thing to say. Indeed, within moral psychology, the language of traits, character, and virtues has been pushed to the margins of academic discourse for many decades. The marginalization of a virtue-centered approach to moral psychology has occurred for at least two reasons. First, real doubts emerged concerning what was taken to be the defining feature of personality traits, namely, that traits show generality and consistency across situations. If Hamish is honest or friendly and is characteristically so, then Hamish might be expected to be honest and friendly all the time, or at least most of the time, in most or all of the situations that require honesty and friendliness. As we will see, however, empirical evidence does not appear to support the common notion that traits adhere to individuals in this way.

Second, the language of virtues, traits, and character is out of step with the metaethical paradigm that has dominated Western reflection on moral matters since the Enlightenment and that has been assumed by virtually all of the major theories of moral psychology. This tradition has been called the *moral law folk theory* (Johnson, 1993), since it underwrites, perhaps implicitly, much of our common understanding of morality in the West. I alluded to this tradition in Chapter 7 when I examined the difference in approach between Kohlberg and Gilligan, but I will have occasion to revisit the issue once again.

For both philosophic and empirical reasons, then, virtues, traits, and moral character have been rather neglected notions in moral psychology. In spite of these twin obstacles, however, there is increasing recognition that personological processes must be integrated in some way into moral psychological theories. There are, once again, both philosophical and empirical reasons for this. On the philosophical front, there is a keener appreciation of the fact that ethical conceptions of what the moral life entails, or what the nature of moral judgment is, must be a psychological possibility for "people like us." It does little good to propose some ethical theory that seems more relevant for abstract entities in some theoretical universe than for warm-blooded psychological persons in the real world. It does little good to propose a model of moral functioning that is unrealistic or implausible given what we know about human rationality. As Owen Flanagan (1991, p. 35) puts it, "Every moral conception owes us at least a partial specification of the personality and motivational structure it expects of morally mature individuals, and that conception will need to be constrained by considerations of realism." In his principle of minimal psychological realism, Flanagan (1991) insists that every moral theory and every projected moral ideal is bound to articulate how the "character, decision processing, and behavior prescribed are possible, or perceived to be possible, for creatures like us" (p. 32). Other ethicists have similarly called for a better specification of psychological processes in moral theory (e.g., A.O. Rorty, 1988; Flanagan & A.O. Rorty, 1990; Goldman, 1993; Johnson, 1993; Wren, 1990; Punzo & Meara, 1993; Brandt, 1970; Thomas, 1988).

On the empirical-psychological front we have already seen in a number of places how the moral self or the responsible self has been implicated in various accounts of moral and prosocial action. What is more, there has always been evidence lurking in the literature to suggest that moral reasoning is associated with a variety of personological dimensions (Haan et al., 1968; Hogan, 1975: Johnson, Hogan, Zonderman, Callens, & Rogolsky, 1981; Lapsley, Harwell, Olson, Flannery, & Quintana, 1984) and ego variables (Sullivan, McCullough & Stager, 1970; Haan, Stroud, & Holstein, 1973; Haan, 1985; Gfellner, 1986).

In more recent research, for example, Daniel Hart has shown that the best predictor of adults' moral reasoning is not their moral reasoning as adolescents, as one might expect, but rather their adolescent scores on measures of "conscience strength" (Hart, 1988) and their preferred use of certain ego defensive strategies in adolescence (Hart & Chmiel, 1993). In the latter study, for example, the tendency to utilize mature defense mechanisms in adolescence was shown to be a better predictor of adult moral reasoning than adolescent moral-reasoning scores. In research that I will examine in Chapter 12, Blasi (1988) has shown that moral and identity concerns interpenetrate in prescribed ways according to which of several developmentally ordered "identity modes" a person uses to define the self.

Similarly, there is broad recognition that self beliefs play a crucial role in human motivation and regulation, including, presumably, moral motivation and moral regulation of behavior, and that the self-system may provide the crucial linkage for integrating diverse areas of psychology (Higgins, 1991). What is more, recent developments in cognitive science have provided alternative ways of conceptualizing moral rationality (Goldman, 1993; Johnson, 1993). Progress in personality and social psychological research has led to a reconceptualization of traits that is more congenial to the research traditions of cognitive psychology (Mischel, 1990; Higgins, 1991; Higgins, King, & Mavin, 1982), which perhaps points the way to a post-Kohlbergian alternative for conceptualizing moral cognition. All of this suggests that a more adequate account of moral psychology must make room for such neglected constructs as self, identity, character, and other markers of personality (Noam & Wren, in press). And it would appear that recent trends in a number of areas within psychology are indeed heralding the return of these notions from the margins of academic discourse.

In the final two chapters I will examine two rather visible approaches to moral personality, the socioanalytic theory of Robert Hogan (Chapter 11) and the more recent writings on moral identity by Augusto Blasi (Chapter 12). I will conclude with an attempt to sketch, in very broad stroke, what recent developments in cognitive science and personality research might have to say about moral psychology and what the post-Kohlbergian landscape might look like.

It will facilitate later discussion of these theories, however, if I first examine in more detail how the characterological approach has become marginalized in moral psychology. This state of affairs must come as a surprise to the reader who is unacquainted with the preoccupations of research psychologists, and therefore it requires some explanation. As I noted earlier, there are both philosophical and empirical reasons for this marginalization. Let's begin by examining the philosophical reasons.

The Marginalization of Moral Character: Philosophical Sources

In Chapter 7, I mentioned a number of dimensions along which virtue-centered and rule-centered ethics could be said to differ. From the time of the Enlightenment virtue ethics has been out of favor in much of Western thought, largely because the classical interest in virtuous character did not seem terribly relevant to the fundamental problem facing Enlightenment philosophers, which was how to secure the objectivity of morals on a firm rational foundation such that our moral convictions might be free of skeptical doubt and the prospect of moral relativism. Such a foundation would ideally show that our moral convictions are grounded by a finite set of moral principles that all rational agents would acknowledge as binding irrespective of tribe, society, religious conviction, culture, and history. Such a foundation would show that the origin of moral rules would be found not in knowledge of human nature, not in an understanding of the human experience, but in the very character of reason itself. This rational foundation would justify our moral convictions. It would defeat skepticism. It would tell us what ought to be done. It would adjudicate the various disputes that are invariably generated by our parochial interests, because the rules of morality are "objective."

The rules of morality are rational and hence are universally applicable, or accessible, to all rational creatures in much the same way that the rules of arithmetic are binding for all rational beings (MacIntyre, 1984). If moral principles exist apart from human experience, they have an objectivity against which our conduct can be appraised. This preoccupation with rational foundations and universal morality eclipsed the traditional concern with moral virtues. The classical interest in virtuous traits that disposes one to live well the sort of life that is good for one to live gives way to the Enlightenment interest in grounding an objective morality that is independent of our private, or collective, conception of what a good life amounts to.

Kant's Approach

The rationalist ethic of Immanuel Kant (1785/1988) is the towering achievement of Enlightenment philosophy and has virtually defined the moral tradition in the West, to such an extent that virtually all of the cognitive developmental theories of moral psychology are Kantian in substance or tone or at least trade on key elements of Kant's metaethics.

Kant's theory of morality was directed toward the discovery of the supreme moral principle (categorical imperative) that a pure will might act upon. A "pure will" is one that always acts from duty, in strict accordance with the dictates of the moral law. Any action performed by such a will, with due consideration of the moral law, would itself be a moral action, since for Kant, the moral status of an action hinges on whether it is derived from the moral principle that commands it. If Jones acts with beneficence and charity because of his generous inclination, his acts have no moral worth. Jones's behavior may be praiseworthy and may be something that we should encourage, but his actions have no moral worth unless done from duty, that is, as the law requires. Similarly, we may be amiable, we may develop our talents, we may be kind and considerate, we may do that which is honorable, and these dispositions may come naturally and automatically to us. Yet if these actions proceed from inclination and not from duty, they have no moral worth.

Hence, in order for an action to have moral worth, it must be done "from duty" (and often contrary to our natural inclination), and our duties are derived from a principle. This suggests that what ennobles our action, what gives it a distinctly moral quality, is not the purpose of the action—not the end we pursue, not the expected effect of our efforts, not the object of our desire. Ends and purposes cannot give our actions moral worth. Rather, moral worth lies in the principle that commands our will without regard to ends. But if ends or purposes do not motivate us to do our duty, then the source of our action must be the principle itself. Duty must be derived from our very respect for the law: "Now an action done from duty must wholly exclude the influence of inclination and with it every object of the will, so that nothing remains which can determine the will except objectively the *law*, and subjectively *pure* respect for this practical law, and consequently the maxim that I shall follow this law even to the thwarting of all my inclinations" (Kant, 1795/1988, p. 25). Such a principle would itself be pure in the sense that it points to a form of knowledge that is not contaminated by anything merely empirical, including such bodily contaminants as feelings, sensations, emotions, and personal inclinations. Consequently, pure moral principles are not derived from experience. In Kant's terms, they are a priori principles. They are purely formal laws, or pure rational concepts that tell us what is required, that is, how to act. But as formal principles, they tell us only about duty as such, that is, what all duties have in common. For example, the injunction "Do that which increases the happiness of the greatest number" is a strictly formal statement of our duty that does not specify the content of any particular action we may want to undertake in support of it (Ebbinghaus, 1954). Hence, a pure will is one that always acts from the duties imposed by a priori moral laws.

Insofar as moral laws are formal, a priori rational concepts, however, they bear no particular relationship to the concrete world of experience that we all live in. Kant did not believe, for example, that the principles of morality could be found in knowledge of human nature. All moral principles exist a priori in reason. We could not derive these principles from what we know about human wills or by abstracting from what is contingent and empirical. Moral principles cannot be derived from particular features of human nature. Indeed, every empirical element contaminates the purity of morals. This is because moral laws must hold good not just for human agents but for all rational agents, they must be valid not only under certain conditions but under all conditions, and they must command not just contingently but with absolute necessity.

Hence moral principles cannot be based on some conception of human reason; they must be based on a general concept of a rational being. If principles are derived from what we know about human personality or from what we know about human nature, then these principles are applicable only to the limits of human personality and nature. They would command not categorically but hypothetically (see further on). "Nor could anything be more fatal to morality than that we should wish to derive it from examples" (Kant, 1795/1988, p. 36). To derive morality from heroic examples of moral action, to suggest that we imitate individuals with noble character, for example, is "fatal" because although our moral saints make visible what the law requires and demonstrate that the moral life is feasible, the true example is to be found in reason alone. The imitation of others can lead us astray if the example is contrary to the "true original which lies in reason" (p. 36).

Perhaps Kant's distinction between noumena and phenomena can help us here. Kant draws a distinction between the empirical realm of sense experience that we ordinary "impure wills" inhabit (the phenomenal world) and the transcendental realm of rational abstraction (the noumenal world) characteristic of pure rational agents (pure wills). Or, to put it differently, Kant distinguishes between two kinds of objects of thought. There are, first, objects that are the concern of the empirical sciences. These objects are "sensible," exist in time and space, are subject to deterministic laws of causality, and the like. He called these objects of thought "phenomena." The phenomenal self is characterized by desires, bodily needs, inclinations, emotions, images, and the like. The phenomenal self is subject to determinisms of the causal universe. The "willing" of the phenomenal self is corrupted by heteronomous influences and is hence impure. A heteronomous influence is any source that lies outside of reason.

In contrast, there are objects of thought that are not sensible, that are not bound by space or time or subject to deterministic laws of causality. These he called "noumena." It is the noumenal agent that is capable of rational willing. The pure will is a "noumenal self" who acts in complete freedom (not being subject to causal necessity). To get from the phenomenal agent, who is specified by various characteristics, to the noumenal agent, we need to abstract from our phenomenal character everything that differentiates us one from another in the world of experience and appearance (Wolff, 1977). The noumenal self abstracts from our spatial-temporal characteristics everything that is particular to us and therefore inessential to our shared essences as rational creatures (Stout, 1981).

How, then, do the a priori principles, not derived from experience, apply to the world of experience? When Jones says, "In this situation, I will do X in order to bring about Y," he clearly makes reference to empirical content. That is, he makes reference to the particularities of a given, concrete situation and a set of actions motivated by his particular purposes. Yet a Kantian moral principle is purely formal. As a formal principle it abstracts from all subjective ends. How, then, can it apply to the situation faced by Jones?

The purpose of moral principles is to evaluate the acceptability of particular maxims. A maxim is a subjective principle of action. It is a rule one makes for oneself, and it applies to the person who "legislates" it (Harrison, 1957). If Jones says, "For the purpose of fitting into my stylish clothes, I will jog every evening at seven o'clock," then he has devised a maxim for his action. A maxim is not a moral principle but may be evaluated by such principles.

In Kant's view, particular maxims, such as the one reached by Jones, can be evaluated in light of the supreme moral principle, the *categorical imperative*. Kant states the principle in one form as "Act only on that maxim through which you can at the same time will that it should become a universal [moral] law" (Kant 1785/1988, p. 49). Another form of the categorical imperative has a metaphoric ring to it: "Act *as if* the maxim of your action were to become through your will a universal *law of nature*" (p. 49; emphasis added).

Both forms of the categorical imperative seem to require that we evaluate the moral status of our maxims by determining if they could serve as a universally valid, objective principle that is binding on the will for all rational creatures. As such, the categorical imperative is a strictly formal principle that determines whether particular maxims can be objectively valid for the decisions we are called upon to make, that is, for the decisions of our will (Ebbinghaus, 1954). A maxim to

the effect that it is permissible to escape the miseries of this life by committing suicide or that one may make false promises to obtain a loan or that one may squan-
der one's talents or that charity and beneficence are not required of us (Kant's
examples) would fail the test of the categorical imperative. In his view, although it
is possible that a universal law of nature does in fact accord with each of these
maxims, no rational agent could actually will that they have universal validity.

Our candidate maxim ("For the sake of fitting into my stylish clothes, I will
jog every evening at seven o'clock") is not, in fact, of the form that would satisfy
the demands of the categorical imperative (and is hence not a moral maxim).
Because the maxim must command universally (be binding on all rational agents),
it cannot be based on any feature or characteristic that is peculiar to me (other
than my rationality). It cannot be based on my bodily feelings, subjective preferences, desires, inclinations, or emotions. What is more, the maxim concerning my
action must be free of any conditions if it is to count as a moral maxim subject to
the supreme moral principle. For example, a maxim of the form "*If* I will X, *then* I
should do Y" does not command unconditionally, since one can avoid doing Y
simply by ceasing to will X. The injunction "do Y" is strictly hypothetical, since it
is contingent on a set of conditions (whether one "wills X").

Note that our candidate maxim is of this form. Kant calls this sort of injunction a "hypothetical imperative." Maxims that fit the form of hypothetical imperatives do not pass moral muster because they are conditioned on our wills. What is
wanted is a moral principle that commands *categorically*, and such a principle would
have to be pure, that is, abstracted from any particular content and free from contingent, subjective influences. Thus the categorical imperative abstracts the form of
duty not only from content (duty as such) but also from all matters of will, that is,
from all purposes and ends, desires and inclinations, since these are what make
imperatives hypothetical (Ebbinghaus, 1954). As Alasdaire MacIntyre (1984, p. 31)
puts it, "To be a [Kantian] moral agent is. . . precisely to stand back from any and
every situation in which one is involved, from any and every characteristic that
one may possess, and to pass judgment on it from a purely universal and abstract
point of view that is totally detached from all social particularity." We have not yet,
however, solved the problem of how to subject a particular maxim to the evaluation of a purely formal moral principle such as the categorical imperative. A
maxim, by definition, is a subjective rule that one makes for oneself. It is a principle of action that hinges on one's particular desires and goals. I have a certain
highly desired end in mind (fitting into stylish clothes), and I engage in certain
actions (jogging) in order to bring it about. As a phenomenal agent, my maxim is
phrased in a deterministic universe subject to the causal laws of nature. It legislates
"for me," in "this world." In contrast, the formal moral principle abstracts from any
particular set of desires, needs, or inclinations that I might have. It abstracts from
my particular preferences. It abstracts from the ends that I would like to see established given the particularities of my life. It legislates not "for me" in "this world"
of causal necessity but for rational "noumenal selves" in the realm of freedom. It is
in this sense that morality is autonomous and objective.

The problem, then, is to show how a purely formal principle applies to the world of experience. According to Mark Johnson (1993), Kant pulls this off metaphorically. The moral law is represented figuratively as a law of nature, as in the second form of the categorical imperative noted previously. That is, treat the moral law as if it were a law of nature. The law of nature is thus used as an illustration (or typification) of the moral law—it is intended as an analogy, or a criterion that people can (and often do) use in order to appraise the moral status of maxims (Kemp, 1958). Given that we have certain ends or purposes, given that it is open to us to engage in certain actions such that our purposes might be realized, and given that we can formulate the relationship between purposes and actions in terms of various rules or maxims, we can then evaluate the moral status of our maxims by asking if we would still be willing to pursue the ends through our actions if our maxim were to become a universal law of nature. Maxims that can be universalized in this way are moral maxims. Maxims that cannot be universalized are nonmoral maxims. As Johnson (1993, p. 72) puts it,

> The figurative test is to ask whether there could exist a system of nature whose "natural" laws were actually those principles we are claiming to be moral laws. If there is something internally inconsistent or contradictory about such a figuratively envisioned natural world, then the proposed moral principle must be rejected. . . By Kant's own description, moral reasoning involves a figurative envisioning of a nonexisting world as a means for judging a proposed action.

Certain of our maxims would fail this figurative test. It is unlikely that we could will, as a natural law, that every rational agent should desire to squeeze into stylish clothes and to take whatever action might bring this about. Hence, we would reject this maxim as a moral principle (although some argue that the categorical imperative, as a rational test of maxims, would *not*, in fact, rule out such trivial maxims; see MacIntyre, 1984, p. 46). However, it is likely (one presumes) that we should accept as morally binding those maxims that assert the importance of keeping promises, developing one's talents, helping others in distress, and forsaking suicide.

My purpose in wading into these complexities is not to explore Kant's ethical theory for its own sake but rather to illustrate how he views the role of personological factors in the process of moral appraisal and deliberation. As we have seen, personal traits that are deeply rooted in our bodily characteristics—our emotions, desires, inclinations, and perceptions and our personal ends and purposes, are viewed as biases and as a source of heteronomous influences from which we must abstract if we are to partake of distinctly autonomous, moral rationality.

Moral Law Folk Theory

That there is protracted conflict between bodily passion and rationality is a theme that is itself deeply rooted in Western thought; indeed, it is a critical assumption of the Judeo-Christian moral tradition (Flew, 1968). As a part of this tradition, Kant's theory makes explicit a set of assumptions about human motivation, the structure of personality, the nature of rationality, and other psychological notions. In other words, most of us endorse, albeit implicitly, a psychological "folk theory" concerning the mind and human nature. This folk theory is woven into our religious intuitions about what it means to be a person, intuitions deeply influenced by the Judeo-Christian tradition in the West.

The psychological folk theory assumes, for example (following Johnson, 1993), that mental life is composed of at least four faculties: perception, passion, will, and reason. Each faculty has a somewhat different role to play within the mind. Perception, for example, receives sense impressions from the body and passes them along to other faculties (e.g., to reason or passion). Reason analyzes, performs calculations, formulates principles. The products of reason are passed along to the will. Reason is such that it exerts influence upon the will. But the will is also influenced by passion, which arises from the body or is activated by a memory trace. Will can usually defeat the force of reason but has a harder go of it against the force of passion. Hence, a strong will is needed to stave off the untoward influence of passion. Oftentimes, the force of reason and the force of passion exert contrary influence upon the will. Hence, the two forces are typically slugging it out within the mind for the control of the will.

According to Johnson (1993), the psychological folk theory is simply assumed and taken for granted by our culturally shared but largely implicit intuitions about morality—what Johnson (1993) calls our "moral law folk theory." The view that we are essentially dualistic in our nature, consisting both of physical (body) and spiritual (mental) dimensions that are in conflict, is one that comes easily to most of us. We assume that our reason formulates general laws about how to act, about what to do and what not to do. We assume that our will can act freely with respect to these general laws. When the will acts against the dictates of reason, we are "immoral." When it chooses to act in accordance with reason, we are "moral." Consequently, our rationality is at the center of our moral life. Our rationality is what sets us apart in creation. Our rationality is what we are "in essence." Morality is thus a deeply rational affair. Passion, in contrast, is to be resisted or checked. Passion (and the body) is the source of error and perdition. Passion is irrational. Passion leads us astray. It is our lower nature, what is unworthy of us (not unlike Freud's id).

Part of our folk tradition, then, is the view that our moral life is a relentless struggle between two kinds of forces, the force of reason and the force of passion. As a result, we "come to experience our moral lives as an ongoing struggle to develop and preserve purity of reason and strength of will in the fact of constant pressures that arise from our embodiment in the world" (Johnson, 1993, p. 17).

Kant's ethical theory simply assumes this tradition, this folk theory, as a background belief. He assumes that humans are the scene of a struggle between two natures, rational and bodily (again, the Freudian image of the struggle between id and ego comes to mind, which too seems to partake of the psychological folk theory). Kant assumes that reason acts as a force and that morality is a system of rules, laws, and principles (Johnson, 1993). He assumes that of the two natures, rationality is that which is essential, higher, and worthy of us; passion is lower, unworthy, and animalistic:

Now reason issues its commands unyieldingly, without promising anything to the inclinations, and, as it were, with disregard and contempt for these claims, which are so impetuous, and at the same time so plausible, and which will not allow themselves to be suppressed by any command. Hence there arises a natural *dialectic*, i.e., a disposition, to argue against these strict laws of duty and to question their validity, or at least their purity and strictness; and, if possible, to make them more accordant with our wishes and inclinations, that is to say, to corrupt them at their very source, and entirely to destroy their worth. (Kant, 1785/1988, p. 30)

Indeed, it is even regrettable that our rational ego is embodied within our physical nature insofar as bodily desires exert an influence that is contrary to reason. "Embodiment, therefore, comes to be regarded as a pressing moral *problem*, on the assumption that, if we were disembodied rational egos with pure wills, we could then act morally by nature" (Johnson, 1993, p. 26), that is, without any sense of obligation. In this case what reason prescribes as objectively necessary would be subjectively necessary as well, and the will would not be commanded by a sense of obligation. The sense of obligation is only required of the agent that objectively knows the good but subjectively is prone to other actions because of contrary inclinations and desires. In this case the will of the person feels the weight of the law as obligation. God has no obligations. God has no duties (Murdoch, 1992).

Perhaps the reader can now detect a contemporary ring in all of this. Kohlberg's theory, for example, trades on many key elements of Kant's theory, not the least of which is the focus on moral reasons and the neglect of emotions; the distinction between form and content; the concern with universality and the autonomy of morality; the definition of moral action as that which is subsumed by a moral principle; the notion that moral principles are automotivating (since reason is a "force"); the use of figurative, other-worldly tests of the morality of decisions (viz., moral musical chairs, the original position, etc.); the embrace of the categorical imperative and the injunction to respect persons as the summit of moral deliberation; and the rejection of examples and imitation in moral education, among others.

Insofar as moral psychology is deeply influenced by the Kantian ethical theory, and the folk tradition of which it is a vivid example, it should now be clear why personological factors, why notions such as virtues and character traits, have been pushed to the margins of contemporary academic discourse. These notions seem deeper rooted in our bodily natures and, as we have seen, the Kantian tradition (and the moral law folk theory) views these sorts of personological factors with grave suspicion. These factors are just the sort of thing the moral point of view is supposed to transcend.

The Moral Point of View

In the standard account, the moral point of view is indifferent to all social particularity, including the characteristics of particular agents; thus it satisfies the demands of impartiality (and universality). Because impartiality demands that one abstract from all that is particular and self-defining and because moral rules must be applicable to all rational moral agents, little concern is evinced for claims regarding particular moral agents and the unique qualities of their personality or character (other than their capacity for rationality), since these factors are the source of heteronomous influence.

Hence, armed with Kantian notions of moral rationality, we understand why Kohlberg would come to disdain any concern with virtues or with traits of character, that is, with the characteristics of particular agents. Who could be interested in the personological dispositions of particular agents if moral rationality requires us to view such things as a source of error and bias or as a source of special pleading? Who could be interested in personal dispositions if moral rationality requires that the particularities of individual character be transcended? Who could be interested in the needs of particular agents and their life projects, desires, and purposes when these things issue in maxims that are only hypothetical and contingent (and are hence "nonmoral")? Who could be interested in the imitation of examples when this is "fatal" to morality? Who could be interested in what "I" must do, even when not formally obliged by a law or principle, when the fundamental question concerns what *any* impartial agent must do (Norton, 1988; Pincoffs, 1983)?

The notion of moral character, then, is out of step with the sort of Kantian moral rationality that Kohlberg builds into principled moral reasoning. It is also out of step with the very core of Kohlberg's research program, which is how to provide the psychological resources by which to combat ethical relativism. It is out of step with his desire to establish psychological foundations (embodied as Stage 6) for moral consensus and agreement.

The Bag of Virtues

There are many thousands of words in the English language that refer to personality traits. The number referring to distinctly virtuous traits, or traits of moral character, must be correspondingly large. Although the classical tradition (e.g., Pieper, 1966) has tended to focus on a small number of cardinal virtues (prudence, courage, justice, temperance), there are clearly numerous other virtues that one may well want to see incorporated into a person of good character. But which ones?

In Kohlberg's view, any composition of a list of desirable virtues must necessarily be arbitrary, since there are so many candidates and we may have favorites. The report cards used by my high school, for example, left room for the teacher to evaluate students on a number of traits, some of which included accuracy, promptness, courtesy, self-control, respect for school property, effort, attitude, cooperation, and preparation. The Panel on Moral Education that was formed in 1988 by the American Association for Curriculum and Development applauded the compilation of 23 core values for use in moral education classes. These values included compassion, courtesy, critical inquiry, due process, equality of opportunity, freedom of thought and action, honesty, human worth and dignity, integrity, justice, knowledge, loyalty, objectivity, order, patriotism, rational consent, reasoned argument, respect for others' rights, responsible citizenship, rule of law, self-respect, tolerance and truth (Saterlie, 1988).

Note that courtesy is the only value held in common by this list and the list of traits favored by my high school. In addition, as Clark Power (1991b) points out, this list excludes 9 out of 11 values touted by the influential work *The Children's Morality Code*, published in 1924 by W. J. Hutchins. The 9 missing values are self-control, good health, kindness, sportsmanship, self-reliance, duty, reliability, good workmanship, and teamwork (Power, 1991b). It is certainly hard to deny that the compilation of favored moral traits or core values has an arbitrary component to it.

But the arbitrary nature of virtue ethics may just be a reason it holds some attraction. Kohlberg writes:

> The attraction of such an arbitrary approach is evident. Although it is true that people often cannot agree on details of right and wrong or even on fundamental moral principles, we all think such traits as honesty and responsibility are good things. By adding enough traits to the virtue bag, we eventually get a list which contains something to suit everyone." (Kohlberg & Turiel, 1971, p. 21; also, Kohlberg, 1972)

In this account, then, virtue is a bag of arbitrarily chosen character traits. Furthermore, and more to the point, Kohlberg argued that the meaning of virtue words is relative to conventional cultural standards and is hence ethically relative:

> Labeling a set of behaviors displayed by a child with positive or negative trait terms does not signify that they are of adaptive or ethical importance. It represents an appeal to particular community conventions, since one person's *"integrity"* is another person's *"stubbornness,"* [one person's] *"honesty* in expressing your true feelings" is another person's *"insensitivity* to the feelings of others." (Kohlberg & Mayer, 1972, p. 479)

The language of character traits and of virtue, then, does not provide what is wanted—a way of protecting the autonomy of morality against all particularities. It does not provide, in short, the necessary ethical and psychological resources by which to combat ethical relativism.

It is also difficult to know just what one is supposed to do with the bag of virtues even if there were consensus about their meaning. According to Power (1991b), value labels are abstractions that cannot guide behavior. They provide no help to those faced with real-life moral decisions. Power (1991b) writes: "Suppose one student sees a peer stealing a radio from a locker. Does the value of loyalty demand reporting the thief to the school authorities or protecting the peer through silence? Many times values come into conflict. Should one be kind and share one's test paper with a student who is flunking, or be honest?" (p. 323). And yet Kohlberg's objections were not entirely conceptual or philosophical. His doubts about the usefulness of character ethics could also be traced to certain empirical literatures within psychology. He could appeal, after all, to the dismal conclusions of the famous Hartshorne and May (1928–1932) studies on character.

In addition, the trait approach to studying personality fell upon hard times beginning in the late 1960s (e.g., Mischel, 1968). Let's see what these literatures implied about the possibility of there being a "moral personality."

The Marginalization of Moral Character: Psychological Sources

If you believe that Jones is an honest fellow, then you probably have every expectation that his honesty will not be restricted to just a few situations—he will be honest in all or most of those situations where honesty is required of him. If he is honest only when his boss is looking but then embezzle a few dollars when the boss turns his back, you will not think much of his honesty. If Jones is honest with his customers but then cheats on his taxes, again, you have reason for withholding your attribution of honesty from him. Let's say that Jones is considered just or courageous, but then we observe that he seems to be just or courageous only when his own affairs are at stake or only when the risks are small or involve no inconvenience. In this case we would wonder just how appropriate it would be to make these attributions about Jones.

These examples illustrate a very common, and traditional, understanding of personality traits. Traits are dispositions to behave in certain characteristic ways. They are adhesive in the sense that they are constitutional aspects of one's personality. They are mental structures that produce uniformities and consistencies in behavior (Allport, 1937). This traditional understanding of traits seems to imply that individuals are best thought of as bundles of stable and enduring trait dispositions that are exhibited across various contexts and in many situations. The typical research strategy was to find out if this was true. That is, first identify a trait of interest, say, honesty or aggressiveness; then observe individuals in numerous situations and contexts and try to predict behavior in these various contexts on the basis of the trait. If Jones is honest, let's see if he is honest in situations A, B, and C.

This was the general research strategy of the Hartshorne and May (1928–1932) studies on character conducted many decades ago. These researchers were interested in demonstrating the traitlike stability of certain character virtues such as honesty, altruism, and caring. With the traditional understanding of trait in mind, these researchers fully expected to find a bimodal distribution of children; there would be some children who were honest and others who were dishonest. When given the opportunity to cheat on an exam, the honest kids would demur and resist temptation; the dishonest kids would cave in and cheat.

But this was not what was found. Whether children cheated depended on a host of situational factors (e.g., whether cheating was easy, whether adults were supervising, whether the test was crucial or important, whether the risk of detection was high or low). Children who resisted cheating in one situation often gave in to temptation in other situations. The authors concluded, with much disappointment, that honesty (for example) was not a stable, traitlike disposition in children. The expectation that traitlike dispositions would show high degrees of cross-situational consistency was not borne out by these early studies.

Yet the full assault on the traditional notion of personality traits did not emerge until the 1960s. In an important monograph Walter Mischel (1968) initiated a significant reevaluation of the classical understanding of global traits and their role in the psychological explanation of personality. This monograph took dead aim at the classical view, shared by both psychodynamic and trait personality theorists, that (1) there are substantial differences in the way people react to the same class of situations and (2) people are characterized by stable, enduring dispositions that generate consistencies in behavior both within and between social situations. Above all Mischel attempted to rescue the individuality of persons from the common view that one's personality could be discerned from just a few signs or behavioral indicators sampled from a limited number of contextual settings. Mischel concluded just the opposite: Knowledge of global personality traits is not useful in predicting behavior across a range of dissimilar situations. Cross-situational consistency of behavior is often very poor: "Individuals show far less cross-situational consistency in their behavior than has been assumed by trait-state theories. The more dissimilar the evoking situations, the less likely they are to produce similar or consistent responses from the same individual" (p. 177). Doubts were also cast on the usefulness of clinical judgments about personality, that is, doubts about the validity of clinical diagnoses that are reached on the basis of a few indirect assessments and doubts about the adequacy of planning specific treatment programs based on the knowledge of global dispositions. Indeed, clinical prediction based on elaborate, and costly, personality diagnostics is notoriously poor. The best predictors of behavior often turn out to be a few simple background variables, indices of past behavior, or the patient's own self-report rather than diagnostic information about underlying personality structure (Meehl, 1954; Sawyer, 1966; Dawes, 1994).

The classical notion, then, that personality traits are stable, enduring dispositions that produce informities in our behavior across disparate situations and environments has fallen on hard times. So too has the allied notion that one's basic character structure can be revealed by a few global trait indicators. But this criticism of the standard notion of personality does not count against the view that there are important continuities in our behavior. Nor does this criticism lead to the unpalatable view that we are held captive by situational variables, responding mechanically in a crude stimulus-response fashion. Indeed, Mischel's (1968) broadside against global traits was often misconstrued as a claim that personal variables don't count in human affairs and all that matters is environmental forces. It was misinterpreted as claiming that there is really no such thing as personality (see, for example, Maddi, 1976). This misreading of Mischel was encouraged by the common view that causal forces reside either in the person *or* in the environment. Hence, under this view, if personality factors are found wanting as an explanation of human behavior, the real culprit must be the environment

But this does not represent Mischel's view. Instead, Mischel (1973) argues that our understanding of personality has to be reconceptualized. It is a mistake, in his view, to phrase the issue in terms of whether person variables *or* situational variables will lead to more reliable behavioral prediction. Rather, attention must be shifted *away* from the traditional notion that social behavior can be adequately predicted with knowledge of a few global dispositional constructs *toward* a dynamic interactional view that emphasizes the transaction between certain person variables and highly specific contextual settings. There is no such thing as context-free traits. Person variables and contextual variables are interactive. Hence, descriptions of personality dispositions must be qualified by reference to local settings and context (Mischel, 1990).

The lack of cross-situational consistency in behavior does not condemn a dispositional approach to personality or deny the existence of individual differences. Rather, it condemns a particular understanding of personality and disposition. The lack of behavioral consistency only undermines the classical view that personality consists of global traits. It undermines the classical view that situations are of little importance other than as a contributor of error, noise,, or bias. Rather than view personality as something one *has* (e.g., global traits) Mischel (1990) argues that personality is better understood as something one *does* in particular settings. That is, instead of being context-free traits that we *have*, person variables consist of various social-cognitive units such as competencies, personal constructs, and encoding strategies (including scripts, schemas, prototypes, and other knowledge structures), expectancies, purposive goals, and the self-regulatory system. These social-cognitive units give us considerable discriminative facility to pick out subtle changes in the features of immediate situations and to respond accordingly. Indeed, it is this discriminative facility that gives rise to apparent cross-situational variability in human behavior, and it is overlooked by the traditional, global trait approach to personality. Mischel's social-cognitive view also suggests, of course, that more attention needs to be devoted to analyzing local features of situations and the way they dynamically interact with these social-cognitive person variables.

Mischel suggests that one way to capture the complexity of dynamic interactions is to view dispositional constructs as conditional if-then propositions that specify the relationship between certain kinds of situations, contexts, or eliciting conditions ("if") and corresponding tendencies toward certain kinds of behavior ("then"). In other words, dispositions are concepts that link two kinds of categories: categories of actions or behaviors and categories of situations or contexts that are correlated with the behaviors in question (Mischel, 1990). These categories are then linked by a rule that specifies the nature of the if-then relationship that is thought to exist between them. Each dispositional construct, then, has three components: a category of acts, a category of contexts or settings, and a proposition that specifies the if-then linkage between acts and settings.

Let's take, by way of example, the following character attribution: Jones is aggressive. In order to understand what it means to say that Jones has a disposition toward aggression, we have to specify the three features of a dispositional construct: (1) the category of acts, (2) the category of contexts or settings, and (3) the conditional if-then rule that links the two categories. Within the category of acts one might list physical aggression (hitting, pushing, throwing objects, slamming doors); one might list verbal aggression (shouting, yelling, cursing, name-calling);

one might also include instances of passive aggression (acts of indirect aggression, for example, forgetting to perform a requested behavior; teasing). Within the category of settings or conditions one would include the variety of events that determine acts of physical, verbal, or passive aggression. Note that within each category (of acts and conditions) there is no definitive list of necessary and sufficient features that constitute aggressive behavior or its determining conditions. Punching might be a better example of aggression than muttering a curse under one's breath; slamming a door might be a better example than sulking; giving someone the silent treatment might be a better example than "forgetting" to take out the garbage.

The point is that a listing of possible aggressive behaviors to be covered by the category acts of aggression is potentially limitless, although some examples of aggression are better than others and would therefore serve as the best examples, or prototypes, of the act in question. The same would be true of the category of situational conditions. Some conditions (e.g., being frustrated, having one's competency tested or challenged) might be better examples of eliciting conditions than other conditions (e.g., being called by a telemarketer; having to wait in a long line; having a manuscript rejected for publication).

The foregoing suggests that the categories of acts and conditions are "fuzzy categories." Take the category "bird." There is no necessary and sufficient criteria that every candidate must possess in order to be subsumed by the category "bird." Should every candidate species chirp, fly, lay eggs, have feathers, build nests, and so on in order to be considered a bird? It seems reasonable to think so. But not all birds chirp; some creatures that do chirp are not birds; not all birds can fly; some creatures that do fly are not birds; not everything that builds a nest or lays an egg is a bird; and feathers are not unique to birds. Consequently, these criteria are neither necessary nor sufficient for assigning category membership. They appear to be merely correlated with the category of bird and probably apply to our best example or prototype of a bird.

We all tend to carry these prototypes around with us. We know that a robin is a better example of a bird than is a penguin. We know that a chair is a better example of furniture than is a nightstand or that an automobile is a better example of vehicle than is a skateboard (e.g., Rosch, 1975; Rosch, Mervis, Gray, Johnson, & Boyes-Braem, 1976). The same is probably true for the disposition "aggressive." Some examples of aggressive actions or of aggressive conditions are better, more central, or more prototypic, than others. There are prototypic features of acts (hitting) and conditions (being highly frustrated) that are correlated with aggression that seem clear and straightforward enough, but at the boundaries it may not be at all clear (it will be "fuzzy") if category membership applies. Is teasing really an act of aggression? Is waiting in line really a frustrating condition?

Finally, one requires a rule that links the two categories. This rule takes the form of an if-then proposition: If some condition C holds, then, with some probability, some behavior B should result. Note that the linking rule is also probabilistic and "fuzzy." We are now left with the following conditional account of dispositions: A dispositional statement (Jones is aggressive) is a concept that consists of a fuzzy condition category linked to a fuzzy behavior category with probabilistic linking propositions. The behavior categories are taken to be only loosely defined, consisting of multiple acts that may vary in their centrality to the category. Likewise, the condition category is only loosely defined, consisting of events or contexts that vary from central or good examples of the condition category to peripheral or poor instances of the category. Also, the linking propositions are taken to be probabilistic, indicating only an imperfect correlation between contexts and behavior. (Wright & Mischel, 1987, p. 1161)

The Wright and Mischel (1987) study is a good illustration of the conditional approach to dispositions and how this approach pegs the search for behavioral consistencies to locally specified conditions. The authors observed children who were "good examples of some psychologically important dispositional categories" (p. 1164), in this case, children who were aggressive and socially withdrawn. These children were observed in numerous situations, across many activities, at a summer camp. Under the classical understanding of trait, one would expect aggressive children to be hostile, bullying, verbally aggressive, and the like across the many activities and situations one might find at a summer camp. That is, one would expect to see "cross-situational consistency." Similarly, one might expect a socially withdrawn child to be easily identified by observers in whatever situation or activity the child was involved with.

But this was not the case. Children judged by adults to be good examples of aggressive and socially withdrawn dispositional tendencies showed considerable variability across situations and activities at the camp. In other words, "aggressive" children were not always aggressive; "socially withdrawn" children were not always socially withdrawn. Instead, whether children exhibited their respective dispositional behaviors depended very much on the situations they found themselves in. When the situation was highly stressful, when the situation challenged their sense of competency, for example, then dispositionally relevant behaviors (aggression, social withdrawal) were more likely to be in evidence. In contrast, when competency demands were low, for example, when the task (e.g., fishing) did not require the child to think rationally, attend to detail, tolerate frustration, deal with peer or adult conflict, or focus on a task while distracted, the child's behavior was indistinguishable from that of children who were less aggressive or socially withdrawn. The trait was not in evidence. Hence, in "easy" situations, dispositional behaviors are unlikely to be observed. It is only when the situation places certain demands upon the child that the disposition in question is likely to be in evidence.

This particular if-then contingency rule has been called the *competency-demand hypothesis*. This hypothesis suggests that stable patterns of individual differences are more likely to be observed in psychologically demanding situations. Let's say Watson faces situation X, say, his boss has asked him to write an important report in an area of his expertise. Writing this report is something Watson wants to do very much. Hence, his motivation is quite high. What is more, he has the skills, training, and competencies required for the task. In this situation whatever Watson does can be predicted from elements of the situation. No dispositional construct needs to be invoked, since Watson is likely to do whatever the situation requires. Hence, knowledge of what the situation requires will probably be a good guide for predicting Watson's eventual behavior. In contrast, when the task places excessive demands on competency, dispositional constructs will play a more prominent role in predicting Watson's behavior. Presumably, the analysis of other traits and virtues, and their eliciting situational conditions, would reveal other sorts of contingency rules.

One important lesson of Mischel's research program is that behavioral consistency is often found in more localized, contextually specific conditions. This does not mean that one should eliminate dispositions, individual differences, or "trait talk" in the attempt to understand of personality. But this finding does severely undermine the classical notion that traits are stable, global, enduring dispositions that show a significant degree of cross-situational consistency. Although Mischel's view on the matter is not the only competitor of the classical theory (e.g., Alston, 1975; Buss & Craik, 1983; Hampshire, 1953), I have perhaps said enough to make the point that any moral theory that focuses on the acquisition of virtues or that focuses on character development, where character is defined in terms of certain highly desirable dispositions or traits, would be hard pressed to find very many resources in the psychological literature to draw upon. As our look at Walter Mischel's research program has illustrated, traits have had an unhappy history in personality research, and there are now significant doubts about the usefulness of global traits for describing any significant feature of human personality, including moral personality. It thus becomes much easier for developmental theories of moral psychology to eschew an interest in moral character or in the role of virtues in our moral life. Not only are there strong ethical-philosophical reasons to distrust the language of moral traits, but now their usefulness as a purely psychological construct is called into question. When doubts about the psychological reality of global traits are coupled with the Kantian themes that inform most developmental theories of moral psychology, themes that treat personological dispositions as a source of error, bias, and heteronomy, the marginalization of a virtue-centered approach to moral psychology becomes more understandable.

As I pointed out earlier, there has been a remarkable shift in ethics away from Kantian themes toward a reconsideration of the classical interest in virtues, which is sometimes referred to as the Aristotelian approach (see, e.g., Aristotle's *Nichomachean Ethics*). Indeed, virtue ethics has made a remarkable comeback in recent years (e.g., French et al., 1988; Porter, 1990; Meilaender, 1984; Kruschwitz & Roberts, 1987; MacIntyre, 1984; Hauerwas, 1979). In concert with this development in ethics has been a general lament over the shabby and dismissive treatment of virtues and character by the cognitive developmental approach (e.g., Philibert, 1975; Dykstra, 1981). As a consequence of these developments, there is now active speculation concerning just how the issues of character and virtue might be reintroduced into moral psychology in a more adequate way. I will revisit Mischel's social-cognitive theory of personality when I attempt to chart what the post-Kohlbergian era in moral psychology might look like.

Before taking up these issues, however, I will examine two additional approaches to moral personality. The first theory was developed in the 1970s by Robert Hogan. As we will see, his socioanalytic theory stands in stark contrast to the cognitive developmental approach to moral development. The second theory is of more recent vintage and is more compatible with the cognitive developmental approach. This theory, developed by Augusto Blasi, views the moral personality in terms of a responsible "self as agent" who develops a moral identity.

11

The Moral Personality: Socioanalytic Theory

Assumptions

In an early paper Robert Hogan (1973) developed a rich, suggestive theory of moral character. This theory made a number of assumptions, a few of which were quite startling to researchers who cut their theoretical teeth within the Kohlbergian, cognitive developmental paradigm. Hogan's theory assumes that purposive behavior is governed by overlapping rule systems and that each rule system is associated with a particular kind of ethic. Athletic activity, for example, is a rule-governed activity that is associated with the ethics of sportsmanship; various kinds of social interaction are rule-governed activities that are associated with the ethics of courtesy and etiquette or, in some circumstances, with the ethics of justice, equity, and fairness. Two quick points can be made thus far. First, morality is a system of rules, and these rules guide purposive behavior. Second, no sharp distinction is drawn between moral rules and other kinds of social rules. Moral rules are not different in kind from manners or expressions of courtesy or from social-conventional rules.

In Hogan's view morality has a "social job to do," the job of regulating conduct. The regulative function of morality is to be understood in terms of certain biological mechanisms. In some ways Hogan's theory articulates an ethological approach to human morality. Because of evolutionary pressure we human beings are disposed to comply with authority. This innate, constitutional motive for compliance is best seen in children. We are also constitutionally disposed toward group loyalty and corresponding altruistic feelings, since self-sacrifice for the sake of the group has survival value and is evolutionarily favored. As a result we are naturally sensitive to group expectations and the demand of our peers, and hence compliance comes easy to us. Indeed, individualism is deviant and unnatural and requires explanation. In other words, we are not born as independent free-standing selves who then have to knuckle under to the demands of the group. Individualism is not the truth of our existence. Social compliance is not what is strange and alien to us as human beings, or contrary to what we are in essence. Rather, compliance is normal and expectable and contributes to individual and group survival; individualism threatens social organization (also, Emler & Hogan, 1991).

Hogan also assumes that much of moral conduct is routine, automatic, ritualized behavior performed for its own sake with the implication that at least some of our moral behaviors have become divorced from whatever larger social purpose they once advanced. Further, Hogan likens moral rules to an internal template that

215

young organisms develop during critical periods. This internal template allows them to evaluate learned responses and to compare them with adult models. In this way moral rules are like innate mechanisms for self-regulation in the sense that they serve as internal standards for self-evaluation and are acquired (internalized) after observing adult models.

Dimensions of Moral Character

Our tendency toward morality, then, is driven by biological mechanisms and by our need to adapt to evolutionary demands upon our species. Morality allows us to adapt at the sociocultural level by regulating and moderating human conduct. What, then, is moral character? For Hogan moral character is a kind of personality structure that encompasses various motives for acting. He draws a Freudian analogy. If we want to understand neurotic symptoms, we must first identify the underlying personality structure. Rupal and Gurpal may both smoke cigars, but for Rupal cigar smoking reflects a neurotic desire for approval; for Gurpal it reflects a neurotic self-destructive tendency. For yet others cigar smoking carries no diagnostic or symbolic value at all, for after all, "sometimes a cigar is just a cigar" (a line often attributed to Freud). Hence what is important is not the symptom but the underlying character structure. Such applies, too, to understanding moral (altruism) and immoral (delinquency, civil disobedience) behavior. Here one must also examine the person's personality structure, his or her character, and character is seen to vary along five dimensions of individual differences.

Moral character, first of all, depends on the amount of *moral knowledge* one has acquired. Acquiring moral knowledge principally revolves around learning three kinds of rules: (1) specific injunctions ("wash your hands before eating"; "don't push your sister"); (2) more general moral rules; and (3) cognitive strategies, or "comparison rules," for evaluating when one's behavior is and is not up to standards. Moral knowledge is critical for two reasons. First, one can follow only the rules that one knows. Second, moral knowledge, particularly knowledge of comparison rules, makes self-criticism and self-regulation possible.

In addition to moral knowledge, internalization of the rules, values, and prohibitions of one's social group is necessary for character development; one must make these rules one's own and view them as personally mandatory. Hogan views this as akin to superego development and calls it *socialization*. Some individuals are well socialized, that is, they show a high degree of willingness to follow rules. Other individuals are less well socialized and thus take a more casual approach to rules. In addition, individuals also vary in their disposition toward empathy (or role-taking or sympathy). Hogan describes empathy as an innate capacity that is elicited by social experience. When the socialization and empathy dimensions of moral development are dichotomized, the following four characterological types are suggested: (1) Individuals who are not socially sensitive, that is, who have poor role-taking or empathic abilities and are not well socialized (low empathy–low socialization), are delinquents. (2) Individuals who are highly socialized but poor in empathy (low empathy–high socialization) are moral realists, that is, are rigid, "stuffy, rule-bound, pedantic prigs" (Hogan 1973, p. 222). (3) Individuals who are highly empathic but not well socialized (high empathy–low socialization) are "le chic" types. That is, they flout rules in a cavalier way. As Hogan puts it, "They are 'emancipated' mildly sociopathic members of normal society, that is, persons who double-park in parking lots, do not return borrowed books, and smoke marijuana" (p. 222). Finally, individuals who are well socialized (and are hence compliant) but also highly sympathetic to the moral frailties of others (high empathy–high socialization) are said to be morally mature.

The fourth dimension of moral character concerns where one stands with respect to the purpose and role of ethics in human affairs. This dimension is anchored by two opposing points of view. One view is broadly Kantian in orientation, the other utilitarian. According to the former view, ethical rules are higher laws that stand over and above human concerns and exist independently of human social life. These higher laws are autonomous of human legislation. One appeals to these higher laws in order to pass judgment on the ordinary legal or social arrangements we might devise or the institutions we might develop. These higher laws are available to us through reason or intuition. Hogan calls this Kantian orientation the "ethics of personal conscience." Presumably, anyone can partake of moral rationality and is free to invoke the force of the moral law upon one's own exercise of reason.

In contrast, the utilitarian tradition suggests that moral rules codify pragmatic arrangements that promote the general welfare of society. Laws are not justified by appeal to ultimate, transcendental higher laws but rather are justified merely on instrumental grounds: Do they advance some purpose that is socially useful? Do they contribute to stability, order, good government, and the like? Hogan calls this perspective the "ethics of social responsibility."

Two Ethical Orientations

Hogan (1970) devised the Survey of Ethical Attitudes in order to identify those who have the disposition to adopt one or the other of these ethical orientations. Here are four examples (out of 35) from the survey:

1. All civil laws should be judged against a higher moral law.
2. Right and wrong can be meaningfully defined only by the law.
3. An unjust law should not be obeyed.
4. Without law the life of man would be nasty, brutish, and short.

If you endorse items 1 and 3, you probably resonate with the ethics of conscience. If you are attracted to items 2 and 4, you align with the ethics of social responsibility.

In Hogan's view, which orientation we find attractive is largely an irrational matter, that is, our preference is derived from the structure of our personality. On the basis of research that correlates the Survey of Ethical Attitudes with various personality measures, Hogan derives the following personological descriptions: If you endorse the ethics of conscience, you are independent, creative, and innovative but also rebellious, impulsive, opportunistic, and irresponsible. Indeed, if you are also nonempathic and hardly socialized, you are probably delinquent, too. Hence, delinquency is compatible with this ethical orientation. If you endorse the ethics of social responsibility you are thoughtful, reasonable, helpful, and dependable but also conventional and resistant to change.

Both perspectives are equally sensitive to injustice but tend to attribute injustice to difference things (Hogan & Dickstein, 1972). Those who endorse the ethics of conscience believe that human nature is basically good and naturally disposed toward benevolence. When things go awry it is because this natural benevolence is distorted by oppressive social institutions. In contrast, those who endorse the ethics of social responsibility view human nature as essentially evil, malevolent, and anti-social, tendencies that must be counteracted and restrained by the institutional forces of society.

Hogan (1973) leaves little doubt where he stands. In his view the lessons of history are quite clear—it is most unrealistic to expect people to be "compassionate, charitable and tolerant." He suggests that "the most we can reasonably expect is that people will comply with the rules, that they will avoid doing evil, that they will not steal our property, molest our families or enslave us" (p. 231). Consequently, just getting people to comply with authority and to obey the rules is about the best we can hope for as a practical end point to moral development.

Which brings us to autonomy, the fifth dimension of character. Hogan finds autonomy in moral affairs to be a "troubling concept." The trouble with autonomy is that the autonomous person who is unsocialized and not empathic can well exercise his or her "personal conscience" but still be "a great rogue and scoundrel" (Hogan, 1973, p. 227). Hogan has clearly confused two meanings of the term "autonomy." He wishes to invoke the Kantian meaning of moral autonomy but conflates it instead with independence of judgment, that is, with the tendency to exercise independent judgment that may well serve selfish and not moral ends. Hence, autonomy is fine, in Hogan's view, just as long as we are also disposed to obey the rules and attend to the needs of others.

Socioanalytic Theory

In a later paper this rather pessimistic account of moral development was dubbed the socioanalytic theory (Hogan, Johnson, & Emler, 1978; see also Hogan, 1974, 1975). The socioanalytic theory clarifies and extends the original formulation in interesting ways. It takes a clearer stand, for example, on three core issues. The first issue concerns the problem of ethical relativism. Moral relativism says not only that different cultures have their own moral arrangements but that there are no objective grounds by which one can evaluate, compare, or choose among the many moral varieties. One set of moral values is as good as any other, since there are no stand-alone criteria that one can appeal to in order to appraise the adequacy of any particular moral position. The authors suggest (as did Kohlberg) that most behavioral theories in psychology would endorse some version of ethical relativism. In contrast, moral absolutism holds that there are indeed universal moral principles that are made known to us through reason and intuition. The cognitive developmental tradition is the best example of moral absolutism within psychology.

Socioanalytic theory embraces a third view, which it calls relative moral absolutism. This view holds that there are certain behaviors that seem required in order to make group living possible and thereby promote the survival of a culture. Other behaviors, if left unchecked, seem to threaten the solidarity of group life and thereby destroy the fabric of society. Those behaviors that promote and destroy group life seem to be the same regardless of what group you have in mind. All societies, then, develop rules concerning behaviors that are to be promoted and behaviors that are to be banned. Consequently, "at a deep level all viable cultures show the same set of rules—rules about lying, cheating, stealing, incest and so on" (Hogan et al., 1978, p. 3). It is in this sense that morality is universal. It just so happens that no society can long endure if it permits incest, lying, cheating, and stealing to go unchecked.

Yet each society also occupies a particular ecological niche. Each society is confronted with a potentially unique set of ecological circumstances to which it must adapt. So each society must also legislate certain rules that promote survival given the particularities of its circumstances. These rules are not to be justified from above, from the "perspective from eternity," that is, according to some sort of transcendental ultimate justification or reference to a supreme moral principle. Rather, the moral rules of society are justified simply in terms of whether they promote cultural survival. This also suggests that moral rules are not timeless. They are valid now just because experience shows that they work. But the future may bring many challenges, and societies may have to discard certain of their moral rules if they are seen to get in the way of cultural adaptation.

The second core issue addressed by socioanalytic theory is the so-called problem of authority. What is the source of our felt sense of moral obligation? There is the utilitarian or social contract view, which says that we tend to our moral obligations because it is in our best interest to do so. By entering into mutual agreements we can maximize the benefits of cooperation while minimizing the burdens. It is in our rational best interest to secure the blessings of civilized life, so we feel obliged to do that which contributes to public order and a well-functioning polity. There is also the higher-law view, which the authors treat as a kind of moral solipsism. Since individuals can decide for themselves what is the higher law, or what moral rationality amounts to, they are then obliged to live according to the dictates of personal conscience. Then there is the view endorsed by socioanalytic theory. People comply with the rules because they want to perceive that their government is legitimate; because compliance will be ensured by force and coercion in any event (indeed, force is the ultimate source of moral obligation—to think that compliance is voluntary is to be greatly mystified); and for unconscious reasons—at a deep level we all fear disorder and desire guidance and direction.

Finally, according to the socioanalytic theory, the development of moral character takes place through an epigenetic process not unlike that in Erikson's stage theory of psychosocial development. Hence, moral development consists of developmental phases that are each characterized by unique psychological challenges. Development is a dialectical transaction between the individual capacities of the developing child and the demands placed upon the child by socialization agents, which is to say that development is a matter of the child accommodating internal conditions to external demands.

The strong focus on evolutionary themes is retained by socioanalytic theory. Moral behavior is rule governed; this system of rules permits cohesive groups to build cultures, organize societies, and thereby adapt to ecological challenges. Hence culture-building and culture-maintaining rules systems have survival value. In short, evolutionary history has favored the emergence of morality. It also provides the basis of human motivation more generally. According to the authors, there are three classes of instinctual motives that give rise to communal behavior and cooperative group living. There is, first, a motivational tendency to seek social approval and social attention. Second, there is a motivational instinct to seek structure, predictability, and order. Part of this instinct involves the tendency to classify, codify, and legislate; to perform rituals; to organize group life in terms of functional roles. Third, socioanalytic theory assumes that we have an instinctual tendency toward aggressive self-expression, which spills out into competitive status-seeking and dominance behavior. Such behavior makes possible the production of status hierarchies and group leadership roles—the presence of which brings order, stability, and predictability to group life.

Phases of Moral Development

What are the phases of moral development? By "moral development" the authors have in mind the gradual elaboration of moral character. The epigenetic image is of a child attempting to adapt, that is, the child attempts to accommodate to the new social demands that each new phase of development entails. The child must construct a character structure that is up to the challenge of each developmental phase.

The first challenge, faced in infancy and the toddler period, is how to assimilate the elements of culture so that one might survive. The infant must become progressively attuned to the various overlapping rule systems that govern his or her life. Language learning is the paradigm case for what the authors have in mind. Parents who teach their child language do not negotiate over the meaning of words but simply tell the child the names of objects, the meaning of words, or the use of language. As the authors put it, "Only children who are able to follow effortlessly the demands, requests and instructions of adults will be able to assimilate their culture and survive" (Hogan et al., 1978, p.8). The child's first task, then, is *rule attunement*—he must become attuned to the rules of adults—and ideally this is accomplished in the context of secure attachment and authoritative parenting.

But the developing child must learn not only how to live with authority but how to live with peers. School-age children are socially awkward and have much to learn not because they are beset with cognitive egocentrism, as Piaget would have it, but because they are inept and inexperienced. They must come to learn *social sensitivity;* that is, they must come to be empathically attuned to the often implicit social expectations of others. This empathic ability allows the child to think in terms of the spirit of the law and to resolve the contradictions that arise when one is caught at the intersection of overlapping rule systems.

Perhaps the attentive reader is detecting a hint of Piaget's theory here. Is not rule attunement just another way of talking about the morality of constraint? Is not social sensitivity just another way of talking about the morality of cooperation? Does not Piaget also claim that important moral lessons are learned in the context of the peer group?

But the authors' view of the role of the peer group in moral development is quite at odds with Piagetian theory (although the difference does appear to be unfairly drawn by the authors). For Piaget, interactions within the peer group motivate the sense of equality, cooperation, solidarity, and justice. Interactions with adults breed heteronomy, moral realism, constraint, and egocentrism. In contrast, the authors suggest that "what children actually encounter in the peer group when adults are not around is bullying, exploitation and persecution. Turn taking and cooperation occur primarily because adults intervene and force children to share, take turns and 'play fair'" (Hogan et al., 1978, p. 10). They go on to suggest that children do learn about justice and reciprocity and fairness, but largely because they know what it means to be treated unjustly and unfairly by older bullies in their neighborhood. Of course, when Piaget was writing about the morality of cooperation, he envisioned a society of peers, that is, a society of equals, and not the case described here, where older children tyrannize younger children.

The third developmental challenge for character development occurs in adolescence. If rule attunement teaches the toddler to live with authority and if social sensitivity teaches the child to live with peers, then the task of adolescence is to live with oneself and to master autonomy. The authors have no patience, however, with what they take to be the cognitive developmental understanding of autonomy. They deny, for example, that autonomous morality means nonconformity or that autonomy somehow entails defiance of conventional authority and social pressure. Rather, for the socioanalytic theorist, autonomy means defending what is highest and ideal in one's culture. The autonomous person does not stand outside of collective values but defends them. Indeed, the autonomous person is committed to conventional standards just because he or she realizes that there can be no ultimate or foundational justification of values. If one value system is as good as another, we might as well defend the values we already have.

The autonomous character is also aware of a few other things. The autonomous person is aware that all philosophies are limited, that one's own values are relative, and that the meaning of life is obscure and justice is often frustrated. Consequently, the autonomous character attempts to cultivate a measure of inner detachment. The autonomous character avoids excessive enthusiasms and violent passions and is perhaps characterized by "the conscious impotence of rage at human folly," as T. S. Eliot (1943, p. 54) put it. The autonomous person clings to the values she has, since these are no more or less valid than any other.

The authors do not entirely eschew identifying moral types. In the previous work Hogan (1973) varied the dimensions of empathy and socialization to yield four moral types: the delinquent, le chic, the morally mature, and the moral realist. In the 1978 paper, however, the authors treat the three developmental phases as dimensions of individual differences and, by varying the loadings on these dimensions, identify three kinds of nonautonomous moral types. If one has high rule attunement but low social sensitivity and low self-awareness, one is a moral realist. The moral realist is very good at following rules and makes for a good bureaucrat and police officer. If one has high rule attunement, high social sensitivity, but low self-awareness, one is a moral enthusiast. Moral enthusiasts appreciate conventional morality and are very empathic and well intentioned. But they lack the sort of perspective that comes with self-awareness; they lack an "internal moral gyroscope"— so they rush about from one moral outrage to the next, taking up one cause, then another. Finally, the moral zealot is one who is characterized by low rule attunement, high social sensitivity, and low self-awareness. The zealot is hostile toward authority, feels injustice keenly, and is prone to aggressive confrontations to advance his or her remedies.

What of the distinction between the ethics of conscience and the ethics of social responsibility? The authors maintain that this dichotomy is one of the great ideological polarities in Western thought and that it is found in most human groups. What is more, this ideological polarity is the result of two broad *personality syndromes* that condition how human nature is construed and the kinds of moral judgments that are reached. Indeed, "moral development is properly considered within the context of personality development as a whole" (Hogan et al., 1978, p. 13).

Empirical Status

The socioanalytic theory has not attracted much research interest since it was first articulated in the 1970s (e.g., Nardi, 1979; Haier, 1977; Nardi & Tsujimoto, 1979; Tsujimoto & Nardi, 1978). I am aware of no sustained research program that is attempting to derive testable empirical hypotheses from this provocative theory. Part of the difficulty is that the developmental claims of the theory are so general that the derivation of fine-grained hypotheses is almost impossible. To chart character development from infancy to adolescence in terms of three broad phases, for example, is surely to miss many details and nuances. Furthermore, many (but not all) developmental intuitions that are found in the theory turn out to be contrary to what is known about the capacities of children. Hogan (1973) suggests, for example, that before children are socialized they are impulsive and egocentric and that empathy is a rather late achievement. But we saw in Chapter 9 that children engage in prosocial behavior from a very early age and have impressive empathic abilities. (Hogan's failure to distinguish among empathy, role-taking, and sympathy is also a problem.)

It is also hard to know what to do with phases of development that also serve as dimensions of individual differences. The derivation of broad character types also seems out of step with contemporary research in personality theory (e.g.,

Mischel, 1990). To view moral behavior as irrational or as just an expression of a personological preference or to reduce moral rationality to simple knowledge about rules does not seem to capture the complexity of human moral functioning. Such a view seems contrary to the notion that rationality is also a deeply entrenched part of what it means to be a person, that moral values make certain claims on us and are potential guides to the formation and expression of our personalities. The notion that we respect authority, follow rules, and crave order because of instinctual motivations buried deep within our evolutionary history is not a view that commands wide assent. Indeed, so much of the theory makes references to unconscious motivations (what is analytic about socioanalysis) that many of its claims cannot be disproved or at least share the same empirical fate as other Freudian artifacts.

If Kohlberg's theory is broadly influenced by Kantian theory, Hogan's theory is influenced by Hobbes (1951/1958). From Hogan we get the image of the world as being a very dangerous place. It is romantic and naive to think that people can be rational, beneficent, prosocial. Experience teaches otherwise. The best we can hope for is to keep the barbarians at the gate by instilling respect for conventional standards, the rule of law, the importance of authority and leadership. Given the historical context in which Hogan's theory was developed, one is tempted to say that it is a reaction to the presumed excesses of the 1960s. This period was, of course, marked by profound sociopolitical change. For many individuals the prospect of a countercultural revolution must have seemed menacing to the extreme. Many were alarmed to see antiwar riots, to see cherished national symbols burned or otherwise desecrated, to see conventional lifestyles mocked, to see patriotism and other official pieties scorned, to see the law flouted, to see civil disobedience on a wide and alarming scale. It did appear that the institutions of society were under siege. Conventional values were being challenged in the name of self-expression, freedom, and autonomy. What is more, many young people, le chic and the moral zealots perhaps, easily invoked the language of higher law and moral autonomy to justify their assault upon traditional values; many of them attempted to stake out the moral high ground by using language that sounded an awful lot like Kohlberg's principled moral reasoner. Taking the law into one's own hands seemed not too far removed from the autonomous person who legislates the moral law for himself. Indeed, it very well seemed that the language of principled morality was being co-opted by a left-wing political movement that challenged conventional values and authority.

Although I doubt Hogan would put it this way, the theory he articulated appears to be a reaction to all these developments. It appears to represent the theoretical revenge of the Silent Majority. If Kohlberg's theory makes liberals feel triumphal, self-satisfied, and comfortable with their moral assertions, Hogan's theory, realistic and hardheaded, would confound them. Indeed, their presumptions about the rational superiority of their higher law would be shown up for what it is, namely, just an irrational preference linked to personological variables and probably a fault in development to boot. Their embrace of nonconformity is just a shallow understanding of autonomy, which really means conforming to ideal conventions. The political demonstrator is not a moral hero. On the contrary, such a person has simply caved in to excessive enthusiasms and has failed to cultivate inner detachment. The true moral hero is one who accepts conventional values, since no others can be shown to be any better. The true moral hero complies with authority and defends cultural standards. The true moral hero wants to survive. The true moral hero is resigned to his or her fate and accepts the fact that the world is not perfect and that injustice often triumphs. The true moral hero is Ecclesiastes, resigned to the lot assigned him, aware that folly is sometimes "promoted to high dignities" (Ecclesiastes 10:7) and that moral exertion is "vanity and chasing of the wind" (2:18).

Hogan's theory appears to be an attempt to reassert the moral imperative to respect law and order, to appreciate conventional standards, and to comply with authority. It does so not so much by making metaethical arguments, that is, not by searching for ultimate justifications in a priori principles, not by any appeal to rational first principles, but rather by grounding the moral imperative in the very stuff of human nature—in biological mechanisms, in unconscious motivations, in instinctual tendencies forged in the heat of evolutionary history. Paradoxically, however, if we attempt to formulate a psychological explanation for moral functioning by grounding it in evolutionary history, the reasons for moral behavior become just as elusive as when we attempt a philosophical explanation by searching for the essence of morality in a transcendental universal reason or in the workings of a pure will.

It is interesting to note that the theories of Kohlberg and Hogan represent opposing options in what Johnson (1993) called the moral law folk theory, which was discussed in Chapter 10. Kohlberg's theory stresses the importance of rationality in moral functioning; Hogan stresses irrationality. Kohlberg focuses on cognitive elements; Hogan focuses on biological elements. Kohlberg emphasizes moral judgment and draws attention to behaviors carefully selected according to reasons self-consciously constructed and to principles self-consciously invoked. He draws attention to the importance of intentions and self-constructed meanings, to the notion that morality is a conscious activity of a rational being. Hogan focuses instead on unconscious motives and the notion that rule-following is an adaptive activity of an instinctual, biological being. Kohlberg's theory emphasizes what is higher in human nature; Hogan emphasizes what is lower.

What seems right about Hogan's theory is its steady insistence that moral functioning cannot be divorced from personality. But this insight is purchased at the steep price of pushing moral rationality to the very margins of the theory. If Kohlberg errs in one direction, Hogan errs in the other. The nature of these errors are revealed by reference to the moral law folk theory. Since the folk theory construes rationality as a property of the mind and personality as the organization of bodily desires and inclinations—and since mind and body, rationality and personality, are contraposed as extreme opposites at war with one another for the control of the will—it becomes more clear how Hogan, whose theory asserts the primacy of personality, could be tempted into denying moral rationality, and how Kohlberg, whose theory has a Kantian flavor, could assert the primacy of reason over the corrupting influence of personological inclinations. In short, asserting the primacy of personality (the body) entails denying rationality (the mind), and vice versa.

What is required is the middle way. What is required is a sophisticated theory of moral personality that does not tempt us to make either/or claims about the rational and personological elements of moral functioning. Fortunately, such a theory is being developed by Augusto Blasi. I take up Blasi's work on the moral personality in Chapter 12.

12

The Moral Self

We have encountered Blasi's work before in our look at moral action. According to his Self Model, the moral agent must work out the following issues in the course of deciding what to do. The agent must first decide on the morally correct action. The agent must then conclude that it is he who is responsible for performing the morally good action. He is motivated to perform this action just because the self is at stake and on the line, just because the self is responsible. Hence, he is motivated because of an internal demand for self-consistency. To reach a judgment that he is responsible to do X but then to fail to do X is to threaten the integrity of the self. Finally, he must inhibit contrary inclinations. He must short-circuit those defensive strategies that might interfere with the felt sense of discomfort that arises from inconsistency.

The Self Model emphasizes responsibility and integrity as key notions underlying moral action. Responsibility entails the obligation to act according to one's judgment. Integrity is the sense of wholeness and personal intactness that results from self-consistent actions, from being true to the self in action. Since his early writings on moral action, Blasi has been working out the implications of the Self Model for other aspects of moral functioning. What is a self? What does it mean to say that the self is responsible? How is personality implicated in self-consistency? What is the proper relationship between personality and rationality? How does the moral personality develop?

Blasi has clear sympathy for the Kohlbergian tradition. In his view the signal achievement of the cognitive developmental approach was its insistence that rationality is the essence of morality. Morality is a cognitive system that allows us to come to grips with the truth of our experience. Morality is one result of our attempt to extract meaning from our social exchanges, and this meaning entails the view that moral action involves intention and knowledge (Blasi, 1989). We come to appreciate the moral quality of an action just when we know something about the agent's point of view. How does the agent construe the situation? What is the agent's understanding of the self or of social relationships? What is the agent's understanding of what he or she is doing? What is the agent's judgment? What are the agent's reasons? (Blasi, 1984). In other words, what the agent knows and what the agent intends are two key considerations that are prior to evaluating a moral action. In Blasi's view, one cannot dispense with the cognitive element in moral psychology. To eliminate reason from morality is to destroy the moral phenomenon itself (Blasi, 1984).

The difficulty, of course, is to retain the emphasis on reason, judgment, and knowledge while at the same time constructing a moral psychology that is also realistic, warm-blooded, and deeply rooted in our personality. The folk-theory dichotomy between reason and personality is present here as well. If one links moral functioning to our deeper human nature, to personality, to the self, to desires and natural inclinations, then one risks divorcing morality from its chief characteristic, which is judgment and reason. This was Hogan's error. However, if one emphasizes reason and judgment as the sole sources of moral motives, then morality is divorced from the person. This was Kohlberg's error. The trick is to ground morality on a conception of personality in such a way that the rational character of morality is not lost. That is, we must somehow show that moral functioning depends on the self but that reason and judgment play a role, too. Blasi's (1984) solution is this: The very construction of the self, the self's very identity, hinges on moral reasons. There is no dichotomy between the self and moral rationality when the self is constructed with reference to moral reasons. When this occurs one can speak of the moral personality.

Does everyone develop a conception of the self guided by moral notions? Does everyone develop a moral personality? This seems implausible. In Blasi's (1984) view the self is not a collection of traits but is rather a way of organizing self-related information. Some information is central, important, and essential for self-understanding; other information is peripheral, unimportant, and nonessential. These dimensions (central-peripheral, important-unimportant, essential-nonessential) are thought to reflect principles of psychological consistency. Some individuals organize self-related information around moral categories; others do not. Some individuals let moral notions penetrate to the essence and core of what and who they are as a person; others have only a glancing acquaintance with moral notions but perhaps choose to define the self in other ways, by reference to other values. One has a moral identity just to the extent that moral notions, such as being good, being just, being fair, are judged to be central, important, and essential to one's self-understanding. One has a moral identity just to the extent that one is committed to living in such a way that one expresses what is central, important, and essential in one's life.

This suggests two things. First, if moral considerations are self-defining, if they are part of the essential self to the extent that self-integrity is seen to hinge on being self-consistent in action, then not to act in accordance with one's identity, not to act with what is essential, important, and central to one's life is to risk losing the self. Second, moral identity is a dimension of individual differences (Blasi, 1984). Presumably, being moral, being just, being fair, may not be part of the identity of some individuals. Moral categories do not penetrate their understanding of who they are as persons, do not influence their outlook on important issues, or do not factor into the important decisions they will be called upon to make. Some individuals may incorporate these categories into their personality to different degrees or may come to emphasize some but not other moral categories. Some individuals, for example, may build compassion into self-identity; others may resonate to fairness; still others, to obedience or temperance or courage and perhaps many other moral virtues.

How is the moral self constructed? In Blasi's (1984) view the moral self is the self whose very identity is constructed by reference to moral categories or under the influence of moral reasons. This suggests that psychological mechanisms denoted as the self and moral principles, reasons, and categories are independent domains and that one domain (morality) has to influence the other (the essential self). Blasi (1984) suggests that this might happen along the following four steps.

Step 1: First one constructs general moral structures, presumably much the way Kohlberg describes the process. Hence, through social interaction, through role-taking opportunities, one develops a certain understanding of social reality. One develops an organized way of thinking through the moral issues. Part of what one comes to know is that there is such a thing as objective reality and that one's appraisal of objective reality is "independent of our *personality biases*" (Blasi, 1984, p. 138; my emphasis). Note that by making our appraisal of the moral landscape independent of our personality biases, Blasi is attempting to maintain the autonomy of morality. That is, there is an objective moral reality, there is truth, and we can apprehend that truth with our cognitive abilities in such a way that it is not otherwise contaminated by personological factors.

Step 2: One's general moral structures then come to influence the construction of certain ideals—ideals of actions, ideals of agents.

Step 3: This generalized understanding of ideals contributes to the construction of the ideal moral self. The ideal moral self then becomes a constituent of the core, essential self and becomes, in addition, a principle of action. As Blasi (1984, p. 131) puts it, "Understanding that a specific ideal is a good for one's becoming already involves a restructuring of the very core of the actual self, introducing in it a new principle of tension between what one understands and what one does."

Step 4: The self now becomes the source of moral judgments. The moral self asks "What must *I* do?" given that moral integrity is the core of what it means to be a person at all. The basis of these judgments is one's very identity, but these judgments are not the simple workings of personality but are instead genuinely cognitive, moral judgments (note the folk-theory dichotomy between "cognitive" and "personality") insofar as the self was constructed under the influence of moral reasons. In other words, just because the source of moral judgments is self-understanding does not mean that moral judging is based on personological factors, since, in this case, the self is the product of moral categories.

It is important to note that moral understanding (Step 1) is prior to moral identity. One first develops moral structures. One first comes to certain moral understandings. These understandings then penetrate the self—leading to a moralization of personality, or of the self. This direction of effect, from moral understanding to moral identity, allows Blasi to assert the autonomy of morality, to assert its "objectivity" from personality biases, as noted previously. In a number of recent writings Blasi (1989, 1991) has described the progressive moralization of the self as a process of integration, whereby moral notions become integrated within the personality. He has also brought significant clarity to the very concept of moral personality (Blasi, 1985). Before we take up the moralization of the self and the integration of the moral personality, let's explore in more detail just how Blasi (1985) understands moral personality.

What Is the Moral Personality?

The term "moral personality" implies that personality is somehow relevant to moral functioning. Only a moral sense that is deeply rooted in one's personality can give rise to moral action or can otherwise sustain the effort to live in fidelity to one's moral commitments. If the capacity for living the moral life is seen to hinge on "person variables," then any adequate moral psychology must be able to specify how personality contributes to moral action. But the expression "moral personality" is not unambiguous. According to Blasi (1985), there are at least three ways of understanding the importance of personality for moral functioning. There is the view, first, that moral functioning requires strong will.

What is strong will? Strong will is composed of those stable dispositions (traits) that play an instrumental role in sustaining effective behavior. Strong will is our "agentic system" (Blasi, 1991), and the dispositions that compose it make it possible for us to carry out our (moral) intentions. These dispositions include the ability to delay gratification; to exercise impulse control; to use defense mechanisms and coping skills; to persevere in the face of adversity; to be courageous; to deploy attentional resources in task-relevant ways; to engage in effective role-taking and information-processing; and more. These instrumental, or "efficiency," variables correspond to our common notion of personality traits, that is, they are stable dispositions for which there are individual differences. These dispositions are also morally neutral in the sense that they can be placed at the service of moral or immoral ends. They are the personological preconditions for sustaining any action at all. Only when these dispositions are placed at the service of moral projects can one legitimately speak about *moral* personality. Which brings us to good will, the second sense of moral personality.

What is good will? Blasi (1985) uses this term to describe the moral self, the self whose very identity is constructed with moral categories. As such, good will is a deep, central, affective and motivational orientation toward morality. Good will is possible when one first (cognitively) realizes what morality amounts to, then attempts to order the element of one's life in light of this understanding. Both strong will and good will are compatible with the view that morality is interpersonal, that is, morality is all about defining our obligations toward one another. Good will can sustain moral action on behalf on another, can make moral action reliable and dependable through its own motivational power (because acting morally is necessary in order to express what is the truth of one's identity, which is to say, with what is essential, important, and central to one's self-understanding) or through its use of strong will. But either way, moral action is carried out because of one's felt obligation to the other. Blasi (1985) suggests that there is yet a third understanding of moral personality that draws attention to the moral value of certain personality characteristics quite apart from any interpersonal considerations. This third option involves the agent alone in her or her personhood and might be called a personal morality. Destroying one's intellectual powers with drugs and alcohol, selling one's freedom, debasing one's dignity—these are inherently immoral. We have a genuinely moral obligation to develop our talents, to seek the truth about ourselves, to live authentically. The personal domain cannot be a refuge from moral obligation. Making decisions about the sort of life one is to live or about the kind of person one wishes to become or attempting to live well the life that is good for one to live involves many personal decisions that do not have an obvious interpersonal component yet involve an inner felt sense of obligation that is genuinely moral nonetheless. In this view the integrity of the self is a moral issue that can be subsumed under the moral injunction to respect persons—since the self is a person, too.

As Blasi (1985) points out, the three meanings of moral personality are not mutually exclusive. Indeed, it is possible to see the three meanings as complementary aspects of one organic whole that is anchored by good will. Good will makes use of strong will, innervates it and gives it meaning. It also motivates the striving for a personal morality and directs its implementation. Given the importance of goodwill one might think that it has been the subject of significant psychological research. But it has not. Blasi (1985) complains that goodwill has been largely neglected in psychological research. The reason for this neglect can be traced to three trends in the scientific study of morality.

The first trend he calls secularization. With the secular trend the concept of morality has been transformed into morally neutral instrumental variables that are necessary for living a well-adjusted life. The secular trend transforms morality into mere character. The moral person is one who possesses strong will. The morality of persons has been reduced to such traits as resistance to temptation, determination, self-control, ego strength, and whatever else contributes to functional adaptation, since these traits are thought desirable in any person of character. When distinctly moral categories are considered, such as empathy, altruism, kindness, they tend to be naturalized by social science researchers. That is, these "moral variables" are treated just like any other natural variable or construct in psychology, which is to say, as a variable whose explanation is to be sought in biological makeup or in experiential history but not by reference to the agent's own judgment or moral intentions. As a consequence these traits are stripped of all moral connotation— they are secularized. No wonder contemporary psychology finds it difficult to reach the good will, for the good will depends upon the agent's own construal of his or own life project.

The second trend Blasi (1985) calls fragmentation. Fragmentation is the notion that there is no stable, unifying center to character or to personality. Personality is simply a catalog of traits and abilities that are functionally independent of one another. And since none of these traits are central, one can study them in isolation. In Blasi's (1985) view fragmentation appeared to become a real option for social science researchers as a result of the Hartshorne and May studies, which suggested that moral personality was at least an elusive and fugitive concept.

Finally, Blasi (1985) argues that social science research has tended to depersonalize morality. Depersonalization is the tendency to deal with moral knowledge and moral issues as if they can be divorced from one's personal life. It is to discuss moral issues in an abstract way, as a professional exercise, as if moral principles have no relevance for one's life other than to provide the ingredients for a good discussion. Just as one can study religion without being religious, so too can one study the functional aspects of moral discussion—namely, how to dissect an argument, how to assume multiple perspectives, how to play moral musical chairs, how to generate reasons, how to listen and persuade, and so on—in a formal exercise that does not penetrate one's life in any interesting way. One can become conversant with moral theories, quote the relevant authorities, and master the relevant literatures but do this in such a way that this knowledge is compartmentalized and split off from one's daily affairs.

Blasi (1985) suggests that of all the extant moral psychologies, the cognitive developmental approach has tended to resist the pull toward secularization and fragmentation. But its measure of academic respectability may have been purchased by its tendency toward depersonalization in moral education (e.g., plus-one moral-discussion strategies):

> If this is indeed the case, it may be possible to articulate the rules by which social sciences regulate their interest in moral functioning: Norms of practical living can be accepted as the subject of research and teaching as long as they are not specifically moral; moral rules can be an acceptable subject for research and teaching as long as they are considered naturalistically and relativistically; the possibility of a universal and objective system of morality can be a proper subject for education and research as long as it is depersonalized. (p. 441)

Blasi's research program attempts to buck the powerful trend toward fragmentation, naturalization, secularization, and depersonalization in moral psychology. He is attempting to assert the primacy of good will in moral functioning and to draw our attention to the essential, responsible self as subject, the moral self. Let's now examine Blasi's (1989, 1991) account of the moralization of the self.

How Is Moral Integration Possible?

The term "integration" is used by Blasi (1991) as a metaphor to convey the idea that personality is unified and coalesces around a center. This center is called self or ego. The self is progressively moralized when the objective values that one apprehends become integrated within the motivational and affective systems of personality and when these moral values guide the construction of the self-concept and one's identity as a person. The foundation of moral integration is understanding because cognition and cognitive development are important to morality (Blasi, 1991). Recall that Blasi's chief problem is to develop a model of moral personality that defends the objective autonomy of morality. In his view the chief characteristic of morality is that it is independent of one's personal needs or one's psychological makeup. Morality and identity, morality and the self, are two separate psychological systems that only gradually come together in an integrated way. If morality and identity were not conceptually independent domains, morality could not come to influence our personality (Blasi, 1991). But moral values do make an objective claim on us. It is precisely because moral values are objective, "out there," independent of our desires, needs, inclinations, independent of our egoistic wishes, tastes, or preferences, that we can feel the weight of obligation. The fact that we are aware that not just any solution to a moral problem will do is an indication that there is an objective component to morality. Whatever else "moral personality" may mean, it cannot mean that our moral sensibilities are constructed by our personality characteristics. It cannot mean that our morality is guided by or otherwise influenced by our personal needs, desires, inclinations, tastes, and preferences or is somehow dependent on our psychological identity (e.g., Gilligan's "different voices"), for this is to say that the source of morality is not "out there" after all, but "in here." This is to say that morality is not objective, independent, and autonomous, something that is to be perceived, grasped, apprehended, understood—terms that convey the cognitive element in moral functioning—but is instead something that is irrational, personal, and idiosyncratic. In short, if moral psychology eliminates or minimizes the cognitive, rational element in moral functioning, then morality has no objective foundations. The autonomous court of appeal does not impose universal obligations upon us quite irrespective of the particularities of our identity, character, and personality.

One problem for moral psychology is to adequately explain this rational, cognitive element. Blasi (1991) does not believe that contemporary cognitive psychology can be of much help, since it tends to model human cognition in terms of impersonal, automatic information-processing. In his view moral knowledge is a possession of an intentional agent who consciously deliberates, makes decisions, and assumes responsibility for the correctness and truth of these decisions (Blasi, 1983a, 1991). This theme is best captured by his analysis of the self as subject, which I will take up in due course.

Given that the self apprehends objective moral values, how is the self thereby moralized, that is, how are moral values integrated within the personality? The integration (or integrity) of the moral personality is revealed, first, by our felt sense of accountability, or by the "ownership" we assert over our actions. Many of us have been in situations when we just could not muster the agency, or the strong will, to put into effect what our good will demanded of us. We desired to do the right thing but were let down by our "agentic system." But when our rational understanding of morality is integrated with our character (strong will, or agentic system), we should feel a sense of ownership over our actions, a sense of mastery over the moral demands that we place upon ourselves, and, consequently, a sense of moral accountability toward ourselves and others (Blasi, 1989, 1991).

Moral integration is also indicated by our ability to use our moral understanding to crowd out the many other motives that could influence our behavior. That is, moral integration is indicated when our behavior is motivated by moral knowledge and is usually experienced as a felt sense of personal obligation. Let's say that we observe a boy, Tommy, share a toy with a classmate. There are at least two things going on here. First, Tommy is sharing the toy because of a spontaneous tendency to share. His act is impulsive, done without much thought. If we ask Tommy why he gave up the toy, he might reply, "Because I wanted to." But there is a second possibility. Tommy could have shared because he knows that it is good and right to share one's belongings. In this case his sharing is motivated not by spontaneous tendencies but by moral knowledge. Tommy's behavior was guided by certain moral standards and the felt sense of obligation to conform to what is morally required. What do children know about personal obligation?

In one study (cited in Blasi, 1991) 6-, 12- and 17-year-old participants were presented with a hypothetical dilemma where the protagonist had to choose between obeying her mother or helping a younger peer who was in distress. Most children opted to help the peer in distress. But when the children were asked if the protagonist was obliged to do what she thought was right, only 12 percent of the 6-year-olds thought so. In contrast, most of the older children thought that the protagonist had a strict obligation to act according to what she thought was right. Blasi (1991) interprets the responses of the 6-year-olds as an indication that their prosocial inclinations are a sort of impulsive, spontaneous tendency that is not yet invested with objective moral standards.

A third indication of moral integration is when moral understanding takes on its own motivational power. Recall that Blasi (1989) argues that morality is independent of personal needs and that, indeed, this independence is one of the defining features of morality. Consequently, if morality is motivating at all, the source of its motivation cannot be anything deeply rooted in us. If we are moral because it satisfies our narcissistic needs or our need for attention or any other personal motive, the autonomy of morality cannot be sustained. It follows, then, that morality must eventually come to take on its own motivational power in its own right and to make certain claims upon us that may well conflict with personal motives. Oftentimes these competing motives are quite compelling, and we may hence fail to choose what we understand to be the correct course of action. If we then feel guilt, shame, regret, hypocrisy, and allied emotions, we can be sure that our moral understanding is well integrated within our personality. If we don't feel these moral emotions, our moral sensibilities are split off from the rest of our personality. This is important to keep in mind just because many popular psychologies tell us that these emotions are dysfunctional and are to be avoided. One is not supposed to feel much guilt or shame or hypocrisy about anything. These things are usually the source of what ails us. But if Blasi is correct, these moral emotions are not a lamentable feature of our personality or pathogenic sign of personal disintegration but are instead a positive sign of moral integration. They are an indication that moral understanding is integrated with our affective system. The writer C. S. Lewis (1956) once wrote that hypocrisy is not always a bad thing and that, indeed, "hypocrisy can do a man good" (p. 192). To be aware that one has fallen short of the mark and to allow this awareness to cut deeply into one's emotional life is certainly uncomfortable and bracing, but it is better to have these feelings than to not have them. As Lewis (1956, p. 192) puts it, "The distinction between pretending you are better than you are and beginning to be better in reality is finer than moral sleuthhounds conceive."

When are emotions integrated with moral understanding? A series of studies by Nunner-Winkler and Sodian (1988) sheds some light on this problem. In one study four-, six-, and eight-year-old children heard a hypothetical story about two children, Florian and Thomas. Thomas had some sweets that Florian liked very much. In one version of the story, Florian stole the sweets and his theft went undetected. In the "moral" version of the story, Florian resisted the temptation to steal. In both versions of the story children were asked: "How does Florian feel now?" "Why?"

It is important to note that children of all ages knew that stealing was wrong. In this sense all of the children had knowledge of the relevant moral rule. But the emotional attributions of the four-year-olds were quite different from the attributions of the older children. The four-year-olds did not seem to believe that whether Florian's behavior was "moral" or "immoral" had much to do with how he would feel. The moral quality of Florian's action was seemingly irrelevant to the emotion he would feel after stealing or not stealing the sweets. Most four-year-olds (74 percent) expected Florian to be happy when he stole the sweet because he got what he wanted. In contrast, only 40 percent of the six-year-olds thought Florian would be happy after stealing, and 90 percent of the eight-year-olds thought Florian would experience a sadness or fear, largely because of moral considerations (viz., stealing is wrong). Further, the majority of four-year olds also thought that Florian would feel sad when he resisted temptation (since he didn't get what he desired); the older children thought he would feel relief or pride. In a subsequent task children were told another hypothetical story about two children who had both stolen a toy car from a friend. One child was said to be happy, the other child, sorry. Who was "worse" (i.e., more culpable), the child who was happy because now he or she had a beautiful car or the child who was sorry for stealing the car from a friend? The results showed that the majority of six-year-olds and virtually all the eight-year-olds judged the happy child to be worse than the sorry child; a majority of four-year-olds thought the two children would feel the same. Indeed, only 35 percent of the four-year-olds judged the happy child to be worse than the sorry child.

Clearly, then, for the young child, the moral quality of an action does not appear to penetrate an agent's emotional life. The integration of moral knowledge (stealing is wrong) with emotional consequences (feeling sorry or bad) does not appear much before age six and is not reliably observed until age eight. But what if the moral transgression is quite severe? Perhaps an incident of minor theft (as in the Florian story) does not quite bring out the moral quality of the action in a way that is compelling for young children. What if the child inflicts serious bodily injury upon another child in order to get what he or she wants? Surely young children could not miss the moral implications of personal assault? In a second study the authors told preschool children a story about a child (John) who pushed another child (Stephen) from a swing, causing Stephen to bleed and cry. Stephen was understandably sad and angry. Why did John do this? In one version of the story, John just wanted to ride on the swing himself ("tangible profit"). In another version, John didn't want to ride on the swing, he just didn't like Stephen and wanted to annoy him ("nontangible profit"). As in the first study, children were asked, "How does John feel now?"

Surprisingly a majority of the preschool children thought that John would be happy after visiting serious distress upon Stephen (the tangibility of the profit did not seem to matter). The moral value of what John did was not easily factored into their appraisal of John's feelings. The authors suggest that when young children make emotional attributions, they tend to neglect morality when the agent's personal motives (what he or she really wants or desires) conflicts with moral standards. That is, "young children expect to be happy whenever they get what they want, regardless of whether this wish is in accordance with moral standards" (Nunner-Winkler & Sodian, 1988, p. 1332). What John did was despicable, sure, but he should have felt happy because he could play on the swing or because he annoyed Stephen just like he wanted. Indeed, a third experiment showed that five-year-olds tend to attribute positive emotions to a child who harms another child only if the harm is inflicted intentionally.

According to Blasi (1989), moral understanding is integrated with personality if it is accompanied by moral emotions. The studies by Nunner-Winkler and Sodian (1988) show that moral emotions are indeed split off from moral understanding in young children but that they progressively converge with development. By eight years of age children are able to utilize emotional consequences (e.g., expected feelings of shame, regret, pride, joy, guilt) as a guide for motivating moral behavior.

I have noted three sources of evidence that point to the integration of personality and moral understanding. The first was the felt sense of accountability; the second was the sense of responsibility and personal obligation; the third was the experience of moral emotions that accompanies moral understanding. The fourth line of evidence comes from Blasi's (1988; Blasi & Milton, 1991) important research on the moral identity of the self as agent.

The Self as Agent

What is the nature of the self whose very identity is constructed under the guidance of moral reasons? Psychological research has tended to conceptualize the self as a kind of cognitive schema that is influential in information-processing (Markus; 1977; Greenwald & Pratkanis, 1984; Rogers, Kuiper, & Kirker, 1977) or else as a concept that is known or discovered through reflection. Similarly, the notion of identity is most often operationalized as a status or category—one has an identity when one has thought about various options and then has made a selection (e.g., Marcia, 1980). Blasi's (1988) approach to the self and his understanding of identity is refreshingly different from these more traditional views. Rather than invoke the self-concept, for example, Blasi insists that the phenomenological aspect of the self best captures the psychological complexity of an intentional subject. In his view we experience ourselves as related to our actions and experiences—not through reflection—but in the very process of acting and experiencing. "Without this relation of ourselves to our acting embedded in each and every action and experience, there would be neither action nor experience, but only processes impersonally occurring within the organism" (Blasi, 1988, p. 229). This he calls the self as subject.

The self as subject can be described along four dimensions. These dimensions constitute the very stuff of subjectivity and are hence present in all of our experiences. The first dimension is *agency*. Agency refers to the degree to which an action is unreflectively grasped as our own. The second dimension is *identity with oneself*, which is the realization that the one who is acting is the very same as the one who is aware. The third dimension is the experience of *unity* among the diversity of one's present activities—"thinking, selecting words, talking, hearing one's voice, and so forth, all belong to the same agent, to the experiencing and acting 'I'" (Blasi, 1988, p. 229). The fourth dimension is *otherness*. Otherness refers to the sense of separate existence, to an awareness that one is a separate agent, different from other agents and different from other objects on which and whom one can perform actions. the self as agent corresponds closely to what we call the existential self, which is the subjective understanding "*that* I exist, I exist separately from other persons, I can cause things to happen in the world. . . ." "The self-as-subject, in sum, is understood here as the specific way by which one experiences oneself as agent, unified in one's agency, different from other agents, and capable to stand back vis-à-vis oneself in reflection" (Blasi, 1988, p. 229).

If the search for identity requires one to answer the question "Who am I?" then the self as subject cannot be irrelevant to how we understand identity. The four dimensions of the self as subject are deeply involved in the search for identity. The sense of agency conveys the feeling that one is responsible for who one is, that one is responsible for the choices and commitments that one makes and for the projects with which one identifies. The sense of otherness conveys the idea that one must gain some distance from one's own past, from the expectations that others have of one, and from the conventional assumptions of one's society. The notion of unity suggests that one's identity should bring a sense of order and coherence to one's self-understanding, that one should act consistently and be faithful to one's commitments. This sense of unity also conveys the idea that one's identity provides a way of experiencing the self. There is a pronounced subjective, experiential sense to having an identity; it feels like an inner sense of continuity, a felt sense of knowing where one is going, of being at home in one's body. It is, in short, a kind of identity with oneself.

Blasi (1988) has designed an interview that invites individuals to reflect on identity issues from the perspective of the self as agent. Four kinds of psychological identity have been identified, each of which corresponds to a particular way of construing and expressing one's identity. These identity modes also appear to emerge developmentally from late childhood through adulthood (Blasi & Milton, 1991). They appear to differ from one another in the degree to which identity is thought to be central in one's personality and in the degree to which one takes ownership for the sort of identity one has. These identity modes are described in Table 12.1. What are the implications of these identity modes for understanding moral integration?

In a preliminary study (Blasi & Glodis, 1990, reported by Blasi, 1991) a sample of adolescent girls and young women were interviewed. After assessing their predominant identity mode, the researchers next asked the participants to consider the case of a hypothetical person who made a decision that ran counter to her ideal. This ideal was also one that the participant endorsed. What emotions would the participant feel if she were in the position of the protagonist? Why would she feel that way? The authors found that participants who were in the management-of-identity mode expressed more negative emotions, made more references to chosen ideals, and more often explained emotional reactions by appealing to the problem of personal inconsistency and lack of integrity. This result suggests not only that one's identity (i.e., one's identity mode) changes and assumes different developmental forms but that each form of identity also varies in the importance it

TABLE 12.1   Modes of Identity

Social role identity
The sense of self is diffused in one's actions, roles, and relationships and is described with simple traits. Identity is defined by reference to external attributes (physical appearance, the relationships one has, etc.). To be sincere means to behave in typical ways or to be truthful about one's actions. The "inner core" of selfhood as a unifying center is not yet identified.

Identity observed
The self is "extracted" from its actions and concentrated, isolated, and differentiated from other psychological processes. It is now spoken of as a whole, entire entity made up of internal, psychological traits (vs. social roles, preferred actions) that are naturally given and unchangeable. It is the "true self"—internal, inaccessible to others, comprising spontaneous emotions and feelings. To be sincere means to behave in ways that correspond to one's inner feelings, the feelings of the true inner self.

Management of identity
The self is still an internal, psychological entity, but it now comprises not so much spontaneous thoughts and feelings but values, ideals, and commitments. To be sincere means to act in ways that reflect deeply felt commitments. Identity is not a "natural given," something to be observed (as in the previous stage), but is rather something that is achieved in action. One has a responsibility, and duty, to shape the self in light of ideals. If one acts contrary to these commitments and ideals, the self is betrayed.

Identity as authenticity
The self confronts the loss of certainty concerning one's goals, commitments, ideals, and beliefs. There is an awareness that one harbors conflicting ideals or irreconcilable goals. One attempts to free the self from conventional views and stereotypes in order to protect independence and self-integrity. The unity of the self now is accomplished by means of a "broad stance" toward the self and world, an openness to experience, a willingness to affirm one's responsibility to recognize the truth about the self and one's world.

Source: Adapted from Blasi (1988, 1991).

has for the self. Much more is at stake for the self in the management-of-identity mode than, say, in a social-role-identity mode and hence the striking pattern of reaction to self-inconsistency and the concern with personal integrity. There is greater personological integration to the extent that identity issues are held to be crucial for the self as subject.

Can morality be constitutive of one's identity, and are there individual differences on this score? As we have seen, according to Blasi's (1984) Self Model of moral identity, Both are possibilities. It is expected that people will differ in their use of moral categories for constructing their identity. The relevant research on this question is not currently available, although as Blasi (1991) notes, there are preliminary suggestions that some individuals do indeed consider moral categories to be central to their identity. Note that such suggestions are not the same as saying that these individuals view morality as important. Virtually everyone thinks that morality is important. But not everyone has to pursue every moral ideal. There are many ways of living a life well, and individuals should be free to select those values that resonate with their self-understanding and to construct their identities accordingly (Blasi, 1991). The implication of this line of research is that individuals who construct their identity on the basis of moral concerns (and hence have a moral identity) may nonetheless still differ in their degree of moral integration, depending on which identity mode best describes them (Blasi, 1991). In other words, there could be at least four ways of having a moral identity, and these correspond with the four identity modes identified by this research program.

Postscript

The Post–Kohlbergian Era in Moral Psychology

I would like to conclude the text by briefly considering some possible new lines of research in moral psychology. It is not usually the business of a textbook to take on this task, largely because the field is dynamic, good ideas abound, and the future cannot always be seen with sufficient clarity to make prognostication worthwhile. Yet I do believe that some trends can already be discerned, at least in their nascent forms, and one can at least suggest some ways to encourage their development.

It should be clear by now that the past 30 years in moral psychology have been dominated by cognitive developmentalism more generally and by Kohlberg's theory in particular. This is not to say that there were not other important research programs being developed during this time, for indeed, as we have seen, the cognitive-learning perspective was emerging from its grounding in traditional social learning theory. Similarly research on prosocial development and altruism, empathy, moral socialization, and related topics attracted considerable interest as well.

In addition, an important literature developed that addressed certain Piagetian moral concepts from an information-processing perspective. Yet cognitive developmentalism continues to be accorded pride of place in most textbooks, and even alternative or rival theories first have to come to grips with the claims, metaphors, and empirical literatures of this paradigm. The fact that Kohlberg's theory was a lightening rod of criticism, that so many theoretical, philosophical, and methodological controversies seemed to swirl around it, simply illustrated its influence.

Not coincidentally, the influence of Kohlberg's theory overlapped significantly with the authority of the Piagetian paradigm. Yet curiously, the evident decline of the Piagetian influence in the study of intellectual development has had few implications for Kohlbergian moral psychology. The decline of the Piagetian paradigm has allowed for other conceptions of rationality to come front and center, many of which have been deeply influenced by developments in cognitive science (Case, 1985; Sternberg, 1984). Yet moral rationality is still mostly a matter of Piagetian cognitive structures developing through stages.

There are perhaps a number of reasons that the theories and tactics of cognitive psychology have not penetrated the study of moral rationality. One reason is that much of the subject matter of cognitive science has not yet been given a developmental grounding. In other words, although much is being learned about adult cognition, the developmental processes by which one attains these adult forms of cognitive functioning have not been completely specified. What is more, at least some of the metaphors of cognitive science (that the mind works like a computer) do not lend themselves to a developmental explanation. There is also the suspicion that the intentional subject invariably gets lost within the architecture and processes of cognitive information-processing. There are worries that moral functioning will be explained in terms of automatic, impersonal processes and thereby lose that sense that morality involves conscious decision-making of a personal self who has deep convictions. These latter notions seem harder to capture in cognitive psychology. The lack of any particular moral-philosophic commitments (e.g., autonomy and objectivity of morality, universality) must also raise suspicions.

Cognitive Science

Although these are not unimportant issues, there are a number of ways in which cognitive science could contribute to moral psychology. Kohlberg has written that stage functions as a kind of lens by which one appraises the dilemmatic features of situations. A virtue-centered moral psychology suggests that what one sees in the moral landscape may well depend on the sort of person one is, which is to say, on one's character. The metaphor of vision—"lens," "seeing"—suggests that moral perception is a psychological process that any account of moral rationality must not neglect (e.g., Blum, 1991).

The notion of schema is often used to account for how we encode and represent social information. According to Taylor and Crocker (1981), schemas have numerous functions: (1) they lend structure to experience; (2) they determine what information will be encoded or retrieved from memory; (3) they affect the speed of problem-solving and the processing of information; (4) they allow the person to fill in missing data in what is perceived; (5) they provide the basis for solving problems, evaluating experiences, setting goals, making plans, anticipating the future, and (6) for developing behavior routines to bring these about. There may be something deeply schematic about the way we appraise moral situations and structure our experience and make decisions, although this is rather unexplored territory in moral psychology.

In addition, it may well be the case that many of the moral concepts that I have examined in this text are better thought of as "fuzzy categories," and that moral cognition is largely driven by prototypes of various kinds. The Kantian injunction to respect persons, which Kohlberg builds into principled moral reasoning, seems unproblematic until one attempts to specify just what a person is. Some of our more contentious moral debates (e.g., abortion) swirl around different perspectives on personhood. Is a fetus a person? Is a newborn a person? At what point in human life is *personality* gained or lost? In other words, by what criteria should we recognize a person. There seem to be rather clear cases of personhood, that is, there are prototypically good examples of personhood, but perhaps there are marginal cases as well where the criteria seem "fuzzy."

As another example, take the very case of what constitutes a moral rule. We saw in Chapter 6 that one of the great issues in contemporary moral psychology is whether there are different domains of knowledge. The domains approach suggests that even young children seem to make distinctions between moral and social-conventional transgressions. Children appear to have implicit knowledge of criteria or rules that allows them to categorize certain events as moral and certain other events as social-conventional or personal. The Kohlbergian tradition tends to argue that the criteria used to make domain distinctions are unreliable, since one can imagine many kinds of situations that seem to be conventional but nonetheless involve important moral considerations as well. Similarly, the virtue-ethics tradition wants to deny that personal issues are beyond the pale of moral appraisal. This domain overlap supposedly counts against the usefulness of the domains approach to social knowledge; this argument has been disputed.

But perhaps this argument is not so much over how to define a moral event but rather how to apply our prototypic moral situation to fuzzy categories. Inflicting injury upon another may be our prototypic moral transgression. Addressing a teacher by his or her first name might fit our prototype of what is a social convention. Whether to keep one's hair long or short might be a prototypically personal issue. But as we move from the prototype (the best example) to the margins of its applicability, we enter into uncharted areas.

Category knowledge is represented as a loose set of features that are correlated only with group membership. The decisions that we make for assigning group membership will be probabilistic. "There will be many ambiguous borderline cases that yield overlapping fuzzy boundaries between categories" (Mischel, 1984, p. 356). If moral knowledge is structured protoptypically we may well wonder just how to apply our moral prototypes to those unusual cases that look like domain overlap. Is wearing a bikini to a funeral a moral or conventional transgression? Is reading pornographic literature a personal or moral issue? This is hard to say insofar as these situations stretch the applicability of our moral, conventional, and personal prototypes.

In some ways this is similar to the point of the monograph by Turiel and others (1991). As we saw in Chapter 6, this monograph showed that there is uniform consensus that killing and rape are always wrong, they are wrong everywhere, and no law can make them right or permissible. These acts, killing and rape, seem to match our prototype of what constitutes a typical moral issue. But other contentious issues, such as abortion or pornography, are nonprototypical if they are evaluated in terms of features that span more than one domain.

In other words, they fit the definition of a moral issue in most, but not all, respects. For most individuals, however, abortion (for example) is the quintessential moral issue of our time, and it seems odd to call it nonprototypical. Turiel and others (1991) suggested that we should reserve the title "moral" to those issues that are prototypic and call other issues something else, yet this conceptual precision seems to be purchased at the cost of violating our intuitive impression that there is something deeply moral about the issue of abortion or gay rights or drug use.

In some ways, trying to carve up social knowledge into domains on the basis of definitions is not unlike trying to come up with the defining features of games (Wittgenstein's example). What is the definition of a game? In what way is pinochle similar to English football? to checkers? to Scrabble? to charades? We quickly come to see that it is difficult to pick out necessary and defining features of a game in order to end up with a useful definition. All games do, however, appear to share family resemblances with other games. We can perhaps sort games into domains. We can identify, for example, card games, lawn and field games, board games, drinking games, and much more. This could be an instructive and useful exercise. But at no time would we be interested in specifying which activity was or was not a game, since necessary and defining features for making this specification are not available.

Perhaps this is the case with many social issues as well. Is abortion a moral issue? In some ways it is our prototypic moral issue. Is avarice a moral issue? In what ways are marital infidelity and theft similar to assault? to cheating on our taxes? to betraying a confidence? Rather than sort these issues into conceptual categories on the basis of necessary and defining features, it might be better to acknowledge that moral issues share a family resemblance, although some issues are better examples than others. When we think of birds, the image of a penguin does not come immediately to mind, but it would be odd to say that the penguin is not a bird just because it doesn't fly. It is a nonprototypic bird, perhaps, but it is still a bird for all that. Similarly, it seems odd not to call abortion a moral issue just because many individuals leave room for personal choice in the matter.

There are currently important research programs in cognitive social psychology and personality that are examining the role of prototypes and fuzzy sets in guiding social perception. These programs are guided by the view that the categories we use to organize our experience are not all-or-none categories but are rather constructed around the best example (or prototype) of the category of event in question. There is indeed evidence that our understanding of persons (Cantor & Mischel, 1977, 1979; Chaplin, John, & Goldberg, 1988), social situations (Cantor, Mischel & Schwartz, 1982), diagnostic categories (Cantor, Smith, deSales French, & Mezzich, 1980), and emotions (Fehr & Russell, 1984) are organized around prototypes. There is also evidence that we judge the consistency of our own actions with respect to a trait or a category of behavior not by looking for cross-situational consistency, that is, not by looking for matches across all conceivable situations, but rather by looking for consistency in those limited number of behaviors that are prototypic for that category (Mischel, 1984).

There are clear implications of this research for how we understand persons, for how we conceptualize moral situations that require a moral response; and for how we appraise character, understand virtue traits, and appraise moral action. But the research literatures of cognitive social psychology have not been used for insights by moral psychologists, and social psychologists and personality researchers have not considered the implications of their work for moral psychology.

Research on the notion of *chronic accessibility* of knowledge seems to hold particular promise (Higgins, 1991; Wyer & Srull, 1981; Srull & Wyer, 1980). It is well known that the meaning and significance of persons, objects, events, and situations (and their interactions) depend upon how these things are represented and categorized. The personal constructs that we use help us extract meaning from our social experience (Kelly, 1955; Mischel, 1973). How these knowledge categories are formed and activated and the factors that determine their accessibility, then, become important issues for understanding social perception and social cognition (Higgins & Bargh, 1987).

There is evidence, for example, that recent activation of a category significantly increases the likelihood that the construct will be used as the basis for subsequent social judgment (e.g., Higgins, Rholes, & Jones, 1977; Bargh, Bond, Lombardi, & Tota, 1986). There is evidence that the more often a category is activated, the longer it will remain predominant in tasks that require categorization (Higgins, Bargh, & Lombardi, 1985). What is more, certain categories seem to be chronically accessible, and there may be individual differences in chronic accessibility that influence social perception and social judgments (Bargh & Pratto, 1986; Bargh & Thein, 1985; Higgins, 1991). That is, there may be individual differences in the readiness with which certain constructs are used.

A study by Higgins and others (1982) is illustrative. In this study participants were asked to write down the trait characteristics of four friends (two male, two female) and of themselves. A trait was considered "accessible" if it was used to describe the self and at least one friend or if it was used to describe at least three friends. Two weeks later the participants returned to take part in an ostensibly different study on person perception (a different "experimenter" was used). Each participant was given an essay that was said to describe another student. The descriptors used in this essay were moderately positive or moderately negative. In addition, the traits were accessible for some but not all of the participants. So as a participant read the essay, he or she encountered traits that were accessible but also some that were relatively inaccessible (the essays were obviously tailored to match the accessible traits of each participant). After a delay, the participants were asked to reproduce the essay word for word and to fully describe the target person. The authors found that information that was not related to the accessible construct tended to be deleted from the participants' impressions of the target person. That is, inaccessible trait-related information tended to be omitted in favor of accessible trait-related information when participants were asked to form an impression of the fellow student. Furthermore, when participants were asked to reproduce the essay, inaccessible trait-related information was more likely to be deleted. Additional research has shown that chronically accessible constructs are stable over years and guide the processing of information about political choices (Lau, 1989); and that chronic-accessibility models are useful for explaining self-inconsistency and the emotional reactions that may result (Strauman & Higgins, 1987).

Once again, this research program is not directed toward understanding moral cognition or moral functioning, yet it seems to provide a rich conceptual framework and an arsenal of research tactics that might prove useful for providing a finer-grain analysis of how moral rationality works. Perhaps the notion of chronic accessibility can help us understand moral identity or the experience of self-betrayal and other moral emotions (shame, hypocrisy) that spring from a felt sense of self-inconsistency. Perhaps it makes more sense to think of traits and virtues and character in terms of personal constructs and the knowledge structures, categories, and schemas that are chronically accessible? Virtuous individuals, then, would be those for whom moral categories are chronically accessible for appraising and interpreting social reality. These are only possibilities, of course, but the post-Kohlbergian era in moral psychology may well see a closer rapprochement with the research traditions of cognitive science, particularly those applications that are found in personality research and social cognition. That a number of philosophers (Flanagan, 1991; Goldman, 1993; Johnson, 1993) are now calling for just this sort of dialogue makes this prospect more likely.

Other Developments

I want to close by recognizing a few additional trends in the moral psychology literature that bode well for the future development of this field. First, there is now a growing literature on the morality of forgiveness in both its philosophical (e.g., Holmgren, 1993) and psychological dimensions (Enright, Gassin, & Wu, 1992; Enright, Santos, & Al-Mabuk, 1989; Enright, Eastin, Golden, Sarinopoulos, & Freedman, 1992; Enright & Study Group, 1991). Developmental studies have charted a stage progression in conceptions of forgiveness, and implications for counseling and conflict resolution are currently being worked out. Justice must make a pact with mercy, indeed (Murdoch, 1992).

Mark Tappan and his colleagues are highlighting the importance of language, dialogue, and narrative structure for conceptualizing moral experience and moral education (Tappan, 1989, 1991; Tappan & Brown, 1989; Brown, Debold, Tappan, & Gilligan, 1991; also, Sharpe, 1992). In their view psychological functioning in general, and moral functioning in particular, are mediated by language, by the way one speaks about lived experience. Here, within the narratives and stories of our lives, in the "voices" we speak, we find the web of relationships, the "interpretive community" that structures and sustains our moral meaning. This research program is a promising extension of Carol Gilligan's pioneering research on the moral "voices" of justice and care that she discovered in the narrative stories of individuals facing real moral dilemmas.

Finally, William Kurtines and his colleagues are developing a psychosocial role theory of moral development that attempts to integrate systems theory, role theory, and the view that human behavior is rule governed (Kurtines, 1986; Kurtines, Mayock, Pollard, Lanza, and Carlo, 1991). This theory argues that the actions and decisions of the moral agent take place within a network of socially constructed rule systems that are open to dynamic, evolutionary change. Individuals have tacit or implicit knowledge of these rule systems, although their rule-using competence can sometimes be frustrated by intervening variables. Sociomoral competence is just one aspect of a larger network of interdependent (linguistic, cognitive, communicative) psychosocial competencies whose development is affected by maturation (genetically influenced structural change, which Kurtines appears to want to link to the cognitive developmental tradition) and learning (conditioning, modeling, imitation).

Hence this theory is an integration of cognitive developmental and learning theory traditions, with a twist. The twist is that developmental maturity is not reached just when the full range of psychosocial competencies come on line. Rather, the processes that have heretofore governed developmental change (maturation, learning) now shift to "co-constructive social evolutionary processes" whereby one "contributes to the subjective construction and intersubjective co-construction of reality" (Kurtines et al., 1991, p. 315). In other words, once a certain level of competency is attained, where competency is defined by the limit of maturational-structural stage and learning processes, further growth is still possible, although the growth will be evolutionary rather than developmental in the sense that the outcome of such a social construction cannot be known in advance. A major point is that one is not constrained by maturational and learning processes, and this is critical from the perspective of social evolution. Our capacity for social evolution has made it possible for the human species to transcend the limits of organic, biological evolution, to understand the forces that shape us, and to control them. Social and cultural evolution is thus a free, open, creative co-construction of reality.Research is currently focused on measurement issues (the various competencies; dimensions of sociomoral knowledge; the various skills required for co-construction, negotiation, and communication) and on charting developmental variations in sociomoral knowledge. But clearly the research program being carried out by Kurtines and his colleagues bears watching as they work out the empirical consequences of this rich, integrative framework.

References

Adams, D. (1993). Love and impartiality. *American Philosophical Quarterly, 30,* 223–234.

Alejandro, R. (1993). Rawls's communitarianism. *Canadian Journal of Philosophy, 23,* 75–100.

Allport, G. W. (1937). *Personality: A psychological interpretation.* New York: Holt

Alston, W. P. (1975). Traits, consistency and conceptual alternatives for personality theory. *Journal for the Theory of Social Behavior, 5,* 17–48.

Ambron, S. A. (1973). *The relation between role-taking and moral judgment in five- and seven-year olds.* Unpublished doctoral dissertation, New York, Columbia University.

Anderson, N. H. (1971). Integration theory and attitude change. *Psychological Review, 78,* 171–206.

Anderson, N. H. (1974). Cognitive algebra: Integration theory applied to social attribution. In L. Berkowitz (Ed.), *Advances in experimental social psychology.* (Vol. 7, pp. 1–101). New York: Academic Press.

Anderson, N. H., & Butzin, C. A. (1978). Integration theory applied to children's judgments of equity. *Developmental Psychology, 14,* 593–606.

Anderson, N. H., & Cuneo, D. O. (1978). The height + width rule in children's judgments of quantity. *Journal of Experimental Psychology: General, 107,* 335–378.

Aristotle. (1985). *Nichomachean ethics* (T. Irwin, Trans.). Indianapolis: Hackett.

Armsby, R. (1971). A reexamination of the development of moral judgments in children. *Child Development, 42,* 1241–1248.

Aron, I. E. (1977). Moral philosophy and moral education: A critique of Kohlberg's theory. *School Review, 85,* 197–217.

Austin, V. D., Ruble, D., & Trabasso, T. (1977). Recall and order effects as factors in children's moral judgments. *Child Development, 48,* 470–474.

Ayer, A. J. (1952). *Language, truth, and logic.* New York: Dover.

Bakan, D. (1966). *The duality of human existence.* Boston: Beacon.

Bandura, A . (1969). Social learning of moral judgments. *Journal of Personality and Social Psychology, 11,* 275–279.

Bandura, A. (1986). *Social foundations of thought and action: A social-cognitive theory.* New York: Prentice Hall.

Bandura, A. (1991). Social cognitive theory of moral thought and action. In W. M. Kurtines & J. L. Gewirtz (Eds.), *Handbook of moral behavior and development: Vol. 1. Theory* (pp. 45–104). Hillsdale, NJ: Lawrence Erlbaum.

Bandura, A., & McDonald, F. J. (1963). The influence of social reinforcement and the behavior of models in shaping children's moral judgments. *Journal of Abnormal and Social Psychology, 67,* 274–281.

Bargh, J. A., Bond, R. N., Lombardi, W. J., & Tota, M. E. (1986). The additive nature of chronic and temporary sources of construct accessibility. *Journal of Personality and Social Psychology, 50,* 869–878.

Bargh, J. A., & Pratto, F. (1986). Individual construct accessibility and perceptual selection. *Journal of Personality and Social Psychology, 22,* 293–311.

248   References

Bargh, J. A., & Thein, R. D. (1985). Individual construct accessibility, person memory, and the recall-judgment link: The case of information overload. *Journal of Personality and Social Psychology, 49,* 1129–1146.

Barnes, E. (1894). Punishment as seen by children. *Pedagogical Seminary, 3,* 235–245.

Barnett, K., Darcie, G., Holland, C. J., & Kobasigawa, A. (1982). Children's cognitions about effective helping. *Developmental Psychology, 18,* 267–277.

Baron, M. (1984).The alleged moral repugnance of acting from duty. *Journal of Philosophy, 81,* 197–220.

Barret, D. E., & Yarrow, M. R. (1977). Prosocial behavior, social inferential ability and assertiveness in children. *Child Development, 48,* 475–481.

Bar-Tal, D. (1976). *Prosocial behavior: Theory and research.* New York: Halstead Press.

Bar-Tal, D. (1982). Sequential development of helping behavior: A cognitive-learning approach. *Developmental Review, 2,* 101–124.

Bar-Tal, D., Raviv, A., & Goldberg, M. (1982). Helping behavior among pre-school children. *Child Development, 53,* 396–402.

Bar-Tal, D., Raviv, A., & Leiser, T. (1980).The development of altruistic behavior: Empirical evidence. *Developmental Psychology, 16,* 516–524.

Baumrind, D. (1971). Current patterns of parental authority. *Developmental Psychology Monographs, 4* (No. 1, Pt. 2).

Baumrind, D. (1973a).The development of instrumental competence through socialization. In A. D. Pick (Ed.), *Minnesota symposium on child psychology* (Vol. 7). Minneapolis: University of Minnesota Press.

Baumrind, D. (1973b). Note. Harmonious parents and their preschool children. *Developmental Psychology, 4,* 99–102.

Baumrind, D. (1986). Sex differences in moral reasoning: Response to Walker's (1984) conclusion that there are none. *Child Development, 57,* 511–521.

Baumrind, D. (1989). Rearing competent children. In W. Damon (Ed.), *Child development today and tomorrow.* San Francisco: Jossey-Bass

Baumrind, D. (1991).The influence of parenting style on adolescent competence and substance use. *Journal of Early Adolescence, 11,* 56–95

Baumrind, D., & Black, A. E. (1967).Socialization practices associated with dimensions of competence in preschool boys and girls. *Child Development, 38,* 291–327.

Bearison, D. J., & Isaacs, L. (1975). Production deficiency in children's moral judgments. *Developmental Psychology, 11,* 732–737.

Becker, L. C. (1991). Impartiality and ethical theory. *Ethics, 101,* 698–700.

Beebe, B., Alson, D., Jaffe, J., Feldstein, S., & Crown, C. (1988).Vocal congruence in mother-infant play. *Journal of Psycholinguistic Research, 17,* 245–259.

Berg-Cross, L. G. (1975). Intentionality, degree of damage and moral judgments. *Child Development, 46,* 970–974.

Berkowitz, L. (1964). *Development of motives and values in a child.* New York: Basic Books.

Berkowitz, M. (1981). A critical appraisal of the educational and psychological perspectives on moral discussion. *Journal of Educational Thought, 15,* 20–33.

Berkowitz, M., & Gibbs, J. (1983). Measuring the developmental features of moral discussion. *Merrill-Palmer Quarterly, 29,* 399–410.

Berkowitz, M., Gibbs, J., & Broughton, J. M. (1980).The relation of moral judgment stage disparity to developmental effects of peer dialogue. *Merrill-Palmer Quarterly, 26,* 341–357.

Berndt, T. (1979). Developmental changes in conformity to peers and parents. *Developmental Psychology, 15,* 608–616.

Bickhard, M. (1978). The nature of developmental stages. *Human Development, 21,* 217–233.

Blasi, A. (1980). Bridging moral cognition and moral action: A critical review of the literature. *Psychological Bulletin, 88,* 1–45.

Blasi, A. (1983a). Moral cognition and moral action: A theoretical perspective. *Developmental Review, 3,* 178–210.

Blasi, A. (1983b). The self and cognition: The role of the self in the acquisition of knowledge and the role of cognition in the development of the self. In B. Lee and G. Noam (Eds.), *Psychosocial theories of the self* (pp. 189–213). New York: Plenum.

Blasi, A. (1984). Moral identity: Its role in moral functioning. In W. M. Kurtines & J. L. Gewirtz (Eds.), *Morality, moral behavior and moral development* (pp. 128–139). New York: Wiley.

Blasi, A. (1985). The moral personality: Reflections for social science and education. In M. W. Berkowitz and F. Oser (Eds.), *Moral education: Theory and application* (pp. 433–443). Hillsdale, NJ: Lawrence Erlbaum.

Blasi, A. (1988). Identity and the development of the self. In D. K. Lapsley & F. C. Power (Eds.), *Self, ego, and identity: Integrative approaches* (pp. 226–242). New York: Springer-Verlag.

Blasi, A. (1989). The integration of morality in personality. In I. E. Bilbao (Ed.), *Perspectivas acerca de cambio moral: Posibles intervenciones educativas* (pp. 119–131). San Sebastian: Servicio Editorial Universidad del Pais Vasco.

Blasi, A. (1990). How should psychologists define morality? or, the negative side effects of philosophy's influence on psychology. In T. Wren (Ed.), *The moral domain: Essays on the ongoing discussion between philosophy and the social sciences* (pp. 38–70). Cambridge: MIT Press.

Blasi, A. (1991). Moral understanding and the moral personality: The process of moral integration. Unpublished manuscript.

Blasi, A., & Glodis, K. (1990). *Response to self-betrayal and the development of the sense of self.* Unpublished manuscript, University of Massachusetts, Boston.

Blasi, A., & Milton, K. (1991). The development of the sense of self in adolescence. *Journal of Personality, 59,* 217–242.

Blatt, M., & Kohlberg, L. (1975). The effects of classroom moral discussion upon children's moral judgment. *Journal of Moral Education, 4,* 129–161.

Blum, L. (1988). Gilligan and Kohlberg: Implications for moral theory. *Ethics, 98,* 472–491.

Blum, L. (1991). Moral perception and particularity. *Ethics, 101,* 701–725.

Boehm, L. (1962). The development of conscience: A comparison of American children of different mental and socioeconomic levels. *Child Development, 33,* 575–590.

Boehm, L. (1966). Moral judgment: A cultural and subcultural comparison with some of Piaget's research conclusions. *International Journal of Psychology, 1,* 143–150.

Boehm, L., & Nass, M. L. (1962). Social class differences in conscience development. *Child Development, 33,* 565–574.

Borke, H. (1971). Interpersonal perception of young children: Egocentrism or empathy? *Developmental Psychology, 5,* 263–269.

Boyd, D. (1976). The problem of sophomoritis: An educational proposal. *Journal of Moral Education, 6,* 36–42.

Boyd, D. (1981). The condition of sophomoritis and its educational cure. *Journal of Moral Education, 10*, 24–39.

Boyd, D. (1986). The ought of is: Kohlberg at the interface between moral philosophy and developmental psychology. In S. Modgil and C. Modgil ·(Eds.), *Lawrence Kohlberg: Consensus and controversy* (pp. 43–64). Philadelphia: Falmer Press.

Boyes, M., & Allen, S. G. (1993). Styles of parent-child interaction and moral reasoning in adolescence. *Merrill-Palmer Quarterly, 39*, 551–570.

Brabeck, M. (1983). Moral judgment: Theory and research on differences between males and females. *Developmental Review, 3*, 274–291.

Brainerd, C. J. (1978). The stage question in cognitive developmental theory. *Behavioral and Brain Sciences, 2*, 173–213.

Brandt, R. B. (1970). Traits of character: A conceptual analysis. *American Philosophical Quarterly, 7*, 23–37.

Bretherton, I., Fritz, J., Zahn-Waxler, C., & Ridgeway, D. (1986). Learning to talk about emotions: A functionalist perspective. *Child Development, 57*, 529–548.

Bretherton, I., McNew, S., & Beeghly-Smith, M. (1981). Early person knowledge as expressed in gestural and verbal communications: When do infants acquire a "theory of mind"? In M. E. Lamb & L. R. Sherrod (Eds.), *Infant social cognition.* (pp. 333–373). Hillsdale, NJ: Lawrence Erlbaum.

Bridgeman, D. L. (1983). Benevolent babies: Emergence of the social self. In D. L. Bridgeman (Ed.), *The nature of prosocial development.* New York: Academic Press.

Brody, G. H., & Schaffer, D. R. (1982). Contributions of parents and peers to children's moral socialization. *Developmental Review, 2*, 31–75.

Broughton, J. M. (1978). The cognitive-developmental approach to morality: A reply to Kurtines and Grief. *Journal of Moral Education, 1*, 81–96.

Broughton, J. M (1981a). Piaget's structural developmental psychology I: Piaget and structuralism. *Human Development, 24*, 78–109.

Broughton, J. M. (1981b). Piaget's structural developmental psychology II: Logic and psychology. *Human Development, 24*, 195–224.

Broughton, J. M. (1983). The cognitive-developmental theory of adolescent self and identity. In B. Lee and G. Noam (Eds.), *Developmental approaches to the self* (pp. 215–266). New York: Plenum.

Brown, L. M., Debold, E., Tappan, M., & Gilligan, C. (1991). Reading narratives of conflict and choice for self and moral voices: A relational method. In W. M. Kurtines & J. G. Gewirtz (Eds.), *Handbook of moral behavior and development: Vol. 2. Research* (pp. 25–62). Hillsdale, NJ: Lawrence Erlbaum.

Bryan, J. H. & London, D. (1970). Altruistic behavior by children. *Psychological Bulletin, 73*, 200–211.

Bryan, J. H., & Walbek, N. H. (1970a). The impact of words and deeds concerning altruism upon children. *Child Development, 41*, 747–757.

Bryan, J. H., & Walbek, N. H. (1970b). Preaching and practicing self-sacrifice: Children's actions and reactions. *Child Development, 41*, 329–353.

Bryant, B. (1982). An index of empathy for children and adolescents. *Child Development, 53*, 413–425.

Bryant, B. K., & Crockenberg, S. B. (1980). Correlates and dimensions of prosocial behavior: A study of female siblings with their mothers. *Child Development, 51*, 529–544.

Buchanan, A. (1977). Categorical imperatives and moral principles. *Philosophical Studies, 31*, 249–260.

Buchanan, J. P., & Thompson, S. K. (1973). A quantitative methodology to examine the development of moral judgment. *Child Development, 44,* 186–189.

Buckley, N., Siegel, L., & Ness, S. (1979). Egocentrism, empathy, and altruistic behavior in young children. *Developmental Psychology, 15,* 329–330.

Buck-Morss, S. (1975). Socioeconomic bias in Piaget's theory and its implications for the cross-cultural controversy. *Human Development, 18,* 35–49.

Burns, N., & Cavey, L. (1957). Age differences in empathic ability among children. *Canadian Journal of Psychology, 11,* 227–230.

Bush, A. J., Krebs, D. L., & Carpendale, J. I. (1993). The structural consistency of moral judgments about AIDS. *Journal of Genetic Psychology, 154,* 167–175.

Buss, D. M., & Craik, K. H. (1983). The act frequency approach to personality. *Psychological Review, 90,* 105–126.

Calhoun, C. (1988). Justice, care, gender bias. *Journal of Philosophy, 85,* 451–463.

Callahan, S. (1991). *In good conscience: Reason and emotion in moral decision-making.* San Francisco: Harper.

Campos, J. J., Campos, R. G., & Barrett, K. C. (1989). Emergent themes in the study of emotional development and emotion regulation. *Developmental Psychology, 25,* 394–402.

Candee, D. (1976). Structure and choice in moral reasoning. *Journal of Personality and Social Psychology, 34,* 1293–1301.

Candee, D., & Kohlberg, L. (1983). Moral reasoning and obedience to authority. In L. Kohlberg, D. Candee, & A. Colby (Eds.), *Recent research in moral development.* Cambridge: Harvard University Press.

Cantor, N., & Mischel, W. (1977). Traits as prototypes: Effects on recognition memory. *Journal of Personality and Social Psychology, 35,* 38–48.

Cantor, N., & Mischel, W. (1979). Prototypes in person perception. In L. Berkowitz (Ed.), *Advances in experimental social psychology* (Vol. 12, pp. 3–52). New York: Academic Press.

Cantor, N., Mischel, W., & Schwartz, J. (1982). A prototype analysis of psychological situations. *Cognitive Psychology, 14,* 45–77.

Cantor, N., Smith, E. E., deSales French, R., & Mezzich, J. (1980). Psychiatric diagnosis as a prototype categorization. *Journal of Abnormal Psychology, 89,* 181–193.

Carlo, G., Knight, G. P., Eisenberg, N., & Rotenberg, K. J. (1991). Cognitive processes and prosocial behaviors among children: The role of affective attributions and reconciliations. *Developmental Psychology, 27,* 456–461.

Carpendale, J.I.M., & Krebs, D. L. (1992). Situational variation in moral judgment: In a stage or on a stage? *Journal of Youth and Adolescence, 21,* 203–224.

Carr, S., Dabbs, J., & Carr, T. (1975). Mother-infant attachment: The importance of mother's visual field. *Child Development, 46,* 331–338.

Case, R. (1985). *Intellectual development: Birth to adulthood.* Orlando, FL: Academic Press.

Chaplin, W. F., John, O. P., & Goldberg, L. R. (1988). Conceptions of states and traits: Dimensional attributes with ideals as prototypes. *Journal of Personality and Social Psychology, 54,* 541–557.

Chapman, M. (1987). Piaget, attentional capacity, and the functional implications of formal structure. In H. Reese (Ed.), *Advances in child development and behavior* (Vol. 20, pp. 289–334). Orlando, FL: Academic Press.

Chapman, M. (1988). *Constructive evolution: Origin and development of Piaget's thought.* Cambridge: Cambridge University Press.

Chapman, M., Zahn-Waxler, C., Cooperman, G., & Iannotti, R. (1987). Empathy and responsibility in the motivation of children's helping. *Developmental Psychology, 23,* 140–145.

Chi, M.T.H., & Ceci, S. J. (1987). Content knowledge: Its role, representation, and restructuring in memory development. In H. Reese (Ed.), *Advances in child development and behavior.* (*Vol. 20,* pp. 91–142). Orlando, FL: Academic Press.

Chodorow, N. (1989). *Feminism and psychoanalytic thinking.* New Haven: Yale University Press.

Cohn, J. F., Campbell, S. B., Matias, R., & Hopkins, J. (1990). Face to face interactions of postpartum, depressed, and nondepressed mother-infant pairs at 2 months. *Developmental Psychology, 26,* 15–23.

Cohn, J. F., & Tronick, E. Z. (1983). Three-month old infants reaction to simulated maternal depression. *Child Development, 54,* 185–193.

Colby, A. (1973). Logical operational limitations on the development of moral judgment. Unpublished doctoral dissertation, Columbia University, New York.

Colby, A. (1978). Evolution of a moral-developmental theory. In W. Damon (Ed.), *New directions for child development.* (*Vol. 2,* pp. 89–105). San Francisco: Jossey-Bass.

Colby, A., & Kohlberg, L. (1987). *The measurement of moral judgment: Vol. 1. Theoretical foundations and research validation.* Cambridge, England: Cambridge University Press.

Colby, A., Kohlberg, L., Gibbs, J., & Lieberman, M. (1983). A longitudinal study of moral judgment. *Monographs of the Society for Research in Child Development, 48* (1–2, Serial No. 200).

Constanzo, P., Coie, J. D., Grumet, J. F., & Farnill, D. (1973). A reexamination of the effects of intent and consequences in children's moral judgment. *Child Development, 49,* 154–161.

Constanzo, P., & Shaw, M. (1966). Conformity as a function of age level. *Child Development, 37,* 967–975.

Cortese, A. J. (1984). Standard issue scoring of moral reasoning: A critique. *Merrill Palmer Quarterly, 30,* 227–247.

Cowan, P. A., Langer, J., Heavenrich, J., & Nathanson, M. (1969). Social learning and Piaget's cognitive theory of moral development. *Journal of Personality and Social Psychology, 11,* 261–274.

Crockenberg, S., & Litman, C. (1990). Autonomy as competence in 2-year olds: Maternal correlates of child defiance, compliance and self-assertion. *Developmental Psychology, 27,* 961–971.

Crowley, P. M. (1968). Effect of training upon objectivity of moral judgment in grade-school children. *Journal of Personality and Social Psychology, 8,* 228–232.

Cummings, E. M., Iannotti, R. J., & Zahn-Waxler, C. (1985). Influence of conflict between adults on the emotions and aggression of young children. *Developmental Psychology, 21,* 495–507.

Cummings, E. M., Zahn-Waxler, C., & Radke-Yarrow, M. (1981). Young children's responses to expressions of anger and affection by others in the family. *Child Development, 52,* 1274–1282.

Curdin, J. (1966). *A study of the development of immanent justice.* Unpublished doctoral dissertation, University of North Carolina, Chapel Hill.

Damon, W. (1971). The positive justice concept from childhood to adolescence: A developmental analysis. Unpublished master's thesis, University of California, Berkeley.

Damon, W. (1973). Early conceptions of justice as related to the development of operational reasoning. Unpublished doctoral dissertation, University of California, Berkeley.

Damon, W. (1975). Early conceptions of positive justice as related to the development of logical operations. *Child Development, 46,* 301–312.

Damon, W. (1977a). Measurement and social development. *Counseling Psychologist, 6,* 13–15.

Damon, W. (1977b). *The social world of the child*. San Francisco: Jossey-Bass.

Damon, W. (1979). Why study social-cognitive development? *Human Development, 22*, 206–211.

Damon, W. (1980). Patterns of change in children's social reasoning: A two-year longitudinal study. *Child Development, 51*, 1010–1017.

Damon, W. (1981). Exploring children's social cognition on two fronts. In J. H., Flavell & L. Ross (Eds.), *Social cognitive development: Frontiers and possible futures* (pp. 154–175). Cambridge: Cambridge University Press.

Damon, W. (1988). *The moral child: Nurturing children's natural moral growth*. New York: Free Press.

Damon, W., & Killen, M. (1982). Peer interaction and the process of change in children's moral reasoning. *Merrill-Palmer Quarterly, 82*, 347–367.

Darley, J., Klossen, E. C., & Zanna, M. (1978). Intentions and their contexts in the moral judgments of children and adults. *Child Development, 49*, 66–74.

Darley, J. M., & Latane, B. (1968). Bystander intervention in emergencies: Diffusion of responsibility. *Journal of Personality and Social Psychology, 8*, 377–383.

Davison, M., & Robbins, S. (1978). The reliability and validity of objective indices of moral development. *Applied Psychological Measurement, 2*, 391–403.

Dawes, R. (1994). *House of cards: Psychology and psychotherapy built on myth*. New York: Free Press.

Denham, S. A. (1986). Social cognition, prosocial behavior and emotion in preschoolers: Contextual validation. *Child Development, 57*, 194–201.

Denham, S. A., Renwick, S. M., & Holt, R. W. (1991). Working and playing together: Prediction of preschool social-emotional competence from mother-child interaction. *Child Development, 62*, 242–249.

DeRemer, P. A., & Gruen, G. E. (1979). Children's moral judgments: The relationship between intentionality, social egocentrism and development. *Journal of Genetic Psychology, 134*, 207–217.

Deutch, F., & Madle, R. A. (1975). Empathy: Historic and current conceptualizations, measurement, and a cognitive-theoretical perspective. *Human Development, 18*, 267–287.

de Vries, B., & Walker, L. J. (1986). Moral reasoning and attitudes towards capital punishment. *Developmental Psychology, 22*, 509–513.

DeVries, R. (1991). The cognitive-developmental paradigm. In W. M. Kurtines & J. L. Gewirtz (Eds.), *Handbook of moral behavior and development* (pp. 7–12). Hillsdale, NJ: Lawrence Erlbaum.

Döbert, R. (1990). Against the neglect of "content" in the moral theories of Kohlberg and Habermas: Implications for the relativism–universalism controversy. In T. Wren (Ed.), *The moral domain: Essays in the ongoing discussion between philosophy and the social sciences* (pp. 71–108). Cambridge: MIT Press.

Dornbusch, S. M., Ritter, P. L., Leiderman, P. H., Roberts, D. F., & Fraleigh, M. (1987). The relation of parenting style to adolescent school performance. *Child Development, 58*, 1244-1257.

Dunn, J., Brown, J., & Beardsall, L. (1991). Family talk about feeling states and children's later understanding of other's emotions. *Developmental Psychology, 27*, 448–455.

Dunn, J., & Kendrick, C. (1982). *Siblings: Love, envy and understanding*. Cambridge: Harvard University Press.

Dunn, J., & Munn, P. (1986). Siblings and prosocial development. *International Journal of Behavioral Development, 9*, 265–284.

Durkheim, E. (1925/1973). *Moral education*. Glencoe, IL: Free Press.

Dworkin, R. (1978). *Taking rights seriously*. Cambridge: Harvard University Press.

Dykstra, C. R. (1981). *Vision and character*. New York: Paulist Press.

Ebbinghaus, J. (1954). Interpretation and misinterpretation of the categorical imperative. *Philosophical Quarterly, 4*, 97–108.

Edwards, C. P. (1975). Societal complexity and moral development: A Kenya study. *Ethos, 3*, 505–527.

Eisenberg, N. (Ed.). (1982). *The development of prosocial behavior*. New York: Academic Press.

Eisenberg, N. (1986). *Altruistic emotion, cognition and behavior*. Hillsdale, NJ: Lawrence Erlbaum.

Eisenberg, N. (1990). Prosocial development in early and mid-adolescence. In R. Montemayor, G. R. Adams, & T. P. Gullota (Eds.), *From childhood to adolescence: A transitional period? Advances in adolescent development* (Vol. 2, pp. 240–268). Newbury Park, NJ: Sage.

Eisenberg, N., Boehnke, K., Schuhler, P., & Silbereisen, R. K. (1985). The development of prosocial behavior and cognitions in German children. *Journal of Cross-Cultural Psychology, 16*, 69–82.

Eisenberg, N., Lennon, R., & Roth, K. (1983). Prosocial development: A longitudinal study. *Developmental Psychology, 19*, 846–855.

Eisenberg, N., Lundy, T., Shell, R., & Roth, K. (1985). Children's justifications of their adult and peer-directed compliant (prosocial and non-prosocial) behaviors. *Developmental Psychology, 21*, 325–331.

Eisenberg, N., & Miller, P. A. (1987). The relation of empathy to prosocial and related behaviors. *Psychological Bulletin, 101*, 91–119.

Eisenberg, N., Miller, P. A., Shell, R., McNalley, S., & Shea, C. (1991). Prosocial development in adolescence: A longitudinal study. *Developmental Psychology, 27*, 849–857.

Eisenberg, N., & Mussen, P. (1989). *The roots of prosocial behavior in children*. Cambridge: Cambridge University Press.

Eisenberg, N., Pasternack, J. F., Cameron, E., & Tryon, K. (1984). The relation of quantity and mode of prosocial behavior to moral cognitions and social style. *Child Development, 55*, 1479–1485.

Eisenberg, N., Shell, R., Pasternack, J., Lennon, R., Beller, R., & Mathy, R. M. (1987). Prosocial development in middle childhood: A longitudinal study. *Developmental Psychology, 23*, 712–718.

Eisenberg-Berg, N. (1976). The relation of political attitudes to constraint-oriented and prosocial moral reasoning. *Developmental Psychology, 12*, 552–553.

Eisenberg-Berg, N. (1979a). Development of children's prosocial moral judgment. *Developmental Psychology, 15*, 128–137.

Eisenberg-Berg, N. (1979b). Relationship of prosocial moral reasoning to altruism, political liberalism, and intelligence. *Developmental Psychology, 15*, 87–89.

Eisenberg-Berg, N., & Hand, M. (1979). The relationship of preschooler's reasoning about prosocial moral conflicts to prosocial behavior. *Child Development, 50*, 356–363.

Eisenberg-Berg, N., & Lennon, R. (1980). Altruism and the assessment of empathy in the preschool years. *Child Development, 51, 552–557*.

Eisenberg-Berg, N., & Mussen, P. (1978). Empathy and moral development in adolescence. *Developmental Psychology, 14*, 185–186.

Eisenberg-Berg, N., & Neal, C. (1979). Children's moral reasoning about their own spontaneous prosocial behaviors. *Developmental Psychology, 15*, 228–229.

Eisenberg-Berg, N., & Roth, K. (1980). Development of young children's prosocial moral judgment: A longitudinal follow-up. *Developmental Psychology, 16*, 375–376.

Eliot, T. S. (1943). *Four Quartets*. San Diego: Harcourt Brace Jovanovich.

Elkind, D., & Dabeck, R. F. (1977). Personal injury and property damage in the moral judgments of children. *Child Development, 48,* 518–522.

Emler, N. P., & Rushton, J. P. (1974). Cognitive-developmental factors in children's generosity. *British Journal of Social and Clinical Psychology, 13,* 277–281.

Emler, N., & Hogan, R. (1991). Moral psychology and public policy. In W. Kurtines and J. L. Gewirtz (Eds.), *Handbook of moral behavior and development* (Vol. 3, pp. 69–94). Hillsdale, NJ: Lawrence Erlbaum.

Enright, R. D. (1981). *Manual for the distributive justice scale.* Unpublished manuscript.

Enright, R. D., Bjerstedt, A., Enright, W. F., Levy, V. M., Lapsley, D. K., Buss, R. R., Harwell, M., & Zindler, M. (1984). Distributive justice development: Cross-cultural, contextual, and longitudinal evaluations. *Child Development, 55,* 1737-1751.

Enright, R. D., Eastin, D., Golden, S., Sarinopoulos, I., & Freedman, S. (1992). Interpersonal forgiveness within the helping professions: An attempt to resolve differences of opinion. *Counseling and Values, 36,* 84–103.

Enright, R. D., Enright, W. F., & Lapsley, D. K. (1981). Distributive justice development and social class. *Developmental Psychology, 17,* 826–832.

Enright, R. D., Enright, W. F., Manheim, L. A., & Harris, B. E. (1980). Distributive justice development and social class. *Developmental Psychology, 16,* 555–563.

Enright, R. D., Franklin, C. C., & Manheim, L. A. (1980). Children's distributive justice reasoning: A standardized and objective scale. *Developmental Psychology, 16,* 193–202.

Enright, R. D., Gassin, E. A., & Wu, C-R. (1992). Forgiveness: A developmental view. *Journal of Moral Education, 21,* 99–114.

Enright, R. D., & Lapsley, D. K. (1980). Social role-taking: A review of the constructs, measures, and measurement properties. *Review of Educational Research, 50,* 647–674.

Enright, R. D., Lapsley, D. K., Harris, D., & Shauver, D. (1983). Moral development interventions in early adolescence. *Theory into Practice, 22,* 134–144.

Enright, R. D., Lapsley, D. K., & Levy, V. (1983). Moral education strategies. In M. Pressley and J. Levin (Eds.), *Cognitive strategy research: Educational applications* (pp. 43–84). New York: Springer.

Enright, R. D., Santos, M., & Al-Mabuk, R. (1989). The adolescent as forgiver. *Journal of Adolescence, 12,* 95–110.

Enright, R. D., & Study Group (1991). The moral development of forgiveness. In W. Kurtines and J. L. Gewirtz (Eds.), *Handbook of moral behavior and development* (Vol. 1, pp. 123–152). Hillsdale, NJ: Lawrence Erlbaum.

Enright, R. D., & Sutterfield, S. J. (1980). An ecological validation of social cognitive development. *Child Development, 51,* 151–161.

Eron, L. D., Walder, L. O., Huesmann, L. R., & Lefkowitz, N. M. (1974). The convergence of laboratory and field studies of the development of aggression. In J. deWit & W. W. Hartup (Eds.), *Determinants and origins of aggressive behavior* (pp. 347–380). The Hague: Mouton.

Fabes, R. A., Eisenberg, N., McCormick, S. W., & Wilson, M. S. (1988). Preschoolers' attributions of the situational determinants of others' naturally occurring emotions. *Developmental Psychology, 24,* 376–385.

Fabes, R. A., Eisenberg, N., Nyman, M & Michealieu, Q. (1991). Young children's appraisals of others' spontaneous emotional reactions. *Developmental Psychology, 27,* 858–866.

Fabes, R. A., Fultz, J., Eisenberg, N., May-Plumlee, T., & Christopher, F. S. (1989). Effects of rewards on children's prosocial motivation: A socialization study. *Developmental Psychology, 25,* 509–515.

Farnill, D. (1974). The effects of social judgment set on children's use of intention information. *Journal of Personality,* 42, 276–289.

Fehr, B., & Russell, J. A. (1984). Concept of emotion viewed from a prototype perspective. *Journal of Experimental Psychology: General, 113,* 464–486.

Feinman, S. (1982). Social referencing in infancy. *Merrill-Palmer Quarterly, 28,* 445–470.

Feinman, S. (1992). *Social referencing and the social construction of reality in infancy.* New York: Plenum.

Feldman, N. S., Klosson, E. C., Parsons, J. E., Rholes, W. S., & Ruble, D. N. (1976). Order of information presentation and children's moral judgments. *Child Development, 47,* 556–559.

Feshbach, N. D., & Roe, K. (1968). Empathy in six-and seven-year olds. *Child Development, 39,* 133–145.

Fischer, K. (1983). Illuminating the processes of moral development. In A. Colby, L. Kohlberg, J. Gibbs, & M. Lieberman (Eds.), A longitudinal study of moral judgment. *Monographs of the Society for Research in Child Development, 48* (Serial No. 200), pp. 97–106.

Flanagan, O. (1982). Moral structures? *Philosophy of the Social Sciences, 12,* 255–270.

Flanagan, O. (1991). *Varieties of moral personality: Ethics and psychological realism.* Cambridge: Harvard University Press.

Flanagan, O., & Rorty, A. O. (Eds.). (1990). *Identity, character and morality: Essays in moral psychology.* Cambridge: MIT Press.

Flavell, J. (1971). Stage-related properties of cognitive development. *Cognitive Psychology, 2,* 421–453.

Flavell, J., Botkin, P. I., Fry, C. L., Wright, J. W., & Jarvis, P. E. (1968). *The development of role-taking and communication skills in children.* New York: Wiley.

Flavell, J., & Wohlwill, J. F. (1969). Formal and functional aspects of cognitive development. In D. Elkind & J. Flavell (Eds.), *Studies in cognitive development* (pp. 67–119). New York: Oxford University Press.

Flew, R. N. (1968). *The idea of perfection in Christian theology.* New York: Humanities Press.

Ford, M. (1979). The construct validity of egocentrism. *Psychological Bulletin, 86,* 1169–1188.

Ford, M. R., & Lowery, C. R. (1986). Gender differences in moral reasoning: A comparison of the use of justice and care orientations. *Journal of Personality and Social Psychology, 50,* 777–783.

Frankena, W. K. (1973). *Ethics.* Englewood, NJ: Prentice-Hall.

French, P. A., Uehling, T. E., & Wettstein, H. K. (Eds.). (1988). *Ethical theory: Character and virtue* (Midwest Studies in Philosophy). Notre Dame, IN: University of Notre Dame Press.

Freud, S. (1923/1961). *The ego and the id.* In J. Strachey (Gen. Ed.), *The standard edition of the complete psychological works of Sigmund Freud* (pp. 12–68). London: Hogarth Press.

Friedman, M. (1985). Abraham, Socrates and Heinz: Where are the women? (Care and context in moral reasoning). In C. G. Harding (Ed.), *Moral dilemmas* (pp. 25–41). Chicago: Precedent.

Friedman, M. (1991). The practice of partiality. *Ethics, 101,* 818–835.

Gabennesch, H. (1990). The perception of social conventionality by children and adults. *Child Development, 61,* 2047–2059.

Geiger, K., & Turiel, E. (1983). Disruptive school behavior and concepts of social convention in early adolescence. *Journal of Educational Psychology, 75,* 677–685.

Gellner, E. (1985). *Relativism and the social sciences.* Cambridge: Cambridge University Press.

Gelman, R., & Baillargeon, R. (1983). A review of some Piagetian concepts. In P. H. Mussen (Ed.), *Handbook of child psychology* (4th ed., Vol. 3, pp. 167–230). New York: Wiley.

Gerson, R. P., & Damon, W. (1978). Moral understanding and children's conduct. In W. Damon (Ed.), *Moral development* (pp. 41–60) (New Directions for Child Development No. 2). San Francisco: Jossey-Bass.

Gewirth, A. (1978). *Reason and morality*. Chicago: University of Chicago Press.

Gewirth, A. (1988). Ethical universalism and particularism. *Journal of Philosophy, 85*, 283–302.

Gewirtz, J. L. (1991). Prologue—Lawrence Kohlberg's life and work from the vantage point of a long-time friend and colleague: A memoir. In W. M. Kurtines & J. L. Gewirtz (Eds.), *Handbook of moral behavior and development: Vol 1. Theory* (pp. 1–6). Hillsdale, NJ: Lawrence Erlbaum.

Gfellner, B. M. (1986). Changes in ego and moral development in adolescents: A longitudinal study. *Journal of Adolescence, 9*, 281–302.

Gibbs, J. (1979). Kohlberg's moral stage theory: A Piagetian revision. *Human Development, 22*, 89–112.

Gibbs, J. (1991). Toward an integration of Kohlberg's and Hoffman's theories of morality. In W. M. Kurtines & J. L. Gewirtz (Eds.), *Handbook of moral behavior and development: Vol. 1 Theory* (pp. 183–222). Hillsdale, NJ: Lawrence Erlbaum.

Gibbs, J., Clark, P., Joseph, J., Goodrick, T., & Makowski, D. (1986). Relations between moral judgment, moral courage, and field independence. *Child Development, 57*, 185–193.

Gibbs, J., & Widaman, K. (1982). *Social intelligence: Measuring the development of sociomoral reflection*. Englewood Cliffs, NJ: Prentice-Hall.

Gilligan, C. (1977). In a different voice: Women's conceptions of the self and of morality. *Harvard Educational Review, 47*, 481–517.

Gilligan, C. (1982). *In a different voice: Psychological theory and women's development*. Cambridge: Harvard University Press.

Gilligan, C., & Attanucci, J. (1988a). Much ado about. . . knowing? noting? nothing? A reply to Vasudev concerning sex differences and moral development. *Merrill-Palmer Quarterly, 34*, 451–456.

Gilligan, C., & Attanucci, J. (1988b). Two moral orientations: Gender differences and similarities. *Merrill-Palmer Quarterly, 34*, 223–237.

Gilligan, C., & Belenky, M. F. (1980). A naturalistic study of abortion decisions. In R. Selman & R. Yandow (Eds.), *Clinical-developmental psychology* (pp. 69–90) (*New Directions for Child Development No. 7*). San Francisco: Jossey-Bass.

Gilligan, C., & Wiggins, G. (1987). The origin of morality in early childhood relationships. In J. Kagan & S. Lamb (Eds.), *The emergence of morality in young children* (pp. 277–305). Chicago: University of Chicago Press.

Gilligan, J. (1976). Beyond morality: Psychoanalytic reflections on shame, guilt and love. In T. Lickona (Ed.), *Moral development and behavior* (pp. 144–158). New York: Holt, Rinehart & Winston.

Ginsberg, H., & Opper, S. (1969). *Piaget's theory of intellectual development*. Englewood Cliffs, NJ: Prentice-Hall.

Glass, G. V., McGraw, B., & Smith, M. L. (1981). *Meta-analysis in social research*. Beverly Hills, CA: Sage.

Goldman, A. I. (1993). Ethics and cognitive science. *Ethics, 103*, 337–360.

Gove, F. L., & Keating, D. P. (1979). Empathic role-taking precursors. *Developmental Psychology, 15*, 594–600.

Gralinksi, J. H., & Kopp, C. B. (1993). Everyday rules for behavior: Mothers' requests to young children. *Developmental Psychology, 29*, 573–584.

Greenwald, A. G., & Pratkanis, A. R. (1984). The self. In R. S. Wyerand T. K. Srull (Eds.), *Handbook of social cognition* (Vol. 3, pp. 129–178). Hillsdale, NJ: Lawrence Erlbaum.

Grinder, R. E. (1964). Relations between behavioral and cognitive development. *Child Development, 35,* 881–891.

Grover, S. (1980). An examination of Kohlberg's cognitive-developmental model of moralization. *Journal of Genetic Psychology, 136,* 137–143.

Gruber H., & Voneche, J. (Eds.). (1977) *The essential Piaget.* New York: Basic Books.

Grueneich, R. (1982a). The development of children's integration rules for making moral judgments. *Child Development, 53,* 887–894.

Grueneich, R. (1982b). Issues in the developmental study of how children use intention and consequence information to make moral judgments. *Child Development, 53,* 29–43.

Grunebaum, J. O. (1993). Friendship, morality and special obligation. *American Philosophical Quarterly, 30,* 51–61.

Grusec, J. (1971). Power and the internalization of self-denial. *Child Development, 42,* 93–105.

Grusec, J. (1991). Socializing concern for others in the home. *Developmental Psychology, 27,* 338–343.

Grusec, J., Dix, T., & Mills, R. (1982). The effects of type, severity, and victim of children's transgressions on maternal discipline. *Canadian Journal of Behavioral Science, 14,* 276–289.

Grusec, J., Kuczynski, L., Rushton, J. P., & Simutis, Z. (1979). Learning resistance to temptation through observation. *Developmental Psychology, 15,* 233–240.

Grusec, J., Kuczynski, L., Simutis, Z., & Rushton, J. P. (1978). Modeling, direct instruction and attributions: Effects on altruism. *Developmental Psychology, 14,* 51–57.

Grusec, J., & Redler, E. (1980). Attribution, reinforcement, and altruism: A developmental analysis. *Developmental Psychology, 16,* 525–534.

Grusec, J., Saas-Kortsaak, J. P., & Simutis, Z. (1978). The role of example and moral exhortation in the training of altruism. *Child Development, 49,* 920–923.

Grusec, J. & Skubiski, S. L. (1970). Model nurturance, demand characteristics of the modeling experiment, and altruism. *Journal of Personality and Social Psychology, 14,* 352–359.

Gunnar, M. R., & Stone, C. (1984). The effects of positive maternal affect on infant responses to pleasant, ambiguous and fear-provoking toys. *Child Development, 55,* 1231–1236.

Gutkin, D. (1972). The effect of systematic story changes on intentionality in children's moral judgments. *Child Development, 43,* 187–195.

Haan, N. (1975). Hypothetical and actual moral reasoning in a situation of civil disobedience. *Journal of Personality and Social Psychology, 32,* 235–270.

Haan, N. (1985). Processes of moral development: Cognitive or social disequilibrium? *Developmental Psychology, 21,* 996–1006.

Haan, N., Smith, M. B., & Block, J. (1968). Moral reasoning of young adults: Political social behavior, family background, and personality correlates. *Journal of Personality and Social Psychology, 10,* 183–201.

Haan, N., Stroud, J., & Holstein, C. (1973). Moral and ego stages in relation to ego processes: A study of "hippies." *Journal of Personality, 41,* 596–612.

Habermas, J. (1983). Interpretive social science vs. hermeneuticism. In N. Haan, R. Bellah, P. Rabinow, & W. Sullivan (Eds.), *Social science as moral inquiry.* New York: Columbia University Press.

Habermas, J. (1990). *Moral consciousness and communicative action.* (C. Lenhardt & S. W. Nicholson, Trans.). Cambridge: MIT Press.

Haier, R. J. (1977). Moral reasoning and moral character: Relationship between the Kohlbergian and Hogan models. *Psychological Reports, 40*, 215–226.

Hampshire, S. (1949). Fallacies in moral philosophy. *Mind, 58*, 466–482.

Hampshire, S. (1953). Dispositions. *Analysis, 14*, 5–11.

Hardwick, D. A., McIntyre, C. W., & Pick, H. L. (1976). The content and manipulation of cognitive maps in children and adults. *Monographs of the Society for Research in Child Development. 41* (3, Serial No. 166).

Hare, R. M. (1952). *The language of morals.* New York: Oxford University Press.

Hare, R. M. (1981). *Moral thinking: Its levels, method and point.* New York: Oxford University Press.

Harris, S., Mussen, P., & Rutherford, E. (1976). Some cognitive, behavioral and personality correlates of maturity and moral judgment. *Journal of Genetic Psychology, 128*, 123–135.

Harrison, J. (1957). Kant's examples of the first formulation of the categorical imperative. *Philosophical Quarterly, 7*, 50–62.

Harrower, M. R. (1934). Social status and the moral judgment of the child. *British Journal of Educational Psychology, 4*, 75–95.

Hart, D. (1988). A longitudinal study of adolescent's socialization and identification as predictors of adult moral judgment development. *Merrill-Palmer Quarterly, 34*, 245–260.

Hart, D., & Chmiel, S. (1993). The influence of defense mechanisms on moral judgment development: A longitudinal study. *Developmental Psychology, 28*, 722–730.

Hartshorne, H., & May, M. (1928–1932). *Studies in the nature of character.* New York: Macmillan.

Hartup, W. W., & Coates, B. (1967). Imitation of a peer as a function of reinforcement from the peer group and rewardingness of the model. *Child Development, 38*, 1003–1016.

Hauerwas, S. (1979). *Character and the Christian life: A study in theological ethics.* San Antonio: Trinity University Press.

Havighurst, R. J., & Neugarten, B. L. (1955). *American Indian and white children: A sociopsychological investigation.* Chicago: University of Chicago Press.

Haviland, J. M. (1971). A developmental study of children's beliefs about punishment. Unpublished doctoral dissertation, Michigan State University, East Lansing.

Haviland, J. M. (1979). Teachers' and students' beliefs about punishment. *Journal of Educational Psychology, 71*, 563–570.

Haviland, J. M., & Lelwica, M. (1987). The induced affect response: 10-week old infants' response to three emotional expressions. *Developmental Psychology, 23*, 97–104.

Hay, D. F. (1979). Cooperative interactions and sharing between very young children and their parents. *Developmental Psychology, 15*, 647–653.

Hay, D. F., Nash, A., & Pedersen, J. (1981). Responses of six-month olds to the distress of their peers. *Child Development, 52*, 1071–1075.

Hedges, L. V., & Olkin, I. (1985). *Statistical methods for meta-analysis.* Orlando, FL: Academic Press.

Hendy, R. & Butter, E. J. (1981). Moral judgments by children of the intentional behavior of friends and strangers. *Journal of Genetic Psychology, 139*, 227–232.

Herskovitz, M. J. (1955). *Cultural anthropology.* New York: Knopf.

Higgins, A. (1991). The just community approach to moral education: Evolution of the idea and recent findings. In W. M. Kurtines & J. L. Gewirtz (Eds.), *Handbook of moral behavior and research: Vol 3. Application* (pp. 111–142). Hillsdale, NJ: Lawrence Erlbaum.

Higgins, E. T. (1981). Role-taking and social judgment: Alternative developmental perspectives and processes. In J. H. Flavell & L. Ross (Eds.), *Social cognitive development: Frontiers and possible futures* (pp. 119–153). Cambridge: Cambridge University Press.

Higgins, E. T. (1991). Personality, social psychology and person-situation-relations: Standards and knowledge activation as a common language. In L. A. Pervin (Ed.), *Handbook of personality: Theory and research* (pp. 301–338). New York: Guilford Press.

Higgins, E. T., & Bargh, J. A. (1987). Social cognition and social perception. *Annual Review of Psychology, 38,* 369–425.

Higgins, E. T., Bargh, J. A., & Lombardi, W. (1985). The nature of priming effects in categorization. *Journal of Experimental Psychology: Learning, Memory and Cognition, 11,* 59–69.

Higgins, E. T., King, G. A., & Mavin, G. H. (1982). Individual construct accessibility and subjective impressions and recall. *Journal of Personality and Social Psychology, 43,* 35–47.

Higgins, E. T., Rholes, W. S., & Jones, C. R. (1977). Category accessibility and impression formation. *Journal of Experimental Social Psychology, 13,* pp. 141–154.

Hildebrandt, D. E., Feldman, S. E., & Ditrichs, R. A. (1973). Rules, models and self-reinforcement in children. *Journal of Personality and Social Psychology, 25,* 1–5.

Hobbes, T. (1651/1958). *Leviathan.* Indianapolis: Bobbs-Merrill.

Hoffman, M. (1960). Power assertion by the parent and its impact on the child. *Child Development, 31,* 129–143.

Hoffman, M. (1963). Child-rearing practices and moral development: Generalizations from empirical research. *Child Development, 34,* 295–318

Hoffman, M. (1975a). Altruistic behavior and the parent-child relationship. *Journal of Personality and Social Psychology, 31,* 937–943.

Hoffman, M. (1975b). Developmental synthesis of affect and cognition and its implications for altruistic motivation. *Developmental Psychology, 11,* 607–622.

Hoffman, M. (1975c). Moral internalization, parental power, and the nature of the parent-child interaction. *Developmental Psychology, 11,* 228–239.

Hoffman, M. (1977). Moral internalization: Current theory and research. In L. Berkowitz (Ed.), *Advances in experimental social psychology* (Vol. 10, pp. 86–135). New York: Academic Press.

Hoffman, M. (1981). Is altruism part of human nature? *Journal of Personality and Social Psychology, 40,* 121–137.

Hoffman, M. (1984). Interaction of affect and cognition in empathy. In C. E. Izard, J. Kagan, & R. B. Zajonc, (Eds.), *Emotions, cognition and behavior* (pp. 103–131). Cambridge: Cambridge University Press.

Hoffman, M. (1987). The contribution of empathy to justice and moral judgment. In N. Eisenberg & J. Strayer (Eds.), *Empathy and its development* (pp. 47–80). Cambridge: Cambridge University Press.

Hoffman, M. (1991). Empathy, social cognition, and moral action. In W. M. Kurtines & J. L. Gewirtz (Eds.), *Handbook of moral behavior and development: Vol. 1. Theory* (pp. 275–301). Hillsdale, NJ: Lawrence Erlbaum.

Hoffman, M., & Saltzstein, H. D. (1967). Parent discipline and the child's moral development. *Journal of Personality and Social Psychology, 5,* 45–57.

Hogan, R. (1970). A dimension of moral judgment. *Journal of Consulting and Clinical Psychology, 35,* 205–212.

Hogan, R. (1973). Moral conduct and moral character: A psychological perspective. *Psychological Bulletin, 79,* 217-232.

Hogan, R. (1974). Dialectical aspects of moral judgment. *Human Development, 17,* 107–117.

Hogan, R. (1975). Moral development and the structure of personality. In D. DePalma and J. Foley (Eds.), *Moral development: Current theory and research* (pp. 153–167). Hillsdale, NJ: Lawrence Erlbaum.

Hogan, R., & Dickstein, E. (1972). Moral judgment and perceptions of injustice. *Journal of Personality and Social Psychology, 23*, 409–413.

Hogan, R. Johnson, J. A., & Elmer, N. P. (1978). A socioanalytic theory of moral development. In W. Damon (Ed.), *Moral development: New directions for child development. No. 2* (pp. 1–18). San Francisco: Jossey-Bass.

Hollos, M., Leis, P., & Turiel, E. (1986). Social reasoning in Nigerian children and adolescents. *Journal of Cross-Cultural Psychology, 17*, 352–374.

Holmgren, M. R. (1993). Forgiveness and the intrinsic value of persons. *American Philosophical Quarterly, 30*, 341–352.

Holstein, C. S. (1976). Irreversible, stepwise sequence in the development of moral judgment: A longitudinal study of males and females. *Child Development, 47*, 51–61.

Hudson, W. D. (Ed.). (1969). *The is-ought question: A collection of papers on the central problem in moral philosophy*. New York: Macmillan.

Hume, D. (1930). *An enquiry into the principles of morals*. Chicago: Open Court.

Hutchins, W. J. (1929). The children's morality code. *Journal of the National Educational Association, 13*, 292.

Huttonlocher, J., & Presson, C. (1973). Mental rotation and the perspective-problem. *Cognitive Psychology, 4*, 277–299.

Iannotti, R. J. (1978). Effects of role-taking experiences on role-taking, empathy, altruism, and aggression. *Developmental Psychology, 14*, 119–124.

Iannotti, R. J. (1985). Naturalistic and structured assessments of prosocial behavior in preschool children: The influence of empathy and perspective-taking. *Developmental Psychology, 21*, 46–55.

Irwin, D., & Moore, S. G. (1971). The young child's understanding of social justice. *Developmental Psychology, 5*, 406–410.

Jahoda, G. (1958). Immanent justice among West African children. *Journal of Social Psychology, 47*, 241–248.

Jensen, A. M., & Moore, S. G. (1977). The effect of attribute statements on cooperativeness and competitiveness in school-age boys. *Child Development, 48*, 305–307.

Johnson, J., Hogan, R., Zonderman, A., Callens, C., & Rogolsky, S. (1981). Moral judgment, personality and attitudes toward authority. *Journal of Personality and Social Psychology, 40*, 370–373.

Johnson, M. (1993). *Moral imagination: Implications of cognitive science for ethics*. Chicago: University of Chicago Press.

Johnson, R. C. (1962a). Early studies of moral judgments. *Child Development, 33*, 603–605.

Johnson, R. C. (1962b). A study of children's moral judgments. *Child Development, 33*, 327–354.

Jose, P. E. (1991). Measurement issues in children's immanent justice judgments. *Merrill-Palmer Quarterly, 37*, 601–617.

Josselson, R. (1988). I and thou revisited. In D. K. Lapsley & F. C. Power (Eds.), *Self, ego, and identity: Integrative approaches* (pp. 91–108). New York: Springer.

Jurkovic, G. J. (1980). The juvenile delinquent as a moral philosopher: A structural-developmental perspective. *Psychological Bulletin, 88*, 709–727.

Kahneman, D., & Tversky, A. (1973). On the psychology of prediction. *Psychological Review, 80*, 237–251.

Kant, I. (1785/1988). *Fundamental principles of the metaphysics of morals* (T. K. Abbott, Trans.). Buffalo, NY: Prometheus Books.

Kapur, N. B. (1991). Why it is wrong to be always guided by the best: Consequentialism and friendship. *Ethics, 101*, 483–504.

Karniol, R. (1978). Children's use of intention cues in evaluating behavior. *Psychological Bulletin, 85*, 76–85.

Karniol, R. (1980). A conceptual analysis of immanent justice responses in children. *Child Development, 51*, 118–130.

Karniol, R. (1982). Settings, scripts, and self-schemata: A cognitive analysis of the development of prosocial behavior. In N. Eisenberg (Ed.), *The development of prosocial behavior*. New York: Academic Press.

Kaye, K. (1982). *The mental and social life of babies*. Chicago: University of Chicago Press.

Keasey, C. B. (1971). Social participation as a factor in the moral development of preadolescents. *Developmental Psychology, 5*, 216–220.

Keasey, C. B. (1972). Young children's attributions of intentionality to themselves and others. *Child Development, 48*, 261–264.

Keasey, C. B. (1977). Young children's attribution of intentionality to themselves and others. *Child Development, 48*, 261–264.

Kegan, R. (1982). *The evolving self*. Cambridge: Harvard University Press.

Kekes, J. (1989). *Moral tradition and individuality*. Princeton: Princeton University Press.

Kelly, G. (1955). *A theory of personality: The psychology of personal constructs*. New York: Norton.

Kemp, J. (1958). Kant's examples of the categorical imperative. *Philosophical Quarterly, 8*, 63–71.

Killen, M. (1990). Children's evaluation of morality in the context of peer, teacher-child and family relations. *Journal of Genetic Psychology, 151*, 395–410.

Killen, M. (1991). Social and moral development in early childhood. In W. M. Kurtines & J. L. Gewirtz (Eds.), *Handbook of moral behavior and development: Vol 2. Research* (pp. 115–138). Hillsdale, NJ: Lawrence Erlbaum.

Kister, M. C., & Patterson, C. J. (1980). Children's conceptions of the causes of illness: Understanding contagion and use of immanent justice. *Child Development, 51*, 839–846.

Kitchener, R. (1980). Piaget's genetic epistemology. *International Philosophical Quarterly, 20*, 377–405.

Kitchener, R. (1983). Developmental explanations. *Review of Metaphysics, 36*, 791–818.

Kitchener, R. (1985). Holistic structuralism, elementarism and Piaget's theory of relationism. *Human Development, 28*, 281-295.

Kitchener, R. (1986). *Piaget's theory of knowledge: Genetic epistemology and scientific reasoning*. New Haven, CT: Yale University Press.

Knight, G. P., & Kagan, S. (1977). Development of prosocial and competitive behaviors in Anglo-American and Mexican-American children. *Child Development, 48*, 1385–1394.

Knight, G. P., Kagan, S., & Buriel, R. (1982). Perceived parental practices and prosocial development. *Journal of Genetic Psychology, 131*, 57–65.

Kochanska, G. (1991). Socialization and temperament in the development of guilt and conscience. *Child Development, 62*, 1379–1392.

Kohlberg, L. (1948). Beds for bananas: A first hand story of the S.S. Redemption and what happened afterwards in Cyprus and in Palestine. *Menorah Journal, 36*, 385–399.

Kohlberg, L. (1958). The development of modes of moral thinking and choice in the years ten to sixteen. Unpublished doctoral dissertation, University of Chicago.

Kohlberg, L. (1969). Stage and sequence: The cognitive-developmental approach to socialization. In D. Goslin (Ed.), *Handbook of socialization theory and research* (pp. 347–480). Chicago: Rand McNally.

Kohlberg, L. (1971). From is to ought: How to commit the naturalistic fallacy and get away with it in the study of moral development. In T. Mischel (Ed.), *Cognitive development and epistemology* (pp. 151–235). New York: Academic Press.

Kohlberg, L. (1972). Indoctrination versus relativity in value education. *Zygon*, pp. 285–309.

Kohlberg, L. (1973a). The claim to moral adequacy of a highest stage of moral development. *Journal of Philosophy, 70*, 630–646.

Kohlberg, L. (1973b). Continuities in childhood and adult moral development revisited. In P. B. Baltes & K. W. Schaie (Eds.), *Lifespan developmental psychology: Personality and socialization*. New York: Academic Press.

Kohlberg, L. (1986). A current statement on some theoretical issues. In S. Modgil and C. Modgil (Eds.), *Lawrence Kohlberg: Consensus and controversy* (pp. 485–546). Philadelphia: Falmer Press.

Kohlberg, L. (1987). The development of moral judgment and moral action. In L. Kohlberg (Ed., with collaborators), *Child psychology and childhood education: A cognitive developmental view* (pp. 259–328). New York: Longman.

Kohlberg, L., Boyd, D., & Levine, C. (1990). The return of Stage 6: Its principle and moral point of view. In T. Wren (Ed.), *The moral domain: Essays in the ongoing discussion between philosophy and the social sciences* (pp. 151–181). Cambridge: MIT Press.

Kohlberg, L., & Gilligan, C. (1971). The adolescent as philosopher: The discovery of the self in a post-conventional world. *Daedalus, 4*, 1028–1061.

Kohlberg, L., Hickey, J., & Scharf, P. (1972). The justice structure of the prison. *Prison Journal, 51*, 3–14.

Kohlberg, L., & Kramer, R. (1969). Continuities and discontinuities in childhood and adult moral development. *Human Development, 12*, 93–120.

Kohlberg, L., Levine, C., & Hewer, A. (1983). *Moral stages: A current formulation and a response to critics.* In J. A. Meacham (Ed.), *Contributions to human development. (Vol. 10).* Basel: Karger.

Kohlberg, L., & Mayer, R. (1972). Development as the aim of education. *Harvard Educational Review, 42*, 449–496.

Kohlberg, L., & Mayer, R. (1987). Development as the aim of education. In L. Kohlberg (Ed., with collaborators), *Childhood psychology and childhood education: A cognitive developmental view* (pp. 45–86). New York: Longman.

Kohlberg, L., & Turiel, E. (1971). Moral development and moral education. In G. Lesser (Ed.), *Psychology and educational practice*. Chicago: Scott Foresman.

Kornblith, H. (1980). Beyond foundationalism and the coherence theory. *Journal of Philosophy, 77*, 597–612.

Kramer, R. (1968). Moral development in young adulthood. Unpublished doctoral dissertation, University of Chicago.

Krause, M., & Meiland, J. W. (Eds.). (1982). *Relativism: Cognitive and moral.* Notre Dame, IN: University of Notre Dame Press.

Krebs, D. (1970) Altruism: An examination of the concept and a review of the literature. *Psychological Bulletin, 73*, 258–302.

Krebs, D., Denton, K. L., Vermeulen, S. C., Carpendale, J. I., & Bush, A. (1991). Structural flexibility of moral judgment. *Journal of Personality and Social Psychology, 61*, 1012–1023.

Krebs, D., & Gillmore, J. (1982). The relationship among the first stages of cognitive development, role-taking abilities, and moral development. *Child Development, 53*, 877–886.

Krebs, D., & Russell, C. (1981). Role-taking and altruism: When you put yourself in the shoes of another, will they take you to their owner's aid? In J. P. Rushton & R. M. Sorrentino (Eds.), *Altruism and helping behavior II*. Hillsdale, NJ: Lawrence Erlbaum.

Krebs, D., & Sturrup, B. (1982). Role-taking ability and altruistic behavior in elementary school children. *Journal of Moral Education, 11*, 94–100.

Krebs, D., Vermuelen, S.C.A., Carpendale, J. I., & Denton, K. (1991). Structural and situational influences on moral judgment: An interaction between stage and dilemma. In W. M. Kurtines & J. L. Gewirtz (Eds.), *Handbook of moral behavior and development: Vol 2. Research* (pp. 139–170). Hillsdale, NJ: Lawrence Erlbaum.

Kruger, A. (1992). The effects of peer and adult-child transactive discussions on moral reasoning. *Merrill-Palmer Quarterly, 38*, 191–211.

Kruschwitz, R. B., & Roberts, R. C. (1987). *The virtues: Contemporary essays on moral character.* Belmont, CA: Wadsworth.

Kuhn, D. (1976). Short term longitudinal evidence for the sequentiality of Kohlberg's early stages of moral judgment. *Developmental Psychology, 12*, 162–166.

Kuhn, D., Langer, J., Kohlberg, L., & Haan, N. (1977). The development of formal operations in logical and moral development. *Genetic Psychology Monographs, 95*, 97–188.

Kuhn, T. (1970) *The structure of scientific revolutions* (2nd ed.). Chicago: University of Chicago Press.

Kurdek, L. A. (1978). Perspective-taking as the cognitive basis of children's moral development: A review of the literature. *Merrill-Palmer Quarterly, 24*, 3–28.

Kurdek, L. A. (1980). Developmental relations among children's perspective-taking, moral judgment and parent-rated behavior. *Merrill-Palmer Quarterly, 26*, 103–121.

Kurdek, L. (1981). Young adult's moral reasoning about prohibitive and prosocial dilemmas. *Journal of Youth and Adolescence, 10*, 263–272.

Kurdek, L., & Rodgon, M. (1975). Perceptual, cognitive and affective perspective-taking in kindergarten through sixth-grade children. *Developmental Psychology, 11*, 643–650.

Kurtines, W. M. (1986). Moral behavior as rule-governed behavior: Person and situation effects on moral decision making. *Journal of Personality and Social Psychology, 50*, 784–791.

Kurtines, W. M., & Greif, E. (1974) The development of moral thought: A review and evaluation of Kohlberg's approach. *Psychological Bulletin, 81*, 453–470.

Kurtines, W. M., Mayock, E., Pollard, S. R., Lanza, T., & Carlo, G. (1991). Social and moral development from the perspective of psychosocial theory. In W. M. Kurtines and J. L. Gewirtz (Eds.), *Handbook of moral behavior and development* (Vol. 1, pp. 153–182). Hillsdale, NJ: Lawrence Erlbaum.

Lakatos, I. (1978). Changes in the problem of inductive logic. In J. Worrall & G. Currie (Eds.), *Mathematics, science, and epistemology* (pp. 128–210) (Imre Lakatos Philosophical Papers Vol. 2). Cambridge: Cambridge University Press.

Lakatos, I., & Musgrave, A. (Eds.).(1970). *Criticism and the growth of knowledge.* Cambridge: Cambridge University Press.

Lane, J., & Anderson, N. H. (1976). Integration of intention and outcome in moral judgment. *Memory and Cognition, 4*, 1–5.

Langer, J. (1969). *Theories of development.* New York: Holt, Rinehart, & Winston.

Lapsley, D. K. (1990). Continuity and discontinuity in adolescents' social cognitive development. In R. Montemayor, G. R. Adams, & T. Gullota (Eds.), *From childhood to adolescence: A transitional period?* (pp. 183–204) (*Advances in Adolescent Development Vol. 2).* Newbury Park, NJ: Sage.

Lapsley, D. K. (1992a). Moral psychology after Kohlberg. Paper presented at the annual meeting of the Midwestern Psychological Association, April, Chicago.

Lapsley, D. K. (1992b). Pluralism, virtues, and the post-Kohlbergian era in moral psychology. In F. C. Power & D. K. Lapsley (Eds.), *The challenge of pluralism: Education, politics, and values* (pp. 169–200). Notre Dame, IN: University of Notre Dame Press.

Lapsley, D. K. (1994). Id, ego, superego. In V. S. Ramachandran (Ed.), *The encyclopedia of human behavior*. San Diego: Academic Press.

Lapsley, D. K., Enright, R. D., & Serlin, R. (1989). Moral and social education. In J. Worell & F. Danner (Eds.), *The adolescent as decision-maker: Applications to development and education* (pp. 111–143). San Diego: Academic Press.

Lapsley, D. K., Harwell, M. R., Olson, L. M., Flannery, D., & Quintana, S. M. (1984). Moral judgment, personality and attitude to authority in early and late adolescence. *Journal of Youth and Adolescence, 13,* 527–542.

Lapsley, D. K., & Serlin, R. (1984). On the alleged degeneration of the Kohlbergian research program. *Educational Theory, 34,* 157–170.

Lapsley, D. K., & Quintana, S. M. (1989). Mental capacity and role-taking: A structural equations approach. *Merrill-Palmer Quarterly, 35,* 143–163.

Latane, B., & Rodin, J. A. (1969). A lady in distress: Inhibitory effects of friends and strangers on bystander intervention. *Journal of Experimental Social Psychology, 5,* 189–202.

Lau, R. R. (1989). Construct accessibility and electoral choice. *Political Behavior, 11,* 5–32.

Laudan, L. (1977). *Progress and its problems: Towards a theory of scientific growth.* Berkeley: University of California Press.

LaVoie, J. C. (1974). Type of punishment as a determinant of resistance to deviation. *Developmental Psychology, 10,* 181–189.

LeMare, L., & Krebs, D. (1983). Perspective-taking and styles of (pro)social behavior in elementary school children. *Academic Psychology Bulletin, 2,* 289–298.

Leming, J. (1978). Intrapersonal variations in stage of moral reasoning among adolescents as a function of situational context. *Journal of Youth and Adolescence, 7,* 405–416.

Leon, M. (1982). Rules in children's moral judgments: Integration of intent, damage and rationale information. *Developmental Psychology, 18,* 835–842.

Lepper, M. (1983). Social-control processes and the internalization of social values: An attributional perspective. In E. T. Higgins, D. N. Ruble, & W. W. Hartup (Eds.), *Social cognition and social development: A socio-cultural perspective* (pp. 294–330). Cambridge: Cambridge University Press.

Lepper, M., & Green, D. (1975). Turning play into work: Effects of surveillance and extrinsic reward on children's intrinsic motivation. *Journal of Personality and Social Psychology, 31,* 479–486.

Lewis, C. S. (1956). *Surprised by joy: The shape of my early life.* New York: Harcourt, Brace, World.

Lewis, M., & Brooks-Gunn, J. (1979). *Social cognition and the acquisition of self.* New York: Plenum.

Levine, C. G. (1979a). The form-content distinction in moral development research. *Human Development, 22,* 225–234.

Levine, C. G. (1979b). Stage acquisition and stage use: An appraisal of stage displacement explanations of variation in moral reasoning. *Human Development, 22,* 145–164.

Lickona, T. (1976). Research on Piaget's theory of moral development. In T. Lickona (Ed.), *Moral development and behavior* (pp. 219–240). London: Holt, Rinehart, & Winston.

Lickona, T. (1980). Democracy, cooperation and moral education. In C. Brusselmans (Ed.), *Towards moral and religious maturity* (pp. 487–515). Morristown, NJ: Silver Burdette.

Lickona, T. (1991). Moral development in the elementary school classroom. In W. Kurtines & J. Gewirtz (Eds.), *Handbook of moral behavior and development: Vol 3. Application* (pp. 143–162). Hillsdale NJ: Lawrence Erlbaum.

Lipscomb, T. J., Larrieu, J. A., McAllister, H. A., & Bregman, N. J. (1982). Modeling and children's generosity: A developmental perspective. *Merrill-Palmer Quarterly, 28,* 275–282.

Livesley, W. J., & Bromley, D. B. (1973). *Person perception in childhood and adolescence*. London: Wiley.

Locke, D. (1976). Cognitive stages or developmental phases? A critique of Kohlberg's stage-structural theory of moral reasoning. *Journal of Moral Education, 8*, 168–181.

Locke, D. (1986). A psychologist among the philosophers: Philosophical aspects of Kohlberg's theory. In S. Modgil & C. Modgil (Eds.), *Lawrence Kohlberg: Consensus and controversy* (pp. 21–38). Philadelphia: Falmer Press.

Lockwood, A. (1978). The effects of values clarification and moral development curricula on school-age subjects: A critical review of recent research. *Review of Educational Research, 48*, 325–364.

Loevinger, J. (1976). *Ego development: Concepts and theories*. San Francisco: Jossey-Bass.

Loevinger, J. (1986). On Kohlberg's contributions to ego development. In S. Modgil & C. Modgil (Eds.), *Lawrence Kohlberg: Consensus and controversy* (pp. 183–193). Philadelphia: Falmer Press.

Louden, R. B. (1984). On some vices of virtue ethics. *American Philosophical Quarterly, 21*, 227–236.

Louden, R. B. (1986). Kant's virtue ethics. *Philosophy, 61*, 473-489.

Ludemann, P. M. (1991). Generalized discrimination of positive facial expressions by seven- and ten-month old infants. *Child Development, 62*, 55–67.

Ludemann, P. M., & Nelson, C. A. (1988). Categorical representation of facial expressions by 7-month old infants. *Developmental Psychology, 24*, 492–501.

Lyons, N. P. (1983). Two perspectives: On self, relationships, and morality. *Harvard Educational Review, 53*, 125–145.

MacIntyre, A. (1959). Hume on "is" and "ought." *Philosophical Review, 68*, pp. 451–468.

MacIntryre, A. (1984). *After virtue* (2nd ed.). Notre Dame, IN: University of Notre Dame Press.

MacRae, R. (1954). A test of Piaget's theories of moral development. *Journal of Abnormal and Social Psychology, 49*, 14–18.

Maddi, S. (1976). *Personality theories: A comparative analysis*. Homewood, IL: Doresy Press.

Malinowski, C. I., & Smith, C. P. (1985). Moral reasoning and moral conduct: An investigation prompted by Kohlberg's theory. *Journal of Personality and Social Psychology, 49*, 1016–1027.

Mannerino, A. P. (1976). Friendship patterns and altruistic behavior in preadolescent males. *Developmental Psychology, 12*, 555-556.

Marcia, J. E. (1980). Identity in adolescence. In J. Adelson (Ed.), *Handbook of adolescent psychology* (pp. 159–187). New York: Wiley.

Markus, H. (1977). Self-schemata and processing information about the self. *Journal of Personality and Social Psychology, 35*, 63–78.

Martin, G. B., & Clark, R. D. (1982). Distress crying in newborns: Species and peer specificity. *Developmental Psychology, 18*, 3–9.

Maruyama, G., Fraser, S. C., & Miller, N. (1982). Personal responsibility and altruism in children. *Journal of Personality and Social Psychology, 42*, 658–664.

May, L. (1985). The moral adequacy of Kohlberg's moral development theory. In C. Hardin (Ed.), *Moral dilemmas* (pp. 115–136). Chicago: Precedent.

Mayer, N. K., & Tronick, E. Z. (1985). Mothers' turn-giving signals and infant turn-taking in mother-infant interactions. In T. M. Field & N. A. Fox (Eds.), *Social perception in infants*. Norwood, NJ: Ablex.

Mayes, L. C., & Carter, A. S. (1990). Emerging social regulatory capacities as seen in the still-face situation. *Child Development, 61*, 754–763.

McDowell, J. (1979). Virtue and reason. *Monist, 62,* 331–350.

McFall, L. (1987). Integrity. *Ethics, 98,* 5–20.

McMains, M. J., & Liebert, R. M. (1968). Influence of discrepancies between successively modeled self-reward criteria on the adoption of a self-imposed standard. *Journal of Personality and Social Psychology, 8,* 166–171.

McNamee, S. (1978). Moral behavior, moral development and motivation. *Journal of Moral Education, 7,* 27–32.

Medinnus, G. R. (1959). Immanent justice in children: A review of the literature and additional data. *Journal of Genetic Psychology, 94,* 253–262.

Meehl, P. (1954). *Clinical versus statistical prediction: A theoretical analysis and review of the literature.* Minneapolis: University of Minnesota Press.

Mehrabian, A., & Epstein, N. A. (1972). A measure of emotional empathy. *Journal of Personality, 40,* 523–543.

Meilaender, G. (1984). *The theory and practice of virtue.* Notre Dame, IN: University of Notre Dame Press.

Merchant, R. L., & Rebelsky, F. (1972). Effects of participation in rule formation in the moral judgment of children. *Genetic Psychology Monographs, 85,* 287–304.

Miller, P. H., Kessel, F. S., & Flavell, J. H. (1970). Thinking about people thinking about people thinking about. . . A study of social cognitive development. *Child Development, 41,* 613–623.

Miller, R. L., Brickman, P., & Bolen, D. (1975). Attribution versus persuasion as a means for modifying behavior. *Journal of Personality and Social Psychology 31,* 430–441.

Mills, R.S.L., & Grusec, J. E. (1989). Cognitive, affective and behavioral consequences of praising dilemmas. *Merrill-Palmer Quarterly, 35,* 299–326.

Mischel, W. (1968). *Personality and assessment.* New York. Wiley.

Mischel, W. (1969). Continuity and change in personality. *American Psychologist, 24,* 1012–1018.

Mischel, W. (1972). Direct versus indirect personality assessment: Evidence and implications. *Journal of Consulting and Clinical Psychology, 38,* 319–329.

Mischel, W. (1973). Toward a cognitive social-learning reconceptualization of personality. *Psychological Review, 80,* 250–283.

Mischel, W. (1979). On the interface of cognition and personality: Beyond the person-situation debate. *American Psychologist, 34,* 740–754.

Mischel, W. (1984). Convergences and challenges to the search for consistency. *American Psychologist, 39,* 351–364.

Mischel, W. (1990). Personality dispositions revisited and revised: A view after three decades. In L. A. Pervin (Ed.), *Handbook of personality: Theory and research* (pp. 111–134). New York: Guilford.

Mischel, W., Jeffrey, K. M., & Patterson, C. J. (1974). The layman's use of trait and behavioral information to predict behavior. *Journal of Research in Personality, 8,* 231–242.

Mischel, W., & Mischel. H. N. (1976). A social-cognitive learning approach to morality and self-regulation. In T. Lickona (Ed.), *Moral development and behavior* (pp. 84–107). New York: Holt, Rinehart, Winston.

Moore, G. E. (1903/1993). *Principia ethica* (Rev. Ed.). Cambridge: Cambridge University Press.

Moran, J. J., & Joniak, A. J. (1979). Effect of language on preference for responses to a moral dilemma. *Developmental Psychology, 15,* 337–338.

Murdoch, I. (1992). *Metaphysics as a guide to morals.* London: Penguin Books.

Mussen, P., & Eisenberg-Berg, N. (1977). *Caring, sharing and helping*. San Francisco: Freeman.

Mussen, P., Harris, S., Rutherford, E., & Keasey, C. B. (1970). Honesty and altruism among preadolescents. *Journal of Personality and Social Psychology, 13*, 289–299.

Najarian-Svajian, P. H. (1966). The idea of immanent justice among Lebanese children and adults. *Journal of Genetic Psychology, 109*, 57–66.

Nardi, P. M. (1979). Moral socialization: An empirical analysis of the Hogan model. *Journal of Moral Education, 9*, 10–16.

Nardi, P. M., & Tsujimoto, R. (1979). The relationship of moral maturity and ethical theories attitude. *Journal of Personality, 47*, 365–377.

Nelson, C. A. (1987). The recognition of facial expressions in the first two years of life: Mechanisms of development. *Child Development, 58*, 889–909.

Nelson, C. A., & Dolgrin, K. G. (1985). The generalized discrimination of facial expressions by seven-month old infants. *Child Development, 56*, 58–61.

Newton-Smith, W. (1981). *The rationality of science*. London: Routledge.

Niiniluota, I. (1984). *Is science progressive?* Dordrecht, Netherlands: Reidel.

Nisan, M. (1987). Moral norms and social conventions: A cross-cultural comparison. *Developmental Psychology, 23*, 719–725.

Nisan, M. (1988). A story of a pot, or a cross-cultural comparison of basic moral evaluations: A response to the critique by Turiel, Nucci, and Smetana (1988). *Developmental Psychology, 24*, 144–146.

Nisan, M., & Kohlberg, L. (1982). Universality and cross-cultural variation in moral development: A longitudinal and cross-sectional study in Turkey. *Child Development, 53*, 865–876.

Nisbett, R. E., & Ross, L. D. (1980). *Human inference: Strategies and shortcomings of social judgment*. Englewood Cliffs, NJ: Prentice Hall.

Noam, G. (1990). Beyond Freud and Piaget: Biographical worlds—interpersonal self. In T. Wren (Ed.), *The moral domain: Essays in the ongoing discussion between philosophy and the social sciences* (pp. 360–400). Cambridge: MIT Press.

Noam, G., & Wolf, M. (1991). Lawrence Kohlberg 1927–1987. In W. M. Kurtines & J. L. Gewirtz (Eds.), *Handbook of moral behavior and moral development: Vol 1. Theory* (pp. 21–24). Hillsdale, NJ: Lawrence Erlbaum.

Noam, G., & Wren, T. (Eds.). (1995). *Morality and the self*. Cambridge: MIT Press.

Noddings, N. (1984). *Caring: A feminine approach to ethics and moral education*. Berkeley: University of California Press.

Norton, D. L. (1988). Moral minimalism and the development of moral character. *Midwest Studies in Philosophy, 13*, 180–195.

Nozick, R. (1981). *Philosophic explanations*. Cambridge: Belknap/Harvard University Press.

Nucci, L. (1981). The development of personal concepts: A domain distinct from moral or societal concepts. *Child Development, 52*, 114–121.

Nucci, L. (1982). Conceptual development in the moral and conventional domains: Implications for values education. *Review of Educational Research, 49*, 93–122.

Nucci, L. (1984). Evaluating teachers as social agents: Students' ratings of domain appropriate and domain inappropriate teacher responses to transgressions. *American Educational Research Journal, 21*, 367–378.

Nucci, L. (1985). Children's conceptions of morality, societal convention and religious prescription. In C. Harding (Ed.), *Moral dilemmas* (pp. 137–174). Chicago: Precedent.

Nucci, L. (1991). Doing justice to morality in contemporary values education. In J. S. Benninga (Ed.), *Moral, character, and civic education in the elementary school* (pp. 21–42). New York: Teachers College Press.

Nucci, L., & Nucci, M. S. (1982a). Children's responses to moral and social conventional transgressions in free play settings. *Child Development, 53*, 1337–1342.

Nucci, L., & Nucci, M. S. (1982b). Children's social interactions in the context of moral and conventional transgressions. *Child Development, 53*, 403–412.

Nucci, L., Guerra, N., & Lee, J. (1989) Adolescent judgments of the personal, prudential and normative aspects of drug usage. Paper presented at the biennial meeting of the Society for Research in Child Development, Kansas City, MO.

Nucci, L., & Turiel, E. (1978). Social interactions and the development of social concepts in preschool children. *Child Development, 49*, 400–407.

Nucci, L., Turiel, E., & Encarnacion-Gawrych, G. E. (1983). Children's social interactions and social concepts: Analyses of morality and convention in the Virgin Islands. *Journal of Cross-Cultural Psychology, 14*, 469–487.

Nucci, L., & Weber, E. K. (1991). The domain approach to values education: From theory to practice. In W. M. Kurtines & J. L. Gewirtz (Eds.), *Handbook of moral behavior and development: Vol. 3. Application* (pp. 251–266). Hillsdale, NJ: Lawrence Erlbaum.

Nummendal, S. G., & Bass, S. C. (1976). Effects of the salience of intention and consequences on children's moral judgments. *Developmental Psychology, 12*, 475–476.

Nunner-Winkler, G., & Sodian, B. (1988). Children's understanding of moral emotions. *Child Development, 59, 1323–1338*.

Oster, H. (1981). "Recognition" of emotional expression in infancy? In M. E. Lamb & L. R. Sherrod (Eds.), *Infant social cognition*. Hillsdale, NJ: Lawrence Erlbaum.

Parke, R. D. (1974). Rules, roles, and resistance to deviation: Recent advances in punishment, discipline and self-control. In A. D. Pick (Ed.), *Minnesota symposia on child psychology* (Vol. 8, pp. 111–143). Minneapolis: University of Minnesota Press.

Parsons, J. E., Ruble, D. N., Klosson, E. C., Feldman, N. S., & Rholes, W. S. (1976). Order effects in children's moral and achievement judgments. *Developmental Psychology, 12*, 357–358.

Patterson, G. R. (1982). *Coercive family processes*. Eugene, OR: Castalia.

Payne, F. D. (1980). Children's prosocial conduct in structured situations and as viewed by others: Consistencies, convergences and relationships with person variables. *Child Development, 51*, 1252–1259.

Percival, P., & Haviland, J. M. (1975). Consistency and retribution in children's immanent justice decisions. *Developmental Psychology, 14*, 132–136.

Pekarsky, D. (1983). Moral choice and education. *Journal of Moral Education, 12*, 3–13.

Peterson, L. (1982). Altruism and the development of internal control: An integrative model. *Merrill-Palmer Quarterly, 28*, 197–222.

Philibert, P. J. (1975). Lawrence Kohlberg's use of virtue in his theory of moral development. *International Philosophical Quarterly, 15*, 455–480.

Phillips, D. C., & Nicolayev, J. (1978). Kohbergian moral development: A progressing or degenerating research program. *Educational Theory, 28*, 286–301.

Piaget, J. (1926). *The language and thought of the child*. London: Routledge & Kegan Paul.

Piaget, J. (1928). *Judgment and reasoning in the child*. London: Routledge & Kegan Paul.

Piaget, J. (1950). *The psychology of intelligence*. London: Routledge & Kegan Paul.

Piaget, J. (1951). *The child's conception of the world*. Savage, MD: Littlefield Adams.

Piaget, J. (1952a). [Autobiography]. In E. G. Boring (Ed.), *A history of psychology in autobiography* (Vol. 4, pp. 237–256). New York: Russell & Russell

Piaget, J. (1952b). *Origins of intelligence*. New York: International Universities Press.

Piaget, J. (1960). The general problem of the psycho-biological development of the child. In J. Tanner & B. Inhelder (Eds.), *Discussions on child development* (Vol. 4, pp. 3–27). New York: International Universities Press.

Piaget, J. (1932/1965). *The moral judgment of the child.* New York: Norton.

Piaget, J. (1952/1965). *The child's conception of number.* New York: Norton.

Piaget, J. (1970). *Genetic epistemology.* New York: Norton.

Piaget, J. (1968/1971). *Structuralism* (trans. C. Maschler). New York: Harper

Piaget, J. (1971a). *Psychology and epistemology.* New York: Viking.

Piaget, J. (1971b) The theory of stages in cognitive development. In D. R. Green (Ed.), *Measurement and Piaget* (pp. 1–11). New York: McGraw Hill.

Piaget, J. (1977). Forward. In H. Gruber & J. Voneche (Eds.), *The essential Piaget* (pp. xi–xii). New York: Basic Books.

Piaget, J., & Inhelder, B. (1967). *The child's conception of space.* New York: Norton.

Piaget, J., & Inhelder, B. (1974). *The child's construction of quantities.* London: Routledge & Kegan Paul.

Pickens, J., & Field, T. (1993). Facial expressions in infants of depressed mothers. *Developmental Psychology, 29,* 986–988.

Pieper, J. (1966). *The four cardinal virtues.* Notre Dame, IN: University of Notre Dame Press.

Pinard, A., & Laurendeau, M. (1969). "Stage" in Piaget's cognitive developmental theory: Exegesis of a concept. In D. Elkind & J. H. Flavell (Eds.), *Studies in cognitive development* (pp. 121–170). New York: Oxford University Press.

Pincoffs, E. (1971). Quandry ethics. *Mind, 80,* 552–571.

Pincoffs, E. (1983). Quandary ethics. In S. Hauerwas and A. MacIntyre (Eds.), *Revisions: Changing perspectives in moral philosophy* (Vol. 3, pp. 92–112). Notre Dame, IN: University of Notre Dame Press.

Piper, A. (1987). Moral theory and moral alienation. *Journal of Philosophy, 84,* 102–118.

Plutchik, R. (1987). Evolutionary bases of empathy. In N. Eisenberg & J. Strayer (Eds.), *Empathy and its development* (pp. 38–46). Cambridge: Cambridge University Press.

Popper, K. (1959). *The logic of scientific discovery.* New York: Basic Books.

Porter, J. (1990). *The recovery of virtue.* Louisville, KY: Westminster/John Knox Press.

Power, F. C. (1979). *The moral atmosphere of a just community high school: A four-year longitudinal study.* Unpublished doctoral dissertation, Harvard Graduate School of Education.

Power, F. C. (1991a). Lawrence Kohlberg: The vocation of a moral psychologist and educator: Pt. 1. In W. M. Kurtines & J. L. Gewirtz (Eds.), *Handbook of moral behavior and development: Vol. 1. Theory* (pp. 25–34). Hillsdale, NJ: Lawrence Erlbaum.

Power, F. C. (1991b). Democratic schools and the problem of moral authority. In W. M. Kurtines & J. L. Gewirtz (Eds.), *Handbook of moral behavior and development: Vol. 3. Application* (pp. 317–334). Hillsdale, NJ: Lawrence Erlbaum.

Power, F. C., Higgins, A., & Kohlberg, L. (1989). *Lawrence Kohlberg's approach to moral education.* New York: Columbia University Press.

Power, F. C., & Kohlberg, L. (1980). Religion, morality and ego development. In C. Brusselmans (Ed.), *Toward moral and religious maturity* (pp. 343–372). Morristown, NJ: Silver Burdett.

Power, F. C., & Reimer, J. (1978). Moral atmosphere: An educational bridge between moral judgment and action. In W. Damon (Ed.), *New directions for child development: Moral development (Vol. 2,* pp. 105–116). San Francisco: Jossey-Bass.

Presbie, R. J., & Coiteux, P. F. (1971). Learning to be generous or stingy: Imitation of sharing behaviors as a function of model generosity and vicarious reinforcement. *Child Development, 42,* 1033–1038.

Puka, B. (1990a). The majesty and mystery of Kohlberg's Stage 6. In T. Wren (Ed.), *The moral domain: Essays in the ongoing discussion between philosophy and the social sciences* (pp. 182–223). Cambridge: MIT Press.

Puka, B. (1990b). Toward the redevelopment of Kohlberg's theory: Preserving essential structure, removing controversial content. In W. Kurtines & J. Gewirtz (Eds.), *Handbook of moral behavior and development: Vol 1. Theory* (pp. 373–394). Hillsdale, NJ: Lawrence Erlbaum.

Punzo, V., & Meara, N. (1993). The virtues of a psychology of personal morality. *Theoretical and Philosophical Psychology, 13,* 25–39.

Radke-Yarrow, M., & Zahn-Waxler, C., with collaborators. (1976). Dimensions and correlates of prosocial behavior in young children. *Child Development, 47,* 118–125.

Radke-Yarrow, M., Zahn-Waxler, C., & Chapman, M. (1983). Children's prosocial dispositions and behavior. In P. H. Mussen (Ed.), *Handbook of child psychology: Vol. 4. Socialization, personality and social development* (pp. 469–545). (E. M. Hetherington, Vol. Ed.). New York: Wiley.

Radnitzsky, G., & Anderson, G. (Eds.) (1978). *Progress and rationality in science.* Dordrecht, Netherlands: Reidel.

Raviv, A., Bar-Tal, D., & Lewis-Levin, T. (1980). Motivations for donation behavior by boys of three different ages. *Child Development, 51,* 610–613.

Rawls, J. (1971). *A theory of justice.* Cambridge: Belknap/Harvard University Press.

Reed, D.R.C. (1991). Rereading "Beds for Bananas" in the post-Kohlbergian era. Paper presented at the annual conference of the Association for Moral Education, November 8, University of Georgia, Athens. Available from the author: Department of Philosophy, Wittenberg University, Springfield, Ohio, 45501.

Reed, T. M., & Hanna, P. (1982). Developmental theory and moral education. *Teaching Philosophy, 5,* 43–54.

Rest, J. (n.d.) The stage concept in moral judgment research. Unpublished manuscript.

Rest, J. (1973). The hierarchical nature of moral judgment. *Journal of Personality, 41,* 86–109.

Rest, J. (1975). Longitudinal study of the Defining Issues Test: A strategy for analyzing developmental change. *Developmental Psychology, 11,* 738–748.

Rest, J. (1979). *Development in judging moral issues.* Minneapolis: University of Minnesota Press.

Rest, J. (1983). Morality. In P. Mussen (Ed.), *Handbook of child psychology:* Vol. 3. Cognitive development (4th ed.; J. Flavell & E. Markman, Vol. Eds., pp. 556–628). New York: Wiley.

Rest, J. (1986a). *Moral development: Advances in theory and research.* New York: Praeger.

Rest, J. (1986b). Moral research methodology. In S. Modgil & C. Modgil (Eds.), *Lawrence Kohlberg: Consensus and controversy* (pp. 455–470). Philadelphia: Falmer Press.

Rest, J., Cooper, D., Coder, R., Masanz, J., & Anderson, D. (1974). Judging the important issues in moral dilemmas: An objective measure of development. *Developmental Psychology, 10,* 491-501.

Rest, J., Davison, M. L., & Robbins, S. (1978). Age trends in judging moral issues: A review of cross-sectional, longitudinal and sequential studies of the Defining Issues Test. *Child Development, 49,* 263–279.

Rest, J., & Narvaez, D. (1991). The college experience and moral development. In W. M. Kurtines & J. L. Gewirtz (Eds.), *Handbook of moral behavior and development: Vol. 2. Research* (pp. 229–248). Hillsdale, NJ: Lawrence Erlbaum.

Rest, J., & Thoma, S. (1985). Moral judgment development and formal education. *Developmental Psychology, 21,* 709–714.

Rest, J., Turiel, E., & Kohlberg, L. (1969). Level of moral judgment as a determinant of preference and comprehension of moral judgments made by others. *Journal of Personality, 37,* 225–252.

Rheingold, H. L. (1982). Little children's participation in the work of adults, a nascent prosocial behavior. *Child Development, 53,* 114–125.

Rheingold, H. L., Hay, D. F., & West, M. J. (1976). Sharing in the second year of life. *Child Development, 47*, 1148–1158.

Rice, M. E., & Grusec, J. (1975). Saying and doing: Effects on observer performance. *Journal of Personality and Social Psychology, 32*, 584–593.

Rogers, T. B., Kuiper, N. A., & Kirker, W. S. (1977). Self-reference and the encoding of self-relevant information. *Journal of Personality and Social Psychology, 35*, 677–688.

Rorty, A. O. (1988). Virtues and their vicissitudes. *Midwest Studies in Philosophy, 13*, 136–148.

Rosch, E. (1975). Cognitive reference points. *Cognitive Psychology, 7*, 532–547.

Rosch, E., Mervis, C. B., Gray, W. D., Johnson, D. M., & Boyes-Braem, P. (1976). Basic objects in natural categories. *Cognitive Psychology, 8*, 382–439.

Rosen, B. (1980). Kohlberg and the supposed mutual support of an ethical and psychological theory. *Journal for the Theory of Social Behavior, 10*, 195–210.

Rosen, B. (1986). Kohlberg and the supposed mutual support of an ethical and psychological theory. *Journal for the Theory of Social Behavior, 10*, 195–210.

Rosenhan, D. L. (1972). Learning theory and prosocial behavior. *Journal of Social Issues, 28*, 151–163.

Rosenhan, D. L., & White, G. M. (1967). Observation and rehearsal as determinants of prosocial behavior. *Journal of Personality and Social Psychology, 5*, 424–431.

Ross, L. (1977). The intuitive psychologist and his shortcomings: Distortions in the attribution process. In L. Berkowitz (Ed.), *Advances in experimental social psychology* (Vol. 10 pp. 173–220). New York: Academic Press.

Rotenberg, K. (1980). Cognitive processes and young children's use of intention and consequences information in moral judgments. *Merrill-Palmer Quarterly, 26*, 359–370.

Rubin, K. (1973). Egocentrism in childhood: A unitary construct? *Child Development, 44*, 102–110.

Rubin, K. (1978). Role-taking in childhood: Some methodological considerations. *Child Development, 49*, 428–433.

Rule, B. G., Nesdale, A. R., & McAra, M. J. (1974). Children's reactions to information about the intentions underlying an aggressive act. *Child Development, 45*, 794–798.

Rumelhart, S. E. (1975). Notes on schemas for stories. In D. L. Bobrow & A. Collins (Eds.), *Representation and understanding: Studies in cognitive science.* New York: Academic Press.

Rushton, J. P. (1975). Generosity in children: Immediate and longterm effects of modeling, preaching and moral judgment. *Journal of Personality and Social Psychology, 31*, 459–466.

Rushton, J. P. (1976). Socialization and the altruistic behavior of children. *Psychological Bulletin, 83*, 898–913.

Rushton, J. P., & Owen, D. (1975). Immediate and delayed effects of TV modeling and preaching on children's generosity. *British Journal of Social and Clinical Psychology, 14*, 309–310.

Rushton, J. P., & Wiener, J. (1975). Altruism and cognitive development in children. *British Journal of Social and Clinical Psychology, 111*, 341–349.

Sagi, A., & Hoffman, M. (1976). Empathic distress in the newborn. *Developmental Psychology, 12*, 175–176.

Saterlie, M. E. (1988). Developing a community consensus for teaching values. *Educational Leadership, 45*, 44–47.

Sawyer, J. (1966). Measurement and prediction, clinical and statistical. *Psychological Bulletin, 66*, 178–200.

Scaife, M., & Bruner, J. S. (1975). The capacity for joint visual attention in the infant. *Nature, 253*, 265–266.

Schank, R. (1975). The structure of episodes in memory. In D. L. Bobrow & A. Collins (Eds.), *Representation and understanding: Studies in cognitive science.* New York: Academic Press.

Schlafli, A., Rest, J., & Thoma, S. (1985). Does moral education improve moral judgment? A meta-analysis of intervention studies using the DIT. *Review of Educational Research, 55,* 319–352.

Schneewind, J. B. (1990). The misfortunes of virtue. *Ethics, 101,* 42–63.

Schwartz, G. M., Izard, C. E., & Ansul, S. E. (1985). The 5-month olds's ability to discriminate facial expressions of emotion. *Infant Behavior and Development, 8,* 65–77.

Searle, J. R. (1969). *Speech acts.* London: Cambridge University Press.

Sears, R. R., Maccoby, E. E., & Levin, H. (1957). *Patterns of child rearing.* Evanston, II: Row, Peterson.

Selman, R. (1971a). The relation of role-taking to the development of moral judgment. *Child Development, 42,* 79–91.

Selman, R. (1971b). Taking another's perspective: Role-taking development in early childhood. *Child Development, 42,* 1721–1734.

Selman, R. (1980). *The growth of intepersonal understanding.* New York: Academic Press.

Selman, R., & Byrne, D. (1975). A structural analysis of role-taking levels in middle childhood. *Child Development, 45,* 803–806.

Selman, R., & Damon, W. (1977). The necessity (but insufficiency) of social perspective-taking for conceptions of justice at three early levels. In D. J. DePalma & J. M. Foley (Eds.), *Moral development: Current theory and research* (pp. 57–73). Hillsdale, NJ: Lawrence Erlbaum.

Senchuk, D. M. (1982). Contra-Kohlberg: A philosophical reinterpretation of moral development. *Educational Theory, 31,* 259–273.

Severy, L. J., & Davis, K. E. (1971). Helping behavior among normal and retarded children. *Child Development, 42,* 1017–1031.

Shantz, C. (1983) Social cognition. In P. Mussen (Ed.), *Handbook of child psychology: Vol. 3. Cognitive development* (J. H. Flavell & E. M. Markman, Vo. Eds., pp. 495–558). New York: Wiley.

Sharpe, R. A. (1992). Moral tales. *Philosophy, 67,* 155–168.

Shweder, R. A. (1982). Beyond self-constructed knowledge: The study of culture and morality. *Merrill-Palmer Quarterly, 28,* 21–69.

Shweder, R. A., Mahapatra, M., & Miller, J. G. (1987). Culture and moral development. In J. Kagan & S. Lamb (Eds.), *The emergence of morality in young children.* Chicago: University of Chicago Press.

Siegel, H. (1981). Kohlberg, moral adequacy, and the justification of educational interventions. *Educational Theory, 31,* 275–284.

Siegel, M., & Storey, R. M. (1985). Day care and children's conceptions of moral and social rules. *Child Development, 56,* 1001–1008.

Siegler, R. S. (1978). The origins of scientific reasoning. In R. S. Siegler (Ed.), *Children's thinking: What develops?* (pp. 109–149). Hillsdale, NJ: Lawrence Erlbaum.

Sigelman, C. K., & Waitzman, K. A. (1991). The development of distributive justice orientations: Contextual influences on children's resource allocation. *Child Development, 62,* 1367-1378.

Simner, M. L. (1971). Newborn's response to the cry of another infant. *Developmental Psychology, 5,* 136–150.

Simpson, E. L. (1974). Moral development research: A case study of scientific cultural bias. *Human Development, 17,* 81–106.

Skinner, B. F. (1971). *Beyond freedom and dignity*. NY: Knopf.

Smetana, J. (1981). Pre-school children's conceptions of moral and social rules. *Child Development, 52,* 1333–1336.

Smetana, J. (1983). Social-cognitive development: Domain distinctions and coordinations. *Developmental Review, 3,* 131-147.

Smetana, J. (1985). Pre-school children's conceptions of transgressions: Effects of varying moral and conventional domain-related attributes. *Developmental Psychology, 21,* 18-29.

Smetana, J. (1989). Toddler's social interactions in the context of moral and conventional transgressions in the home. *Developmental Psychology, 25,* 499–508.

Smetana, J., & Braeges, J. L. (1990). The development of toddler's moral and conventional judgments. *Merrill-Palmer Quarterly, 36,* 329–346.

Smetana, J., Kelly, M., & Twentyman, C. T. (1984). Abused, neglected and nonmaltreated children's conceptions of moral and social conventional transgressions. *Child Development, 55,* 277–287.

Smith, C. L., Gelfand, D. M., Hartmann, D. P., & Partlow, M.E.Y. (1979). Children's causal attributions regarding helping behavior. *Child Development, 50,* 203–210.

Snarey, J. (1985). Cross-cultural universality of social-moral development: A critical review of Kohlbergian research. *Psychological Bulletin, 97,* 202–232.

Snarey, J., Reimer, J., & Kohlberg, L. (1984). The socio-moral development of kibbutz adolescents: A longitudinal, cross-cultural study. *Developmental Psychology, 21,* 3–17.

Song, M-J., Smetana, J., & Kim, S. Y. (1987). Korean children's conceptions of moral and conventional transgressions. *Developmental Psychology, 23,* 577–582.

Srull, T. K., & Wyer, R. S. (1980). Category accessibility and social perception. *Journal of Personality and Social Psychology, 38,* 841–856.

Staub, E. (1970). A child in distress: The influence of age and number of witnesses on children's attempt to help. *Journal of Personality and Social Psychology, 14,* 130–140.

Staub, E. (1971). Helping a person in distress: The influence of implicit and explicit "rule" of conduct on children and adults. *Journal of Personality and Social Psychology, 17,* 137–144.

Staub, E. (1987). Commentary on Part I. In N. Eisenberg & J. Strayer (Eds.), *Empathy and its development* (pp. 103–118). Cambridge: Cambridge University Press.

Staub, E., & Sherk, L. (1970). Need for approval, children's sharing behavior, and reciprocity in sharing. *Child Development, 41,* 243–253.

Steinberg, L., Elman, J. D., & Mounts, N. S. (1989). Authoritative parenting, psychosocial maturity and academic success among adolescents. *Child Development, 60,* 1424–1436.

Steinberg, L., Mounts, N. S., Lamborn, S. D., & Dornbusch, S. M. (1991). Authoritative parenting and adolescent adjustment across various ecological niches. *Journal of Research on Adolescence, 1,* 19–36.

Sternberg, R. J. (Ed.). (1984). *Mechanisms of cognitive development.* New York: Freeman.

Sternberg, R. J. (1989). Domain generality versus domain specificity: The life and impending death of a false dichotomy. *Merrill-Palmer Quarterly, 35,* 115–130.

Sternlieb, J. L., & Youniss, J. (1975). Moral judgments one year after intentional or consequence modeling. *Journal of Personality and Social Psychology, 31,* 895–897.

Stocker, M. (1976). The schizophrenia of modern ethical theories. *Journal of Philosophy, 73,* 453–466.

Stout, J. (1981). *The flight from authority: Religion, morality and the quest for autonomy.* Notre Dame, IN: University of Notre Dame Press.

Strauman, T. J., & Higgins, E. T. (1987). Automatic activation of self-discrepancy and emotional syndromes: When cognitive structures influence affect. *Journal of Personality and Social Psychology, 53,* 1004–1014.

Strayer, J. (1980). A naturalistic study of empathic behaviors and their relation to affective states and perspective-taking skills in preschool children. *Child Development, 51,* 815–822.

Sullivan, E. (1977). A study of Kohlberg's structural theory of moral development: A critique. *Human Development, 20,* 352–376.

Sullivan, E. V., McCullough, G., & Stager, M. A. (1970). A developmental study of the relationship between conceptual, ego and moral development. *Child Development, 4,* 399–412.

Suls, J. M., & Gutkin, D. C. (1976). Children's reactions to an actor as a function of expectations and the consequences received. *Journal of Personality, 44,* 149–162.

Suls, J. M., & Kalle, R. J. (1978). Intention, damage and age of transgressor as a determinant of children's moral judgment. *Child Development, 49,* 1270–1273.

Suls, J.M., Gutkin, D. & Kalle, R.J. (1979). The role of intentions, damage and social consequences on the moral judgment of children. *Child Development, 50,* 874–877.

Suppe, F. (1977). *The structure of scientific theories* (2nd ed.). Urbana: University of Illinois Press.

Surber, C. (1977). Developmental processes in social inference: Averaging of intentions and consequences in moral judgment. *Developmental Psychology, 13,* 654–665.

Surber, C. (1982). Separable effects of motives, consequences and presentation order on children's moral judgment. *Developmental Psychology, 18,* 257–266.

Tappan, M. B. (1991). Narrative, language and moral experience. *Journal of Moral Education, 20,* 243–256.

Tappan, M. B. (1989). Stories lived and stories told: The narrative structure of late adolescent moral development. *Human Development, 32,* 300–315.

Tappan, M., & Brown, L. (1989). Stories told and lessons learned: Towards a narrative approach to moral development and moral education. *Harvard Educational Review, 59,* 182–205.

Taylor, C. (1989). *Sources of the self: The making of modern identity.* Cambridge, MA: Harvard University Press.

Taylor, S. E., & Crocker, J. (1981). Schematic bases of social information-processing. In E. T. Higgins, C. P. Herman, and M. P. Zanna (Eds.), *Social cognition: The Ontario symposium* (Vol. 1, pp. 89–134). Hillsdale, NJ: Lawrence Erlbaum.

Tesser, A., Gatewood, R., & Driver, M. (1968). Some determinants of gratitude. *Journal of Personality and Social Psychology, 9,* 233–236.

Thoma, S. J., & Rest, J. (1986). Moral judgment, behavior, decision-making and attitudes. In J. R. Rest (Ed.), *Moral development: Advances in theory and research* (pp. 133–175). New York: Praeger.

Thoma, S. J., Rest, J., & Davison, M. L. (1991). Describing and testing a moderator of the moral judgment and action relationship. *Journal of Personality and Social Psychology, 61,* 659–669.

Thomas, L. (1988) Rationality and affectivity: The metaphysics of the moral self. *Social Philosophy and Policy, 5,* 154–172.

Thomas, L. (1993). The reality of the moral self. *Monist, 76,* 3–21.

Thompson, R. A. (1987). Empathy and emotional understanding: The early development of empathy. In N. Eisenberg & J. Strayer (Eds.), *Empathy and its development* (pp. 119–145). Cambridge: Cambridge University Press.

Tisak, M. (1986). Children's conceptions of parental authority. *Child Development, 57,* 166–176.

Tisak, M., & Turiel, E. (1988).Variation in seriousness of transgressions and children's moral and conventional concepts. *Developmental Psychology, 24,* 352–357.

Trainer, F. E. (1977). A critical analysis of Kohlberg's contributions to the study of moral thought. *Journal for the Theory of Social Behavior, 7,* 41–63.

Trivers, R. L. (1971). The evolution of reciprocal altruism. *Quarterly Review of Biology, 46,* 35–57.

Tsujimoto, R., & Nardi, P. M. (1978). A comparison of Kohlberg's and Hogan's theories of moral development. *Journal of Social Psychology, 41,* 235–245.

Turiel, E. (1966). An experimental test of the sequentiality of developmental stages in the child's moral judgments. *Journal of Personality and Social Psychology, 3,* 611–618.

Turiel, E. (1974). Conflict and transition in adolescent moral development. *Child Development, 45,* 14–29.

Turiel, E. (1975). The development of social concepts: Mores, customs and conventions. In D. J. DePalma & J. M. Foley (Eds.), *Moral development: Current theory and research* (pp. 7–38). Hillsdale, NJ: Lawrence Erlbaum.

Turiel, E. (1978). The development of concepts of social structure: Social convention. In J. Glick & A. Clarke-Stewart (Eds.), *The development of social understanding* (pp. 25–107). New York: Gardner.

Turiel, E. (1977). Conflict and transition in adolescent moral development: II. The resolution of disequilibrium through structural reorganization. *Child Development, 48,* 634–637.

Turiel, E. (1983a). *The development of social knowledge: Morality and convention.* Cambridge: Cambridge University Press.

Turiel, E. (1983b). Domains and categories in social cognitive development. In W. Overton (Ed.), *The relationship between social and cognitive development* (pp. 53–89). Hillsdale, NJ: Lawrence Erlbaum.

Turiel, E. (1989). Domain-specific social judgments and domain ambiguities. *Merrill-Palmer Quarterly, 35,* 89–114.

Turiel, E., & Davidson, P. (1986). Heterogeneity, inconsistency, and asynchrony in the development of cognitive structures. In I. Levin (Ed.), *Stage and structure: Reopening the debate* (pp. 106–143). Norwood, NJ. Ablex.

Turiel, E., Hildebrandt, C., & Wainryb, C. (1991). Judging social issues. *Monographs of the Society for Research in Child Development, 58* (2, Serial No. 224).

Turiel, E., Killen, M., & Helwig, C. C. (1987). Morality: It's structure, functions and vagaries. In J. Kagan & S. Lamb (Eds.), *The emergence of morality in young children* (pp. 155-243). Chicago: University of Chicago Press.

Turiel, E., Nucci, L. P., & Smetana, J. (1988). A cross-cultural comparison about what? A critique of Nisan's (1987) study of morality and convention. *Developmental Psychology, 24,* 140-143.

Turner, T. (1973). Piaget's structuralism. *American Anthropologist, 75,* 351–373.

Tversky, A., & Kahneman, D. (1974). Judgment under uncertainty: Heuristics and biases. *Science, 185,* 1124–1131.

Ugurel-Semin, R. (1952). Moral behavior and moral judgment of children. *Journal of Abnormal Social Psychology, 47,* 463–474.

Underwood, B., & Moore, B. (1982). Perspective-taking and altruism. *Psychological Bulletin, 91,* 143–173.

Urburg, K. & Docherty, E. M. (1976). Development of role-taking skills in young children. *Developmental Psychology, 12*, 198–203.

Vasudev, J. (1988). Sex differences in morality and moral orientation: A discussion of the Gilligan and Attanucci study. *Merrill-Palmer Quarterly, 34*, 239–244.

Vikan, A. (1976a). Moral judgment as a function of role-playing instructions. *Journal of Genetic Psychology, 128*, pp. 109–122.

Vikan, A. (1976b). Objective and subjective responsibility in moral judgment as a function of enactment of role polarities. *Journal of Genetic Psychology, 128*, 153–161.

Walden, T. A. (1982). Mediation and production deficiencies in children's judgments about morality. *Journal of Experimental Child Psychology, 33*, 165–181.

Walker, L. J. (1980). Cognitive and perspective-taking prerequisites for moral development. *Child Development, 51*, 131–139.

Walker, L. J. (1982). The sequentiality of Kohlberg's stages of moral development. *Child Development, 53*, 1330–1336.

Walker, L. J. (1983). Sources of cognitive conflict for stage transition in moral development. *Developmental Psychology, 19*, 103–110.

Walker, L. J. (1984). Sex differences in the development of moral reasoning: A critical review. *Child Development, 55*, 677–691.

Walker, L. J. (1986). Sex differences in the development of moral reasoning: A rejoinder to Baumrind. *Child Development 57*, 522–526.

Walker, L. J. (1989). A longitudinal study of moral reasoning. *Child Development, 60*, 157–166.

Walker, L.J. (1991). Sex differences in moral reasoning. In W. M.Kurtines & J. L. Gewirtz (Eds.), *Handbook of moral behavior and development: Vol. 2. Research* (pp. 333–364). Hillsdale, NJ: Lawrence Erlbaum.

Walker, L. J., de Vries, B., & Bichard, S. L. (1984). The hierarchical nature of stages of moral development. *Developmental Psychology, 20*, 960–966.

Walker, L. J., & Richards, B. S. (1976). The effects of a narrative model on children's moral judgments. *Canadian Journal of Behavioral Science, 8*, 169–177.

Walker, L. J., & Richards, B. S. (1979). Stimulating transitions in moral reasoning as a function of stage of moral development. *Developmental Psychology, 15*, 95–103.

Walker, L. J., de Vries, B., & Trevethan, S.D. (1987). Moral stages and moral orientations in real life and hypothetical dilemmas. *Child Development, 58*, 842–858.

Walker, L. J., & Moran, T. J. (1991). Moral reasoning in a communist Chinese society. *Journal of Moral Education, 20*, 139–154.

Walker, L. J., & Taylor, J. H. (1991a). Family interactions and the development of moral reasoning. *Child Development, 62*, 264-283.

Walker, L. J., & Taylor, J. H. (1991b). Stage transitions in moral reasoning: A longitudinal study of developmental process. *Developmental Psychology, 27*, 330–337.

Walters, G. C., & Grusec, J. (1977). *Punishment.* San Francisco: Freeman.

Wellman, H. M., Larkey, C., & Somerville, S. C. (1979). The early development of moral criteria. *Child Development, 50*, 869–873.

Werner, H. (1957). The concept of development from a comparative and organismic point of view. In D. B. Harris (Ed.), *The Concept of development.* (pp. 125–148). Minneapolis: University of Minnesota Press.

Weston, D. R., & Turiel, E. (1980). Act-rule relations: Children's conceptions of social rules. *Developmental Psychology, 16*, 417–424.

White, G. M. (1972). Immediate and deferred effects of model observation and guided and unguided rehearsal on donating and stealing. *Journal of Personality and Social Psychology*, *21*, 139–148.

Williams, B. (1981). *Moral luck*. Cambridge: Cambridge University Press.

Witherell, C. S., & Edwards, C. P. (1991). Moral versus social-conventional reasoning: A narrative and cultural critique. *Journal of Moral Education*, *20*, 293–304.

Wittgenstein, L. (1958). *Philosophical investigations* (2nd ed., G.E.M. Anscombe, Trans.). New York: Macmillan.

Wolff, R. (1977). *Understanding Rawls*. Princeton: Princeton University Press.

Wren, T. (Ed.). (1990). *The moral domain: Essays in the ongoing discussion between philosophy and the social sciences*. Cambridge: MIT Press.

Wright, J. C., & Mischel, W. (1987). A conditional approach to dispositional constructs: The local predictability of social behavior. *Journal of Personality and Social Psychology*, *53*, 1159–1177.

Wyer, R. S., & Srull, T. K. (1981). Category accessibility: Some theoretical and empirical issues concerning the processing of social stimulus information. In E. T. Higgins, C. P. Herman, and M. P. Zanna (Eds.), *Social cognition: The Ontario symposium* (Vol 1., pp. 161–197). Hillsdale, NJ: Lawrence Erlbaum.

Zahn-Waxler, C., Friedman, S. L., & Cummings, E. M. (1983). Children's emotions and behaviors in response to infant's cries. *Child Development*, *54*, 1522–1528.

Zahn-Waxler, C., Radke-Yarrow, M. (1982). The development of altruism: Alternative research strategies. In N. Eisenberg-Berg (Ed.), *The development of prosocial behavior*. New York: Academic Press.

Zahn-Waxler, C., Radke-Yarrow, M., & Brady-Smith, J. (1977). Perspective-taking and prosocial behavior. *Developmental Psychology*, *13*, 87–88.

Zahn-Waxler, C., Radke-Yarrow, M., & King, R. A. (1979). Child-rearing and children's prosocial initiations toward victims of distress. *Child Development*, *50*, 319–330

Zillman, D., & Bryant, J. (1975). Viewer's moral sanction of retribution in the appreciation of dramatic presentations. *Journal of Experimental Social Psychology*, *11*, 572–582.

About the Book and Author

This is the first book to integrate a comprehensive review of the psychological literatures with allied traditions in ethics. Moral rationality and decision-making; the development of the sense of fairness and justice, and of prosocial dispositions; as well as the notion of moral self and moral identity and their relation to issues of character and virtue are fully discussed in the rich contexts provided by psychological and philosophical paradigms. Lapsley emphasizes parenting and educational strategies for influencing moral behavior, reasoning, and character development, and charts a line of research for the "post-Kohlbergian era" in moral psychology.

This book will be an invaluable text for advanced courses in moral psychology, as taught in departments of psychology, education, and philosophy. It will also prove to be a standard reference work for researchers and ethicists alike.

Daniel K. Lapsley is associate professor of psychology at Brandon University in Canada. He has taught previously at the University of Wisconsin at Madison and at the University of Notre Dame.

Name Index

Subject Index

DATE DUE